VERNON FISHER

M. GEORGIA HEGARTY DUNKERLEY
CONTEMPORARY ART SERIES

V E R N O N

F I S H E R

INTRODUCTION BY Frances Colpitt
INTERVIEW WITH Michael Auping
FOREWORD BY Ned Rifkin

UNIVERSITY OF TEXAS PRESS, AUSTIN

This series was made possible through the generosity of Michele Dunkerley. Publication of this book was funded in part by The Eugene McDermott Foundation.

Printed in China
First edition, 2010

♾ The paper used in this book meets the minimum requirements of ANSI/NISO Z39.48-1992 (R1997) (Permanence of Paper).

Designed by Lindsay Starr

Library of Congress Cataloging-in-Publication Data

Fisher, Vernon, 1943–
Vernon Fisher / introduction by Frances Colpitt; interview with Michael Auping; foreword by Ned Rifkin. — 1st ed.
p. cm. — (M. Georgia Hegarty Dunkerley contemporary art series)
Includes bibliographical references.
ISBN 978-0-292-72323-8 (cloth : alk. paper)
1. Fisher, Vernon, 1943—Themes, motives.
I. Auping, Michael. II. Title.
N6512.F575A4 2010
709.2—dc22 2010006151

An earlier version of Michael Auping's interview with Vernon Fisher was originally published in *30 Years: Interviews and Outtakes* by Prestel. Courtesy of the Modern Art Museum of Fort Worth, 2007.

For Julie Bozzi

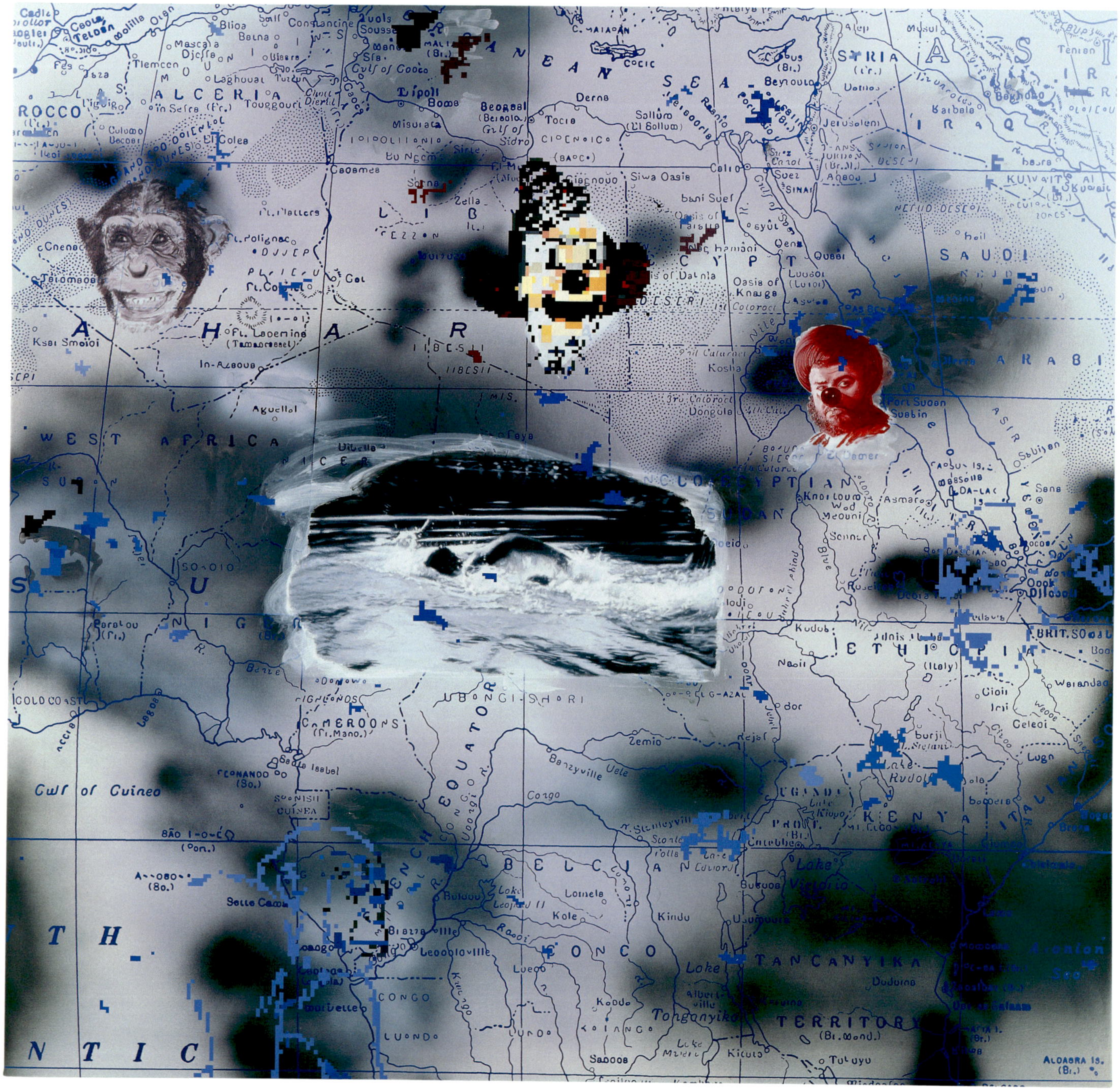

In the Shadows of Corruption and Death 2007

CONTENTS

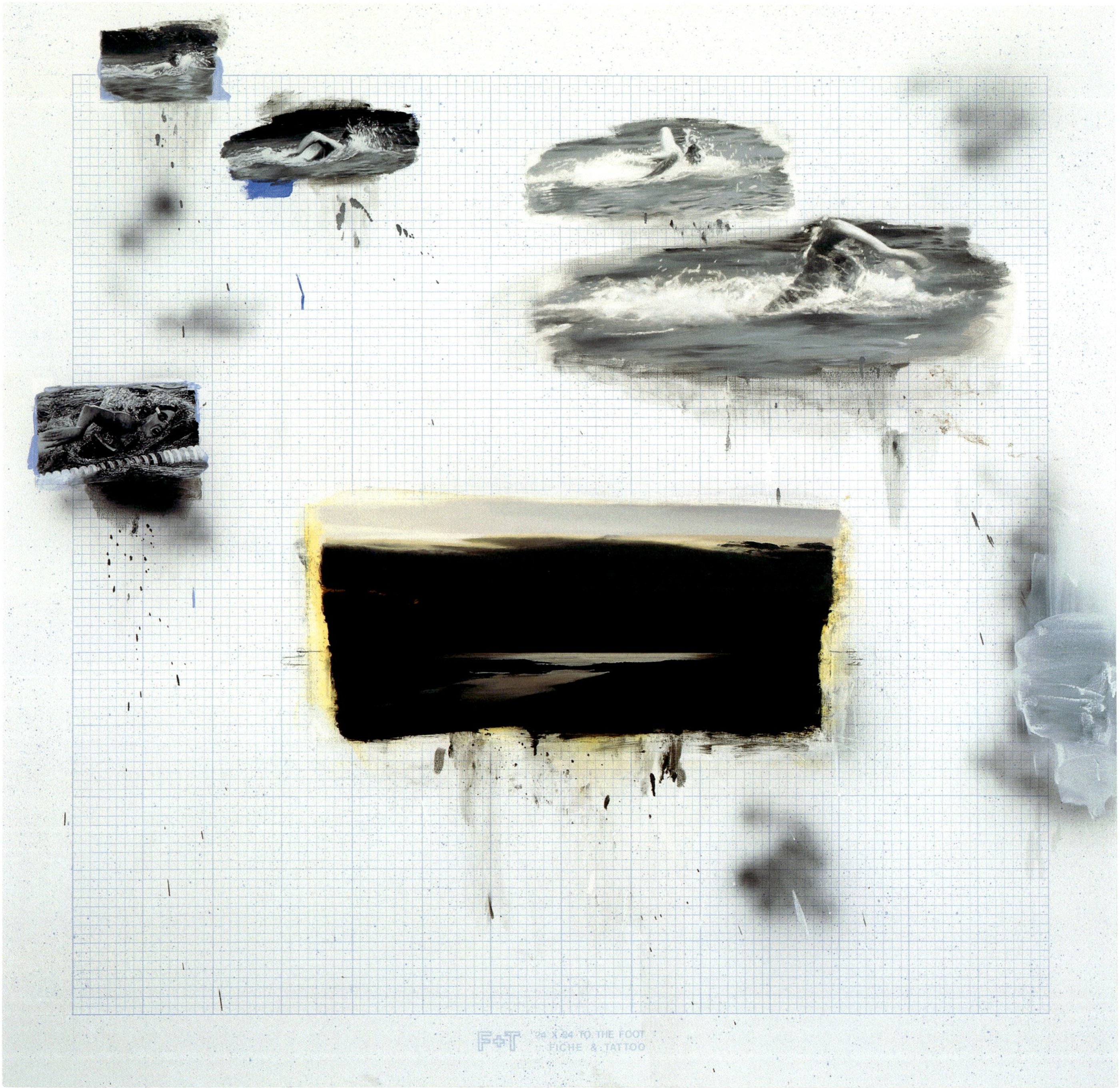

Upstream 2005

FOREWORD

ARTIST AS ATHLETE

Quite recently, Vernon Fisher, a good and close friend for over three decades, came to stay at my new home in Austin. Having moved to Austin only a couple of months earlier, I had managed to persuade Vernon into being my very first overnight guest with the promise that we would be able to watch our beloved Dallas Cowboys' game on *Monday Night Football* on my new, large format, flat-screen television, especially purchased for occasions such as this.

Just before Vernon's visit, a new piece of furniture arrived for my living room, a console upon which this new acquisition would sit. In order to get the furniture into place, I had to unplug the television and its many components (e.g., cable wire, digital box, etc.), which I had somehow managed to install a few weeks before without a hitch. Because I knew that Vernon would be disappointed not to watch the game on the large screen, I did what I could to put everything in good working order. Alas, I could not successfully re-create the proper arrangements of the plugs and the wires. (Secretly, I hoped that Vernon would be able to figure how restore the set to functional operation, since he was, after all, an internationally renowned artist whose work used any number of unusual techniques to realize his various objects.) Teasing me incessantly, Vernon could not stop giving me grief about my failure to make it right the entire time we watched the game upstairs on the other, *smaller* set. The episode reminded me of Vernon's text from *Baseball Cap* (1977), a photo and word piece whose last sentence is also the final paragraph: "I keep trying to make things come out right, but I always seem to get sidetracked."

Baseball Cap was given to me as a thirtieth birthday present in November of 1979 by my then-wife. Not only did she select it for me because I greatly admired the work when I had first seen it in Dallas at the Delahunty Gallery, but I was also beginning to know the artist and had recently written an article on his art in a national publication. Vernon lived nearby in Sherman, Texas, and was teaching at Austin College at the time. I was a second year professor of art at the University of Texas at Arlington. In addition to our mutual engagement with contemporary art, Vernon and I learned that we also shared a passion for most sports.

A few days ago I celebrated my sixtieth birthday. I have *Baseball Cap* in a prominent place in my home where I get to see it every day. After Vernon's visit, I realized that in the doubling of my life, the closing line of his narrative from over thirty years ago makes more than twice as much sense to me. I realized that Vernon Fisher is an "artist/athlete" in a way that never truly occurred to me until this time.

As an undergraduate student at Hardin-Simmons College in Abilene, Texas, Vernon had competed on the track team as a middle-distance runner. Although hardly an Olympic threat, Fisher had a highly competitive drive that often defines a key aspect of the personality of an athlete. However, unlike many jocks, Vernon also developed a serious appreciation of sports, understanding the nuances of gamesmanship and the "flaws" in various approaches to coaching or managerial decision making. (Over the intervening years, Vernon has become an avid and serious golfer.) But more than athletic prowess itself, Vernon incorporates something of a competitor's approach to his art; if something is good, he diligently works to make it better and continues to work out the possibilities. It's *not* "winning," to paraphrase the famous old adage, but "*how* he plays the game."

Vernon is an intensive sportsman and a relatively good sport. (But don't let those "nice guy" Texas Baptist manners fool you; he will *never* forgive me for consistently beating him at ping-pong in his studio many years ago.) However, Vernon Fisher the artist/athlete is also a *killer*. Not unlike the punishing outside linebacker in football or the driving power forward in basketball who intimidate their opponents with their aggressive physical prowess, Vernon asserts his finesse and style with his remarkable intelligence, his agile command of literature and literary criticism, his impressive recall of several film genres, and his rigorous sourcing of cultural images of times gone by. He is a brilliant and cunning tactician of visual compositions, allusions, and insights. However, more than anything else, Vernon will engage you with his soulful and poignant sense of how very fallible we humans always are. His influences range widely, from the early television antics of the Mouseketeers to the Three Stooges. But it is his application of pressure, much like that of a fine defender in sports, which triggers the complexity of our responses.

Triumphs? Vernon has had considerably more than most artists of his generation. He probably holds the record for being the only artist to have been selected for every major group exhibition at a New York art museum in one year, including the Whitney Biennial, the Guggenheim Emergent Americans, and the Hirshhorn's Directions exhibitions. He has also represented the United States in an international art exhibition in New Delhi soon after For many years, he exhibited his newest works at one of the most important galleries in New York, as well as at numerous other galleries throughout this country and Europe. His art is included in many of the finest museums of contemporary art in this country and beyond.

But Vernon has also been a committed artist and teacher. There are legions of younger artists who have benefited from what was described in one New York art review as his "acrobatic intelligence." Like his good and longtime friend Dave Hickey, Vernon enjoys the fact of his rootedness in the Fort Worth area (he grew up in nearby Granbury, Texas) and relates to a wide variety of things that are palpably curious within his native landscape and urban world. From what I have witnessed, Vernon relishes that he can make art of international repute from the place he regards as a nourishing source of inspiration. Obviously, he ventures far and wide, researching topics as diverse and far-flung as Heisenberg's uncertainty principle to ELF, a band of radio frequencies used to communicate

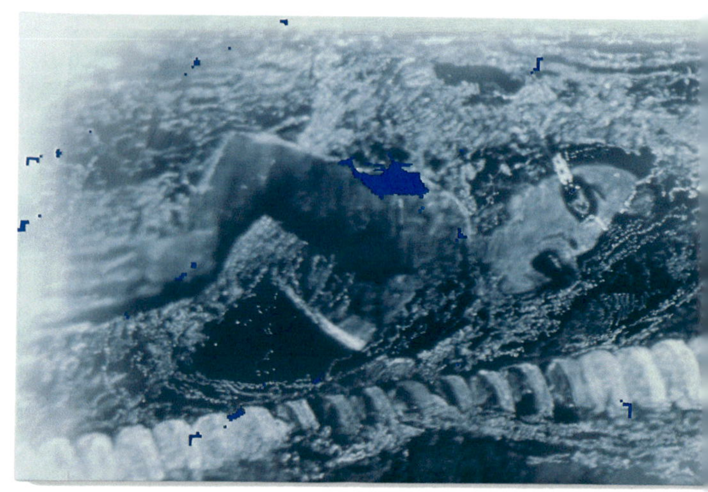

with submarines. But just as he loyally pulls for the Dallas Cowboys and Texas Rangers (and even the Dallas Mavericks), he is still making his best cuts and moves in his Fort Worth studio.

As you review the works represented in this handsome volume, consider the blurry world of presumptive certainty within the scope of chaotic information and imagery that gluts our senses in the post-Internet world we inhabit. Take pleasure in the prescience of Vernon Fisher's musings and explorations over the past thirty-plus years on the curiosities he discerns in the foibles of human behavior.

Whatever Vernon attempts to do, he does so with profound conviction, an investigative hunger, and an excitement about what he has discovered through his own probes, investigations, and analyses. To extend the crippling sports analogy, if I were a captain in the choose-up game of "art world," I know I would always want to have Vernon playing the key position and batting cleanup. (And this from a "manager" who cannot seem to hook up his own television "system"!)

NED RIFKIN
Director, Jack S. Blanton Museum of Art;
Professor, Department of Art and Art History,
University of Texas at Austin

NOVEMBER 19, 2009

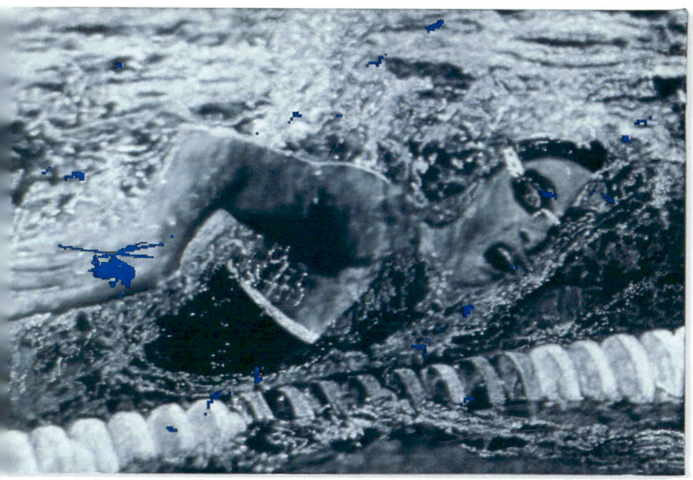

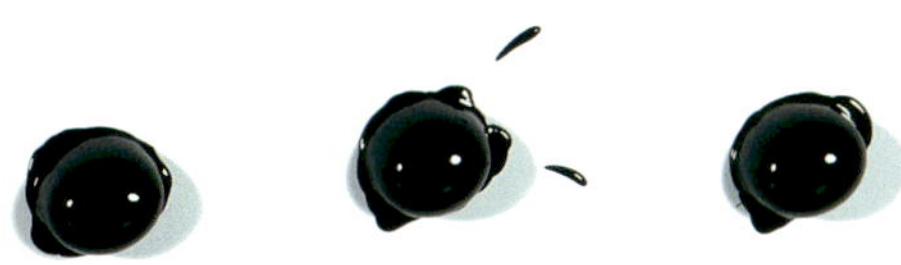

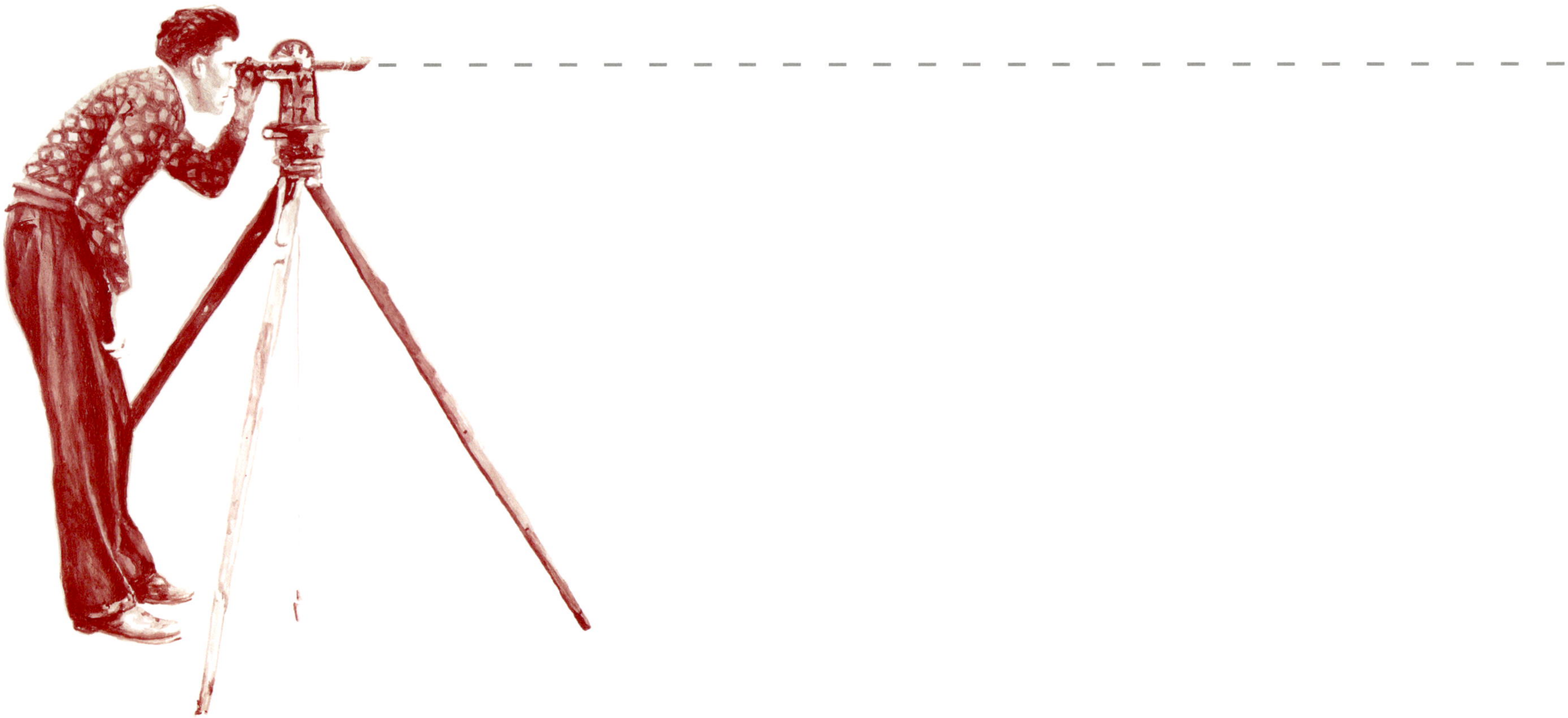

VERNON FISHER

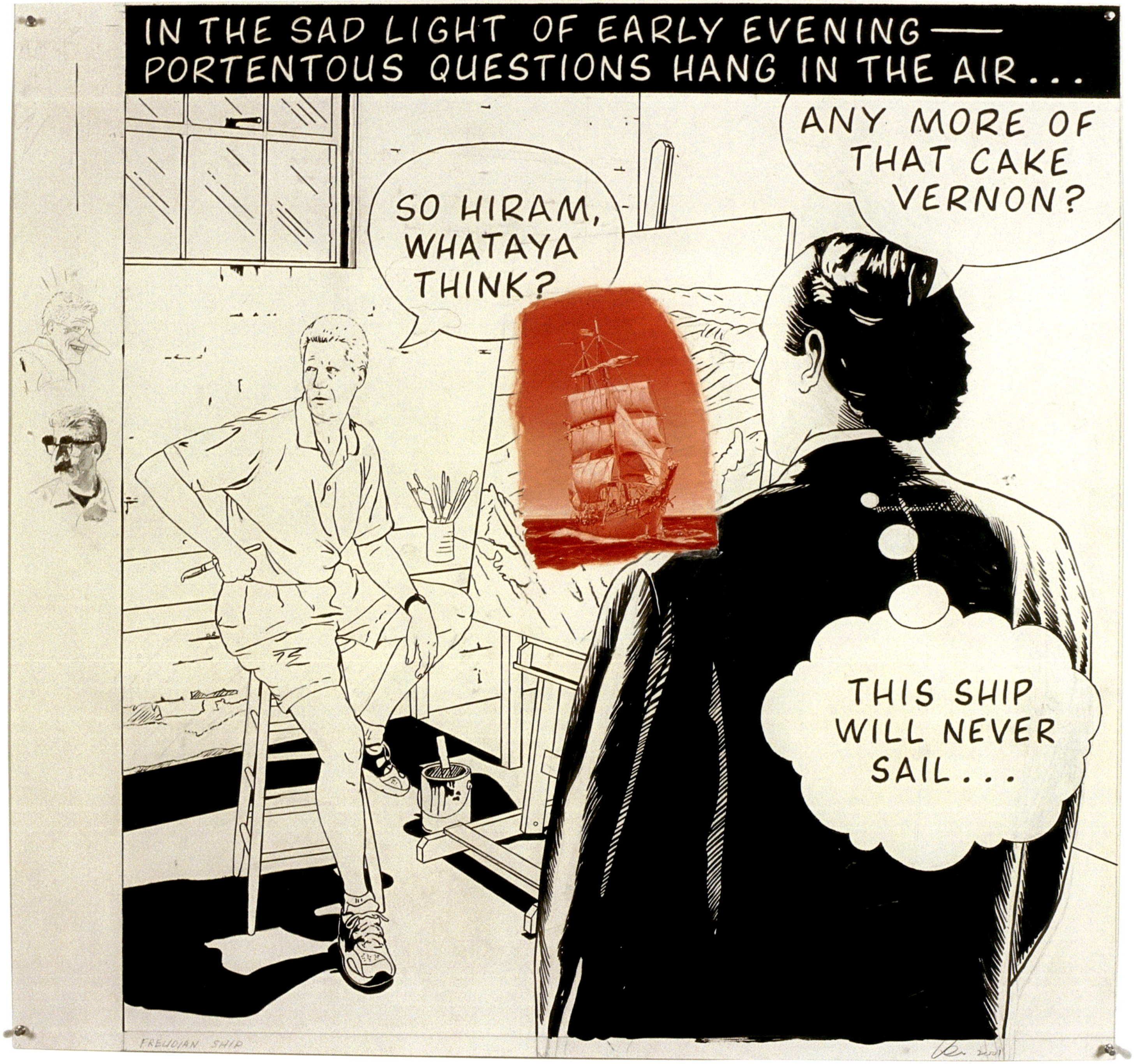

Freudian Ship 2001

INTRODUCTION

FRANCES COLPITT

During the heady years of art's radical transformation by postmodernism, Vernon Fisher, not yet age forty, was swept into the spotlight. In the three years from 1980 to 1982, he had solo exhibitions at museums and galleries in Düsseldorf, Rotterdam, New York City, Dallas, and Houston and participated in twenty-five group shows in cities as far-ranging as Tyler, Texas and New Delhi, India. Although it was clearly not calculated to illustrate the nascent theories of postmodernism, Fisher's brash and innovative multimedia work reflected many of the movement's major concerns. Incorporating photography, painting, sculptural elements, found objects, and written language, his art was tuned in to the breakdown of monolithic modernism, which was predominantly abstract, driven by the desire for formal unity, and propelled by the singular trajectory of history known as the mainstream. Still based in his native Fort Worth, Texas, Fisher's career and artworks represent the openness, multiplicity, and decentralization of postmodernism.

Now at some distance from the disconcerting origins of postmodern art, we can summarize its fundamental differences from modernism. In many ways, postmodernism was an explicit rejection of modernist principles, which contemporary artists felt were not only hidebound but also restrictive, as if modernism had hardened into a set of rules. Given the valorization of form over content, the quality and aesthetic value of a modern work of art were determined by its wholeness, equilibrium, and the harmonious relationship of parts to the whole. In reaction, postmodernists offered multiplicity and fragmentation, which reflected the messy and complicated nature of real life. The patchwork effect and disjunctive syntax of pastiche, which Fredric Jameson was the first to recognize as a hallmark of postmodernism, was preferred to the synthetic unity of modernist collage.[1] Incorporating pastiche into his own work, Fisher explains that the viewer is "encouraged to think about the piece as a series of discrete wholes rather than as parts of a larger whole. [It] has more in common with the way a film is constructed, as a series of scenes than, say, the way a cubist collage is constructed."[2] Pastiche also encouraged the inclusion of imagery from seemingly unrelated sources or time periods and an array of styles and techniques and rejected the modernist tenets of flatness, spatial coherence, and compositional unity. A consistent goal of modernism, according to its leading spokesman Clement Greenberg, was the elimination of anything not essential to the medium, such as narrative subject matter in painting and ornamentation in architecture.[3] Mies van der Rohe's motto, "Less is more," not only encouraged architectural simplification, it defined the whole of the modernist project. In reaction to this reductive sensibility, Fisher countered, "If less is more, then more is more, too."[4]

In the scenario of the modernist avant-garde, the reductive process was based on an optimistic belief in progress and the advancement of art over time. Postmodernism's loss of faith in progress accompanied a parallel breakdown in modern art's trajectory. A leveling out of the mainstream hierarchy in which only one style of art making and a few innovative artists prevailed at any given time led to the pluralism of the 1970s, focusing attention on a variety of approaches by stylistically diverse artists, some of whom were located outside of the center of the art world in New York. Decentralization extended to the loss of "the conception of a unique self and private identity, a unique personality and individuality, which can be expected to generate its own unique vision of the world and to forge its own unique, unmistakable style," Jameson observed. "The 'death' of the subject itself [results in] the *decentering* of that formerly centered subject or psyche."[5] Self-expression is no longer possible—if indeed it ever was— without a whole, centered individual to do the expressing.

The impossibility of speaking from an authoritative, centered self led Roland Barthes to conclude that "it is language which speaks, not the author." The author or artist is a modern construct whose function it is to hold a text or a body of work together: "We know now that a text is not a line of words releasing a single 'theological' meaning (the 'message' of the Author-God) but a multidimensional space in which a variety of writings, none of them original, blend and clash."[6] Barthes's structural interpretations of literature and film provide insights into the constructed nature not only of the text, but also representation, identity, and the concept of reality itself. The destination of the constructed text is, according to Barthes, a reader who is "no longer a consumer, but a producer of the text."[7] In contrast to the closed, author-driven, "readerly" work, the "writerly" text engages the reader in an open-ended field of meaning. It is just this approach that generates the most rewarding interpretations of Fisher's "writerly" works, which function as texts produced by the viewer through an active engagement with pictures and words.

Demonstrating the fragmentation of authorial identity and the viewer's responsibility for the construction of meaning, Fisher's *Hills Like White Elephants* (1991) was one of several important installations created around the time of his first retrospective.[8] Conceived for the Center for Contemporary Art in Sacramento, California, variations of the project were also presented in Los Angeles and Dallas. Ostensibly a group show, *Hills Like White Elephants* included thirteen artworks attributed to Fisher and three alter egos: Werner Fiche, M. Moon, and Consuelo Tattoo. Ernest Hemingway's 1927 short story "Hills Like White Elephants," here "revised" by Consuelo Tattoo, provided the title for the exhibition. Tattoo's revision of the story, which was painted directly on the gallery wall, eliminated Hemingway's original dialogue, leaving only scenic descriptions and the narration of the characters' actions. Hemingway's short story, already a narrative based on what is not said, describes a conversation between an American man and a young woman drinking in a bar at a Spanish train station. As they sip beer, their conversation alludes to an operation that is never identified. Meaning occurs in between what is stated, and has to be deduced or "written" by the reader. Rewriting Hemingway and reiterating his strategy, Fisher/Tattoo creates a second-order text by deleting the dialogue.

The other "artists" in the exhibition were distinguished by their attitudes toward their subjects. A serious German concerned with issues of mortality, Fiche was represented by two works, one of which included a realistic, life-size skeleton with black metal labels reading "pine," "clay," "rain," "bread," "salt," etc., attached to the bones. Moon, identified as a "romantic pragmatist" in the exhibition's

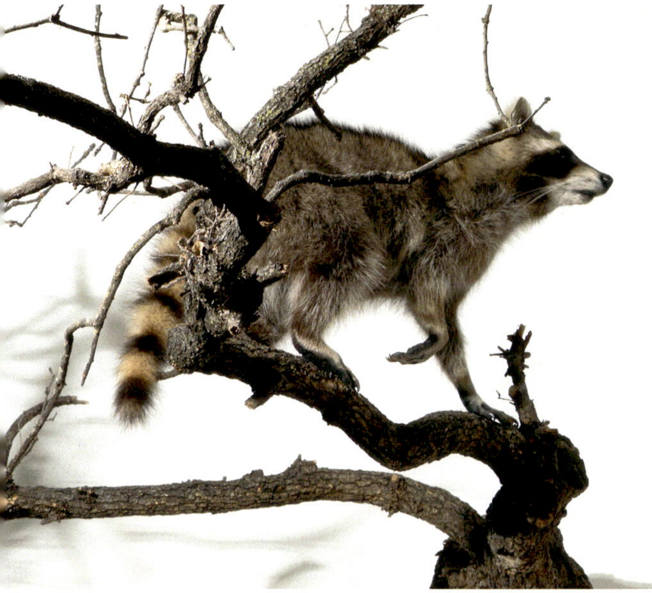

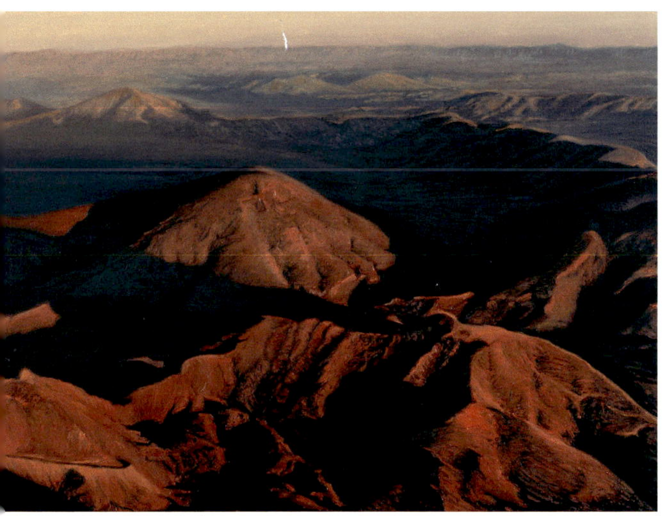

brochure, was credited with a naturalistic oil painting titled *Framed Landscape*, a bird's-eye view of a barren, golden-red mountain range. Deep shadows and glowing peaks suggest illumination by a setting sun. Tattoo also contributed an abstract version of the sublime, an airbrushed painting of ethereal blue circles in a concentric pattern. Only after seeing the title, *That's All Folks*, on the side of the painting does the viewer recognize the valediction at the end of Looney Tunes cartoons as the source for the circles. Tattoo's *After Malevich* also offers the tantalizing possibility of transcendence in reductive abstraction. The two-part relief includes a finely crafted small black cross reminiscent of the Russian artist's spiritual symbols. Countering the idealism of the modernist promise, a stuffed raccoon is perched on a tree branch attached to the wall above the cross. As a whole, *Hills Like White Elephants* was riddled with uncertainty, extending even to its fictitious creators. Conceived as different components of Fisher's artistic self, they exemplify the composite nature of postmodern identity and the "death of the author."[9]

Born in Fort Worth, Texas, Vernon Fisher was raised in Granbury, a nearby small town. After studying literature as an undergraduate in Abilene, Texas, he changed his major to art and became an abstract painter. He continued his studies at the University of Illinois, Urbana-Champaign, receiving his MFA in 1969. He returned to Texas and began teaching at Austin College in Sherman, Texas, north of Dallas. In 1974, at a formative period in his career, Fisher received a grant from the National Endowment for the Arts, which, in allowing him to travel for a year visiting artists and exhibitions, provided a postgraduate education for the young artist. Although he continued to travel and exhibit his work internationally, Fisher lived in Fort Worth and taught at the University of North Texas in Denton. He retired as Regents Professor of Art in 2005. Fisher has met the challenge of living in the generally conservative climate of Texas by creating a conceptually challenging body of work that reflects his good humor and appreciation of life's daily absurdities.

Narrative is a structural model for all of Fisher's works. "We are narratizing creatures," he once told interviewer Matthew Bourbon; "anything is susceptible to becoming fictive."[10] According to psychologist Julian Jaynes, narratization, "an extremely complex set of patterning abilities," is the process of consciousness working to explain our encounters with the world. "We are constantly [narratizing] whenever we are being conscious." Jaynes continues: "A stray fact is narratized to fit with some other stray fact. A child cries in the street and we narratize the event into a mental picture of a lost child and a parent searching for it."[11] The evocative imagery of Fisher's paintings and installations take advantage of the narratizing tendency, offering the promise of interpretation by making connections between things. If the facts—or in Fisher's case,

After Malevich, detail 1991
Framed Landscape, detail 1991

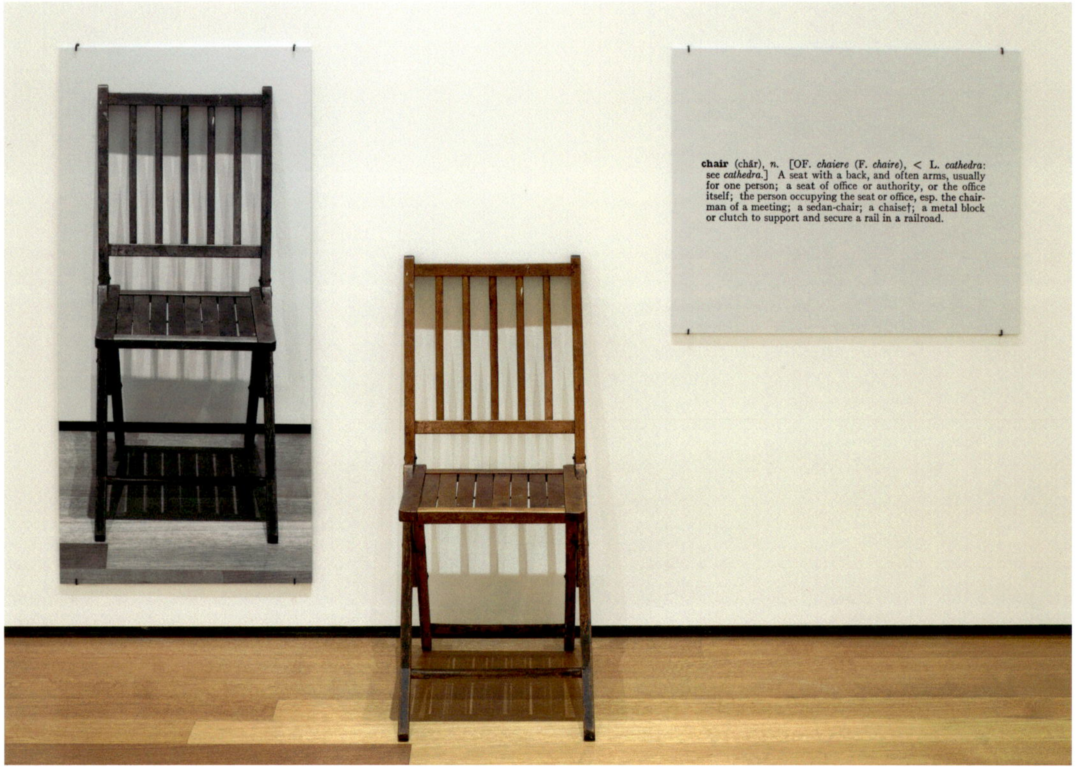

One and Three Chairs 1965
Joseph Kosuth

the images and texts—are incompatible, conciliation occurs through the construction of a narrative to account for them. As a narrative of the exotic and uncanny, Joseph Conrad's 1902 novella *Heart of Darkness* often serves as a model and source of inspiration for Fisher's work. In its depiction of the colonization of Africa and the ivory trade, *Heart of Darkness* probes the concept of otherness and the very human emotion of fear evoked by the unknown. The novella is structured as a story within a story, providing a key to understanding Fisher's own approach to picture making. The character of the novella's central figure, Kurtz the ivory hunter, is constructed from stories told to the narrator, Marlow, who relates them, along with his own climactic encounter, to his fellow sailors, including the unnamed narrator of the frame story. *Heart of Darkness* only allows the reader direct access to Kurtz on his deathbed. As a framed narrative (recalling *Framed Landscape*), the text depends on the individual narrator's point of view. The novella's moral position on race and imperialism is never made explicit; as a writerly text, its meaning emerges from what is unspoken and in between.

The activity of story writing served as a springboard for Fisher's first mature body of work in the mid-1970s. Discouraged with a series of large abstract paintings on vinyl, he began making small books containing written texts. Larger works followed, featuring longer texts superimposed on paintings of banal snapshots. Fisher discovered a way to sand the surface of the painted paper over plastic letters so that the letters of the text literally puncture the paintings. Reflecting on the ironies of everyday life and its existential absurdities, Fisher's stories relate poignant predicaments and melancholic disappointments, "where things aren't working out as planned."[12] Language was widely used in visual art at this time; thus, Fisher's early work was associated with both narrative art, which used pictures to tell stories, and conceptual art, such as that of Joseph Kosuth. Relying on words, often combined with photographic imagery to convey an aesthetic or visual idea, conceptual art is not necessarily narrative. Resistant to narrative interpretation, Kosuth's use of dictionary definitions involves the presentation of an idea (the representation, meaning, and use of an object, for instance, exemplified by the three components of his *One and Three*

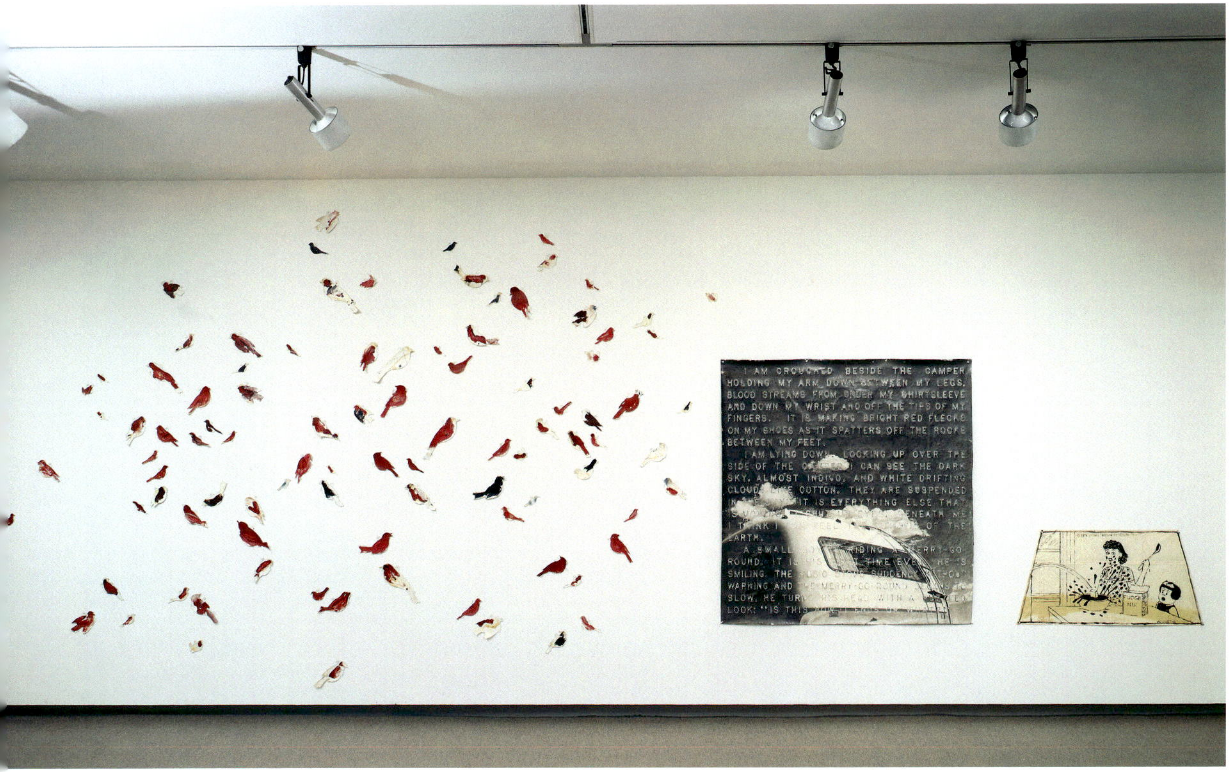

84 Sparrows 1979

Chairs, 1965) rather than the creation of a "text." Fisher's work, however, is more literary in its use of "texts" rather than simple language. In Fisher's practice, the narrative text opens a "methodological field" with multiple meanings, irreducible to any one.[13] In contrast to *One and Three Chairs*, the three horizontally aligned components of Fisher's *84 Sparrows* (1979) create a linear, "sequential order of three very dissimilar elements,"[14] which are visually and conceptually disjunctive but linked by a narrative thread. On the left side of the work, a group of red birds, individually cut out of canvas, is stapled to the wall. On the right is a trapezoidal-shaped drawing of a cartoon panel depicting an astonished Nancy and Aunt Fritzi from the comic strip *Nancy* splashed with chocolate fudge by a free sample of soap thrown into their mixing bowl by a vendor outside the kitchen window. In the center, a photorealistic drawing of the back of a round-roofed camper provides the background for a sanded story describing blood running down the narrator's arm, his sensation of the earth's movement, and a moment of childhood innocence:

> I am crouched beside the camper holding my arm down between my legs. Blood streams from under my shirt-sleeve and down my wrist and off the tips of my fingers. It is making bright red flecks on my shoes as it spatters off the rocks between my feet.
>
> I am lying down. Looking up over the sides of the camper I can see the dark sky, almost indigo, and white drifting clouds like cotton. They are suspended in the sky: it is everything else that is moving. I shut my eyes. Beneath me I think I can feel the turning of the earth.
>
> A small boy is riding a merry-go-round. It is his first time ever. He is smiling. The music stops suddenly without warning and the merry-go-round begins to slow. He turns his head with a puzzled look: "Is this how it ends or what?"

As a text of images as well as of words, *84 Sparrows* offers a field of meaning to be deciphered. It evokes a variety of connections, especially relating to the drops of blood, from the red paint on the birds to the splatters of fudge. The mystery surrounding the unknown causes of the bleeding and the spattering, echoed by the child's bewildered state in the written story, establish the narrative thread.

Along with the structure of narrative, Fisher's works often employ a pedagogical instrument in a supporting role. Blackboards, maps, globes, graph paper, and rulers allow him to "start with something we know."[15] Recalling Jasper Johns's description of his flags and targets as "things the mind already knows,"[16] Fisher's familiar subjects ease viewers into a complex narrative of competing signifiers. "Serv[ing] as potent reminders of our efforts to pin things down, to 'locate ourselves' in the world," he explains, the organizational structures anchor scattered, seemingly arbitrary images, such as cartoon characters or landscape vignettes.[17] The images are secured to the support in the way flags are pinned to a map or equations limned on a chalkboard. Their location appears natural and familiar, without regard for the coherent placement of figures in space in illusionistic painting. Rulers also pin things down, creating the impression of accuracy and credibility. With a story describing an invasion of wasps in the artist's studio, *Wasp Killer* (1979) includes a yardstick, (presumably the one used to kill the wasps) attached to the bottom edge of the left panel, as if to verify the truth of the text through objective affirmation. Fisher's sculpture *Heart of Darkness* (1986), based on a model demonstrating the size of a one-meter cube, includes a ruled measure on one edge of a gridded cube. A maroon vignette of a desert landscape is painted on the opposite corner, spreading onto two sides and the top of the box so that its spatial illusion is completely legible from only one vantage point. A folding ruler, suspended from the lower edge of a painting of faraway mountains and a gleaming river in *Victoria* (1997) suggests the futility of quantifying a distant vision. Due to the natural fallibility of memory and the idiosyncrasy of subjective points of view, there is no singularly true way of accounting for the past. As Fisher says, "What you see always depends on where you stand."[18]

Written short stories began to disappear from Fisher's work in the mid-1980s but the palimpsest effect of layered narratives remained. Blackboards, which Fisher first used in *I Try to Be Objective* (1980) and *Show and Tell* (1981), replaced the photo-based paintings as the physical support for the works and proved to be fertile grounds for fields of disparate images. Although blackboards were also used by Cy Twombly and Joseph Beuys, for whom the classroom associations and didactic implications were meaningful, Fisher uses the blackboard as a specific metaphor for the mind. Displaying partially erased words and hand-rendered pictures of all types from the schematic to the photographic, Fisher's blackboard paintings explore the complexities of time and memory. "Blackboards seem to have, in addition to the obvious pedagogical associations, affinities with the process of thought and memory," he explains.[19] Echoing the temporal distance and degrees of uncertainty in memories, the legibility of the pentimenti ranges from the clarity of highly detailed drawings to the near obscurity of smudges and erasures. Whether they are realistic images and identifiable words or abstract mathematical equations and geometric diagrams, the types of inscriptions on Fisher's blackboards suggest the varieties of memories that occupy the human mind.

Fisher's blackboard paintings were originally painted with slating, a type of paint used to resurface or replace slate blackboards in the classroom. The slating was applied to Masonite panels mounted on elaborate wooden supports with a grid of diagonal struts visible from the side. *Scenes from the American West* (1986), an early blackboard painting that includes a hand-painted image of a drained swimming pool, is shaped like the head of Mickey Mouse; in place of Mickey's eyes are holes that reveal the underlying trestlework. The first stand-alone blackboard painting, *Spider* (1986), is also backed by wooden scaffolding, which supports an actual bathroom sink (recalling elementary-school plumbing) attached to the front of the painting. A highly illusionistic drawing of a rib cage is centered on an erased field that includes an angled skyscraper, a circular pattern of rotating spheres labeled "orbit of moon," mathematical notations, and fragments of writing. In the upper right, a red monochrome vignette depicts a man releasing a weather balloon.

Fisher drew and wrote on his blackboard paintings with white oil stick, which he washed down with solvents to give the impression of erasures. In the 1990s, he substituted black acrylic paint for slating and canvas for the Masonite without

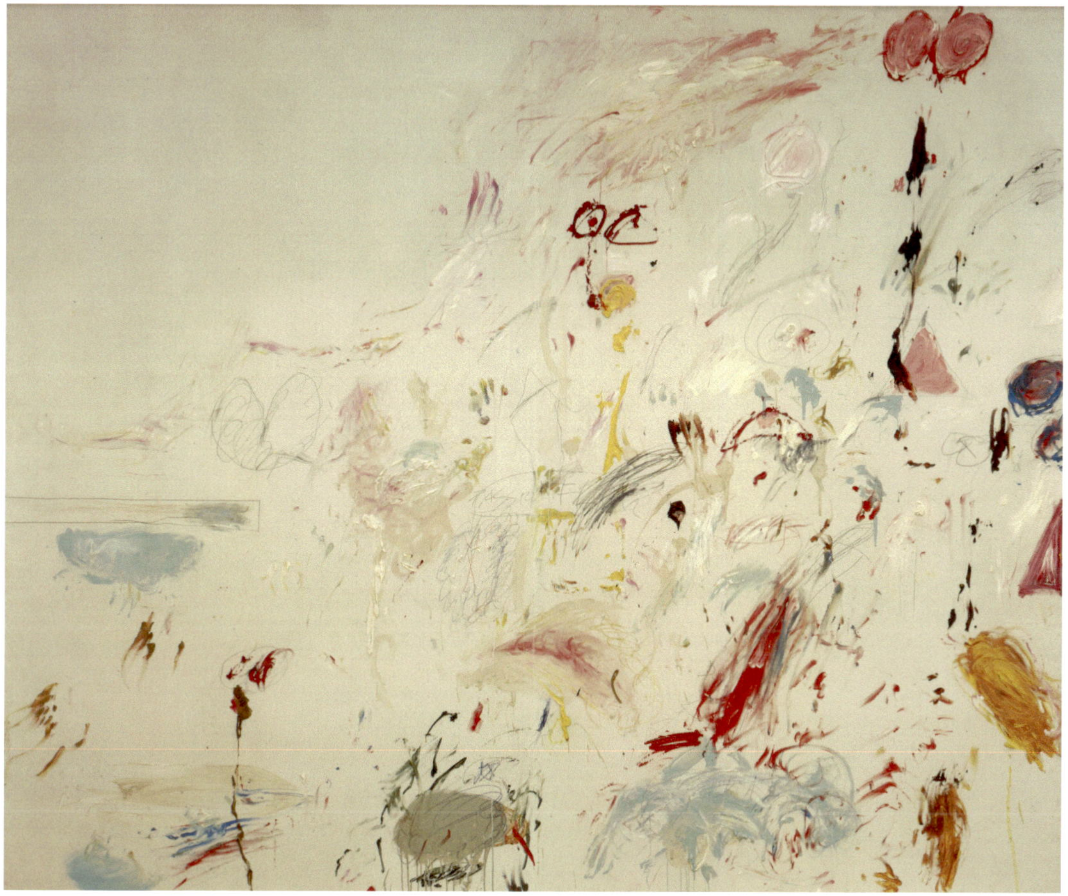

undermining the illusion of an actual blackboard. The illusion is reinforced by including sticks of chalk, eventually replaced by cast epoxy facsimiles, in attached chalk trays or in piles on the floor. Because the chalk markings range from the unfinished to the erased, they appear to be in progress, suggesting that the artist might soon return to his scribbles and calculations. The appearance of suspended activity has also led to the mistaken assumption that the works are intended to be participatory. In 1990, for example, assured by the curator that viewers would know better, Fisher left a just-finished chalk drawing in the Projects Gallery at the Museum of Modern Art only to later learn that a visitor had attempted to complete his drawing for him.[20]

The temporality invoked by the partially erased words, numbers, and diagrams is echoed in the two basic types of ready-made images: line drawings based on comic strips, textbooks, and other drawn illustrations, and painted vignettes derived from photographs. Considerably altered and adjusted through many years of use, Fisher's source materials are housed in both his computer and in an archive of file folders containing thousands of images culled from newspapers, magazines, encyclopedias, textbooks, postcards, and snapshots. In contrast to the simplicity of Fisher's line drawings and cartoons, the monochromatic vignettes are carefully rendered in oil paint to retain the spatial and three-dimensional illusions of their photographic sources. Originally inspired by the sight of spot repairs on old cars in the numerous body shops surrounding his studio in Fort Worth, these vignettes appear as floating, cloud-like patches with blurred white edges. Similar to the speech and thought balloons used in cartooning, the vignettes introduce additional images that create competing narratives in the manner of stray memories or distractions from the business at hand. Their appearance startles but their subject matter, drawn from the collective American consciousness, always seems familiar. The actions, events, and sites depicted in the vignettes also reflect the artist's interest in the operations of the imaginative mind.

Bay of Naples 1961
Cy Twombly

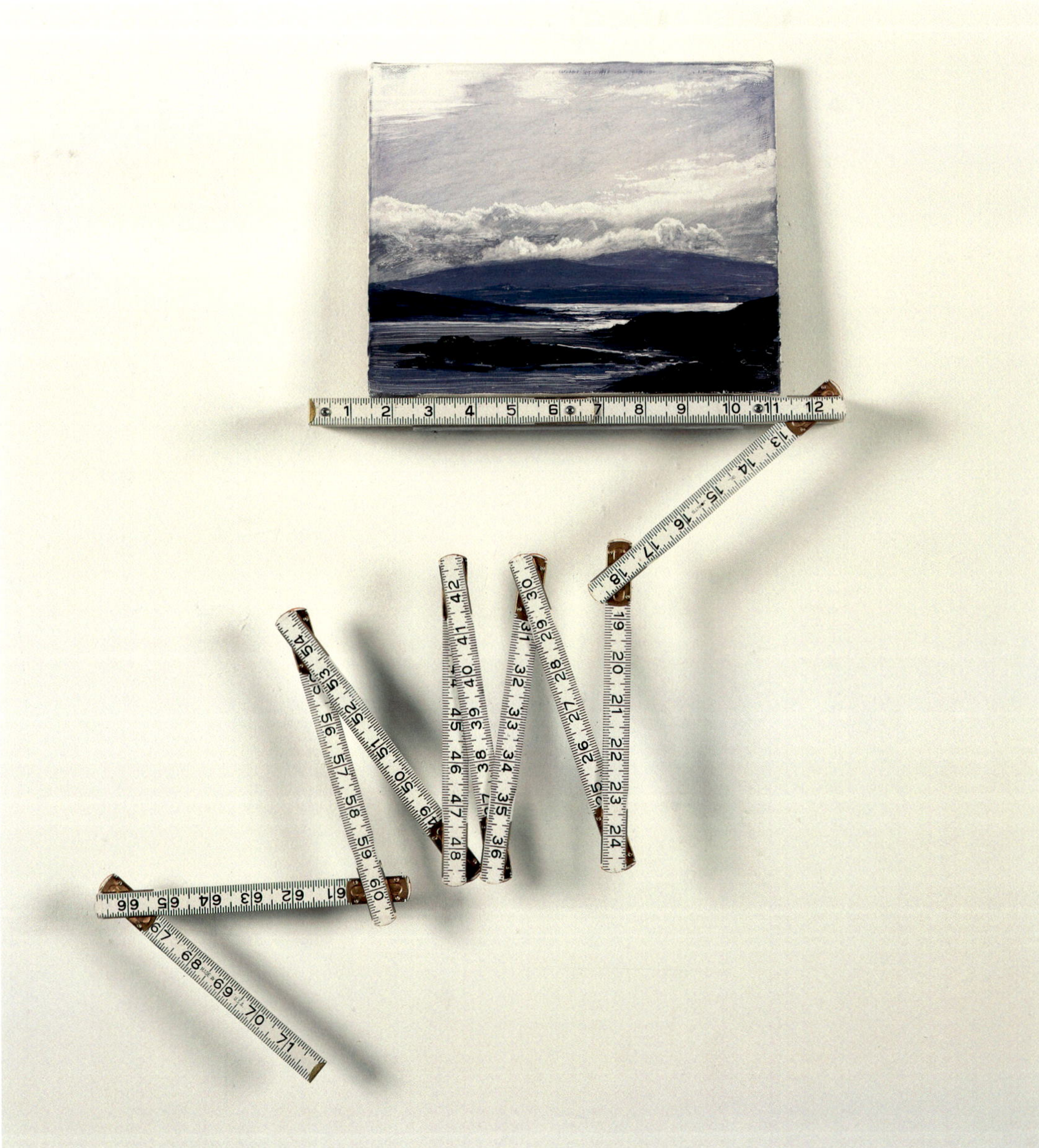

Numerous vignettes of water, including oceans, rivers, waterfalls, and pools, and activities such as swimming and parachuting suggest free-floating and transcendent states of mind. Scientific experiments, explorers, observatories, and land-surveying equipment act as metonyms for the search for meaning. Images of war, such as exploding planes and sinking ships, connote what Fisher describes as "anxious mental states."[21]

Land- and seascapes appear frequently, with the illusion of deep space often intervening between the viewer and the subject of the scene. The vignettes resemble faded photographs "situated formally and thematically in an inaccessible past," as Madeleine Grynsztejn has observed.[22] A recurring subject, which appears in vignettes as well as in stand-alone paintings, is the mountainous landscape, seen from a great distance and raked by dusky light. The two versions of this landscape, the cool, dark mountain range with a winding river in the foreground of *Victoria*, and the arid craggy peaks in *Framed Landscape*, are more painterly than Fisher's typical vignettes. Although sometimes rendered in monochrome, the landscapes are more frequently painted in luminous, softly blended colors. The mountains' physical distance from us implies their temporal distance such that we are, as Dave Hickey observed, "seeing the past in the distance."[23] Reminiscent of the expansive American vision of the Hudson River school, the landscape vignette opens a spatial and temporal gap in a painting that is otherwise present and current.

Victoria 1997

Fisher is partial to comic-book characters from the classic era of cartooning, recalling the simplicity and innocence of youth. Serving not only to represent distant memories, they are, like the maps and blackboards, "something we know." With well-established identities, the personalities and expressive gestures of each character function as emotive punctuation. Although both are mice, for example, the innocent Mickey Mouse and the scheming Ignatz from the *Krazy Kat* comic strip carry very different associations. Nancy, Aunt Fritzi, and Sluggo, the characters in Ernie Bushmiller's broadly drawn comic strip *Nancy* encounter each day with wide-eyed good humor.[24] In the context of Fisher's work, Nancy is "a kind of existential observer whose round-mouthed surprise at life's unpredictability punctuates the scrambled narrative," notes Richard Flood.[25] Although Fisher's comic-book characters are often produced by his own hand, he sometimes degrades scans of the images in Photoshop and then transfers these images to a painting using computer-cut stencils and an airbrush. In early paintings and wall texts, silkscreen printing produced comparable results. Following the examples of Andy Warhol and Robert Rauschenberg, Fisher used the silkscreen to facilitate the transfer and reproduction of ready-made, albeit often altered or hand-drawn, imagery.

Fisher's images, like his blackboard paintings, probe the operations of memory and its relationship to history. Resembling familiar pictures, they may be derived from previously published photographs that we have encountered or they might simply conjure up a type of image—a crashing war plane or a car speeding into the distance—that filled mid-century magazines and newspapers and which reside in our collective memory. Unlike many artists who maintain an archive of source materials to serve as models, inspirations, or critical appropriations, Fisher's use of images is semiotic. Upon their contextualization in a work of art, the images are endowed with meaning and function as if they were words or punctuation marks in a sentence. With no investment in the novelty of the images, Fisher uses the same sources repeatedly, whenever and wherever they are appropriate, much in the same way a writer uses words.[26] The repetition of depictions occurs not only throughout his entire body of work but also in individual pieces. In *Swimming Lesions* (1994), a large-scale installation at Blue Star Art Space in San Antonio, Texas, Fisher presented six tableaux linked by the evocation of memory. At the installation's center was a twelve-foot-high, forty-foot-wide two-sided blackboard wall covered with an expanse of erasures and random information, including numerous images of water. Only after studying both sides of the wall would the viewer realize that the apparently arbitrary information on the front was repeated, with extremely subtle differences, on the back. Throughout the installation, objects, images, and snippets of text appeared in a variety of contexts, gently jostling the memory.

Parallel Lines (1988), at the Hirshhorn Museum and Sculpture Garden in Washington, D. C., also established formal and conceptual relationships across the space of the museum. Eight blackboard drawings were executed directly on the walls of the exit door alcoves on two floors of the circular building. On the second floor were paintings representing a child's perspective on a topic, while on the third floor, a related issue was presented from an adult's point of view. As in *Swimming Lesions*, the entire work could not be experienced at once and had to be assembled in the mind as the viewer moved through the installation. Chalk drawings of circles and spheres, including an orbiting moon, a spinning top, a beach ball, a mine floating on water, and numerous representations of globes echoed the circular structure of the Hirshhorn building. An illustration, reminiscent of children's books from the 1950s, depicted a man showing a boy how to carve a jack-o'-lantern. On the floor above, representing the adult perspective, a globe replaced the pumpkin. Segmenting and privatizing the world, carving the globe is a metonym for aggressive international colonization, foreshadowing the primary subject of the artist's later work: narratives of conquest, exemplified chillingly by Conrad's *Heart of Darkness*.

"Destination Tokyo," a three-paragraph story rendered in white letters on the black doors of the Hirshhorn's freight elevator, was one of two textual components in *Parallel Lines*. The overall narrative of the story recounts a mother's reading lesson to her son on a rainy afternoon; however, the last line, where the son's attention wanders, alludes to the 1943 movie *Destination Tokyo* about the USS *Copperfin*'s secret mission to Japan. The corresponding text on the third floor was "ELF," a deadpan description of extremely low-frequency (ELF) radio signals used by the Navy to communicate with nuclear submarines. Fisher's narrative texts frequently contain a humorous, ironic, or melancholic plot twist. In "ELF" the irony is that the system's sensitivity has led radio operators to mistake their own heartbeats for these crucial communication signals. Contextualized by the museum's location in Washington, D. C., the headquarters of the military-industrial complex spawned by World War II, *Parallel Lines* addressed the national myth of America triumphant, bolstered by advanced weaponry and codified in both Hollywood and journalistic depictions.

With some changes, the "ELF" wall text also appeared in Fisher's 1988 exhibition at the Dallas Museum of Art, *Lost for Words*. The Dallas installation included the previously mentioned sculpture, *Heart of Darkness*. A pair of surveyors with a surveyor's level and measuring staff were painted on one long wall in the museum's main concourse, one at each end of the ramp leading to the galleries. *Pluto*, another wall painting, contained two interwoven and incomplete drawings of dogs: a blue connect-the-dots image of Disney's Pluto, and a series of black splotches. The black-and-white splotch pattern was derived from a perception test known as the "Dog Picture" or "Dalmatian in the Snow," which demonstrates the capacity for forming gestalts. In this context, "ELF" contributed to a meditation on relative legibility, decoding, and inevitable misreadings, which functioned as one of the exhibition's narrative threads.

Fisher's blackboard installation at the Museum of Modern Art in New York, *Movements Among the Dead* (1990), included an upside-down, elongated version of "Dalmatian in the Snow" painted inside a white ellipse. A wall text described Pavlov training a dog to associate cookies with circles projected onto a screen. When ellipses were projected, no treats were dispensed. As the projected images were progressively compressed into circles, the dog went wild. To illustrate the transformation described in the story, a surveyor's level was placed in the center of the gallery and aimed at a parabolic mirror reflecting the Dalmatian on the adjacent wall. Viewers saw the ellipse corrected into a circle and the dog right side up. Behind the mirror, a vignette depicted an image of two explorers in pith helmets riding in a canoe paddled by a dark-skinned native. Based on an encyclopedia illustration, the boat is reiterated in Fisher's later works, such as *The Single-State Assumption* (2005), which is in his series of punctuation paintings.

Words, equations, geometric diagrams, water images (including sea shells and swimmers), and anatomical drawings remain in the pentimenti and scattered vignettes in Fisher's portable chalkboard paintings. In *Evidence of Houdini's Return* (1994), a partially erased and disconnected arm, head, and male torso with an upside-down Mickey Mouse head in place of genitals, occupy different areas of the ground. Vignettes include a ball floating on water (first seen at the Hirshhorn) and a beaker of white liquid with a few mysterious black shapes floating in it. This last vignette is based on Fisher's staged photograph of a Mickey Mouse toy submerged in milk with just the tips of his ears visible and his nose pressed against the glass. An abstract counterpoint, flat brown and black squares appear above a tempting chalk tray projecting from the center of the picture. The palimpsest of drawn and painted images offers the challenge of decipherability and the opportunity for the viewer to unscramble the work's "evidence," rather than to hunt for the artist's intentions or uncover his feelings.

Reinforcing the metaphorical relationship of the blackboard to the narratizing process of consciousness, anatomical illustrations of brains appear in Fisher's later-1990s blackboard paintings. In *Model Citizens* (1997), multiple chalk drawings of brains seen from the front and back and in isomorphic projection are juxtaposed with deep blue vignettes of a Japanese plane crashing into the ocean and of a sinking ship. Clouds of smoke billowing from the explosions recall the brain's puffy wrinkles. *Streams* (1997) includes several line drawings of the brain along with a more modeled version with dark crevices. A distinctly drawn head, with neck musculature

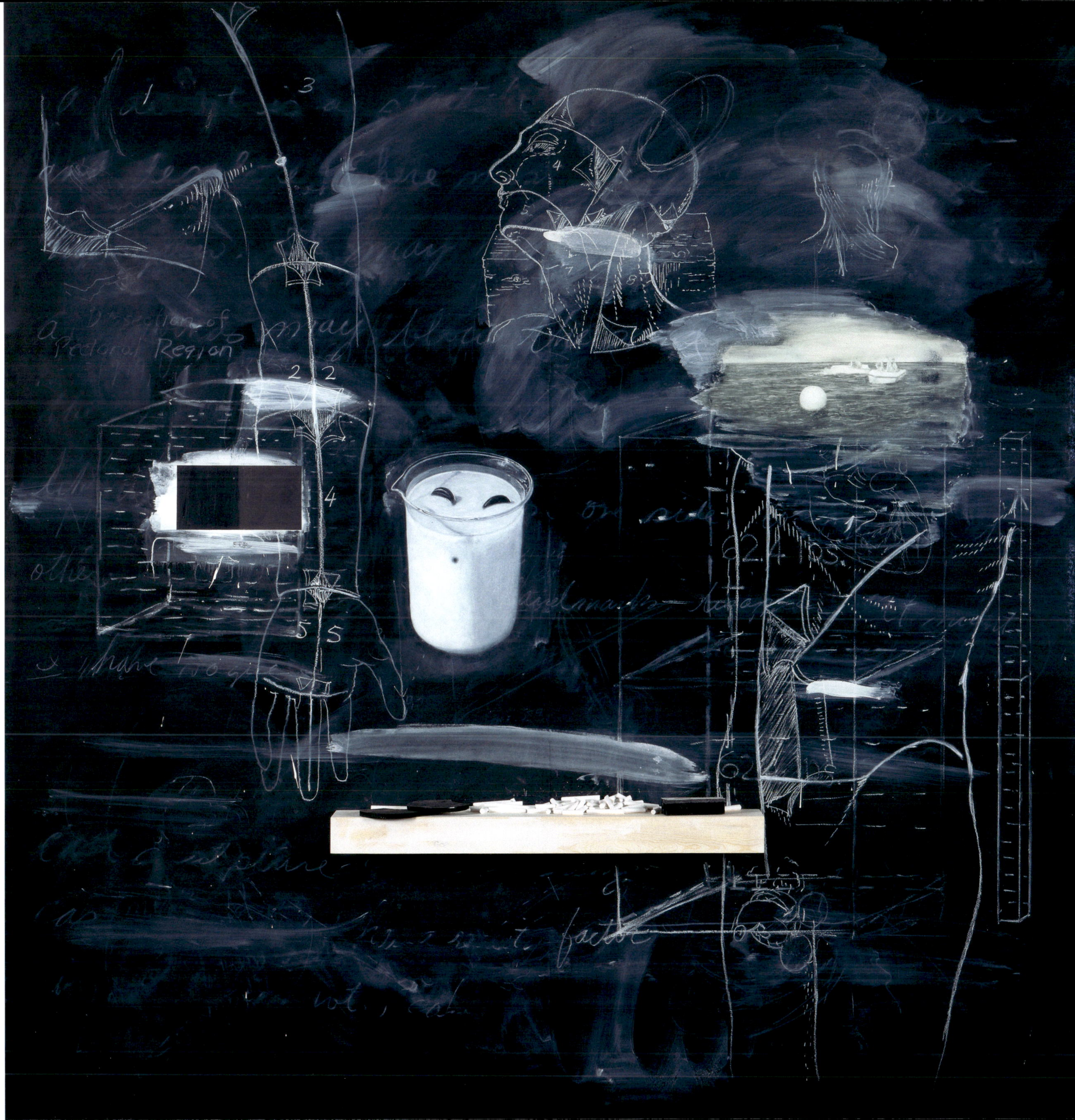
Dissection of
Pectoral Region

outlined, is shown in the process of vomiting. In contrast to this detailed illustration, two smaller cartoon-like faces with a few strokes for hair appear to the left. Beneath are barely legible bits of writing and an erased image of another face and neck. In the center of the painting is a photorealistic vignette depicting a man washing his eyes under a faucet. Rhyming visually with the flow of the fluid disgorged by the vomiting head, water streams across the figure's face. Beneath the painting sit stacks of artificial chalk and real blackboard erasers. Like most of Fisher's blackboard paintings, *Streams* includes a variety of forms of communication and drawing styles, ranging from the naturalistic to the schematic. Each approach is specific to the type of information conveyed. One has the quality of an illustration in a medical book, another the comic effect of caricature, and yet another a primitive denotation of death (crosses in place of eyes). There is no evidence of a single masterful hand, the mark of individuality prized for its authenticity by connoisseurs, but rather a variety of expressions, recalling *Hills Like White Elephants*.

Maps, much like blackboards, are susceptible to revision. Borders are shifted, place names changed, and highways constructed, but the accuracy of a map is taken for granted. Casting doubt on presumptions of permanence and credibility, the maps in Fisher's paintings are outdated and evocative of a resonant era in our recent geographical past. In two instances he combines the map and blackboard in the manner of pull-down maps used in classrooms. Maps of the Pacific Ocean between China and Australia with locations and demarcations from World War II appear in *Swimming from Australia to Japan* (1993) and *Painting in the Pacific* (1994). Suspended in front of handmade blackboards, the trompe l'oeil maps are painstakingly fabricated by hand. Their artificiality is revealed by the curve and dip of the painted map's edges, which is retained from the source of the image—a photocopy of a two-page spread in a book. The wooden pull bar at the bottom of the map faithfully repeats the distortion. A surprising and delightful detail in *Swimming from Australia to Japan* that doesn't make itself immediately apparent is the depiction of the island of Japan in the shape of Godzilla, the Japanese movie monster.

In recent works, the nineteenth-century map of colonial Africa provides a framework for narratives alluding to controversial issues raised by Conrad's *Heart of Darkness* and Darwin's *Descent of Man* (1871). Fisher addressed the topic of Africa's primal otherness as early as 1980 in *Tarzan's Adventure*, which includes a four-paragraph story recalling the narrator's penchant for televised *Tarzan* movies as a child. "I'm still drawn to them," he writes. "It's as though they constitute for me a kind of primary reality, and seeing them now, thirty years later, is like experiencing again the innocent, balmy days of childhood." Images of a swimming Johnny Weissmuller and white men in pith helmets, mostly photographed from a television screen, appear in many paintings as well. All of Fisher's African paintings use a similar section of a colonial map representing the heart of Africa, with the Belgian Congo toward the bottom and Libya at the top. Countries, deserts, rivers, and Lake Victoria (the putative subject of the 1997 painting *Victoria*) are identified by name. *Private Africa* (1995), the first painting to use this map, depicts a blue parachutist and a large waterfall on the site of Victoria Falls, suggesting a thrilling and unconventional descent through space. Although the title refers to the privatization of the country's resources by European colonization, it reflects on a personal level Fisher's childhood introduction to the "Dark Continent" through slide lectures presented by missionaries in his mother's church.[27]

In contrast to the cool black, white, and blue colors of *Private Africa*, *Out of Africa* (2007) is detailed in red on a mottled orange ground. The text on the map, having been degraded in Photoshop, is partially illegible; as the font size decreases, the letters become rounder and begin to break apart. Visual noise is created by stray pixels (small groups of squares made with thick red or black paint), and airbrushed gray puffs, which create a patina of age and disintegration analogous to the fraying of the colonial myth. At the center, an elliptical vignette *en grisaille* depicts the back of a fake gorilla, looming above the roof of an industrial building with crisscrossing power lines in the distance. The vignette was derived from the artist's snapshot of an advertising inflatable at a local haunted house attraction.

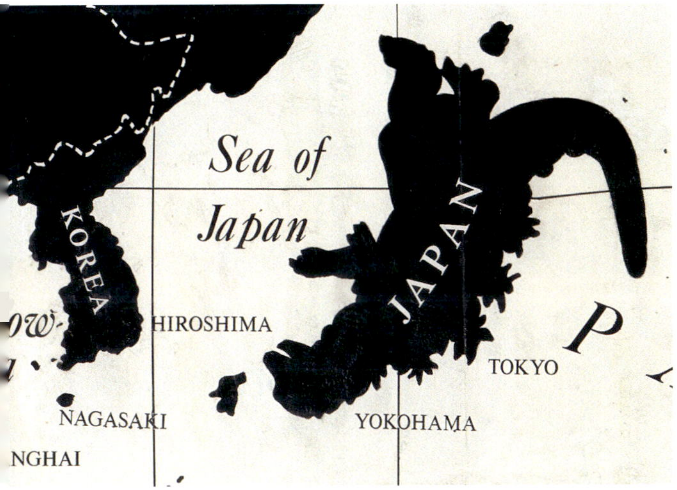

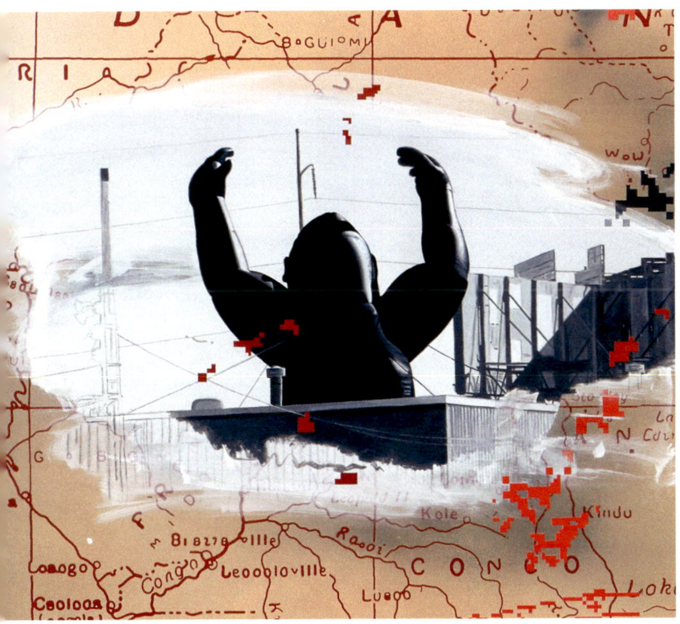

This postmodern King Kong is accompanied by six depictions of primates dispersed across the surface of the map. Resembling a mask, one gorilla head is illusionistically rendered by hand while the others are flatly stenciled. An orange vignette of two pith-helmeted characters in chest-high water (Jane's father, James Parker, and his partner in the ivory business, Harry Holt, from the original *Tarzan* movies) is on the upper left; the disembodied heads of Parker and Holt float in the upper right corner. Their individual identities (whether as characters or actors) are less important than their narrative signification as "great white hunters," referencing the activities of exploration and exploitation in literature (*Heart of Darkness*, 1902), film (*Tarzan the Ape Man*, 1932), and history (Karen Blixen's 1937 memoir of colonial Kenya, *Out of Africa*). Along with the mask-like quality of one ape's head, the artificial, air-filled gorilla recalls the fictionalization of Africa in movies such as *King Kong* (1933) and *Mighty Joe Young* (1949) in which the giant ape represents the dark and barbaric unknown.

In 2007 the African paintings were exhibited with a painted wall text based on the description of Kurtz's death in *Heart of Darkness*. Taken from an early draft of the novella, the section appears to be in a state of revision with handwritten notes, jokes, and puns actually written by Fisher. On the wall, the text was interrupted in the center by a rectangular painting of a ship sailing at night, alluding to Marlow's steamboat on which Kurtz uttered his chilling last words: "The horror, the horror." Large black quotation marks and a comma, both cast in epoxy, bracketed the painting. The punctuation elements are a device Fisher uses to establish the authenticity of an attribution and compare the narrative possibilities of representational painting and written language. A related text painting by Fisher, *Map* (1997), tells the story of a couple lost in the desert. When the woman identifies their location on a map "in a large, coral-shaded area" she jokes, "we're in the pink." None of the names of towns, "Abu Bahr, Abu Njaym, Abu Tij . . . were familiar and there were no names in the areas of coral." Her musings on the significance of the map's colors recall Marlow's recollection of the colored shapes on an African map in *Heart of Darkness*: "However, I wasn't going into any of these. I was going into the yellow. Dead in the center."

As if to provide the couple in Fisher's *Map* with an alternative form of navigating the desert, uncannily lifelike cast epoxy flies arranged in the configuration of the constellations were superimposed on the wall text. Also flecked with artificial flies, a series of reductive abstract paintings known as "Zombies" was also exhibited with *Map* in 1997. The Zombies are horizontally divided, bichromatic abstractions with crackled surfaces resembling a dry lakebed or peeling plaster wall. Their titles are based on the names of North African cities (like the towns in the text piece), positing the paintings as a precedent to the African map series, despite their obviously

Swimming Between Australia and Japan, detail 1993
Out of Africa, detail 2007

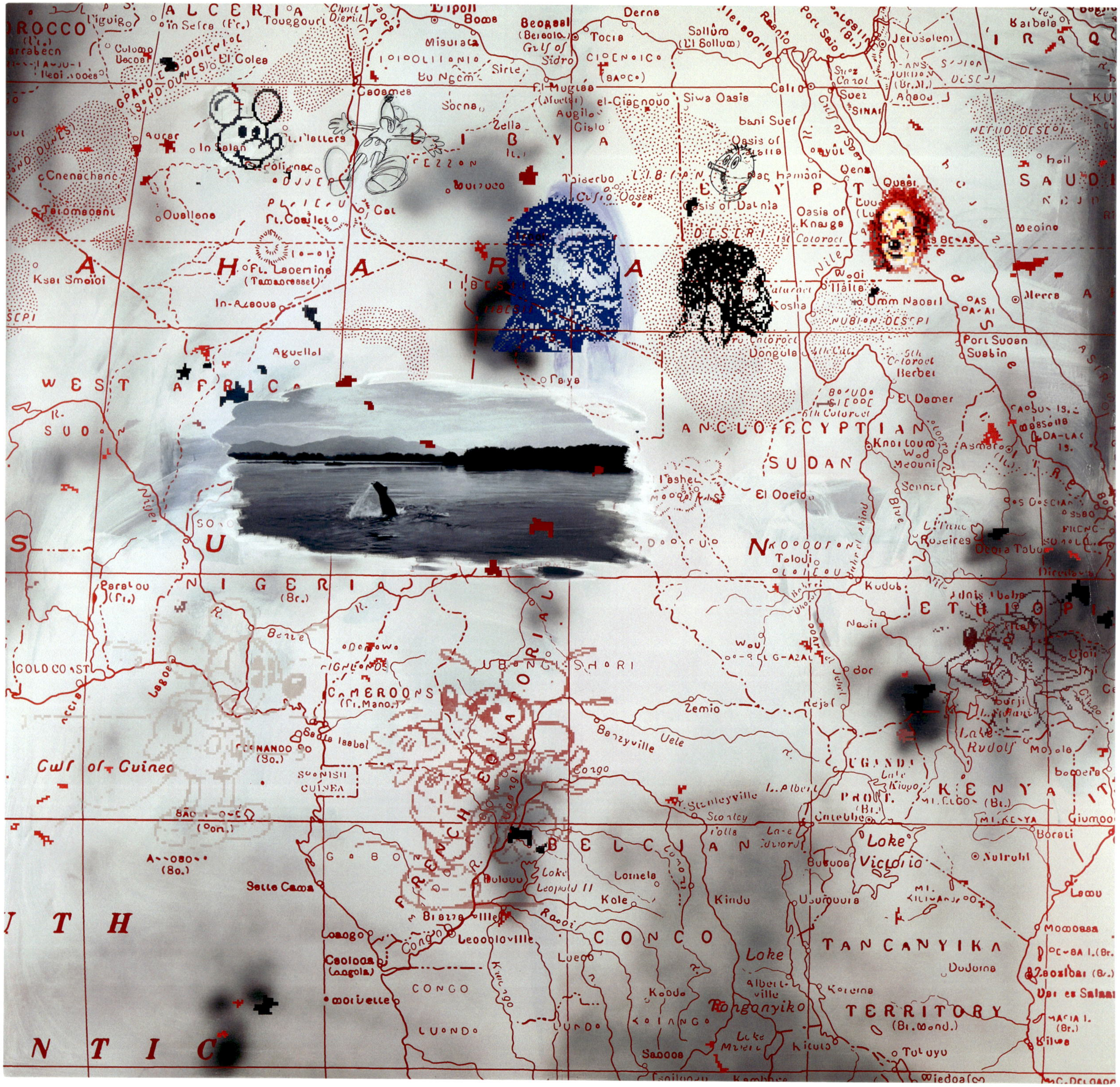

ALGERIA
Derna
Siwa Oasis
Cairo
Jerusalem
LIBYA
SAUDI
EGYPT
SAHARA
WEST AFRICA
ANGLO-EGYPTIAN
SUDAN
El Obeid
Port Sudan
NIGERIA
GOLD COAST
CAMEROONS
Gulf of Guinea
SPANISH GUINEA
FRENCH EQUATORIAL
ETHIOPIA
UGANDA
KENYA
BELGIAN
CONGO
Lake Victoria
Lake Rudolf
Zemio
Leopoldville
Kindu
Kole
Lake Tanganyika
TANGANYIKA TERRITORY
Nairobi
Mombasa
Zanzibar
Dar es Salaam
Kilwa
Setté Cama
NTIC
TH

visible differences. According to Fisher, the inspiration for the series was a scene in Michelangelo Antonioni's *The Passenger* of an insect crawling up a wall in a cheap hotel in North Africa.[28] As with all of Fisher's work, the meaning is not the same as that of the source of the images; it is not a matter of simple decoding. Several commentators have interpreted the title of the series as a reference to the death of painting and the end of modernism, but such a blanket proclamation is atypical of the subtle wit and multivalence of Fisher's oeuvre. The Zombies provoke a dialogue of nature and culture in which nature, represented by the flies, operates on its own terms. Flies appear to land on nearby walls as well as on paintings without regard for the cultural distinction between the two. They also act as interruptions and distractions from the rarified experience of modernist abstraction. "I prefer a high noise to signal ratio," Fisher has said, alluding to the working of the human mind.[29] Consciousness is constantly interrupted by stray thoughts just as flies flit from surface to surface. Buddhists describe this jumping from thought to thought as "monkey mind," a condition Fisher both acknowledges with good-natured acceptance and purposefully invokes in his work.

Fisher also uses simulated graph paper as a background for seemingly unrelated images, imposing order on everyday chaos. Using a cut-vinyl stencil, he transforms a canvas ground into drafting paper, adding an official-looking logo at the bottom. The logo, F + T Fiche & Tattoo, refers to the artist's alter egos, the angst-ridden Werner Fiche and the irreverent Consuelo Tattoo. Cartoon characters, movie stars, comedians, and landscape vignettes from Fisher's pictorial archive appear randomly placed, heedless of the graph paper's organizational grid. The process of making the painting begins with the selection of one image, such as a portrait by Raphael, a worried Mickey Mouse, or Marlon Brando in *A Streetcar Named Desire*. In a "metonymic slide," the expressive quality or implied narrative content of one image suggests the next, which leads to the next, and so on, like the children's game of "Gossip."[30] This metonymic slide from one image to the next is similar to a process of visual rhyming. In interviews, Fisher frequently acknowledges this process, noting for example that in *Ellipse* (2000), the form of an ellipse connects images of the Hindenburg and a manhole from a Nancy cartoon.[31] Fisher is fond of spherical shapes, matching a parachute with a domed observatory in *Objects in a Field* (1986) for instance. He is especially interested in spherical shapes that are composed of crescent-shaped segments: "What interests me about the parachute is the way it's constructed, with all these sections sewn together and reaching a point. It's the way a lot of rounded things are constructed: orange sections, pumpkins, globes, umbrellas."[32] Scalloped seashells and parachutes in *Parrot* (2002), for example, formally echo one another and provide a pseudo-logical connection for a seemingly arbitrary array of images. The titular reference to Darwin's theory of evolution is illustrated in *Descent of Man* (2007) by the diving swimmer, which recalls the modernist trope of linear progress in art history as well as evolution.

In an elaborate metonymic slide, Fisher uses the documentary effect of photography and verifiable dates of historical events to rhyme fiction with fact in his 1992 installation, *Moonrise, Hernandez, N.M., 1951*. The installation included a wall text and two color photographs of books open to pages radically altered by Fisher. In the first picture, a reproduction of Ansel Adams's *Moonrise* is accompanied by text recounting the tale of Ernesto, an ostensible resident of Hernandez, who is having difficulties with his television set as he watches the horror film, *The Wolf Man*. In the second picture, the book is open to a dozen entries footnoting the first picture. The footnotes, for example, explain that Ernesto's difficulties are taking place on the day after Halloween 1951, ten years to the day that Adam's photograph was made. They also explain that Ernesto actually appears in the original Adam's photograph, "though he is very, very small—just a few hundred grains of silver at the most," making reference to the metallic crystals that create a photographic image on paper. In place of illustrations on the books' recto pages are photographs of actual pieces of Halloween candies—an orange circus peanut and four jelly orange slices—casting shadows onto the pages.

The chains of associations that inform Fisher's works are literary as well as visual. A former English

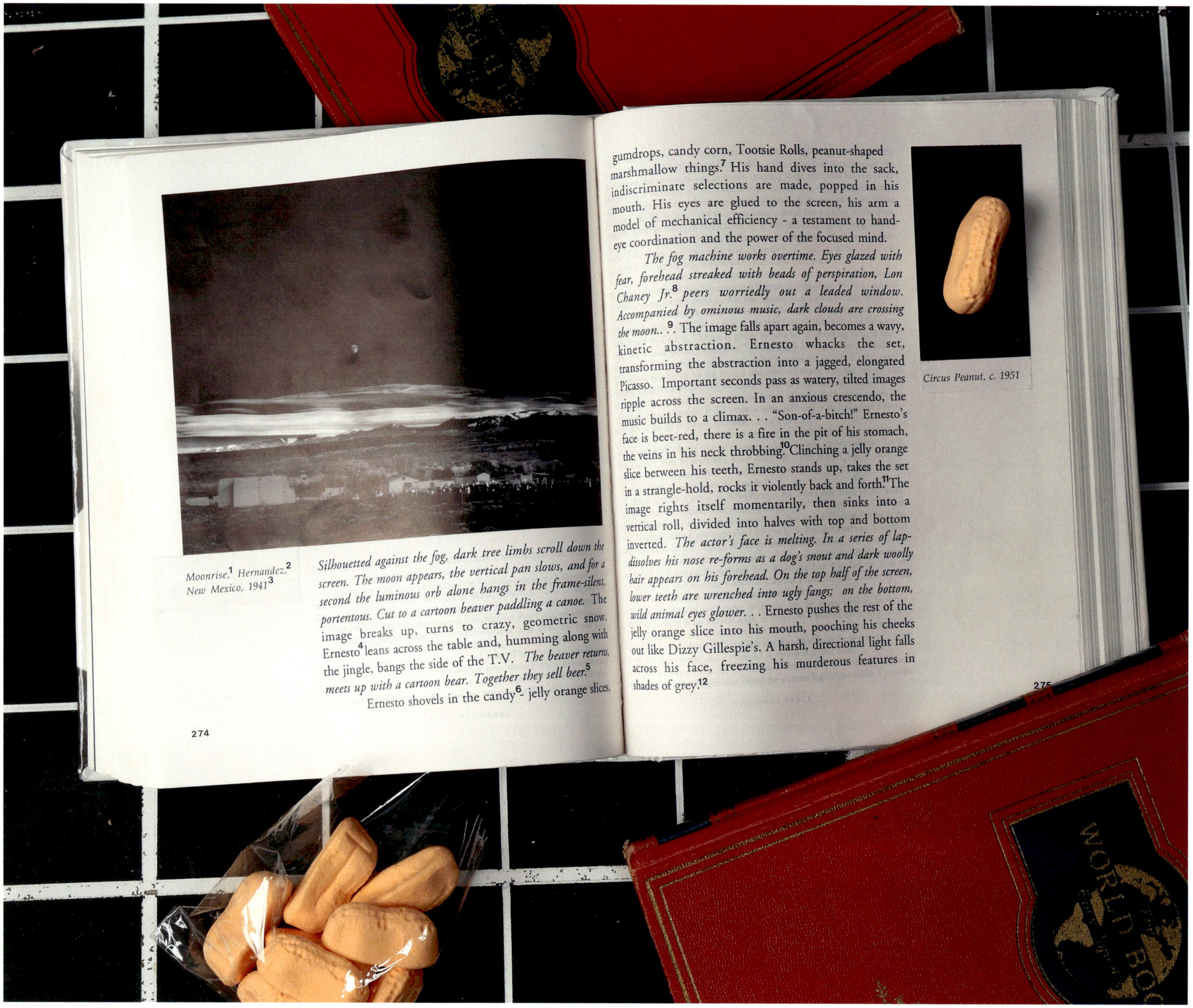

Moonrise, Hernandez, N.M., 1951 1992

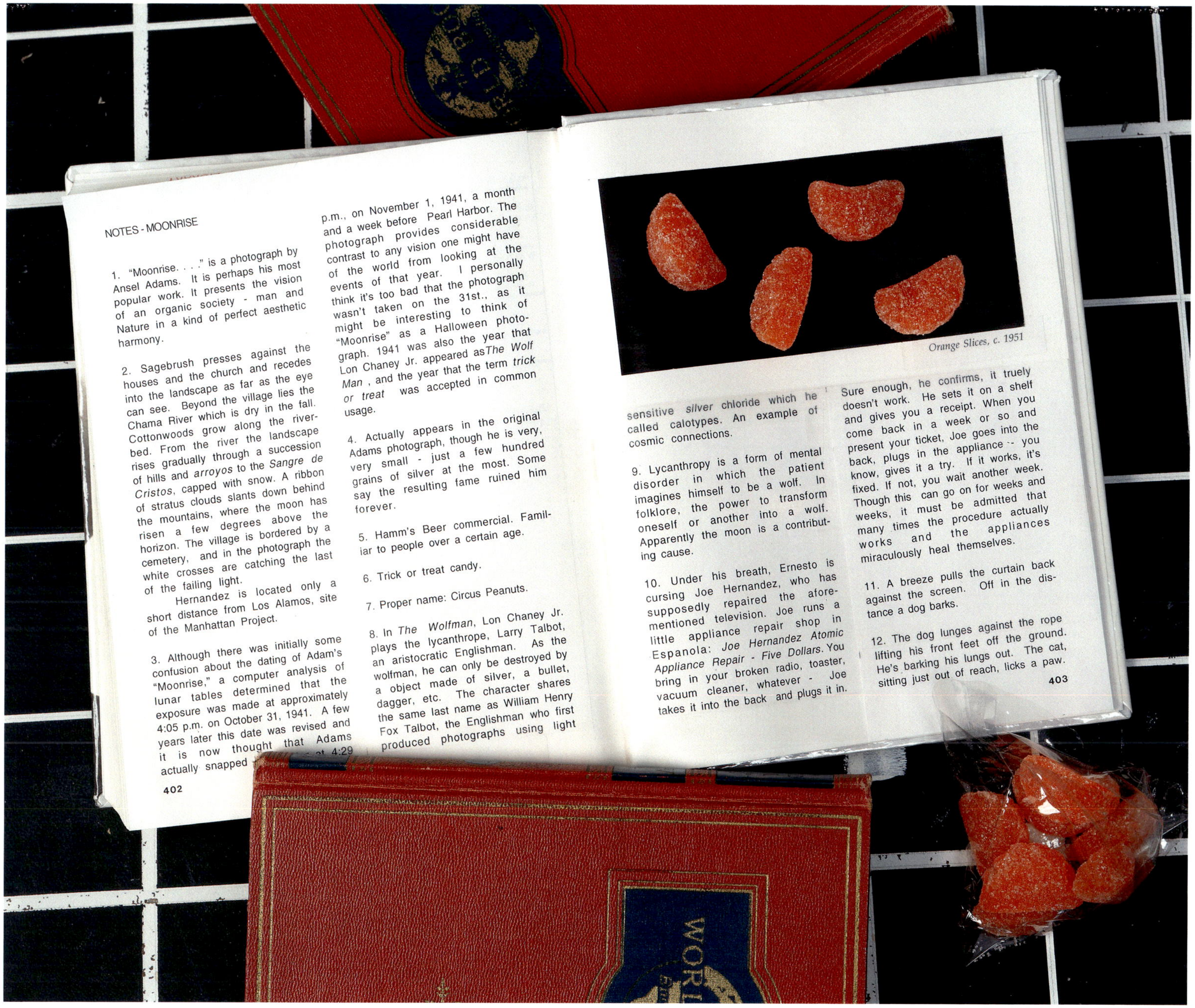
NOTES - MOONRISE
1. "Moonrise. . . ." is a photograph by Ansel Adams. It is perhaps his most popular work. It presents the vision of an organic society - man and Nature in a kind of perfect aesthetic harmony.
2. Sagebrush presses against the houses and the church and recedes into the landscape as far as the eye can see. Beyond the village lies the Chama River which is dry in the fall. Cottonwoods grow along the river-bed. From the river the landscape rises gradually through a succession of hills and arroyos to the Sangre de Cristos, capped with snow. A ribbon of stratus clouds slants down behind the mountains, where the moon has risen a few degrees above the horizon. The village is bordered by a cemetery, and in the photograph the white crosses are catching the last of the failing light.
Hernandez is located only a short distance from Los Alamos, site of the Manhattan Project.
3. Although there was initially some confusion about the dating of Adam's "Moonrise," a computer analysis of lunar tables determined that the exposure was made at approximately 4:05 p.m. on October 31, 1941. A few years later this date was revised and it is now thought that Adams actually snapped
402
p.m., on November 1, 1941, a month and a week before Pearl Harbor. The photograph provides considerable contrast to any vision one might have of the world from looking at the events of that year. I personally think it's too bad that the photograph wasn't taken on the 31st., as it might be interesting to think of "Moonrise" as a Halloween photograph. 1941 was also the year that Lon Chaney Jr. appeared asThe Wolf Man , and the year that the term trick or treat was accepted in common usage.
4. Actually appears in the original Adams photograph, though he is very, very small - just a few hundred grains of silver at the most. Some say the resulting fame ruined him forever.
5. Hamm's Beer commercial. Familiar to people over a certain age.
6. Trick or treat candy.
7. Proper name: Circus Peanuts.
8. In The Wolfman, Lon Chaney Jr. plays the lycanthrope, Larry Talbot, an aristocratic Englishman. As the wolfman, he can only be destroyed by a object made of silver, a bullet, dagger, etc. The character shares the same last name as William Henry Fox Talbot, the Englishman who first produced photographs using light
Orange Slices, c. 1951
sensitive silver chloride which he called calotypes. An example of cosmic connections.
9. Lycanthropy is a form of mental disorder in which the patient imagines himself to be a wolf. In folklore, the power to transform oneself or another into a wolf. Apparently the moon is a contributing cause.
10. Under his breath, Ernesto is cursing Joe Hernandez, who has supposedly repaired the aforementioned television. Joe runs a little appliance repair shop in Espanola: Joe Hernandez Atomic Appliance Repair - Five Dollars. You bring in your broken radio, toaster, vacuum cleaner, whatever - Joe takes it into the back and plugs it in.
Sure enough, he confirms, it truely doesn't work. He sets it on a shelf and gives you a receipt. When you come back in a week or so and present your ticket, Joe goes into the back, plugs in the appliance -- you know, gives it a try. If it works, it's fixed. If not, you wait another week. Though this can go on for weeks and weeks, it must be admitted that many times the procedure actually works and the appliances miraculously heal themselves.
11. A breeze pulls the curtain back against the screen. Off in the distance a dog barks.
12. The dog lunges against the rope lifting his front feet off the ground. He's barking his lungs out. The cat, sitting just out of reach, licks a paw.
403

major, Fisher has never lost his love of literature, which continues to inspire not only the narrative content of his works but the ways in which they are structured. He is especially influenced by the logical, concrete, and yet startling metaphors that are typical of seventeenth-century metaphysical poetry. Employing the metaphysical conceit, the poet provides insights into complex emotional states through previously unimaginable comparisons. One of the best-known metaphysical poems, John Donne's "The Flea," equates the insect's ingestion of blood with lovemaking. Attempting to convince his beloved that sex should not be shameful, the speaker argues that physical coupling is comparable to the mingling of their blood inside the flea that has bitten them both. In a similar manner, Fisher associates seemingly unrelated images and narratives such as Adams's *Moonrise* and a narrative about a fictional character watching *The Wolf Man*, complete with footnotes, to evoke otherwise indescribable feelings.

Such resonances continue in the newest paintings, which have battlefield maps as their backgrounds. Captions along the bottom edges of these paintings are adapted from the book *The 99 Critical Shots in Pool*. Conveying a sense of order, specificity, and precision, the book's title mirrors the obsessive detail of the maps. The battlefield as a metaphor for painting is romanticized in critic Harold Rosenberg's comparison of the abstract expressionist canvas to an arena in "The American Action Painters" (1952). Planning a battle and composing a painting depend on strategies that adapt to events as they unfold. In *Jocko at Dover* (2009), Nancy and Sluggo, with stars above their heads, and a clown are depicted on a World War II battlefield map of Europe, comically personifying defeat. The map traces the Allied evacuation following the Battle of Dunkirk in 1940, when Winston Churchill sent a flotilla of small boats to rescue 330,000 soldiers trapped by the Germans. White letters at the bottom of the map read, "Running English, also known as natural English, adds speed to the cue ball and widens the angle after the ball hits the cushion." Analogizing the strategies of pool and war, the map's caption creates a pun on the speedy retreat of the "running" English soldiers, represented by a tangle of battle lines and directional arrows.

The disparate images in Fisher's paintings are often bound together with drips and smudges of paint or erasures. Ironically recalling the improvisational methods of the abstract expressionists, the drips in Fisher's works signify a spontaneous process and are self-conscious attempts to unify the scattershot pastiche of seemingly unrelated figures. Reminiscent of Cy Twombly's compositions, with small explosions of gestural activity dispersed across the surface, Fisher's compositions also recall Arshile Gorky's organizational method, which was described by Clement Greenberg as "spotting." Gorky's compositions entail, as Greenberg explains, "the adjustment of spots or isolated areas of color," which are united by scumbling the edges of forms or washing transparent pigments over them. "Thus the 'spots,' which strike us first, seem indissolubly welded to the background on one and the same plane, instead of floating over it."[33] In Fisher's paintings erasures, stray pixels, scratches, and other forms of static serve a similar purpose.

Many of Fisher's works throughout his career have contained allusions to Hollywood films, tapping our collective knowledge of actors' identities and motion picture narratives. Like Cindy Sherman and David Salle, Fisher unpacks representations of the past by excavating the history of movies. Acting as clues to their cinematic origins, scratches and static often mar the surfaces of Fisher's film-based paintings such as *Rampaging Bikers* (1999), featuring Marlon Brando, *An American Tragedy* (2005), featuring Shelley Winters, and the *Angel Face* series (2002), based on the 1952 film starring Robert Mitchum and Jean Simmons. In the latter, snippets of invented or borrowed text appear along the bottom edge to caption and recontextualize the imagery. Appearing to have been sloppily typed and edited, with strikeovers and flying caps, the texts have a stuttering quality at odds with Mitchum's suave appeal. In *Scale* (2002), the text "Well, Frank, since you asked—it is smaller than I imagined," appears beneath a picture of Mitchum leaning over the windshield of Simmons's convertible. A vignette of a giant octopus and rabbit from Fisher's snapshot of miniature golf statuary at Goony Golf in Galveston, Texas, serves as a thought balloon for the

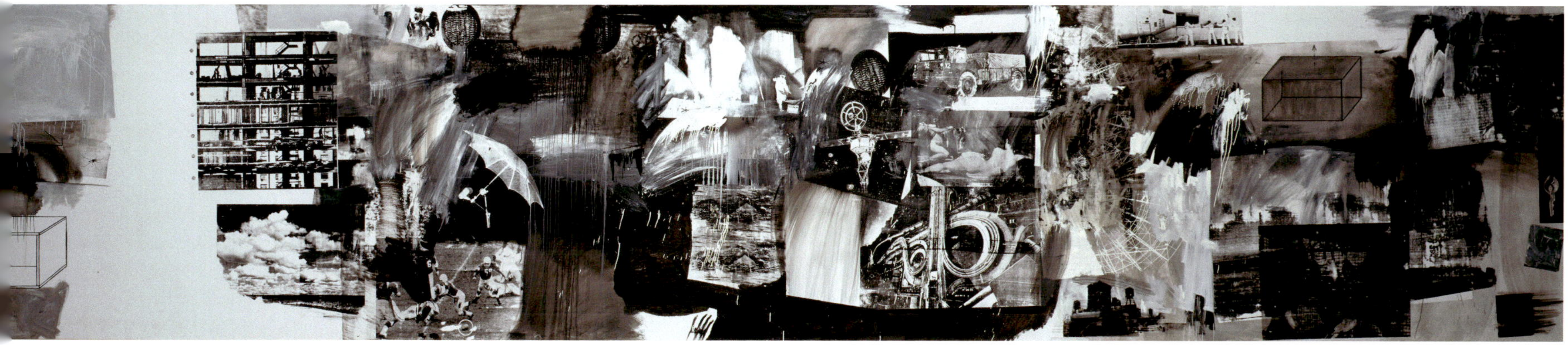

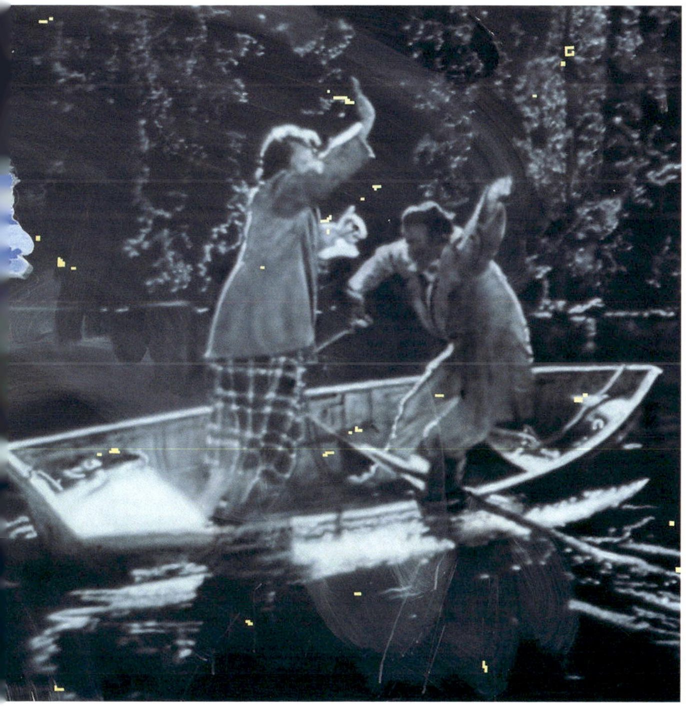

apparently confused Mitchum. An unusual palette of pink, blue, and orange as well as floating, dream-like vignettes of palm trees recast the series' film noir narratives as tropical fantasies.

A three-part work, *An American Tragedy* includes a painting of a black-and-white film still on the left, a sculptural plastic comma in the center, and a cutout drawing of a storm cloud on the right. Re-creating the climactic scene in *A Place in the Sun* (1951), a movie based on Theodore Dreiser's novel *An American Tragedy*, the painting depicts Shelley Winters's character Alice and Montgomery Clift's character George falling out of a boat. Inset on the far left is a blue vignette of a melting block of ice. Although seemingly arbitrary, the three representations—ice, boat on a lake, and cloud—refer to the physical states of water in the process of transformation—solid, liquid, and vapor—which are in turn equated with Alice's imminent death. Between the scene of the crime and the cloud, the comma supplies a pregnant pause (Alice was indeed pregnant, much to George's dismay) and recalls the literary source of the cinematic image. The series of punctuation paintings also includes *Death of Marat* (2002–2003), in which parentheses made out of cast black epoxy bracket a small landscape painting reminiscent of *Victoria*'s river and distant mountains. On the painting's left, a cutout cartoon-like drawing of a spilled can of paint, similar to the melting ice in *An American Tragedy*, alludes to an unhappy ending. Bearing white stripes that suggest the reflection of light, the puddle of black paint is a cartoon version of the luminous river represented in the landscape. *Death of Marat* is a wistful caricature of the tragic serenity evoked by its namesake, Jacques-Louis David's depiction of the assassinated revolutionary in his bath.

Many interpretations of Fisher's work acknowledge its similarities to Robert Rauschenberg's, both

Barge 1962–1963
Robert Rauschenberg

American Tragedy, detail 2005

in their imagery (comics and parachutes among the most obvious) and operational models of memory. The old lace, scraps of clothing, postcards, and newspaper clippings in Rauschenberg's collages are evocative fragments of the past held together by a patina of age and disuse. Described by Leo Steinberg as "a symbolic continuum of litter," a work by Rauschenberg is dense with materials unlike Fisher's two-dimensionally oriented paintings.[34] But both artists present the viewer with layered and colliding forms that require sorting and unpacking through temporal and visual leaps of the imagination. In contrast to the singularity and immediacy of modern works of art, theirs are organized on the discursive model of syntax. While Rauschenberg retained the unifying or "gluing" effect of collage (*coller* means "to glue"), his introduction of the syntactic approach allowed Fisher and other postmodernists to overcome the formalist impasse by reintroducing narrative and narrative structure in art. Fisher's early pieces, such as *84 Sparrows*, were intentionally constructed like sentences to initiate a linear, left-to-right reading that occurs in time. Although no longer horizontally strung out across the wall, the subsequent works retain a multiple, sequential quality, directing the viewer from larger to smaller units and central to peripheral images. Rauschenberg's works also require, according to Rosalind Krauss, "a part-by-part, image-by-image reading." "The encounter with one image after another," she continues, results in "a kind of temporal unfolding that [is] like that of hearing or reading a sentence."[35] However, the sentence is not reducible to "the sum of the words which compose it," as Barthes has shown, nor is narrative "reducible to the simple sum of its sentences." Rather than the word or image, the building block of a narrative is the "connoted value" of motifs and concepts. The syntax of connotations determines the "narrative thread" projected by the reader onto the text.[36] Although differing in form and content, the narratives in Rauschenberg's and Fisher's works resist reduction to simple sums of images. Their resistance to reduction extends to the level of the story, which is simply one component of narrative. Acknowledging that "it remains impossible to read a Rauschenberg, if by reading we mean the extraction from a text of a coherent, monological message," several critics have argued that Rauschenberg's "dumping grounds" of cultural detritus are analogous to memory, consciousness, and "the mind itself."[37]

Despite the possibility of interpretation offered by words, syntactic structures, and representational images, Fisher's narratives defy closure and are not reducible to simple meanings. The temptation to seek a coherent message is everywhere and yet it is consistently thwarted. Instead, as Barthes urged:

> Everything is to be *disentangled*, nothing *deciphered*; the structure can be followed, "run" (like the thread of a stocking) at every point and at every level, but there is nothing beneath: the space of writing is to be ranged over, not pierced; writing ceaselessly posits meaning ceaselessly to evaporate it, carrying out a systematic exemption of meaning.[38]

Rewarding patient disentanglement, the rich indeterminateness of Fisher's works is the very substance of the conscious mind.

NOTES

1. Fredric Jameson, "Postmodernism and Consumer Society," in *The Anti-Aesthetic*, ed. Hal Foster (Seattle: Bay Press, 1983), 112–119.
2. "Interview: Vernon Fisher and Kathy Halbreich," in *Mediums of Language* (Cambridge: MIT, 1982), n. p.
3. Clement Greenberg, "Modernist Painting," in *The Collected Essays and Criticism*, vol. 4, ed. John O'Brian (Chicago: University of Chicago Press, 1993), 86.
4. This comment appears in several interviews with the artist, who attributes it to Dave Hickey.
5. Jameson, "Postmodernism," 114; Fredric Jameson, *Postmodernism, Or the Cultural Logic of Late Capitalism* (Durham, NC: Duke University Press, 1991), 15.
6. Roland Barthes, "The Death of the Author," in *Image-Music-Text*, trans. Stephen Heath (New York: Noonday Press, 1977), 143–146.
7. Roland Barthes, *S/Z*, trans. Richard Miller (New York: Hill and Wang, 1974), 4.
8. The catalogue accompanying the exhibition, *Vernon Fisher*, by Hugh M. Davies and Madeleine Grynsztejn, includes essays and an interview about Fisher's work prior to 1989. The introduction to the present monograph focuses primarily on the artist's work since that period.

9. A Gentleman Scholar [Dave Hickey], "Fisher's Sublime: Incarnations of the Boundless Self," in *Hills Like White Elephants* (Sacramento: Center for Contemporary Art, 1991), n. p. Fisher substantiated the characterizations of his alter egos in conversation with the author, March 16, 2009.
10. Matthew Bourbon, "An Artist's Vantage: A Conversation with Vernon Fisher," *NY Arts*, February 2001, 21.
11. Julian Jaynes, *The Origin of Consciousness in the Breakdown of the Bicameral Mind* (New York: Houghton Mifflin, 1976), passim. Jaynes's book was a major influence on Fisher as a young artist.
12. Vernon Fisher, in *30 Years: Interviews and Outtakes*, by Michael Auping (Fort Worth: Modern Art Museum of Fort Worth, 2007), 148. An expanded version of Fisher's interview is reprinted in this volume.
13. Barthes, "From Work to Text," in *Image-Music-Text*, 157–159. Kosuth's later work incorporating the writings of Freud, for example, is more open to textual interpretation.
14. Vernon Fisher, "Interview with Vernon Fisher," *Vernon Fisher*, 90.
15. Conversation with the artist, March 16, 2009.
16. Quoted in Leo Steinberg, *Other Criteria: Confrontations with Twentieth-Century Art* (New York: Oxford University Press, 1972), 31.
17. Vernon Fisher, "*House of Cards*," unpublished statement, 2009.
18. Conversation with the artist, June 23, 2009.
19. Vernon Fisher, e-mail to Mary Donne, Charles Cowles Gallery, New York, 2003.
20. Conversation with the artist, March 16, 2009.
21. Conversation with the artist, June 23, 2009.
22. Madeleine Grynsztejn, "Telltale Signs: The Art of Vernon Fisher," in *Vernon Fisher*, 19.
23. Dave Hickey, "The Code of the West," in *Vernon Fisher*, 26.
24. Auping, *30 Years*, 150–151.
25. Richard Flood, *Vernon Fisher/Keith Haring* (Rotterdam: Galerie T'Venster, 1982), 4.
26. Conversation with the artist, June 23, 2009. For an extensive examination of individual images that serve as often-repeated sources, see Valerie Loupe Olsen, *Vernon Fisher's File 00* (Houston: The Glassell School of Art of the Museum of Fine Arts, Houston, 2000).
27. Conversation with the artist, March 13, 2009.
28. Fisher, e-mail to the author, May 26, 2009. Fisher notes that flies are commonly featured in memento mori paintings as reminders of mortality.
29. Bourbon, "An Artist's Vantage," 21.
30. Vernon Fisher, Artist's Statement, *NY Arts*, March–April 2007.
31. Auping, *30 Years*, 149–150.
32. Fisher, in *Vernon Fisher*, 82.
33. Clement Greenberg, "Review of an Exhibition of Arshile Gorky," in *The Collected Essays and Criticism*, vol. 2, 220.
34. Steinberg, *Other Criteria*, 89.
35. Rosalind Krauss, "Rauschenberg and the Materialized Image," *Artforum* 13 (December 1974): 37.
36. Barthes, "Structural Analysis of Narratives," in *Image-Music-Text*, 82–93.
37. Craig Owens, *Beyond Recognition: Representation Power and Culture* (Berkeley: University of California Press, 1992), 76–77. See also Steinberg, *Other Criteria*, 88; Krauss, "Rauschenberg and the Materialized Image," 41; Douglas Crimp, *On the Museum's Ruins* (Cambridge: MIT Press, 1993), 44–64.
38. Barthes, "The Death of the Author," 147.

ILLUSTRATIONS

Kosuth, Joseph (1945–) © ARS, NY. *One and Three Chairs* (1965). Wooden folding chair, photographic copy of a chair, and photographic enlargement of a dictionary definition of a chair. Chair, 32 3/8" × 14 7/8" × 20 7/8"; photo panel, 36" × 24 1/8"; text panel, 24" × 24 1/8". Larry Aldrich Foundation Fund. Location: The Museum of Modern Art, New York, NY, U.S.A. Photo Credit: Digital Image © The Museum of Modern Art/Licensed by SCALA/Art Resource, NY.

Cy Twombly, *Bay of Naples* (1961). Oil, crayon, and pencil on canvas, 7' 11 3/8" × 9' 9 3/4". © Cy Twombly. Courtesy of the Menil Collection

Robert Rauschenberg, *Barge* (1962–1963). Oil and silkscreened ink on canvas, 6' 8 1/4" × 32' 2". Guggenheim Bilbao Museoa and Solomon R. Guggenheim Museum, New York with additional funds contributed by Thomas H. Lee and Ann Tenenbaum; the International Director's Council and Executive Committee Members, 1997. © Estate of Robert Rauschenberg/ Licensed by VAGA, New York, NY.

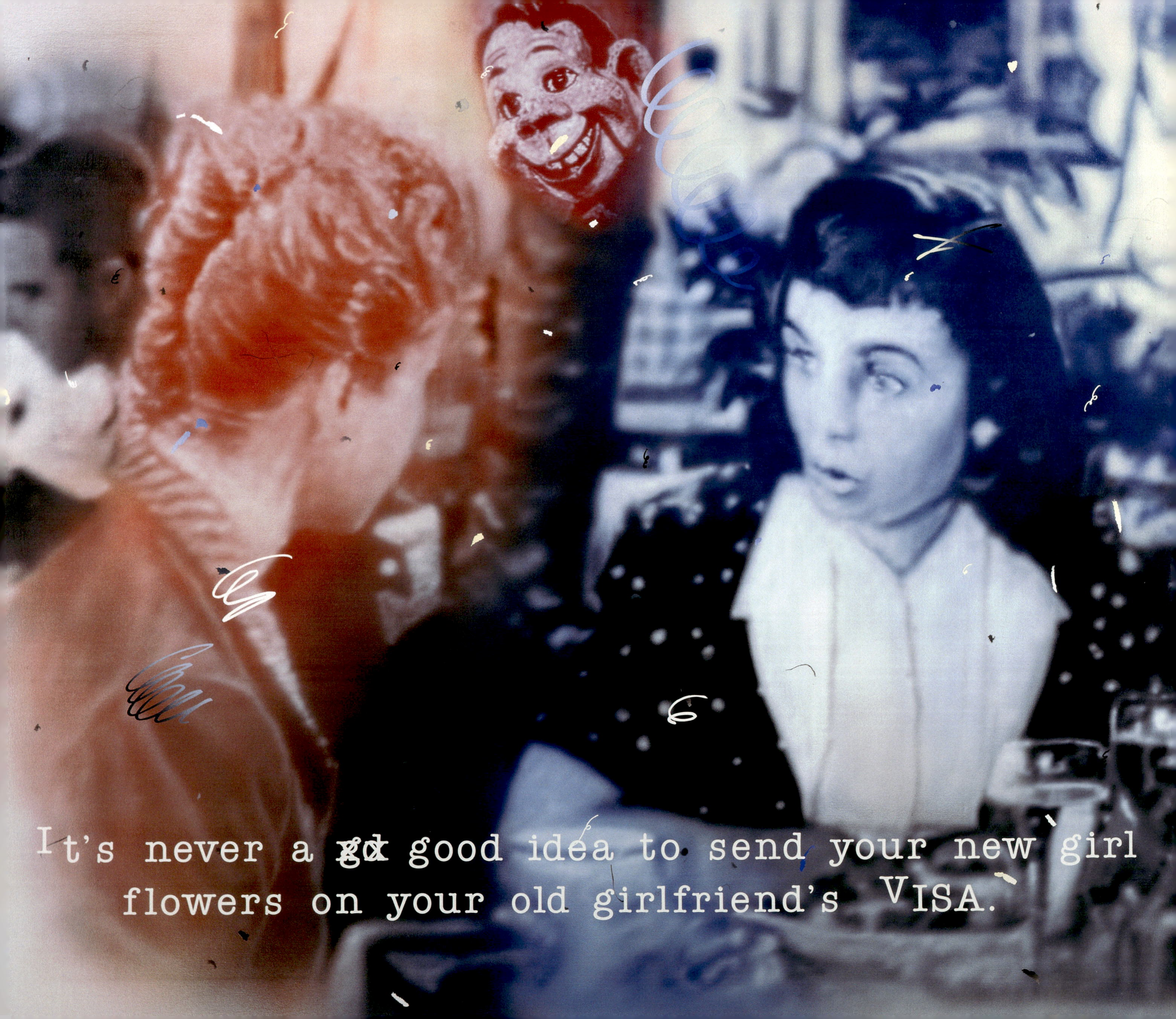
It's never a ~~gd~~ good idea to send your new girl
flowers on your old girlfriend's VISA.

INTERVIEW

WITH MICHAEL AUPING

PART I: FEBRUARY 29, 2007

Michael Auping: I was thinking about how we tend to think categorically, i.e., how we assume that popular imagery died out with pop art but that there may have been residual elements in conceptual stuff in the '70s. I think we are still in a very pop moment right now, but I wouldn't have said that about the '70s. There is Baldessari and Ruscha, but . . . To get to the point, what was the value of popular imagery for you in the early work? Do you think that Texas has its own brand of popular imagery?

Vernon Fisher: I was never interested in popular imagery for its own sake; that is, I never saw myself dragging "low" into an elevated context like the pop artists. I was, however, interested in what I saw around me, and though there was the occasional ironic detail like the Dairy Queen sign saying, "God Bless Anita Bryant," for the most part the imagery was pretty ordinary. For the stories I was writing, that was kind of the point.

In many respects, the stories, which tended to come first, led me to the imagery I used. Just as LeWitt's [dictum] "the idea becomes the machine which makes the art" led the conceptualists to unpredictable visual forms, the stories I wrote led me to imagery that otherwise would have been hard to imagine.

MA: I've read a lot of your stories and one of the things I like about them is how dysfunctional they are in terms of a narrative. It's like the detective saying to the suspect, "It seems to me, Mac, there are a lot of holes in your story." If, as you say, the image comes out of the story, how do you derive an image from a dysfunctional narrative unless you have seen this image out there on the road on the way to the story?

VF: I had been an abstract painter in the years before I began the narrative work and one of the first things I noticed when I began writing (perhaps because it felt so strange and slightly uncomfortable) was that in writing fiction you had to proceed through the world on the way to feeling, that is, the realm of objects and events. Maybe that accounts for the "popular" flavor you're picking up in the work. And I must admit, there are more than a few stories with a kind of "Kmart" setting. At the time, I was renting a house for 75 bucks a month so Kmart was a good part of what I knew—along with cars that broke down frequently. I'm attracted to the ordinary and to trash, but I don't have any feel or enthusiasm for the commercial. Perhaps my associating the pop artists primarily with the latter is misplaced. I don't really know. Or maybe the difference is between "Kmart" as setting and Kmart as subject.

As far as the texts go, there are more than a few stories where "things aren't working out as planned," or where the narratives are loopy and kind of drifting. Is that what you mean by dysfunctional? As far as combining image and text, I didn't want to just illustrate the story and because of that I was oftentimes attracted to images that were relatively inert. Other stories, in turn, suggested excessively dramatic images: ships sinking, missiles launching, H-bomb explosions, etc. I tended to work the extremes. I wanted an initial disconnect between what you read and what you saw—think of the voiceover of Sissy Spacek in *Badlands*. The relation of text to image was always complicated. To finally get to the point, at the time I felt that somehow the text "justified" the image and that that made it different, at least in motivation, from pop art. Looking back today, I still would make that argument though less strenuously.

MA: On the phone you mentioned Kmart realism and Bobbie Ann Mason. Could you elaborate on that, or on any commercial or genre literary influences? It's always hard to get artists to talk about sources or influences, but since you like to write stories and since an interest in writing almost always means there has been an interest in reading, what reading has affected-inspired your art the most?

VF: I mentioned Bobbie Ann Mason as a writer whose work has been described as "Kmart realism." She is probably most known for her novel *In Country*, which was made into a movie with Bruce Willis. Basically, she writes about the working class in rural Kentucky where she lives—people who do their laundry at Laundromats. In that, she's not unlike a lot of other writers—Raymond Carver comes to mind. I have an attraction to that subject matter myself and have written my share of pieces featuring Dairy Queens, grocery stores, Laundromats, third-rate motels, etc.

As to a "pop" literature, I'm having a hard time thinking of any writer whose work might be considered "pop." I guess Donald Barthelme, who makes a kind of textual collage of high and low, might be a candidate. Attitude toward the material is important, I think. I guess I want to maintain a distinction between "camp" and "ironic," though I pray to God you don't ask me to define either one.

I do think I understand what you're getting at. In art, Andy Warhol more than anyone opened the doors to this material. The literary lineage is more complicated, though Flannery O'Connor is certainly lurking back there somewhere.

My reading has always been pretty eclectic, but during the time you're speaking of, Don DeLillo's *White Noise*, Joan Didion's *The White Album*, and most of Richard Brautigan stand out. Obviously I was attracted to ironists, and I read Brautigan to learn how to "write short." Later I read everything by T. C. Boyle as it came off the press. Currently I'm reading Jonathan Lethem and David Mitchell.

MA: Switching gears to specific images, the cartoon character Nancy shows up a number of times in your work. What does her image represent for you? As cartoon images go, she is a pretty strong female figure. Could we call her Kmart feminism? Do you think of her as having a meaning beyond simply being a formal device? I'm looking at *Ellipse,* where she is paired with a Nazi zeppelin.

VF: In *Ellipse*, as is typical of my pieces, there are several intersecting "stories": the Hindenburg image (even pictured aloft as in *Ellipse*, we're conscious of its catastrophic end); the "ellipse" text, which, in my version, begins as a straightforward dictionary definition then devolves into a kind of stream-of-consciousness narrative; and the Nancy cartoon (the manhole where she's lost her ball is essentially an ellipse as shown in perspective). In addition, the cartoon's frame is tilted to parallel the orientation of the Hindenburg in flight. The point of intersection is, of course, the ellipse. Taken together, the piece becomes a meditation on meaning.

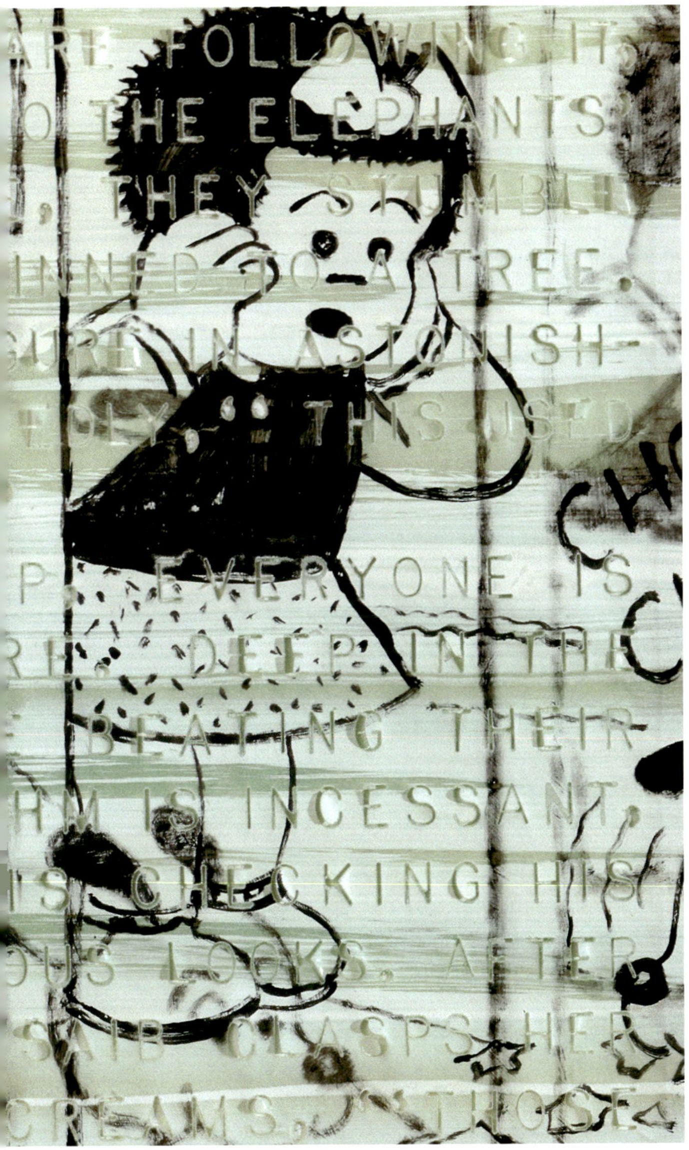

Tarzan's Adventure Window, detail 1980

Over the years, I've used not only Nancy and her gang, but Mickey Mouse, Donald Duck, and several other Disney characters; the Three Stooges, Huntz Hall and Leo Gorcey of the Bowery Boys; Frankenstein, the Wolf Man, and stereotypical characters from genre movies—film noir, Westerns, etc. Maybe they serve as a counterbalance in pieces whose tone is otherwise relatively serious; I don't know. Their presence does tend to undermine the authority of the piece, rendering their meanings somewhat inconclusive.

And Nancy? Well, I kind of stumbled onto Nancy. I was working on the piece that turned out to be *84 Sparrows* and looking for images to bracket the photograph of a camper with sanded-through text when I came across a Nancy comic strip depicting a bar of soap flying through the window (someone was distributing free samples, apparently) and landing in a bowl of chocolate fudge Aunt Fritzi was making, splashing all over her while Nancy looks on in amazement. As the camper text describes a tragic accident (with blood spattering onto the rocks, etc.), it occurred to me that the Nancy cartoon could be seen as essentially a banal version of the same thing. I liked that it departed from the rather grave tone of the story—providing an alternative view, if you will. This may have had something to do with an idea that persisted in a lot of stories I wrote in those days: the notion that the universe is arbitrary and capricious—no one's "up there" looking out for us—and at some level, funny. Something along the line of "the joke's on us." Some time later Janet Kutner pointed out in a review that the arc of the soap flying through the air echoes the shape of the camper top, so there was an unforeseen formal justification as well. This was in 1979, and as you know, Nancy's been a frequent component of my work ever since.

There's a lot I like about Nancy. She's kind of odd looking and simplified, and I like the way each frame is organized in a kind of asymmetrical balance. It's also a strip you always read because you don't want to miss the day it might actually be funny. For years these were my standard replies to queries about Nancy. Later, years later actually, I began to realize that there was a psychological relationship to the strip as well—that the characters were stand-ins for my family: Aunt Fritzi for my mother who, when I was a kid, looked a lot like her; and Nancy, in her wide-eyed wonder, for my little sister who was mentally handicapped. Apparently there's a kind of survivor's guilt that accompanies being the "normal one," and putting Nancy in my pieces was a way of bringing her along with me.

MA: Is Mickey your favorite? Everybody loves Mickey. I never really thought that much of him as a character compared to Pluto and some others, but I do have a soft spot in my heart for Mickey because in his very first couple of cartoons he smoked. You gotta like a mouse who smokes and then goes on to found the Mickey Mouse Club.

VF: Mickey smoked? That breaks my heart. Mickey only appeared a couple of times prior to the blackboards. Once, in *On the Waterfront*, a narrative piece about going to a crumbling drive-in movie somewhere out in West Texas where he comprises one of three text panels; and in *Annette*, where, to be fair, he doesn't appear in person, but is represented by a photograph of me wearing a Mickey Mouse Club hat. In the blackboards, however, he begins to show up regularly, appearing perhaps dozens of times.

There's a lot about Mickey that makes him useful. He's everywhere—everyone knows what he looks like, so any deviation from form or character is immediately apparent. And do people really love Mickey? He's been used as a shill for powerful corporations almost from birth (though I guess you can't really blame Mickey for that; I mean, I don't. I kind of feel sorry for him . . .). Nevertheless, he's a treacly character, almost completely without depth, not nearly as complex as Donald Duck with his anger issues, for example, or leaving the Disney studio, any of the Looney Tunes characters. That sentiment is reflected, I think, when people disparage something by calling it "Mickey Mouse." But he *is* a star, and being typecast as he is, he's extremely useful to appropriate, as a whole constellation of expectations walk out on stage with him.

But the main reason I use him is he's easy to draw. He's constructed almost entirely of circles, his design owing a lot more to Euclid than to order Rodentia, and you can draw him with just a few quick marks. This became important to me when I was doing the blackboards, as the size of the chalk itself, the way it comes, carries with it certain expectations. Chalk doesn't really lend itself to detail, for example, and the moment you break from these expectations, the piece ceases to be convincing as a chalk drawing on blackboard slating. In addition, there's a kind of gestural feel to the chalkboards, owing mainly to the erasures, but also to "drawing from the shoulder" in the manner of the abstract expressionists—a kind of mark making to which Mickey lends himself graciously.

PART II: OCTOBER 26–31, 2009

Michael Auping: Besides Mickey [Mouse], there are a number of recurring images and themes in your stories. In many cases, the backdrop is a blackboard. It is the consuming image. For our generation it is clearly a reference to learning, but I think we all bring something more specific to it. I, for instance, had a love-hate relationship with being asked to go up to the blackboard. I didn't like my handwriting. Can you talk about when you first engaged the image of the blackboard?

Vernon Fisher: The blackboard first appeared as an occasional component of the narrative paintings in 1980. In early instances they were blank; that is, there was no faux chalk drawing. In contrast to the familiar and conversational character of the other components in these early pieces, the blackboard parts felt singular, obdurate, and remote. I could have painted a minimalist panel, I suppose, but for some reason it seemed important that all the components came from the ordinary and recognizable world. Anyway, I thought of those early blackboards as representative of those parts of the world that don't bend to our will, those things that will be here long after we're gone—mountains, oceans, etc. I believe some of that quality remains, even in the later drawn-on blackboards.

MA: The blackboards I'm most familiar with do have drawing on them.

VF: It was probably inevitable that I would draw on them (they seem almost to demand it), and I did beginning the following year. The impulse originally came out of wanting them to be more real. As one almost never encounters a clean blackboard, it meant recreating the look of the smeared and partially erased marks that characterize a blackboard in use. Finding a way to create that look using permanent materials was an exciting moment for me. I began to understand that partially erased images have very different meanings from intact images and that in that context even untouched chalk marks acquire a kind of fragility. That's what most attracts me to the blackboard—its apparent

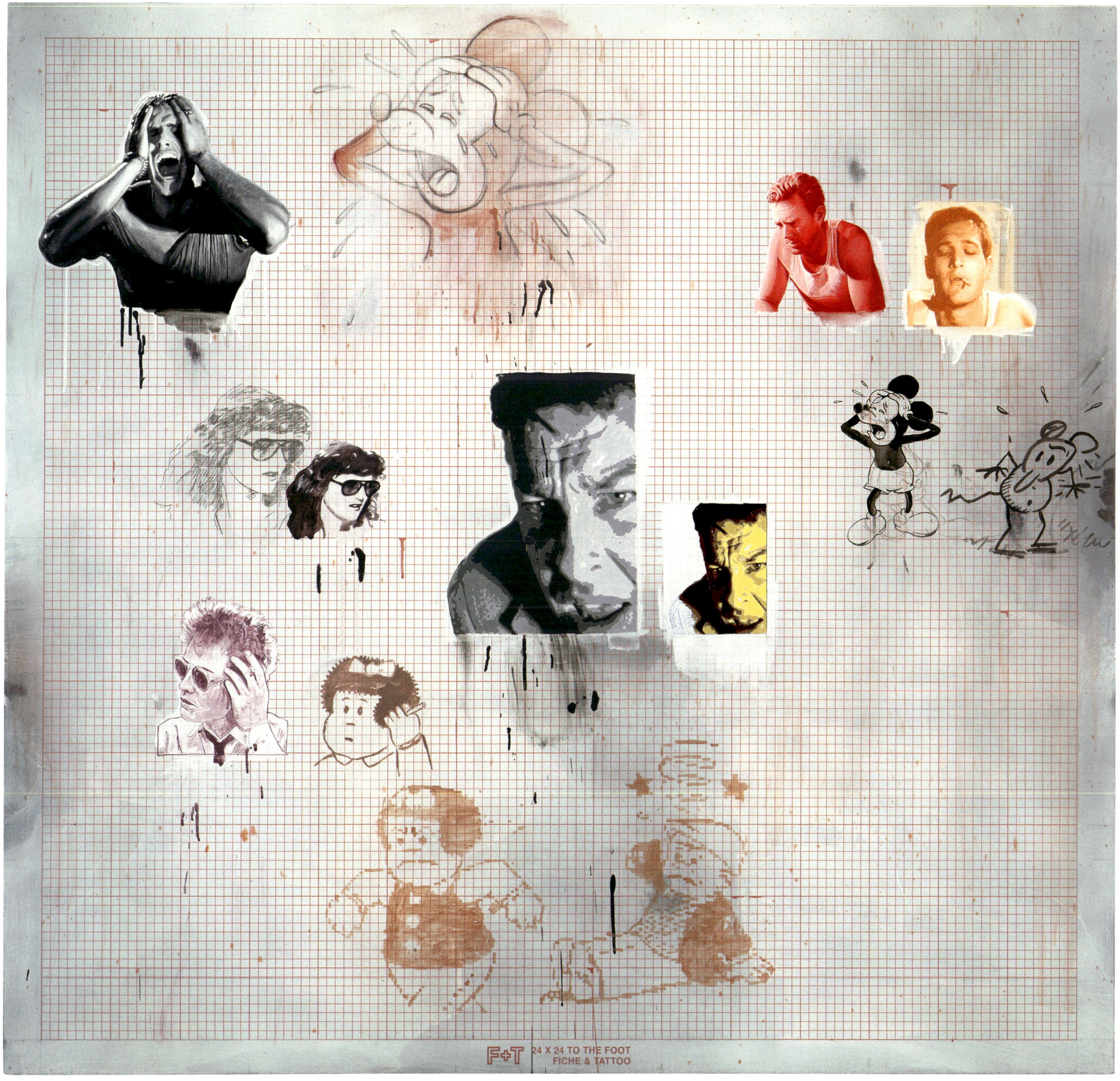
F+T
24 X 24 TO THE FOOT
FICHE & TATTOO

vulnerability—looking so susceptible to being smudged or erased. It's a kind of memento mori, really, accomplished by demonstration rather than by picturing.

MA: You've stayed with the blackboards for a long time.

VF: I made the first stand-alone blackboard in 1986, and have been making them on and off ever since. The blackboard just lends itself so well to my interest in the tentative and fluid quality of the mind at work. Apparently random and disordered notations, for example, are not unexpected on a blackboard because we're used to the notion that blackboards are where ideas are worked out and that blackboards are often shared with others. In that respect, I've never thought of the marks as entirely my own. I've always seen them as partially the residue of other's notations. Drawing on the blackboards, especially in the early stages, can feel a little like an actor playing a role. It's a way of being expressive without being self-conscious.

MA: It's funny that you don't mention the blackboard as a teaching device, a platform for delivering insight. Maybe because it is so obvious a reference. It also seems a little ironic because you are one of those rare artists that have managed to be a successful (i.e., engaged) teacher and have a serious career as a professional artist.

VF: I'm aware of the pedagogical associations of blackboards. I can't control what associations others bring to them, but I prefer the blackboard of the science lab—speculative notations in a state of revision. I do a lot of things in the presentation to encourage non-pedagogical readings—imagery, scale, shape, and the underlying trestlework structure, for example.

MA: I once heard Dave Hickey get up in front of a group of studio professors and tell them they are not professional artists because if they were, they wouldn't be teaching. They would be in the studio with assistants, dealing with dealers and making things for an art world market. I know there are exceptions (Baldessari, et al.), but a discussion of the blackboards gives me a chance to ask you what you think the relationship is between teaching and art; can art actually be taught?

VF: I've heard Dave make that speech as well. He treats me as an exception, at least when I'm present. In any case, I believe he's exaggerating for rhetorical effect though I tend to agree with him in principle. And no, I don't think that art can be taught, but I do think young artists can be coached.

MA: Although this may sound sacrilegious in this age of high conceptualism, did you ever encourage them to develop certain physical skills?

VF: At UNT I did occasionally teach painting technique. At the more advanced levels where I taught, the students were already pretty well prepared. In any case, technique is always relative to an end in view. Most of the time I concentrated on my strengths in analytical and conceptual approaches.

MA: Many people think of you as a conceptual artist, but you spend a lot of time hand painting images. Some might ask, "Why bother?" Find an image and just place it there (collage, digitally, however is most expedient). Do you want to talk about why it is important for you to paint the image?

VF: My work, beginning with the narrative paintings, has been about stretching the interpretative field. Early on, I realized that I wanted the work to incorporate multiple categories of representation/presentation: illusion, depiction, objecthood, replication, abstraction, text, and so forth. I'm intrigued by the notion of multiple and sometimes competing semiotic levels. The hand-painted vignettes are a component of that strategy. The vignettes are often romanticized, and painting them by hand makes them even more so (they can feel very much like a throwback). They embody feelings that are significantly different from the rest of the painting. The degree to which they are different is what makes them attractive and useful.

PLATES

Annette 1977

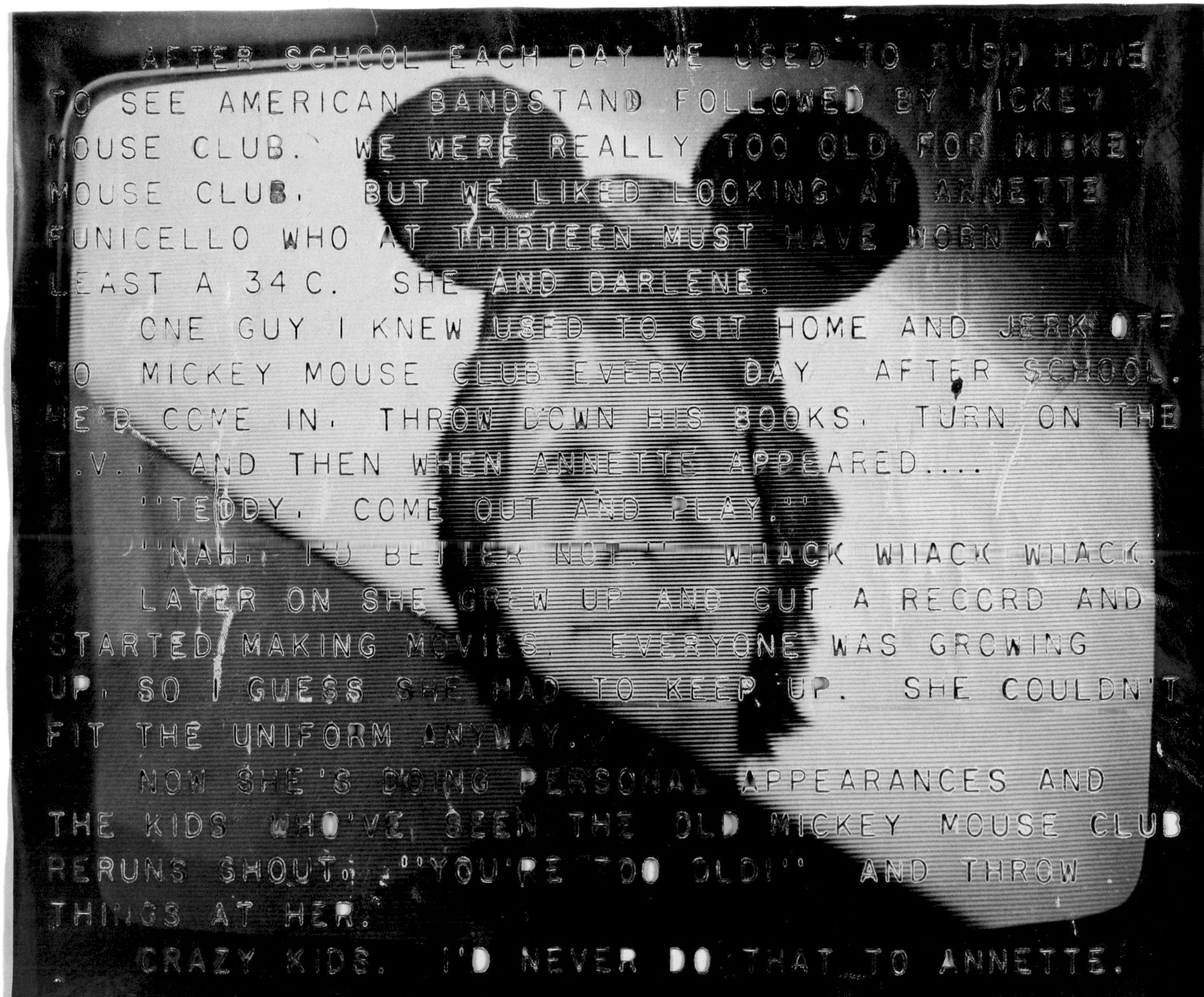
AFTER SCHOOL EACH DAY WE USED TO RUSH HOME
TO SEE AMERICAN BANDSTAND FOLLOWED BY MICKEY
MOUSE CLUB. WE WERE REALLY TOO OLD FOR MICKEY
MOUSE CLUB, BUT WE LIKED LOOKING AT ANNETTE
FUNICELLO WHO AT THIRTEEN MUST HAVE WORN AT
LEAST A 34 C. SHE AND DARLENE.
ONE GUY I KNEW USED TO SIT HOME AND JERK OFF
TO MICKEY MOUSE CLUB EVERY DAY AFTER SCHOOL.
HE'D COME IN, THROW DOWN HIS BOOKS, TURN ON THE
T.V., AND THEN WHEN ANNETTE APPEARED....
"TEDDY, COME OUT AND PLAY."
"NAH, I'D BETTER NOT." WHACK WHACK WHACK.
LATER ON SHE GREW UP AND CUT A RECORD AND
STARTED MAKING MOVIES. EVERYONE WAS GROWING
UP, SO I GUESS SHE HAD TO KEEP UP. SHE COULDN'T
FIT THE UNIFORM ANYWAY.
NOW SHE'S DOING PERSONAL APPEARANCES AND
THE KIDS WHO'VE SEEN THE OLD MICKEY MOUSE CLUB
RERUNS SHOUT, "YOU'RE TOO OLD!" AND THROW
THINGS AT HER.
CRAZY KIDS. I'D NEVER DO THAT TO ANNETTE.

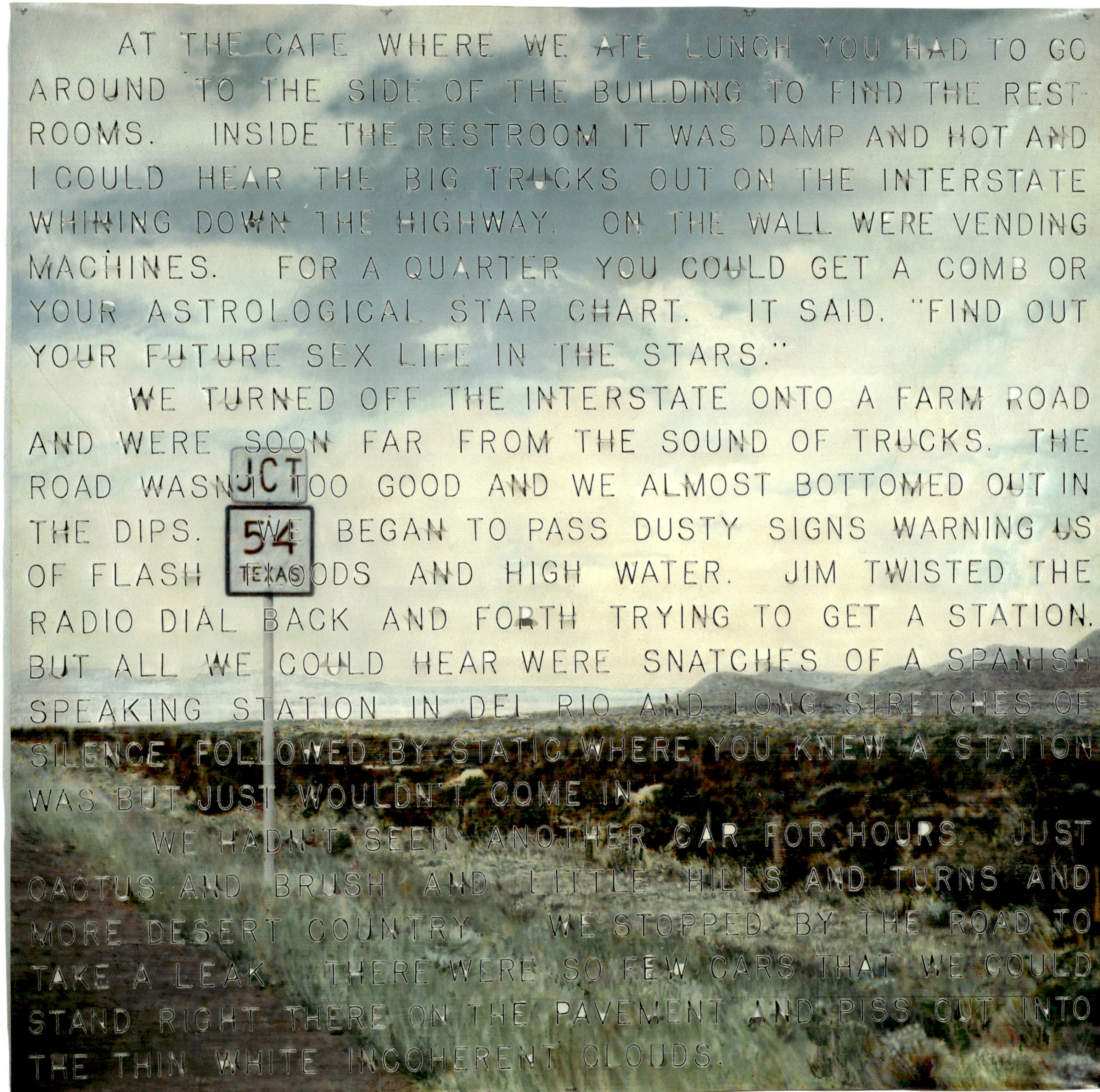
AT THE CAFE WHERE WE ATE LUNCH YOU HAD TO GO AROUND TO THE SIDE OF THE BUILDING TO FIND THE REST-ROOMS. INSIDE THE RESTROOM IT WAS DAMP AND HOT AND I COULD HEAR THE BIG TRUCKS OUT ON THE INTERSTATE WHINING DOWN THE HIGHWAY. ON THE WALL WERE VENDING MACHINES. FOR A QUARTER YOU COULD GET A COMB OR YOUR ASTROLOGICAL STAR CHART. IT SAID, "FIND OUT YOUR FUTURE SEX LIFE IN THE STARS."
WE TURNED OFF THE INTERSTATE ONTO A FARM ROAD AND WERE SOON FAR FROM THE SOUND OF TRUCKS. THE ROAD WASN'T TOO GOOD AND WE ALMOST BOTTOMED OUT IN THE DIPS. WE BEGAN TO PASS DUSTY SIGNS WARNING US OF FLASH FLOODS AND HIGH WATER. JIM TWISTED THE RADIO DIAL BACK AND FORTH TRYING TO GET A STATION, BUT ALL WE COULD HEAR WERE SNATCHES OF A SPANISH SPEAKING STATION IN DEL RIO AND LONG STRETCHES OF SILENCE FOLLOWED BY STATIC WHERE YOU KNEW A STATION WAS BUT JUST WOULDN'T COME IN.
WE HADN'T SEEN ANOTHER CAR FOR HOURS. JUST CACTUS AND BRUSH AND LITTLE HILLS AND TURNS AND MORE DESERT COUNTRY. WE STOPPED BY THE ROAD TO TAKE A LEAK. THERE WERE SO FEW CARS THAT WE COULD STAND RIGHT THERE ON THE PAVEMENT AND PISS OUT INTO THE THIN WHITE INCOHERENT CLOUDS.
JCT
54
TEXAS

Junction 54 1977
84 Sparrows 1979

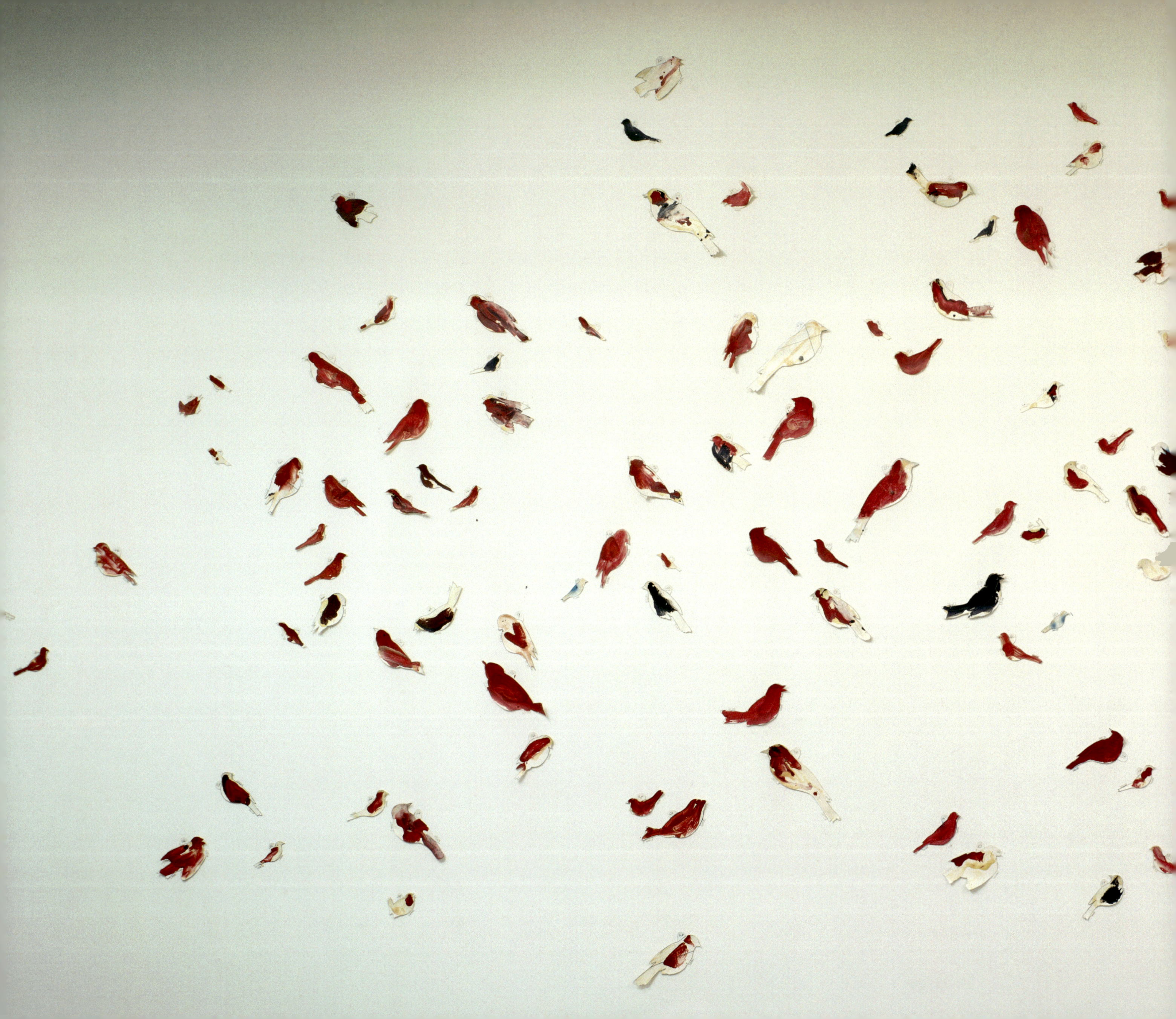

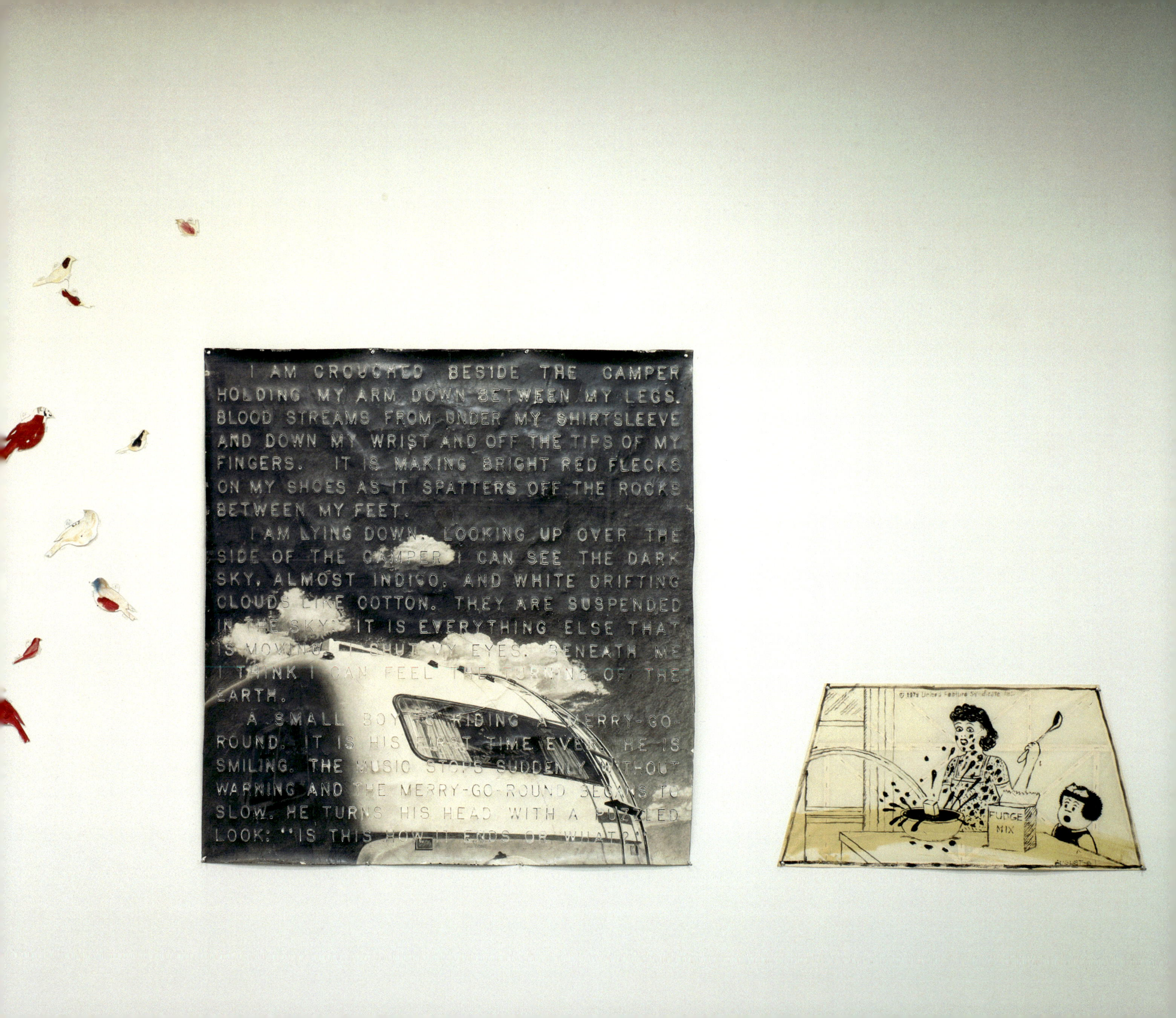
I AM CROUCHED BESIDE THE CAMPER
HOLDING MY ARM DOWN BETWEEN MY LEGS.
BLOOD STREAMS FROM UNDER MY SHIRTSLEEVE
AND DOWN MY WRIST AND OFF THE TIPS OF MY
FINGERS. IT IS MAKING BRIGHT RED FLECKS
ON MY SHOES AS IT SPATTERS OFF THE ROCKS
BETWEEN MY FEET.
I AM LYING DOWN. LOOKING UP OVER THE
SIDE OF THE CAMPER I CAN SEE THE DARK
SKY, ALMOST INDIGO, AND WHITE DRIFTING
CLOUDS LIKE COTTON. THEY ARE SUSPENDED
IN THE SKY; IT IS EVERYTHING ELSE THAT
IS MOVING. I SHUT MY EYES. BENEATH ME
I THINK I CAN FEEL THE TURNING OF THE
EARTH.
A SMALL BOY IS RIDING A MERRY-GO-
ROUND. IT IS HIS FIRST TIME EVER. HE IS
SMILING. THE MUSIC STOPS SUDDENLY WITHOUT
WARNING AND THE MERRY-GO-ROUND BEGINS TO
SLOW. HE TURNS HIS HEAD WITH A PUZZLED
LOOK: "IS THIS HOW IT ENDS OR WHAT?"
FUDGE
MIX

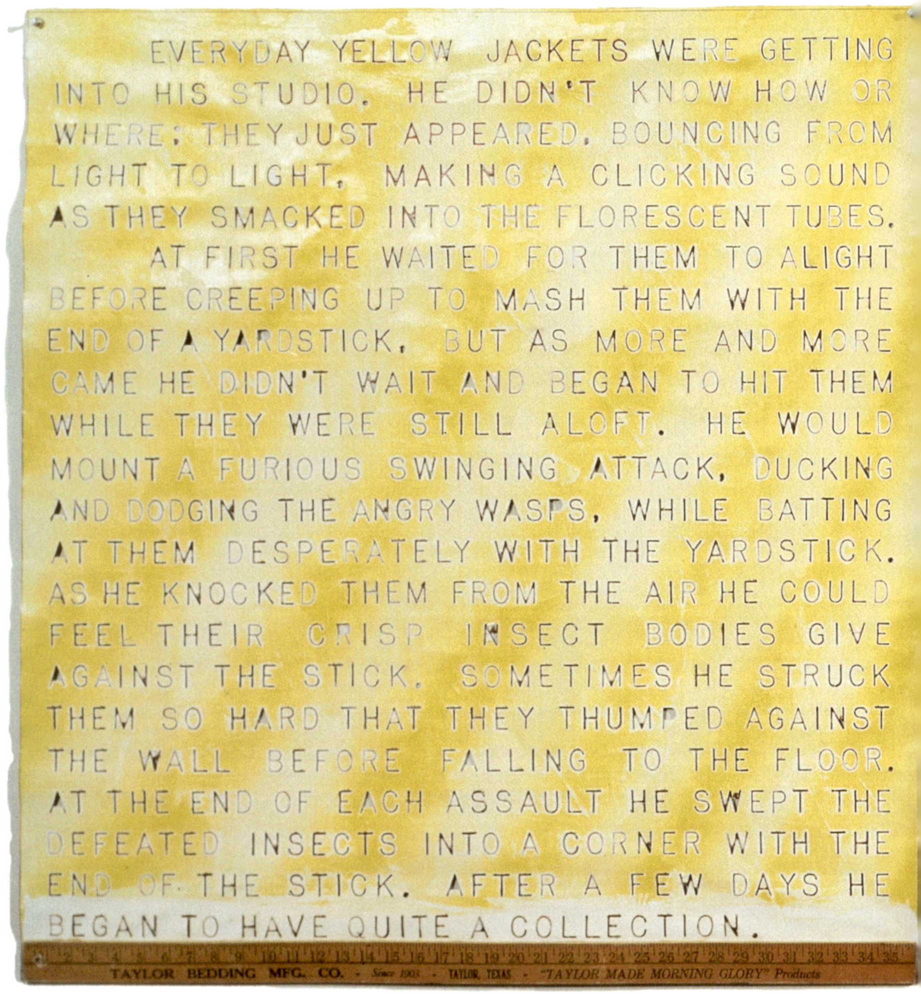

Wasp Killer 1979

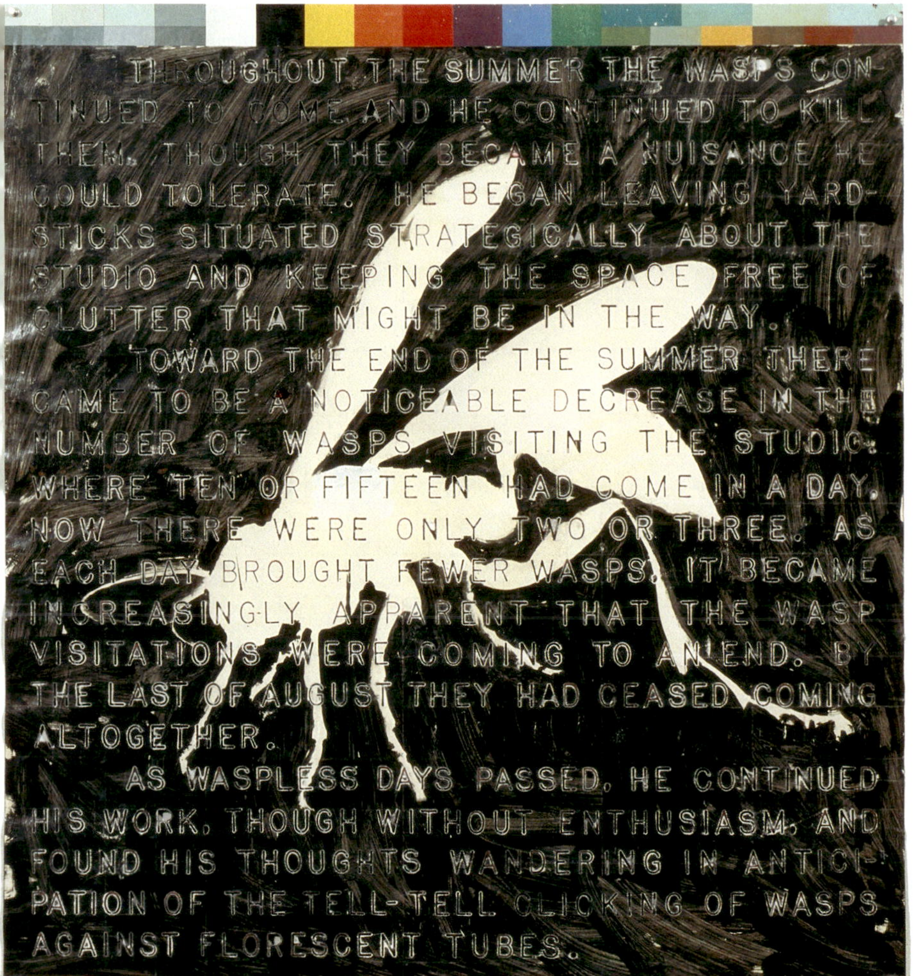
THROUGHOUT THE SUMMER THE WASPS CON-
TINUED TO COME AND HE CONTINUED TO KILL
THEM. THOUGH THEY BECAME A NUISANCE HE
COULD TOLERATE. HE BEGAN LEAVING YARD-
STICKS SITUATED STRATEGICALLY ABOUT THE
STUDIO AND KEEPING THE SPACE FREE OF
CLUTTER THAT MIGHT BE IN THE WAY.
TOWARD THE END OF THE SUMMER THERE
CAME TO BE A NOTICEABLE DECREASE IN THE
NUMBER OF WASPS VISITING THE STUDIO.
WHERE TEN OR FIFTEEN HAD COME IN A DAY,
NOW THERE WERE ONLY TWO OR THREE. AS
EACH DAY BROUGHT FEWER WASPS, IT BECAME
INCREASINGLY APPARENT THAT THE WASP
VISITATIONS WERE COMING TO AN END. BY
THE LAST OF AUGUST THEY HAD CEASED COMING
ALTOGETHER.
AS WASPLESS DAYS PASSED, HE CONTINUED
HIS WORK, THOUGH WITHOUT ENTHUSIASM, AND
FOUND HIS THOUGHTS WANDERING IN ANTICI-
PATION OF THE TELL-TELL CLICKING OF WASPS
AGAINST FLORESCENT TUBES.

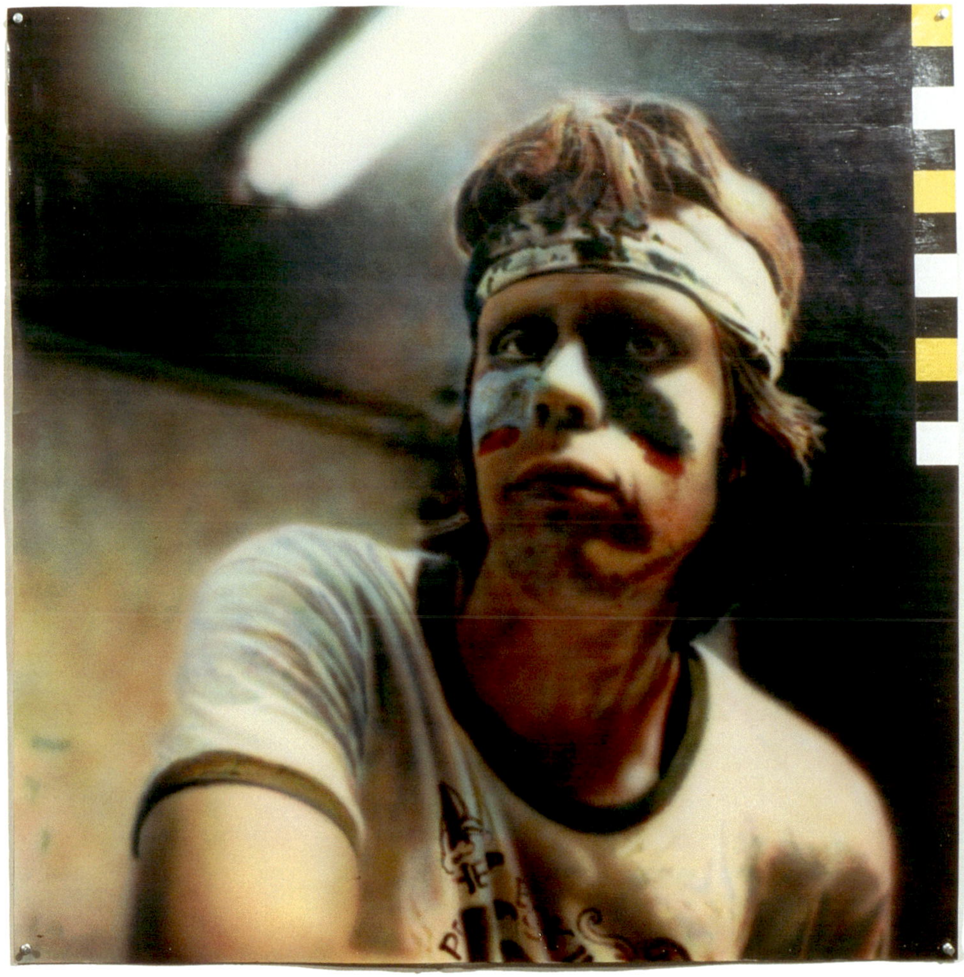

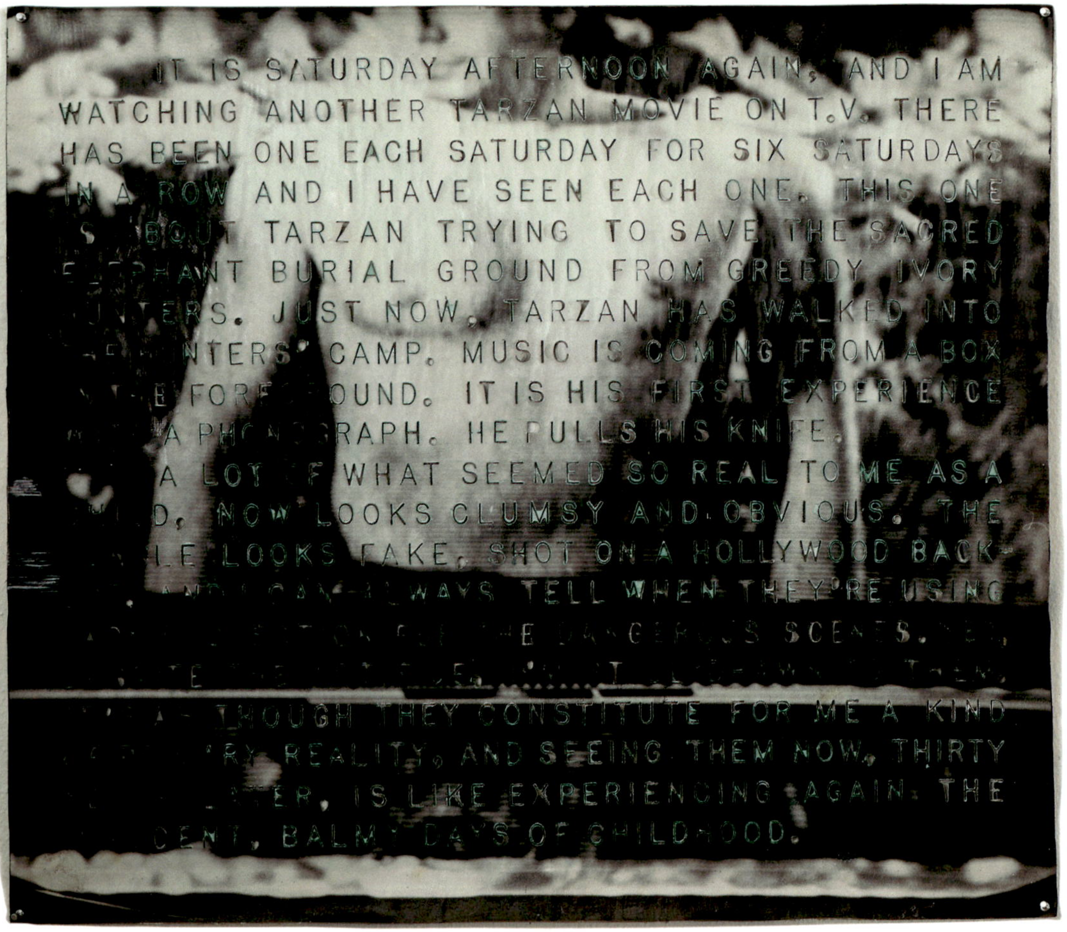
IT IS SATURDAY AFTERNOON AGAIN, AND I AM
WATCHING ANOTHER TARZAN MOVIE ON T.V. THERE
HAS BEEN ONE EACH SATURDAY FOR SIX SATURDAYS
IN A ROW AND I HAVE SEEN EACH ONE. THIS ONE
TARZAN TRYING TO SAVE THE SACRED
BURIAL GROUND FROM GREEDY IVORY
JUST NOW, TARZAN HAS WALKED INTO
CAMP. MUSIC IS COMING FROM A BOX
IT IS HIS FIRST EXPERIENCE
HE PULLS HIS KNIFE.
A LOT OF WHAT SEEMED SO REAL TO ME AS A
NOW LOOKS CLUMSY AND OBVIOUS. THE
LOOKS FAKE, SHOT ON A HOLLYWOOD BACK-
TELL WHEN THEY'RE USING
THE DANGEROUS SCENES.
THOUGH THEY CONSTITUTE FOR ME A KIND
REALITY, AND SEEING THEM NOW, THIRTY
IS LIKE EXPERIENCING AGAIN THE
BALMY DAYS OF CHILDHOOD.

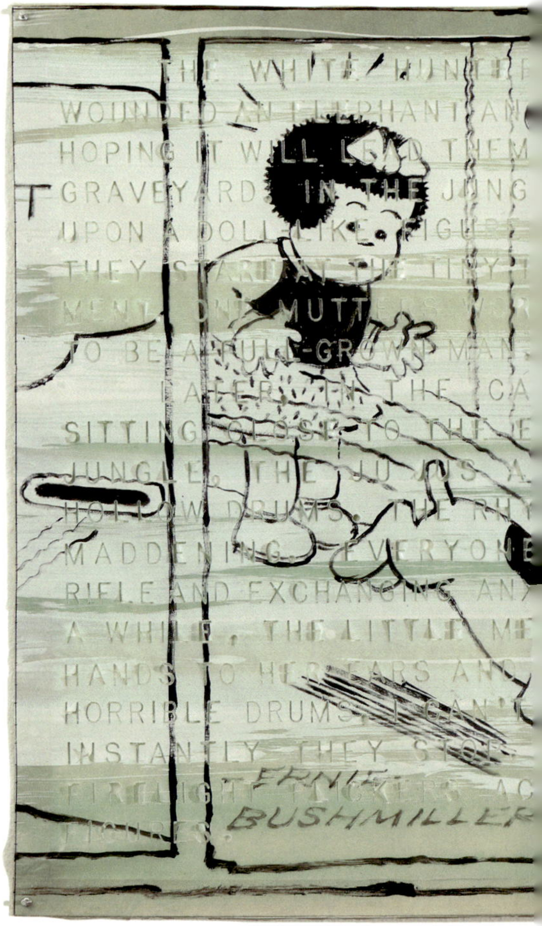
THE WHITE
WOUNDED AN ELEPHANT AN
GRAVEYARD. IN THE JUNG
TO BE A FULL-GROWN MAN.
SITTING
MADDENING. EVERYONE
RIFLE AND EXCHANGING
HORRIBLE DRUMS.
INSTANTLY THEY
ERNIE BUSHMILLER

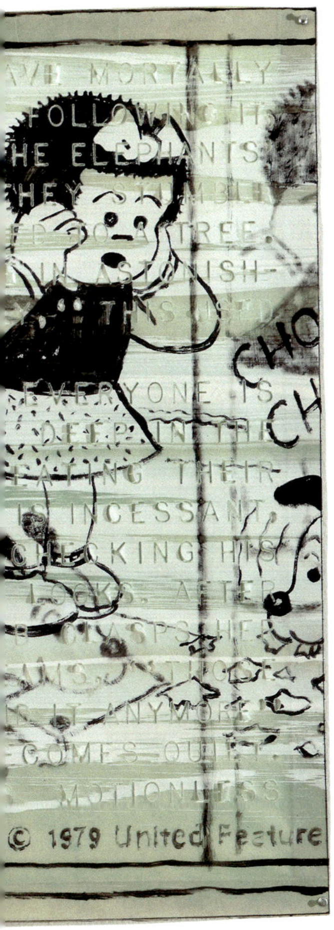

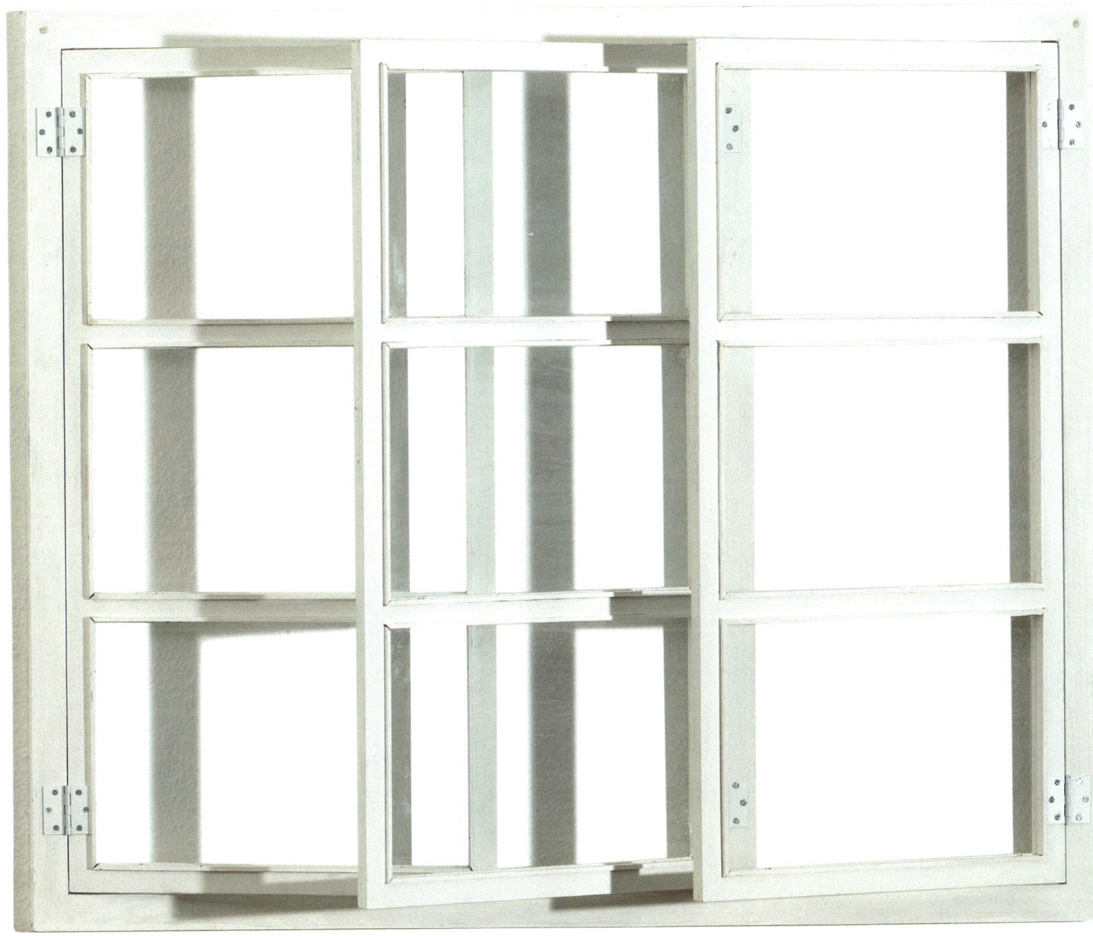

Tarzan's Adventure Window 1980

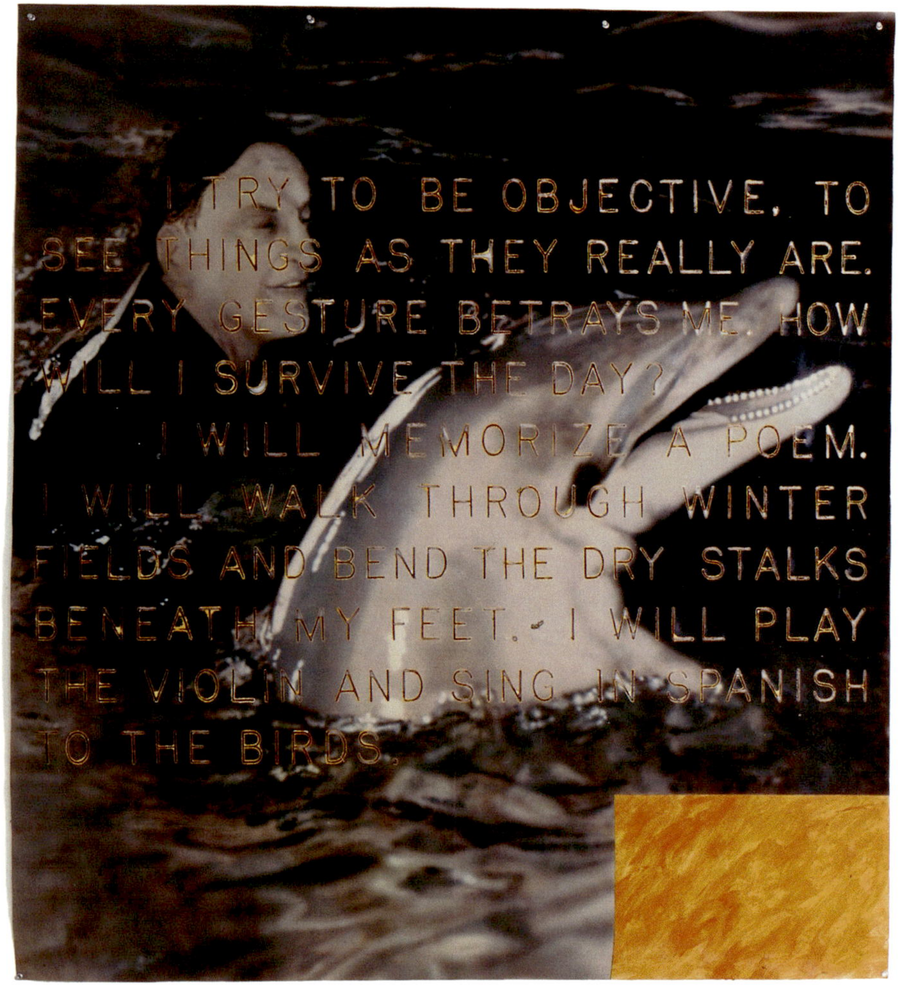
I TRY TO BE OBJECTIVE, TO
SEE THINGS AS THEY REALLY ARE.
EVERY GESTURE BETRAYS ME. HOW
WILL I SURVIVE THE DAY?
I WILL MEMORIZE A POEM.
I WILL WALK THROUGH WINTER
FIELDS AND BEND THE DRY STALKS
BENEATH MY FEET. I WILL PLAY
THE VIOLIN AND SING IN SPANISH
TO THE BIRDS.

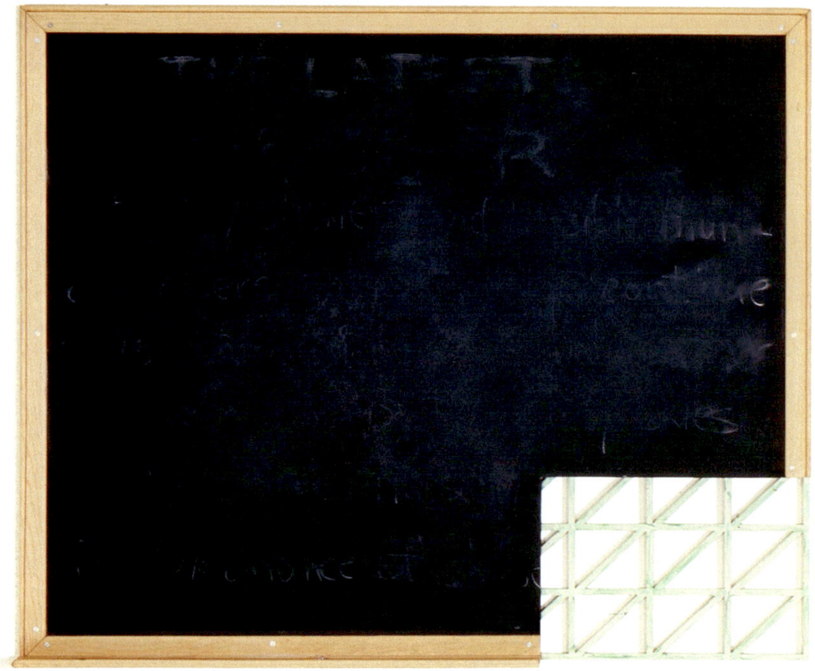

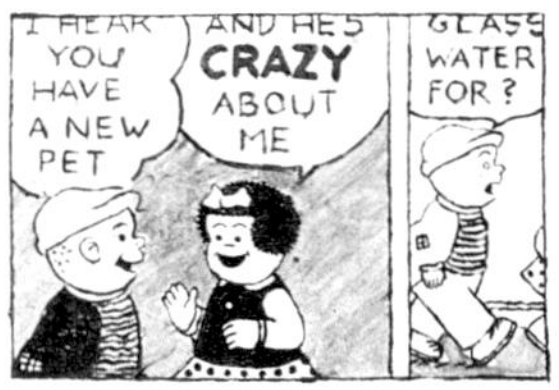
I HEAR YOU HAVE A NEW PET
AND HE'S CRAZY ABOUT ME
GLASS WATER FOR?

Pollock 1981

I told her the story of Jackson Pollock at a party, pissing in Peggy Guggenheim's fireplace.
"Gee, I wish I had the nerve to do that," she said.
"Well, you could," I said, "but it wouldn't look quite the same."

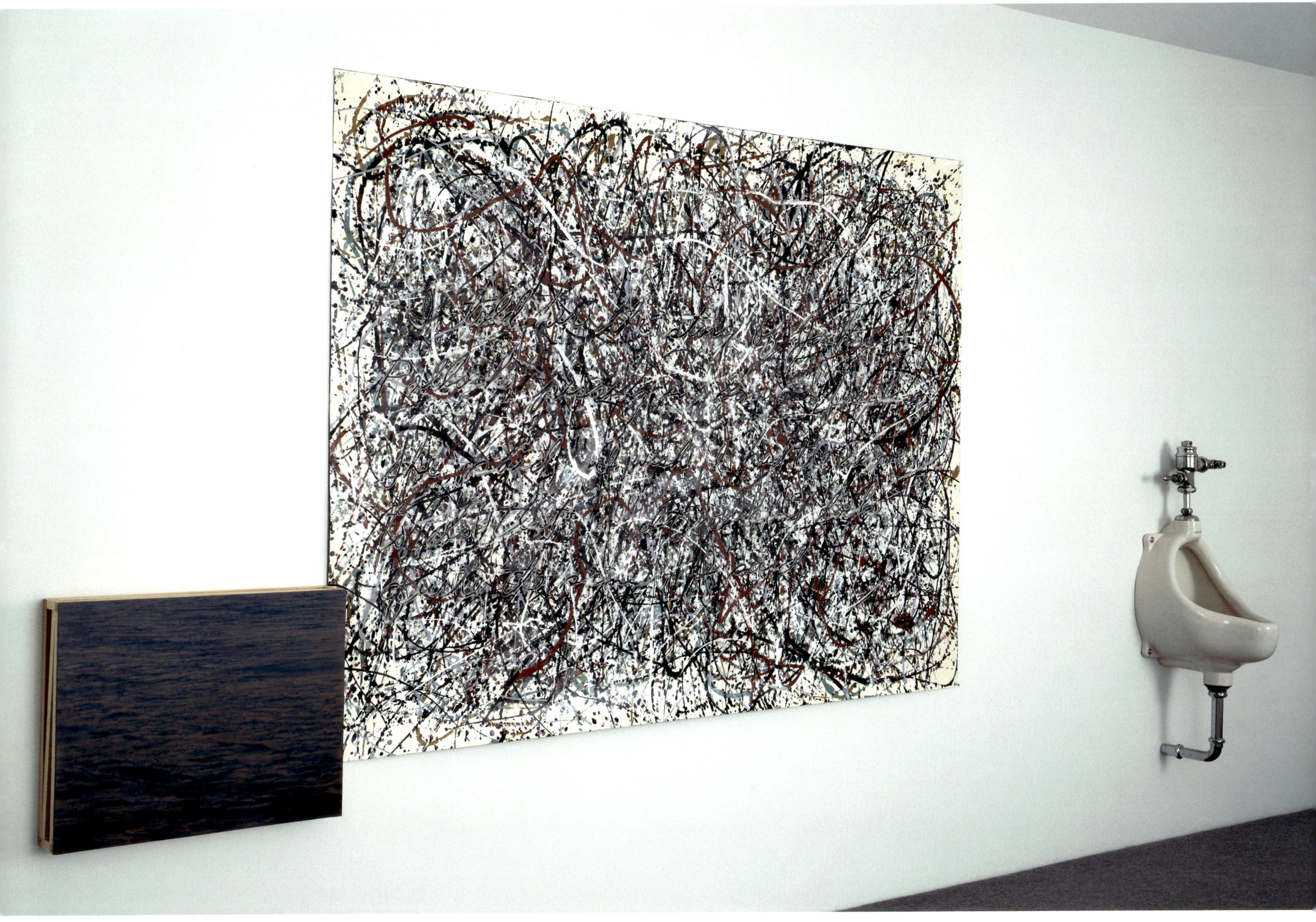

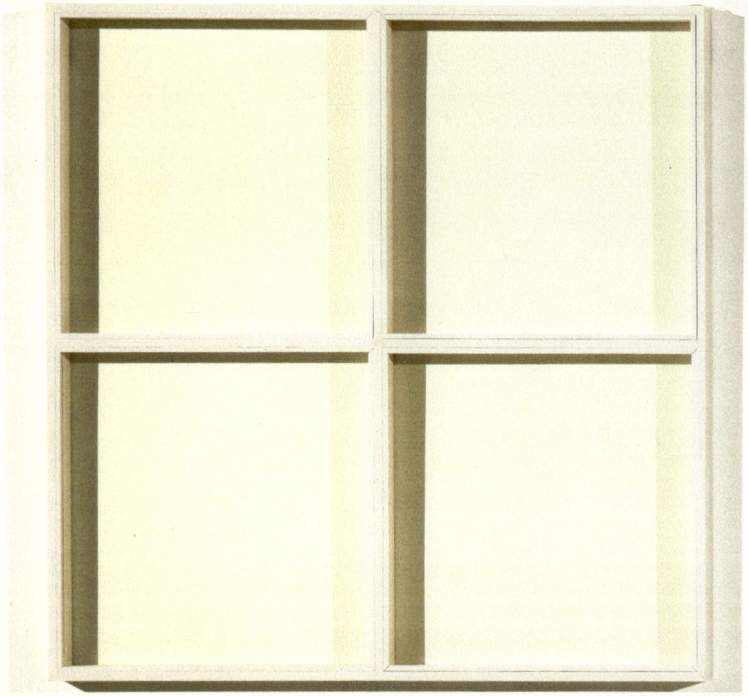

It is Saturday afternoon again, and I am watching another Tarzan movie on T.V. There has been one each Saturday for six Saturdays in a row and I have seen each one. This one is about Tarzan trying to save the sacred elephant burial ground from greedy ivory hunters. Just now, Tarzan has walked into the hunters' camp. Music is coming from a box in the foreground. It is his first experience with a phonograph. He pulls his knife.

A lot of what seemed so real to me as a child, now looks clumsy and obvious. The jungle looks fake, shot on a Hollywood backlot, and I can always tell when they're using back projection for the dangerous scenes. Yet, despite the artifice, I'm still drawn to them. It's as though they constitute for me a kind of primary reality, and seeing them now, thirty years later, is like experiencing again the innocent, balmy days of childhood.

The white hunters have mortally wounded an elephant and are following it, hoping it will lead them to the elephants' graveyard. In the jungle, they stumble upon a doll-like figure pinned to a tree. They stare at the tiny figure in astonishment. One mutters worriedly, "This used to be a full grown man."

Later, in the camp, everyone is sitting close to the fire. Deep in the jungle, the Ju Jus are beating their hollow drums. The rhythm is incessant, maddening. Everyone is checking his rifle and exchanging anxious looks. After a while, the little memsaib clasps her hands to her ears and screams, "Those horrible drums, I can't stand it anymore." Instantly, they stop. It becomes quiet. Firelight flickers across motionless figures.

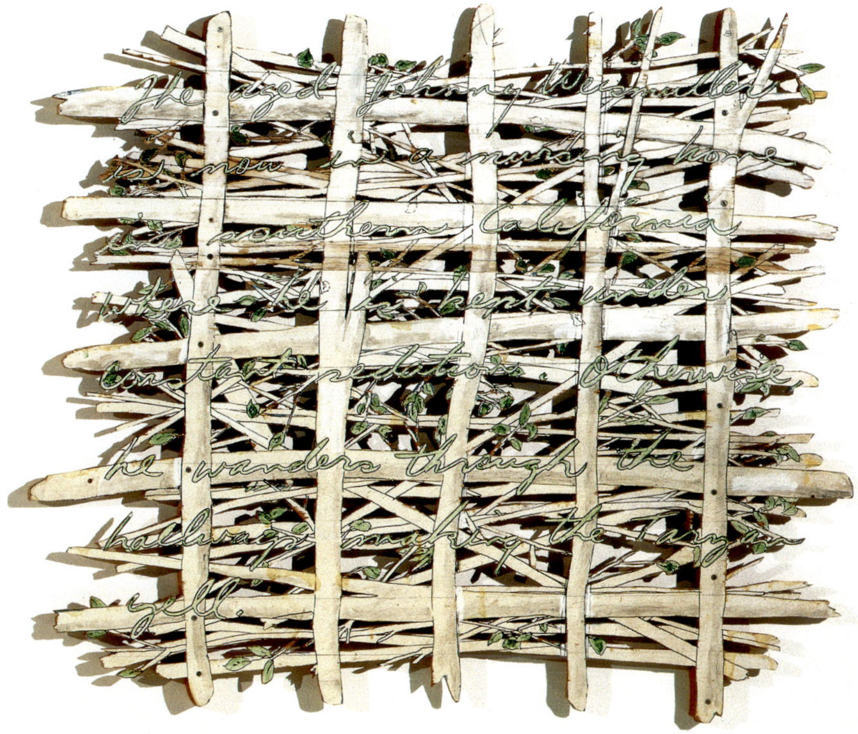

Tarzan's Adventure I 1981

Red and Yellow, Black and White 1982
Detail

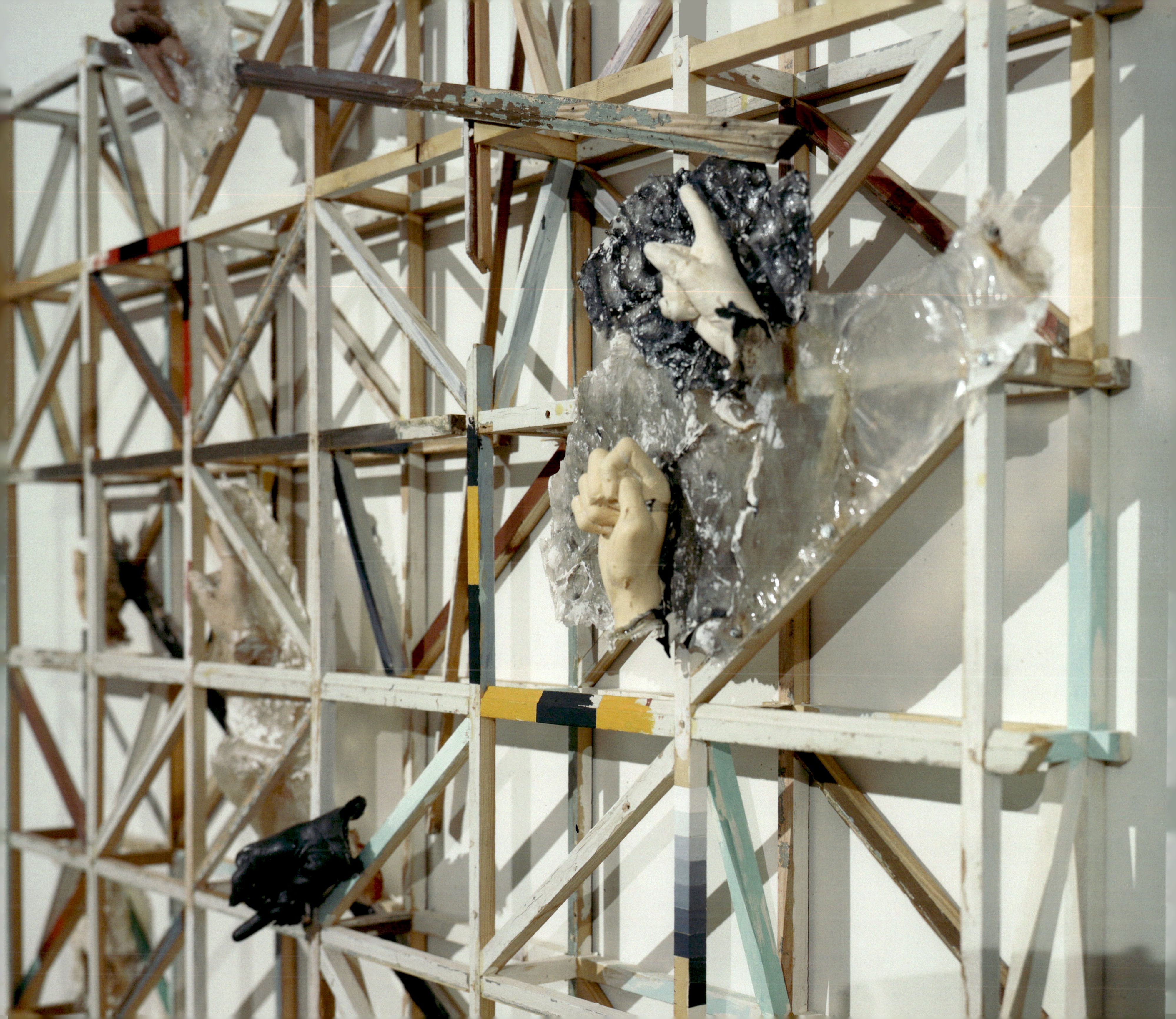

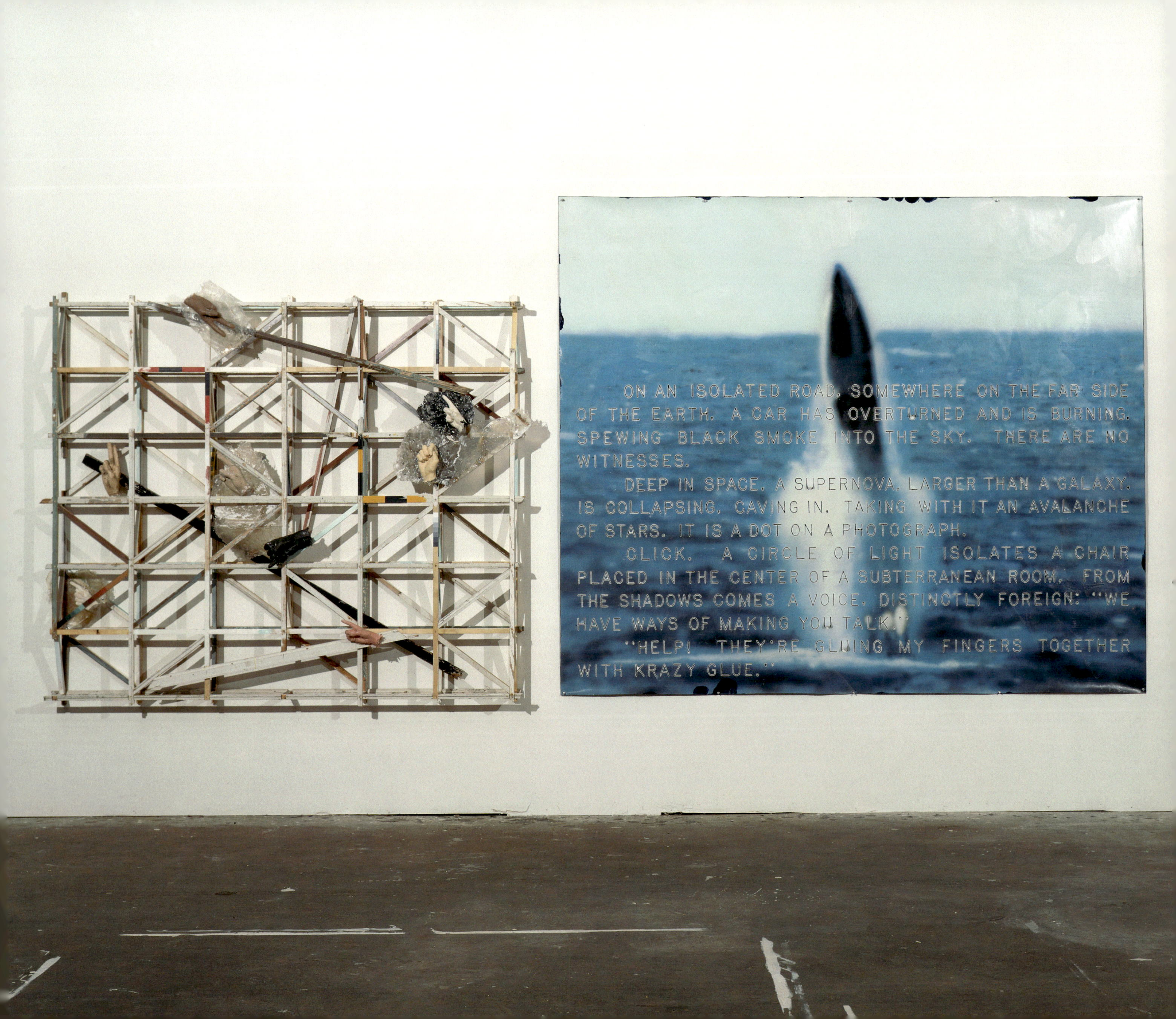
ON AN ISOLATED ROAD, SOMEWHERE ON THE FAR SIDE
OF THE EARTH, A CAR HAS OVERTURNED AND IS BURNING,
SPEWING BLACK SMOKE INTO THE SKY. THERE ARE NO
WITNESSES.
DEEP IN SPACE, A SUPERNOVA, LARGER THAN A GALAXY,
IS COLLAPSING, CAVING IN, TAKING WITH IT AN AVALANCHE
OF STARS. IT IS A DOT ON A PHOTOGRAPH.
CLICK. A CIRCLE OF LIGHT ISOLATES A CHAIR
PLACED IN THE CENTER OF A SUBTERRANEAN ROOM. FROM
THE SHADOWS COMES A VOICE, DISTINCTLY FOREIGN: "WE
HAVE WAYS OF MAKING YOU TALK."
"HELP! THEY'RE GLUING MY FINGERS TOGETHER
WITH KRAZY GLUE."

On an isolated road, somewhere on the far side of the earth, a car has overturned and is burning, spewing black smoke into the sky. There are no witnesses.

Deep in space, a supernova, larger than a galaxy, is collapsing, caving in, taking with it an avalanche of stars. It is a dot on a photograph.

Click. A circle of light isolates a chair placed in the center of a subterranean room. From the shadows comes a voice, distinctly foreign: "We have ways of making you talk."

"Help!" They're gluing my fingers together with Krazy Glue."

Red and Yellow, Black and White 1982

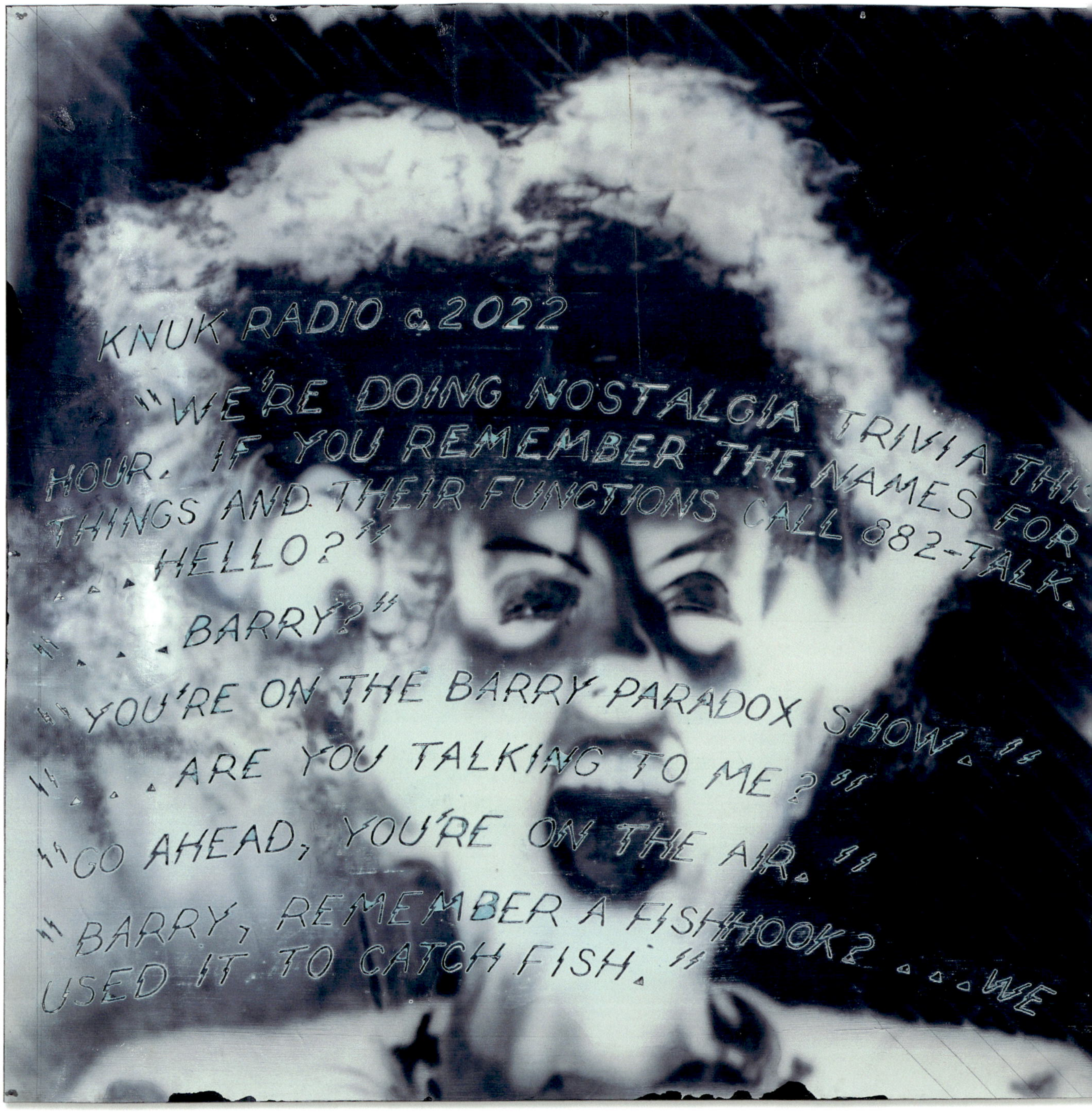
KNUK RADIO c.2022
"WE'RE DOING NOSTALGIA TRIVIA THIS
HOUR. IF YOU REMEMBER THE NAMES FOR
THINGS AND THEIR FUNCTIONS CALL 882-TALK.
"...HELLO?"
"...BARRY?"
"YOU'RE ON THE BARRY PARADOX SHOW."
"...ARE YOU TALKING TO ME?"
"GO AHEAD, YOU'RE ON THE AIR."
"BARRY, REMEMBER A FISHHOOK? ...WE
USED IT TO CATCH FISH."

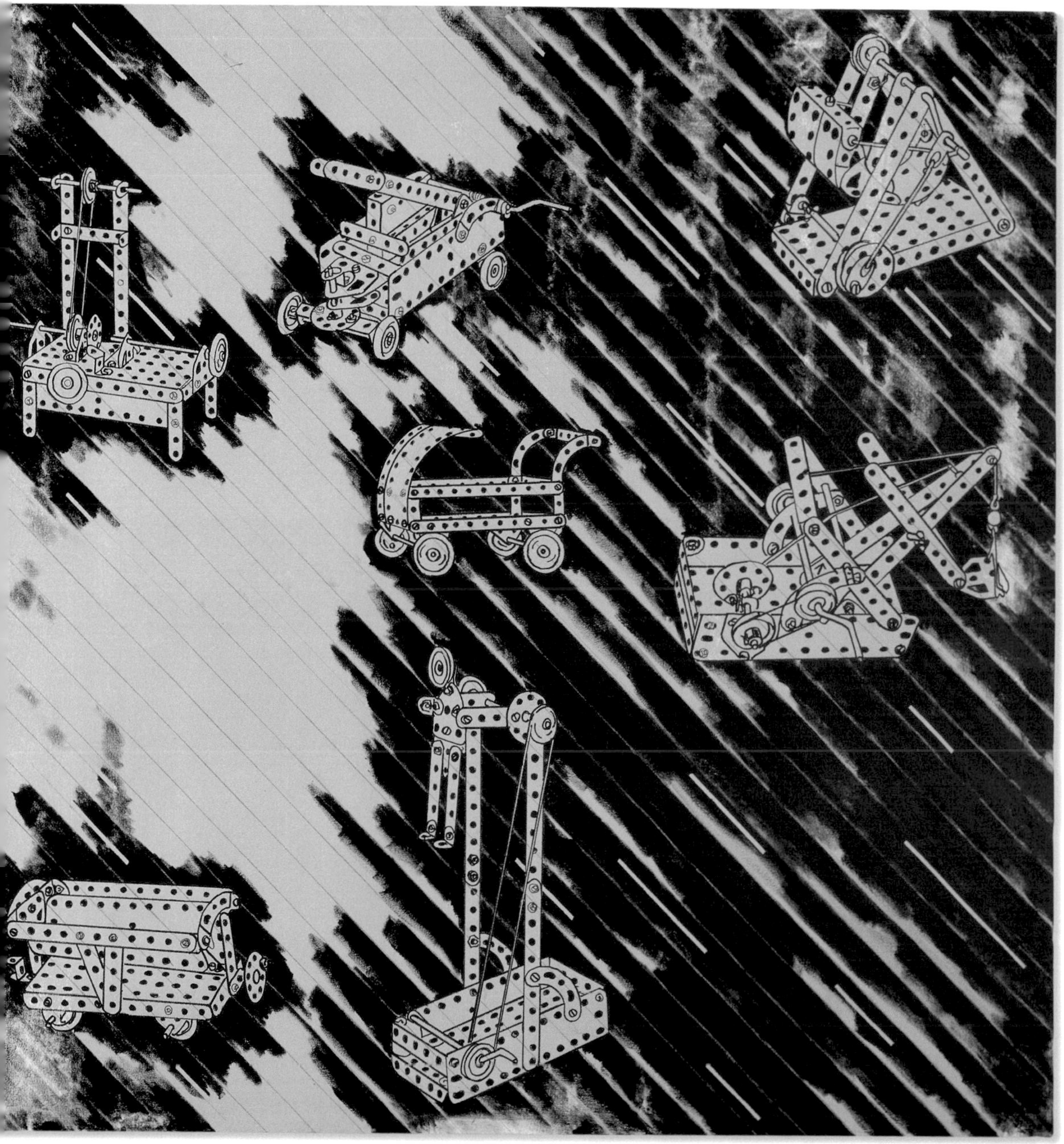

Bridge 1983

White Clouds / Black Sky 1984

We wind down out of the mountains, down through the jungle growth, tall trees strewn with vines, multicolored birds and monkeys, down onto the plains of grass and palms. As we descend, it gets warmer and we shed clothing as we go. Malagar, our driver, who is taking meditation seminars with Mahrajneesh, says back over his shoulder, "When it is finish, I am seeing heaven in just one second. I am being anywhere I want to be."

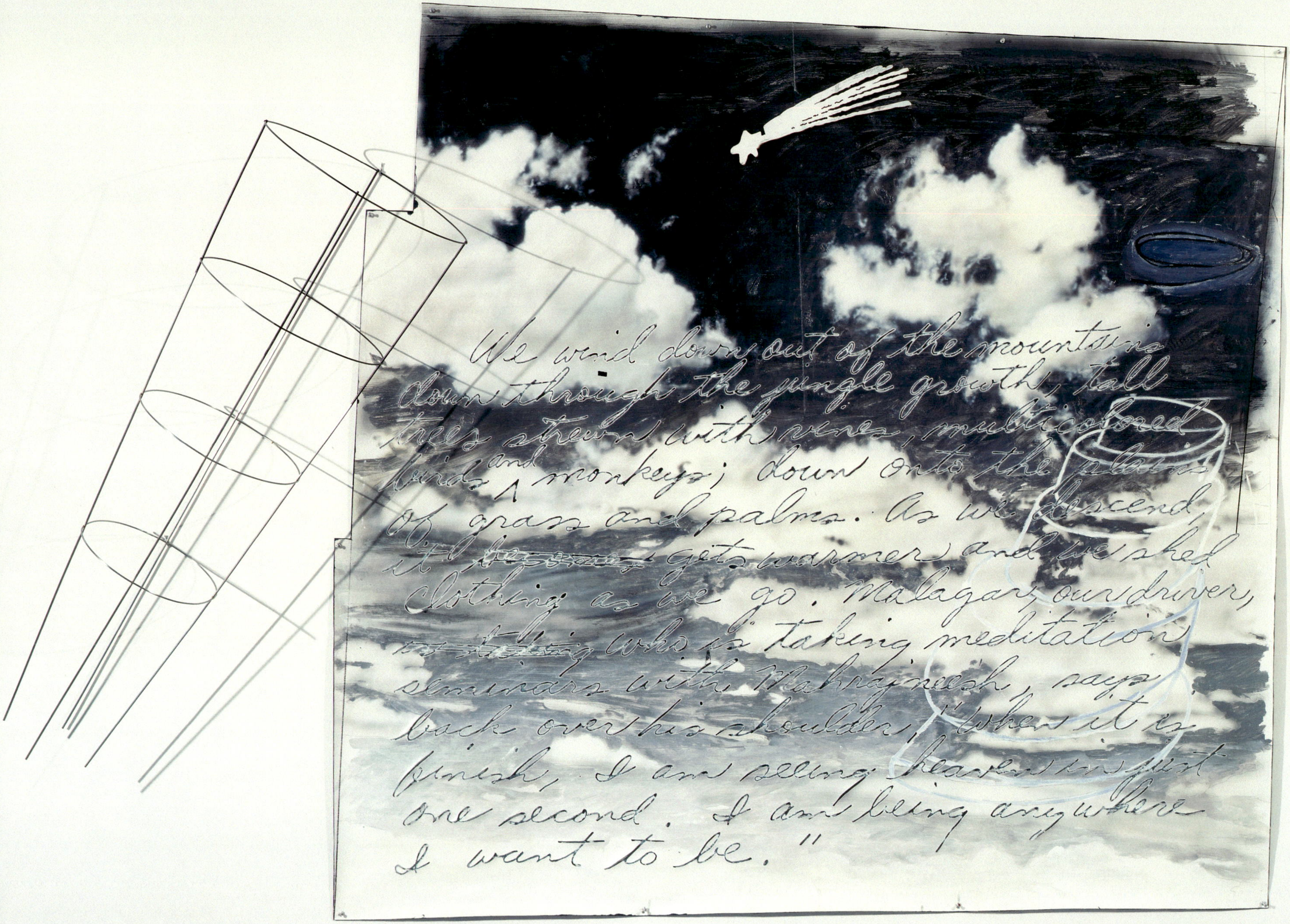
We wind down out of the mountains
down through the jungle growth, tall
trees strewn with vines, multicolored
birds and monkeys; down onto the plains
of grass and palms. As we descend
it gets warmer and we shed
clothing as we go. Malagan, our driver,
who is taking meditation
seminars with Mahrajneesh, says
back over his shoulder, "when it is
finish, I am seeing heaven in just
one second. I am being anywhere
I want to be."

My friend is having a problem with her husband. He is always disappearing without warning. He'll go down to the store for a pack of cigarettes and not return for days or even weeks. When he gets back, there are always several hundred more miles on the car, and all the radio select-o-buttons have been changed. Although she regards this activity as highly questionable, she doesn't want to appear distrustful, so she doesn't know exactly what to do. Lately, she has been spending most of her time driving around the country looking for the one location where all the select-o-buttons match up with local frequencies.

Stickchart Navigation 1983

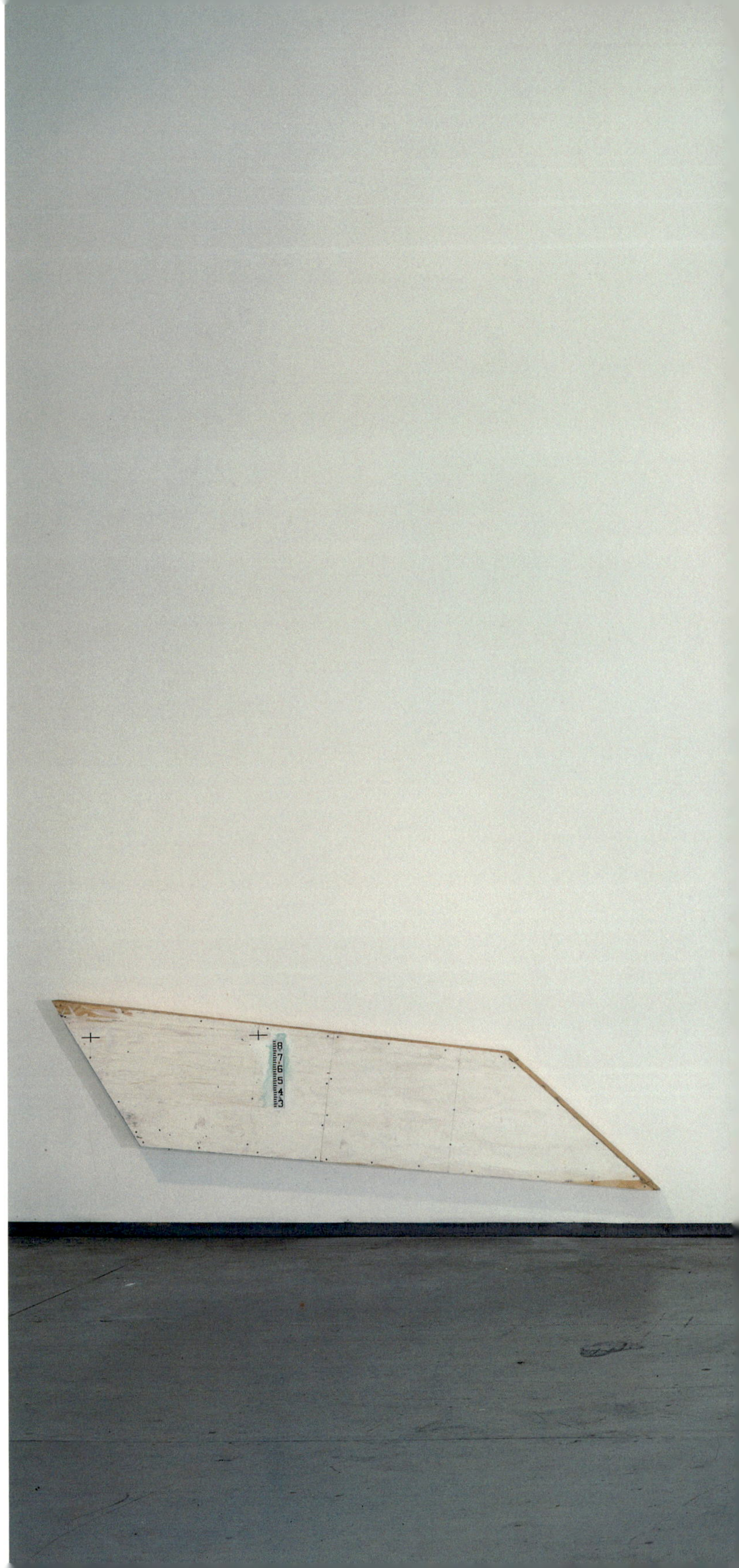

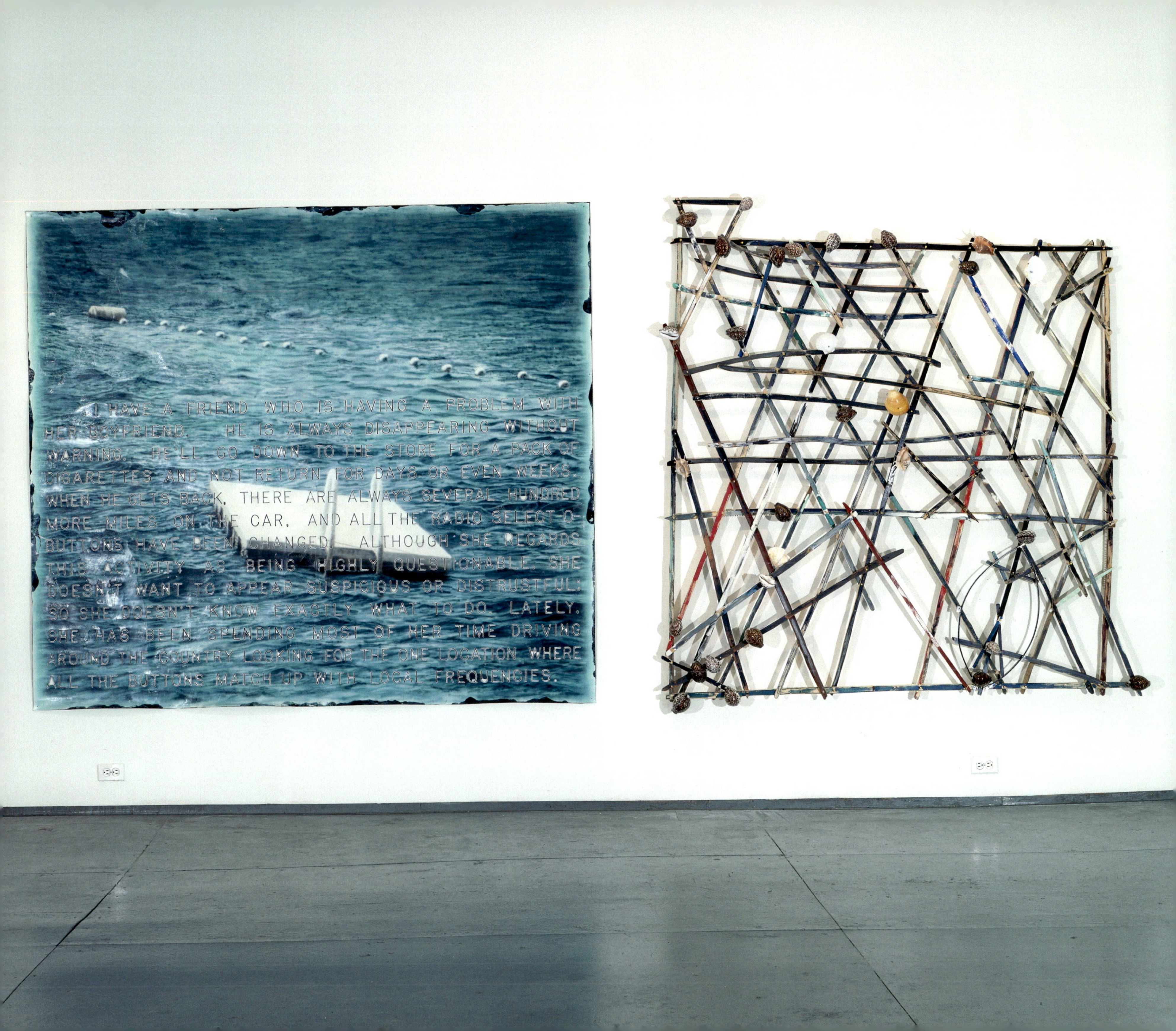
I HAVE A FRIEND WHO IS HAVING A PROBLEM WITH
HER BOYFRIEND. HE IS ALWAYS DISAPPEARING WITHOUT
WARNING. HE'LL GO DOWN TO THE STORE FOR A PACK OF
CIGARETTES AND NOT RETURN FOR DAYS OR EVEN WEEKS.
WHEN HE GETS BACK, THERE ARE ALWAYS SEVERAL HUNDRED
MORE MILES ON THE CAR, AND ALL THE RADIO SELECT-O-
BUTTONS HAVE BEEN CHANGED. ALTHOUGH SHE REGARDS
THIS ACTIVITY AS BEING HIGHLY QUESTIONABLE, SHE
DOESN'T WANT TO APPEAR SUSPICIOUS OR DISTRUSTFUL;
SO SHE DOESN'T KNOW EXACTLY WHAT TO DO. LATELY,
SHE HAS BEEN SPENDING MOST OF HER TIME DRIVING
AROUND THE COUNTRY LOOKING FOR THE ONE LOCATION WHERE
ALL THE BUTTONS MATCH UP WITH LOCAL FREQUENCIES.

Basutoland 1986

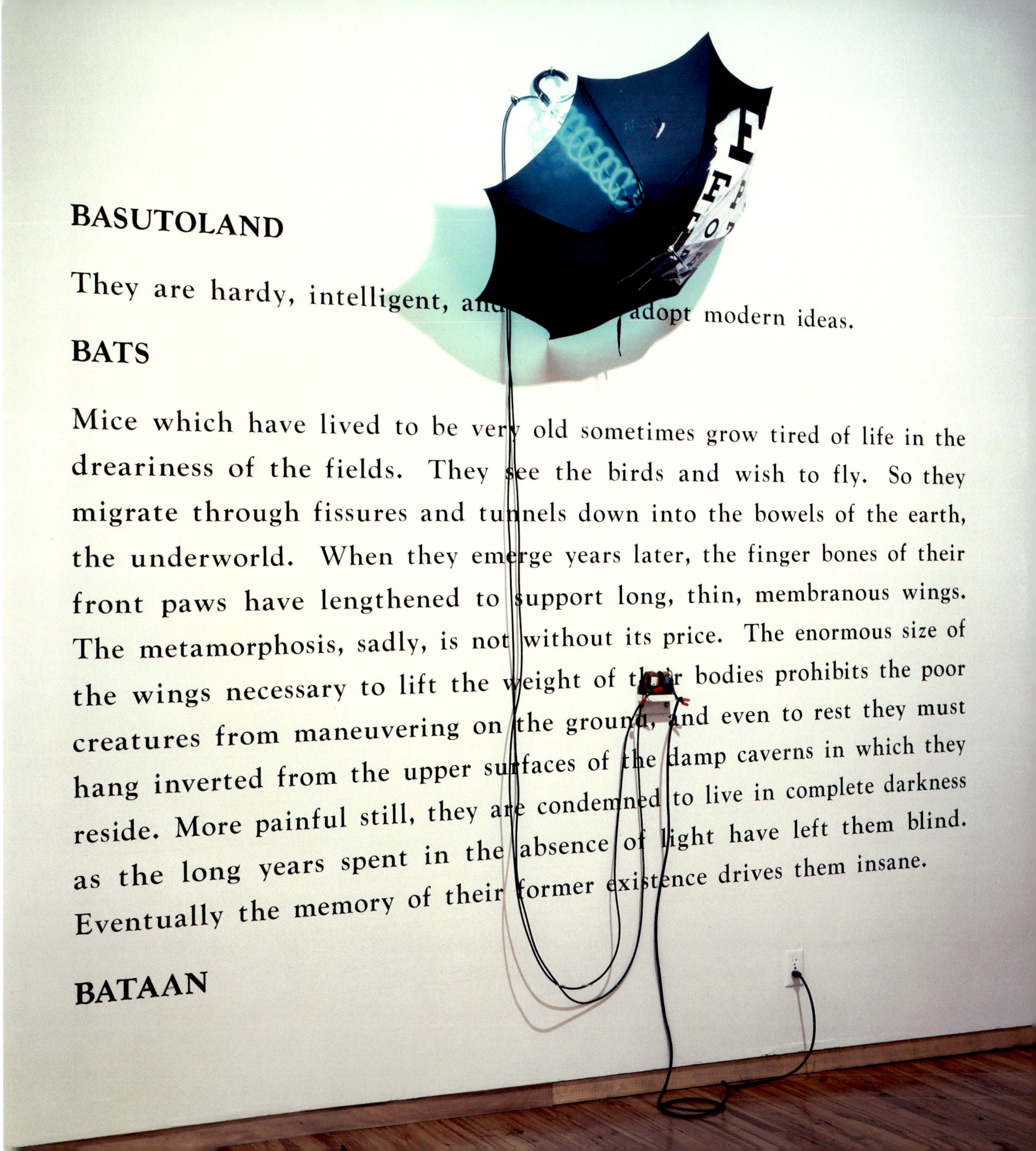
BASUTOLAND
They are hardy, intelligent, an
adopt modern ideas.
BATS
Mice which have lived to be very old sometimes grow tired of life in the dreariness of the fields. They see the birds and wish to fly. So they migrate through fissures and tunnels down into the bowels of the earth, the underworld. When they emerge years later, the finger bones of their front paws have lengthened to support long, thin, membranous wings. The metamorphosis, sadly, is not without its price. The enormous size of the wings necessary to lift the weight of their bodies prohibits the poor creatures from maneuvering on the ground, and even to rest they must hang inverted from the upper surfaces of the damp caverns in which they reside. More painful still, they are condemned to live in complete darkness as the long years spent in the absence of light have left them blind. Eventually the memory of their former existence drives them insane.
BATAAN

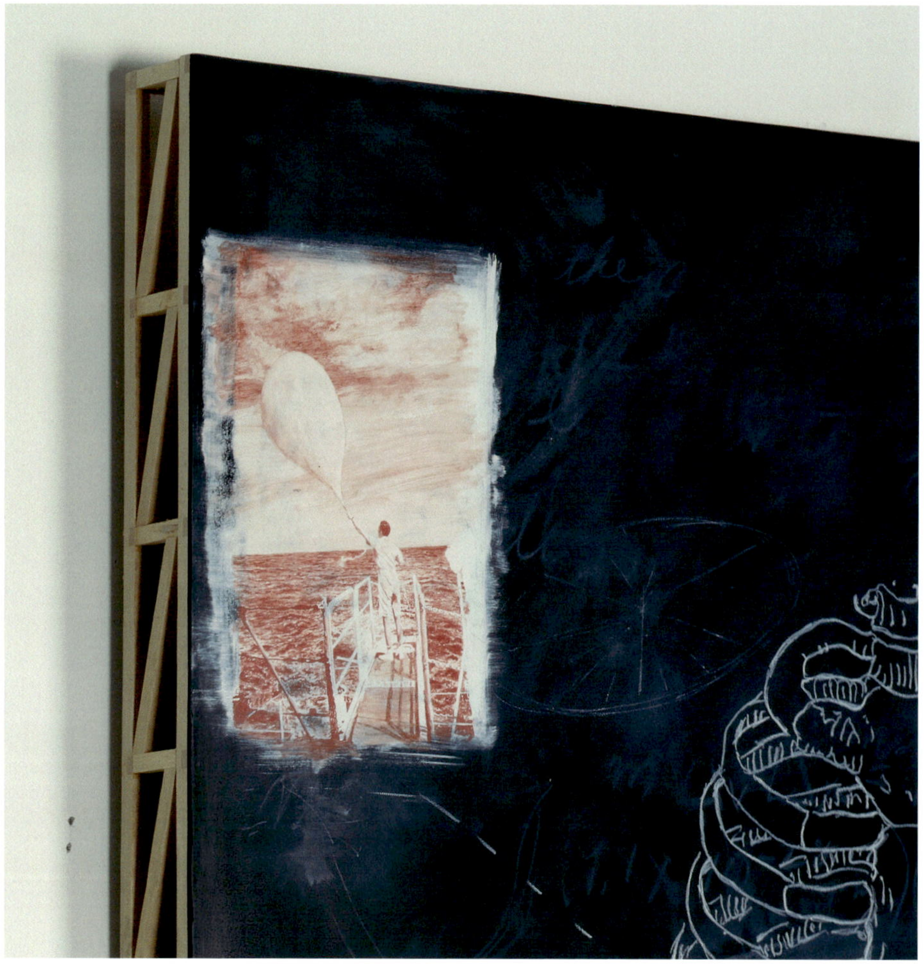

Spider 1986

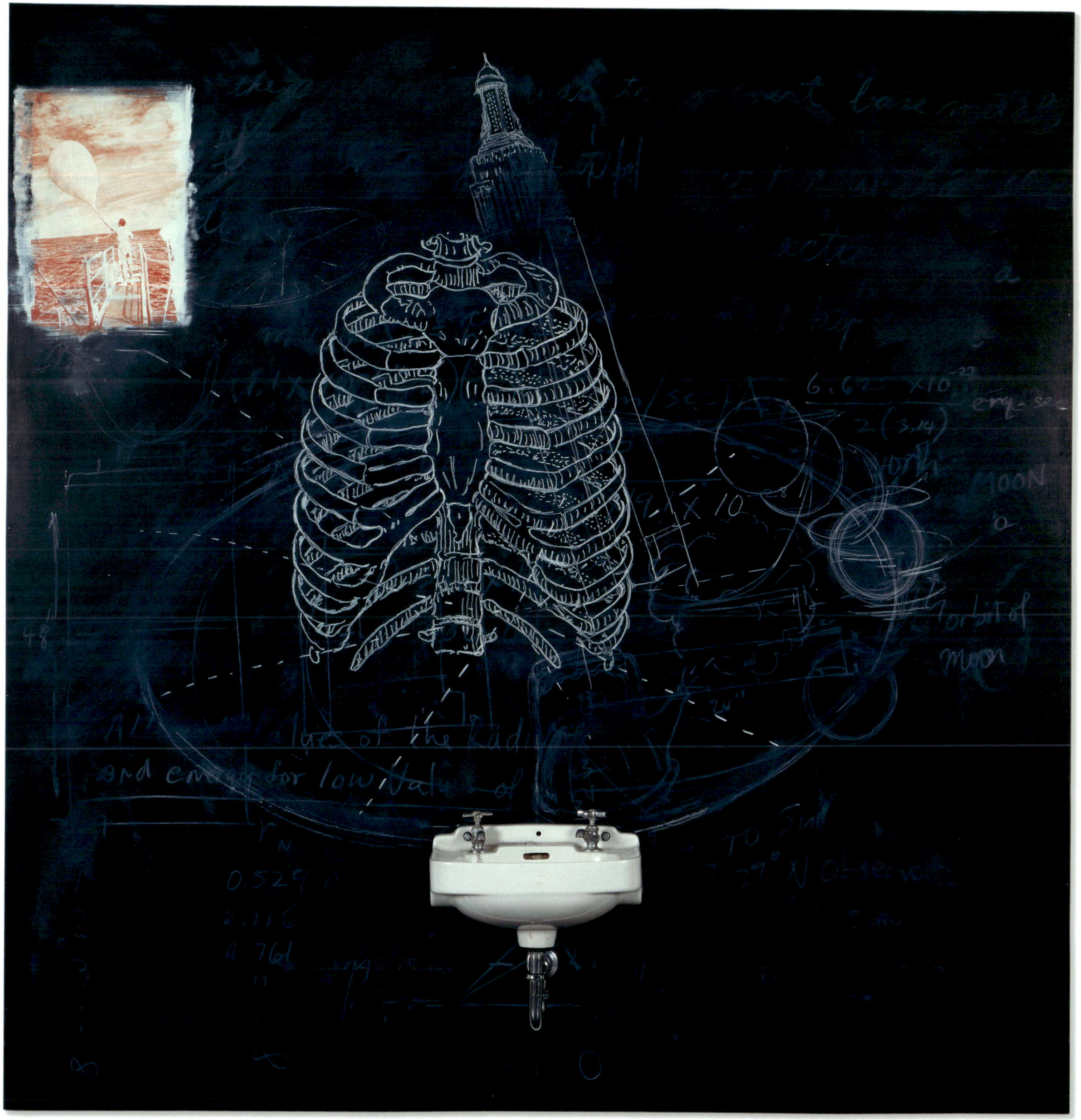
MOON
orbit of
moon

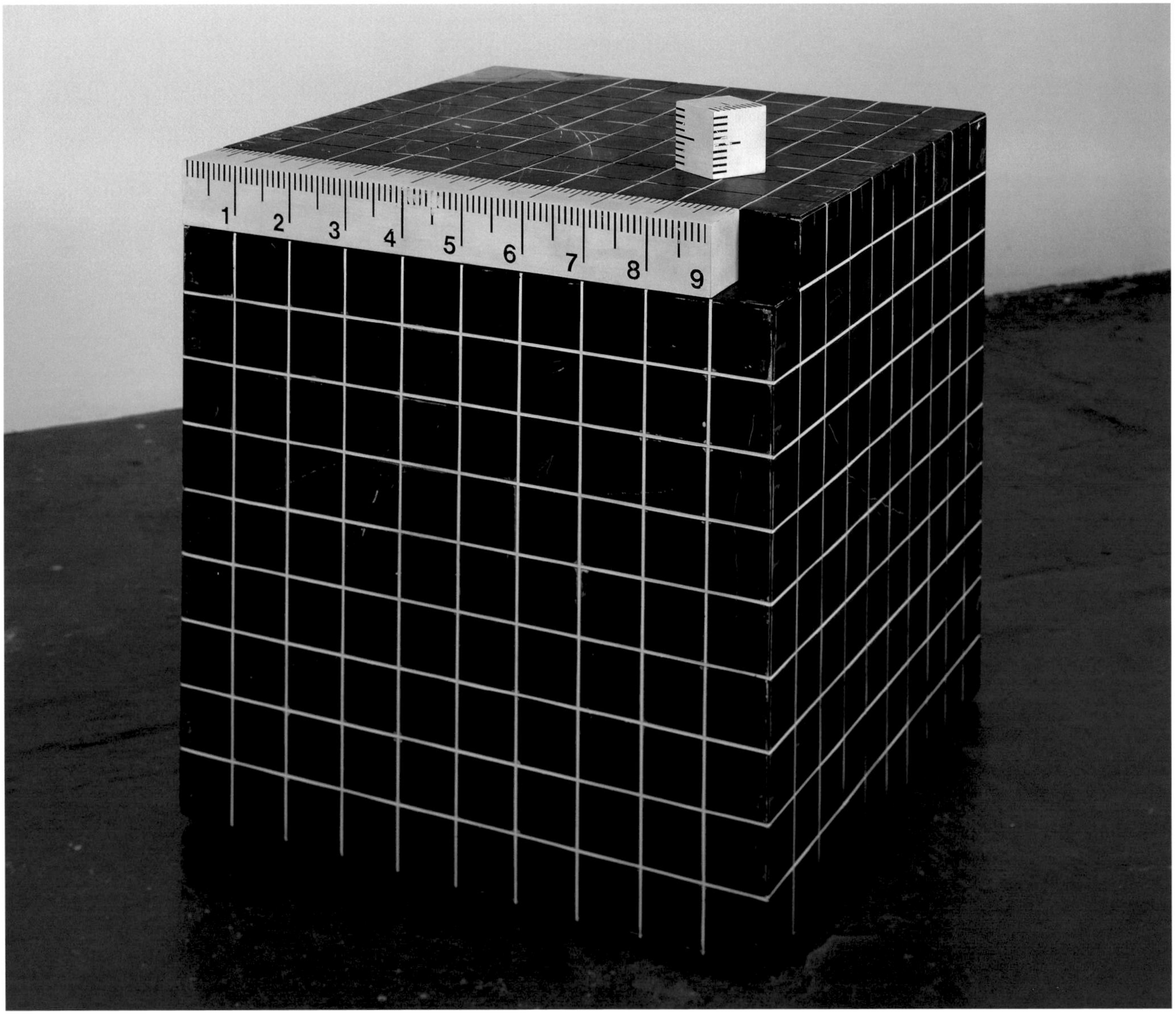
1 2 3 4 5 6 7 8 9

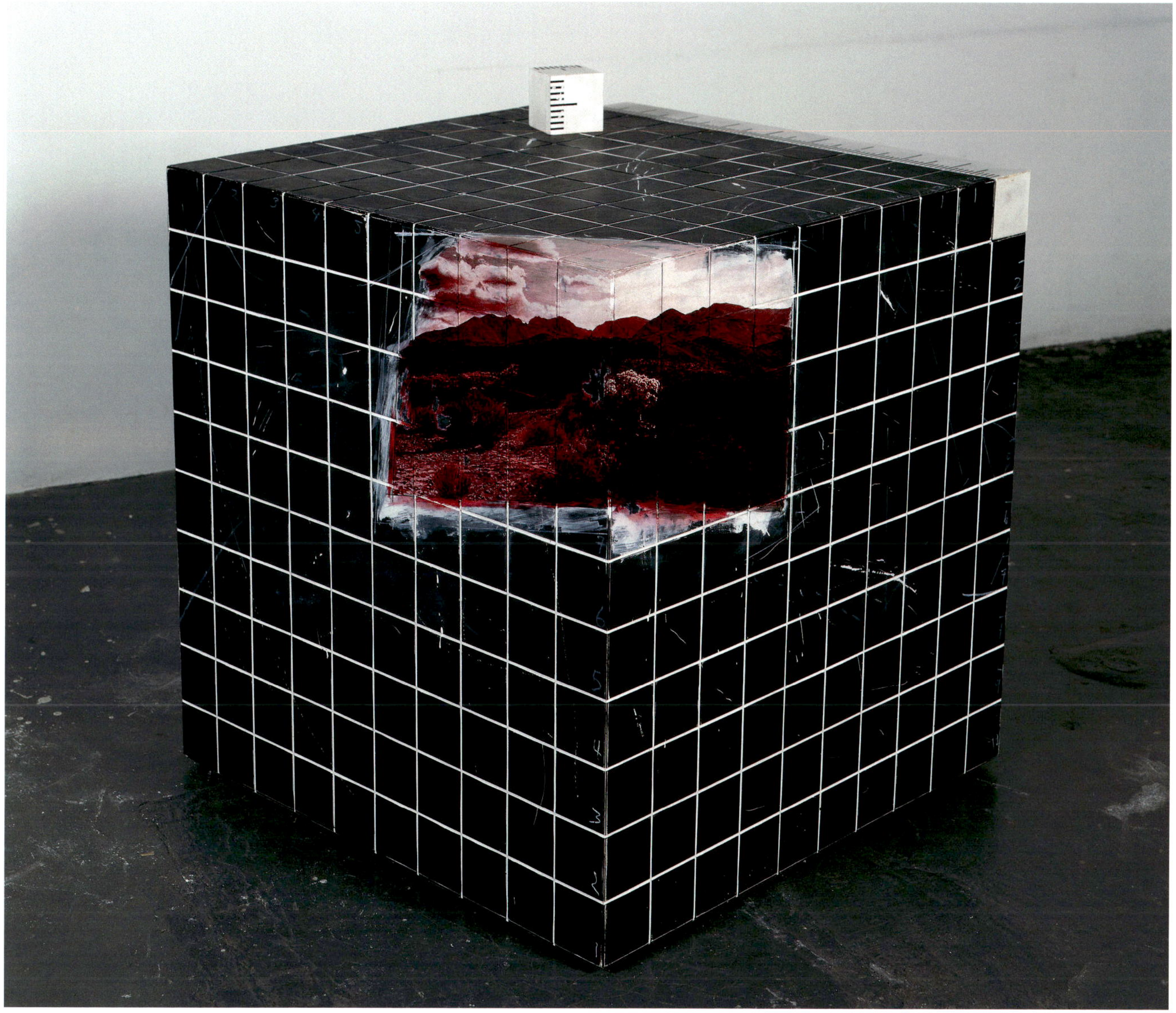

Heart of Darkness 1986

Objects in a Field 1986

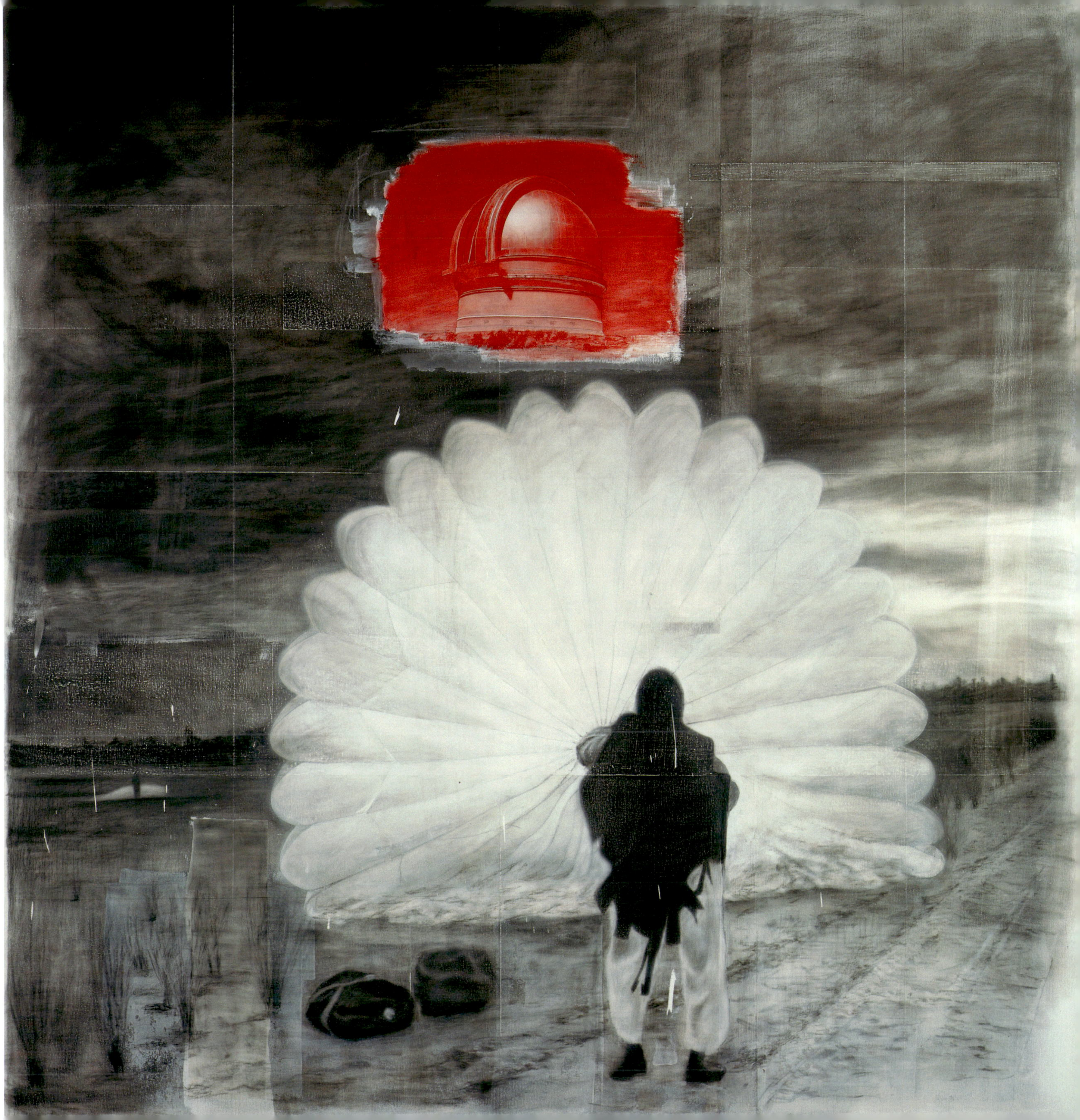

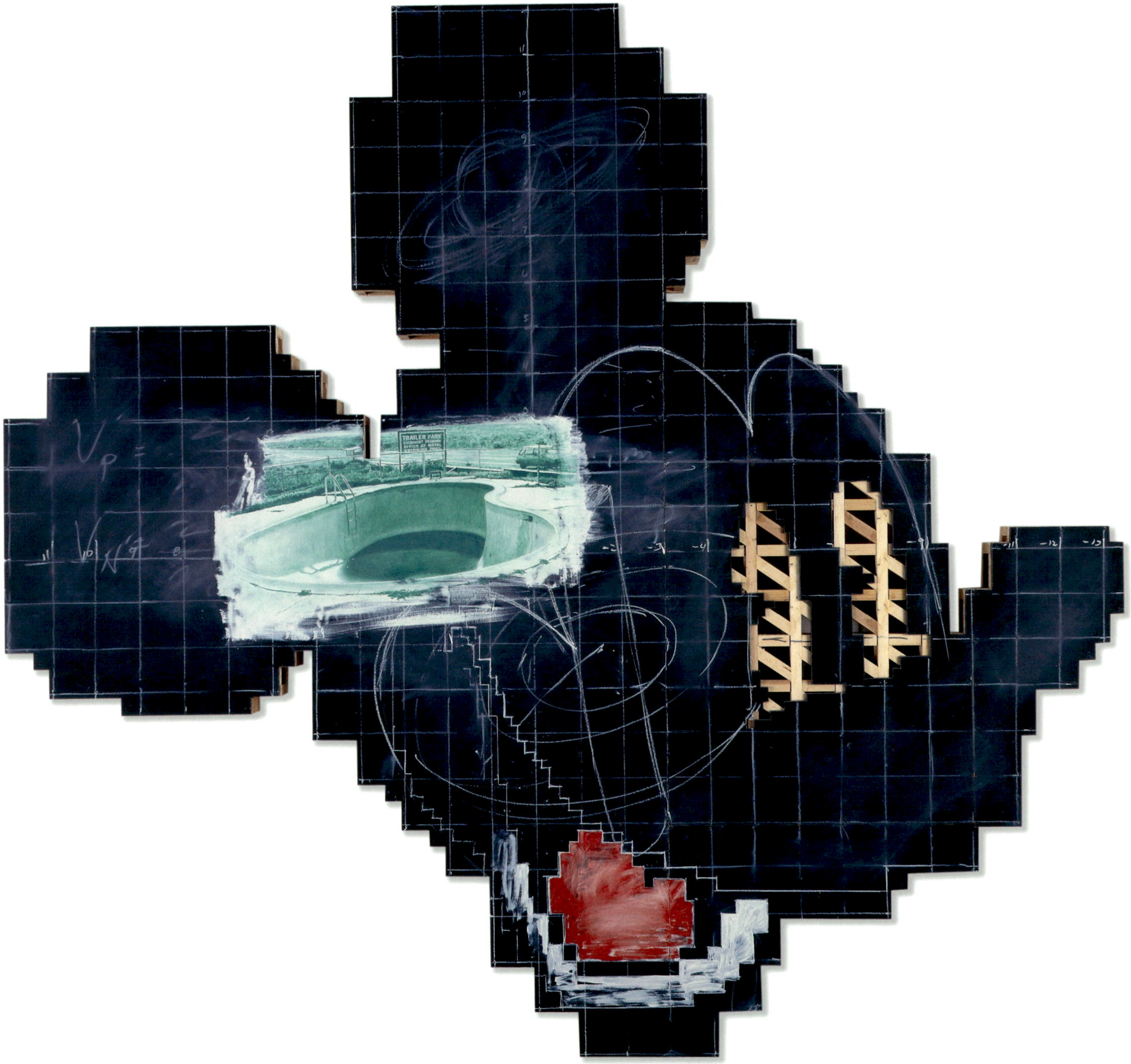
TRAILER PARK

Scenes from the American West 1986

Pumpkin Field 1986

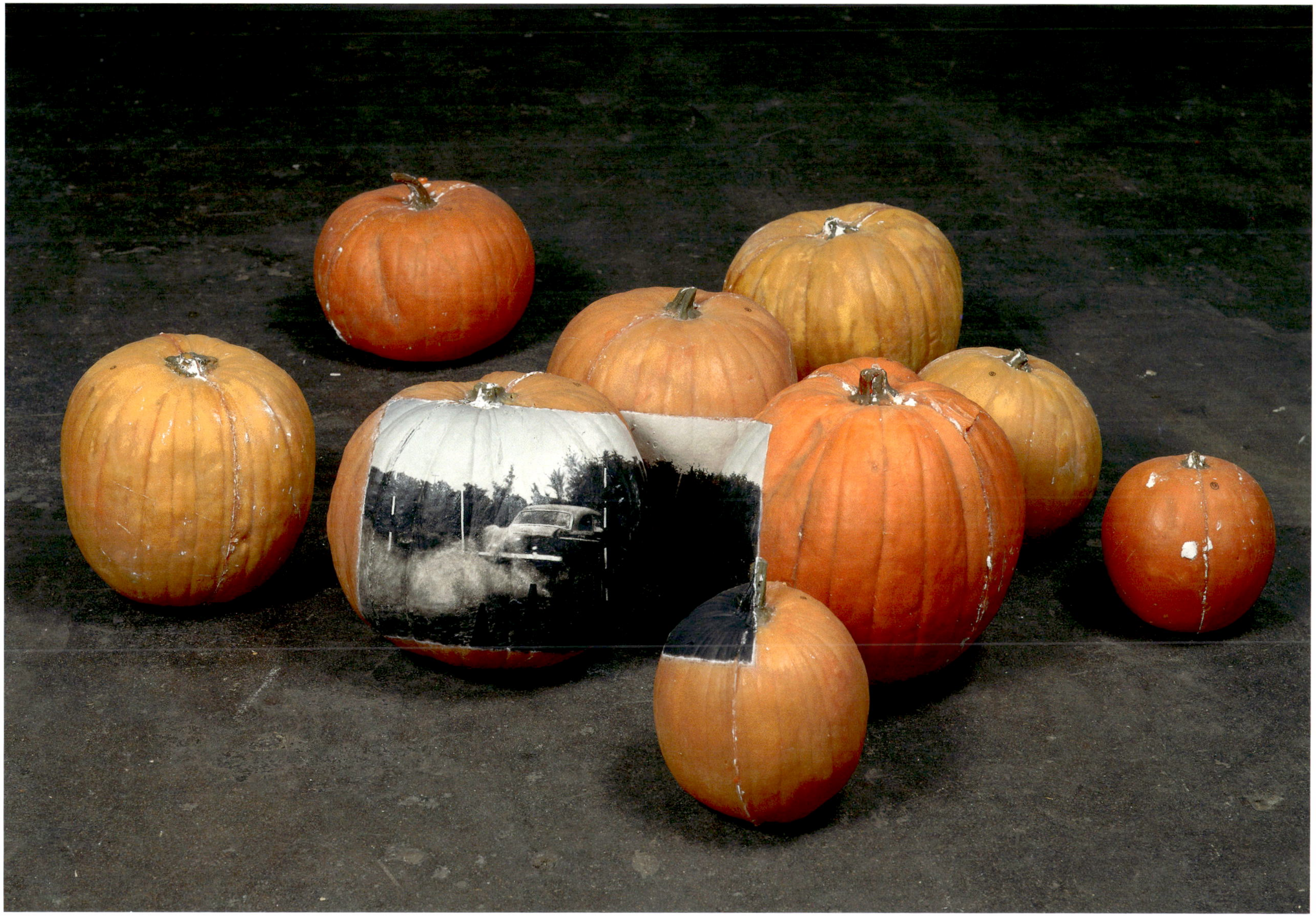

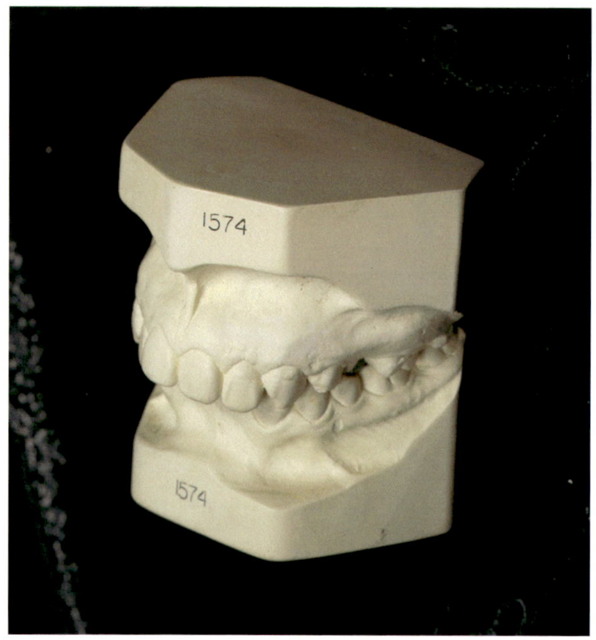

Complementary Pairs 1987

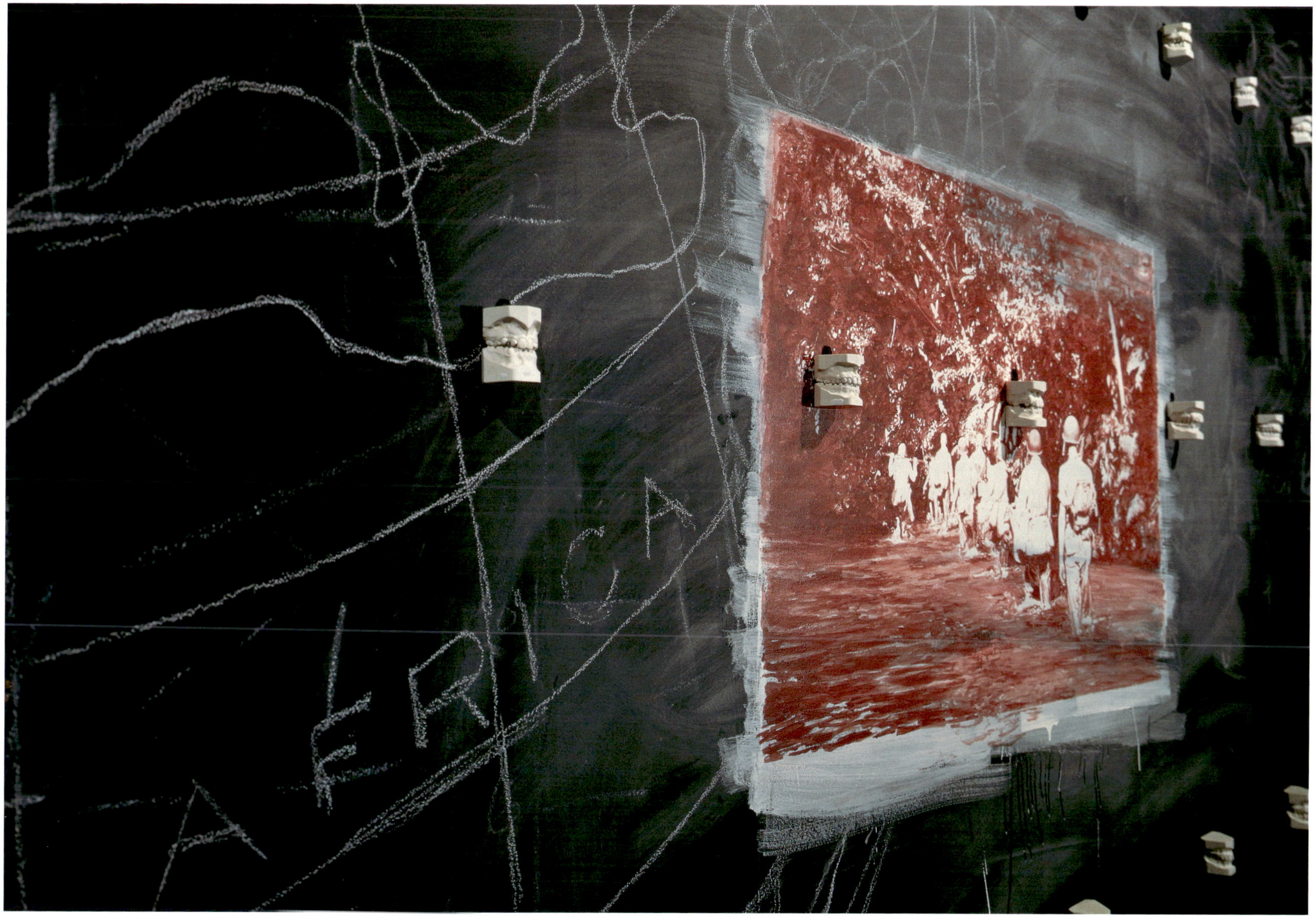
AFRICA

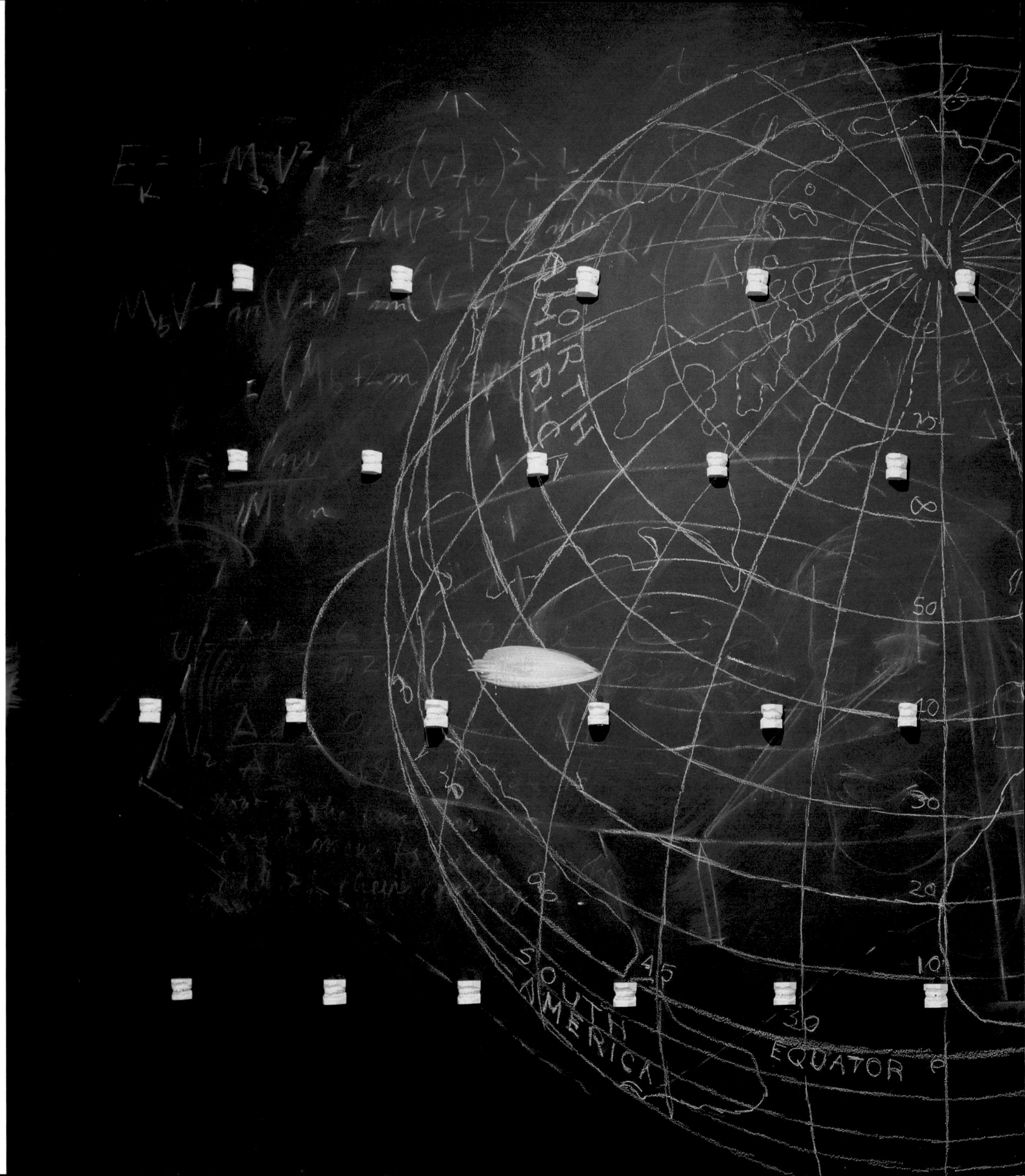
NORTH AMERICA
SOUTH AMERICA
EQUATOR
N

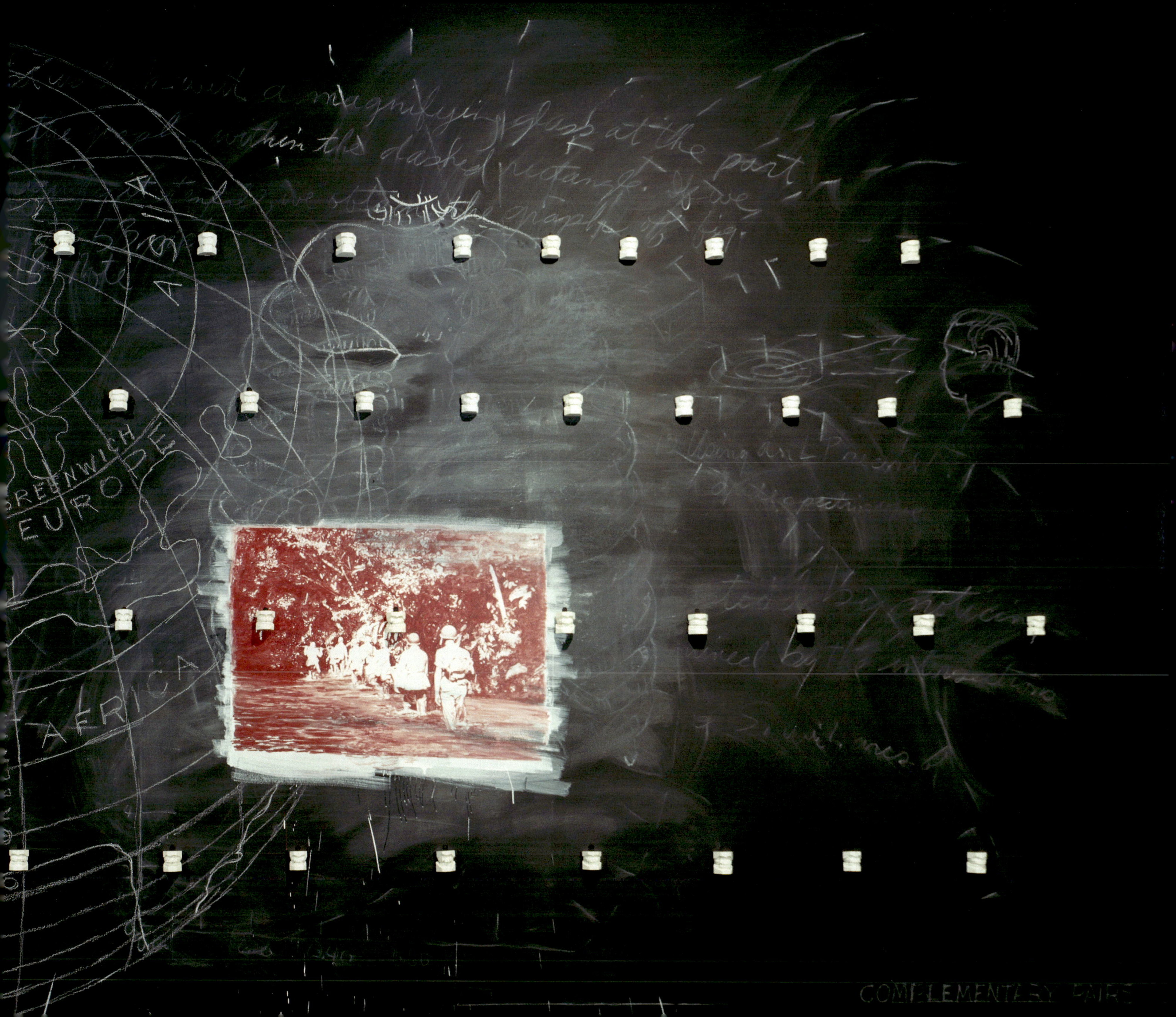
GREENWICH
EUROPE
AFRICA
COMPLEMENTARY PAIRS

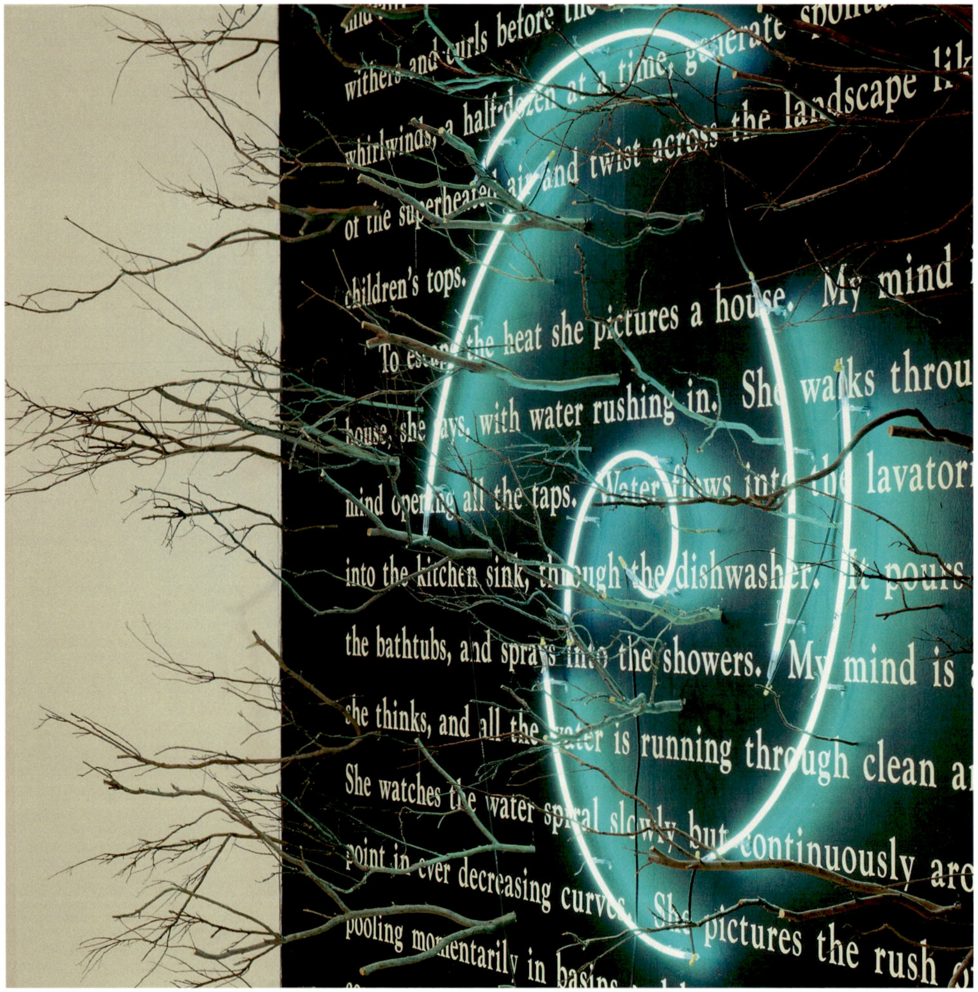

The Coriolis Effect 1987

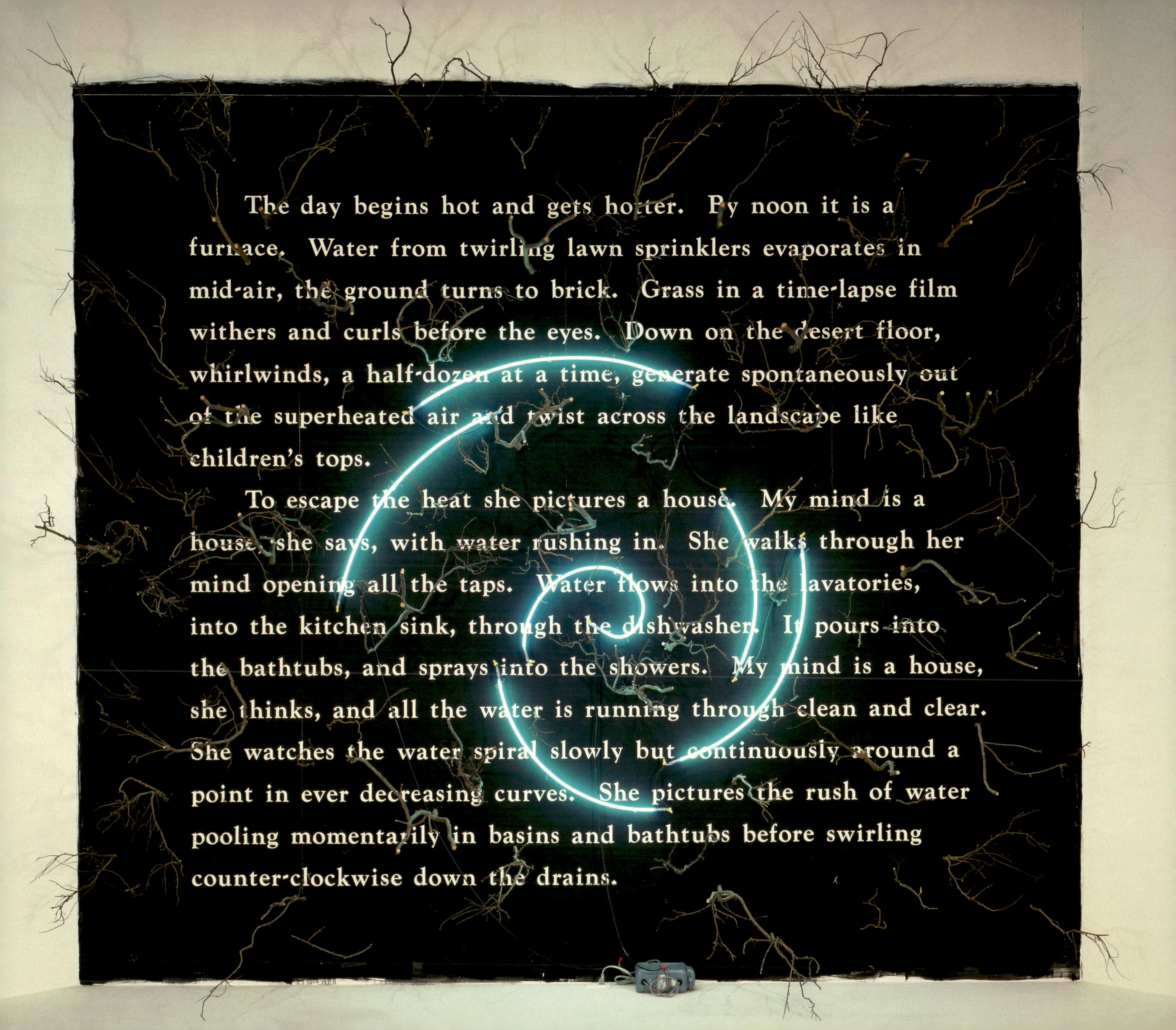
The day begins hot and gets hotter. By noon it is a
furnace. Water from twirling lawn sprinklers evaporates in
mid-air, the ground turns to brick. Grass in a time-lapse film
withers and curls before the eyes. Down on the desert floor,
whirlwinds, a half-dozen at a time, generate spontaneously out
of the superheated air and twist across the landscape like
children's tops.
To escape the heat she pictures a house. My mind is a
house, she says, with water rushing in. She walks through her
mind opening all the taps. Water flows into the lavatories,
into the kitchen sink, through the dishwasher. It pours into
the bathtubs, and sprays into the showers. My mind is a house,
she thinks, and all the water is running through clean and clear.
She watches the water spiral slowly but continuously around a
point in ever decreasing curves. She pictures the rush of water
pooling momentarily in basins and bathtubs before swirling
counter-clockwise down the drains.

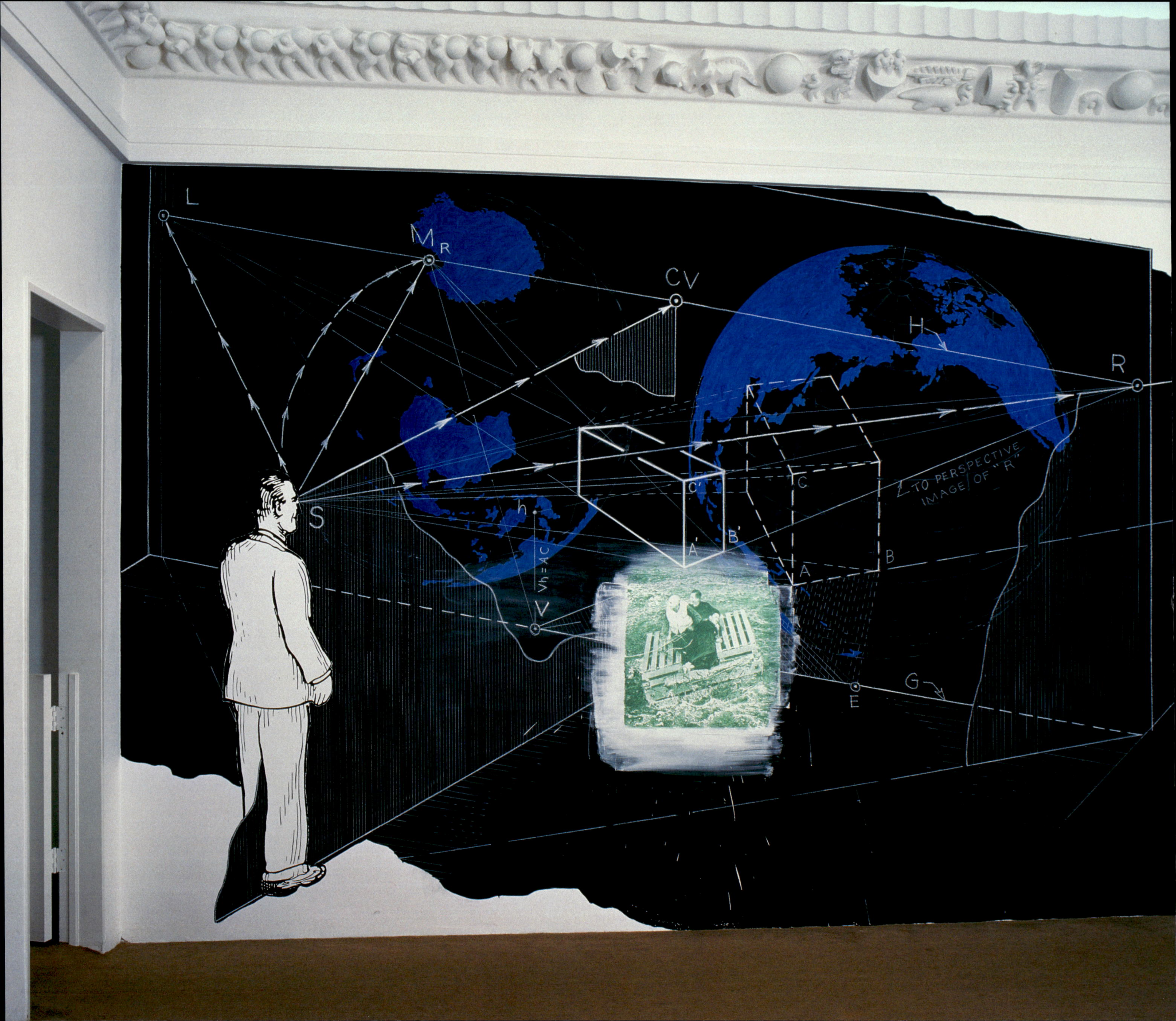
L
MR
CV
H
R
S
h
Vh=AC
V
C'
C
B'
B
A'
A
E
G
TO PERSPECTIVE IMAGE OF "R"

Perdido en el Mar 1987–1988

Perdido en el Mar 1987–1988

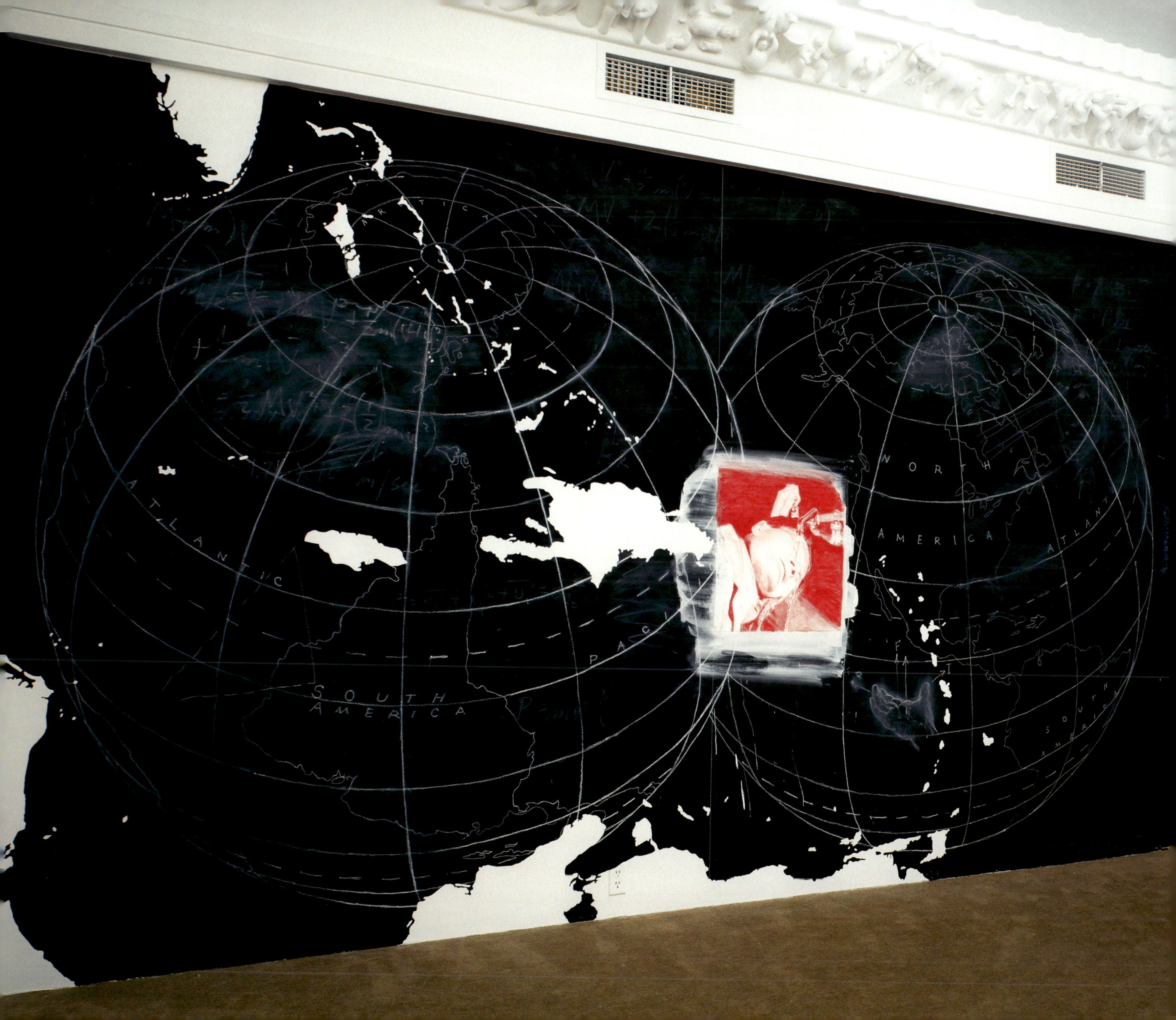
ATLANTIC
SOUTH
AMERICA
NORTH
AMERICA
SOUTH
AMERICA

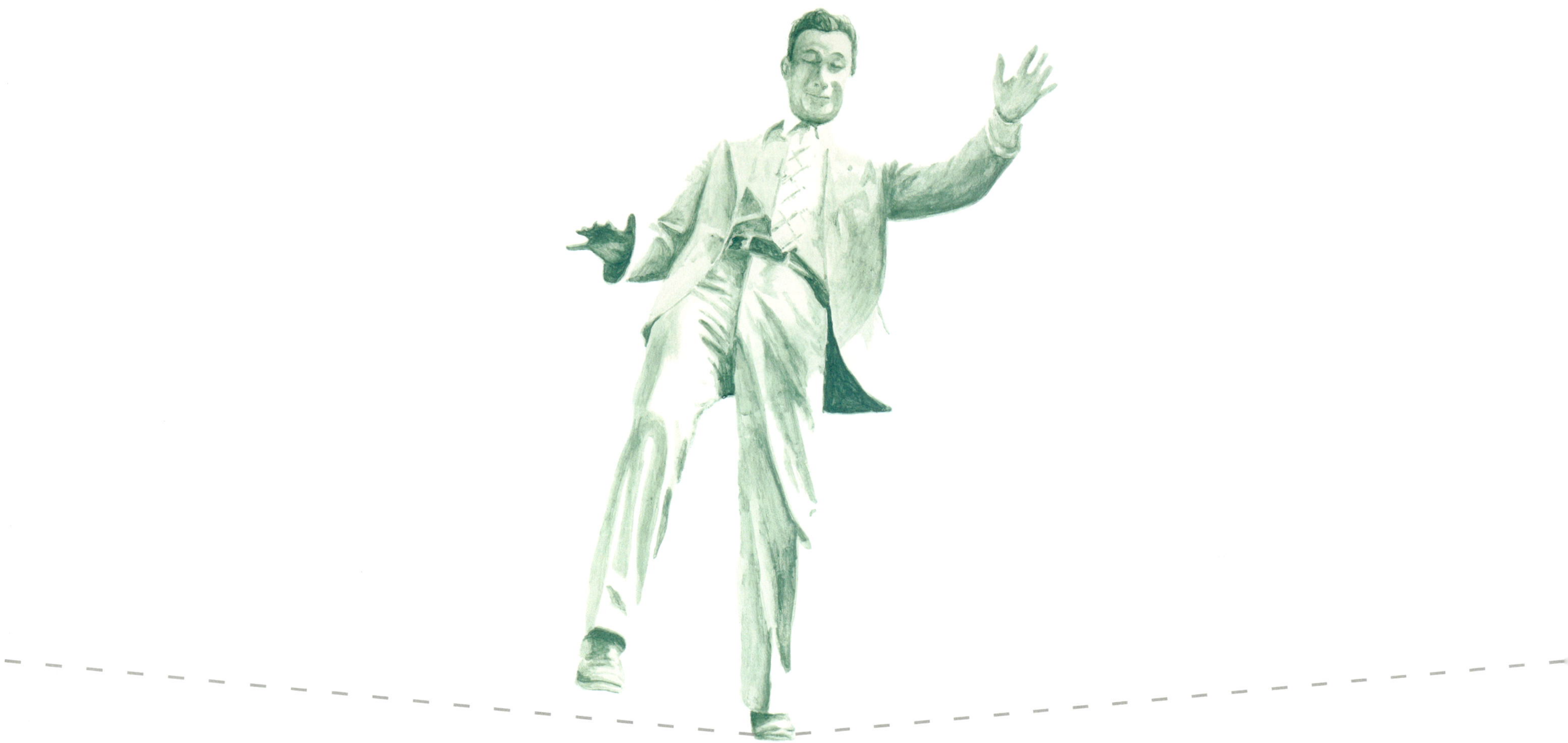

LOST FOR WORDS

Dallas Museum of Art, Dallas, Texas
January 23–April 17, 1988

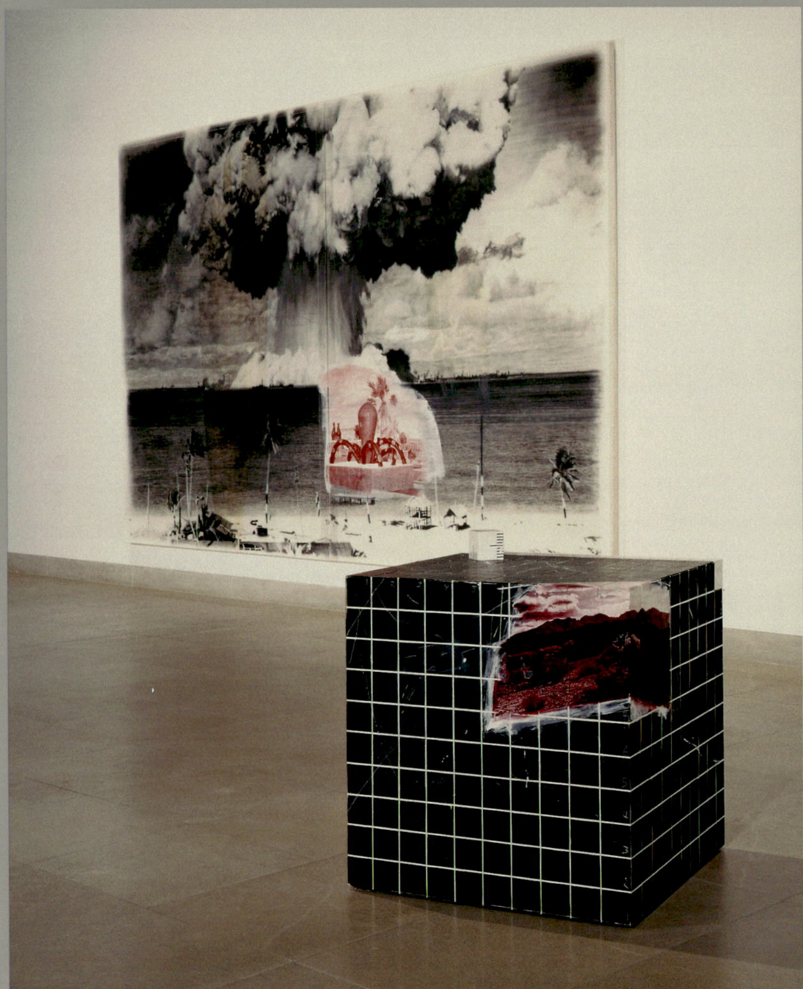

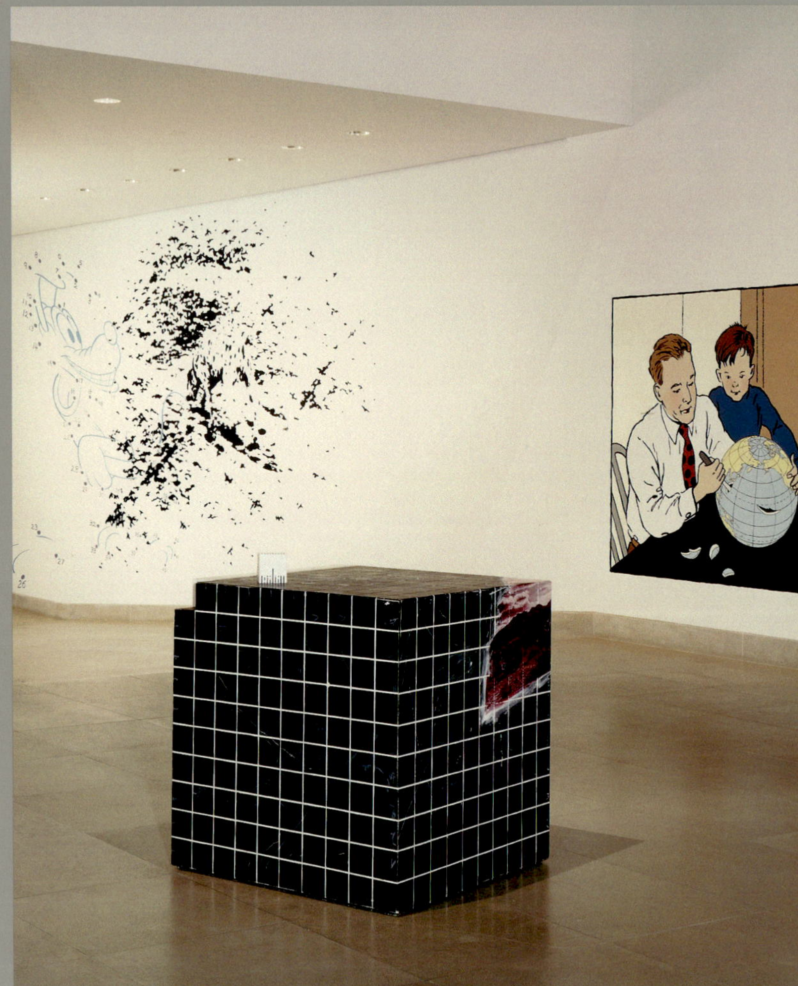

Installation views

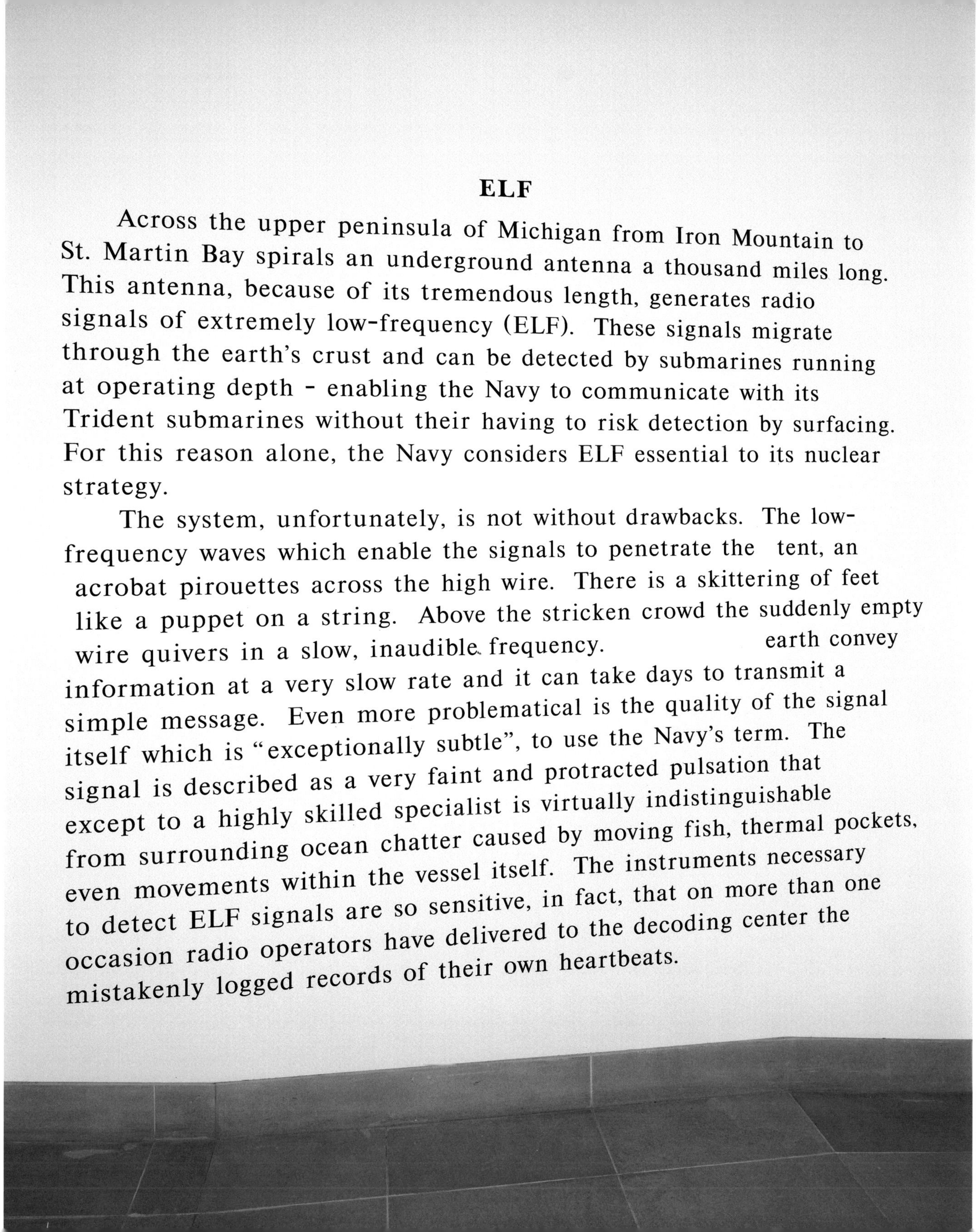
ELF
Across the upper peninsula of Michigan from Iron Mountain to
St. Martin Bay spirals an underground antenna a thousand miles long.
This antenna, because of its tremendous length, generates radio
signals of extremely low-frequency (ELF). These signals migrate
through the earth's crust and can be detected by submarines running
at operating depth - enabling the Navy to communicate with its
Trident submarines without their having to risk detection by surfacing.
For this reason alone, the Navy considers ELF essential to its nuclear
strategy.
The system, unfortunately, is not without drawbacks. The low-
frequency waves which enable the signals to penetrate the tent, an
acrobat pirouettes across the high wire. There is a skittering of feet
like a puppet on a string. Above the stricken crowd the suddenly empty
wire quivers in a slow, inaudible frequency. earth convey
information at a very slow rate and it can take days to transmit a
simple message. Even more problematical is the quality of the signal
itself which is "exceptionally subtle", to use the Navy's term. The
signal is described as a very faint and protracted pulsation that
except to a highly skilled specialist is virtually indistinguishable
from surrounding ocean chatter caused by moving fish, thermal pockets,
even movements within the vessel itself. The instruments necessary
to detect ELF signals are so sensitive, in fact, that on more than one
occasion radio operators have delivered to the decoding center the
mistakenly logged records of their own heartbeats.

ELF 1988

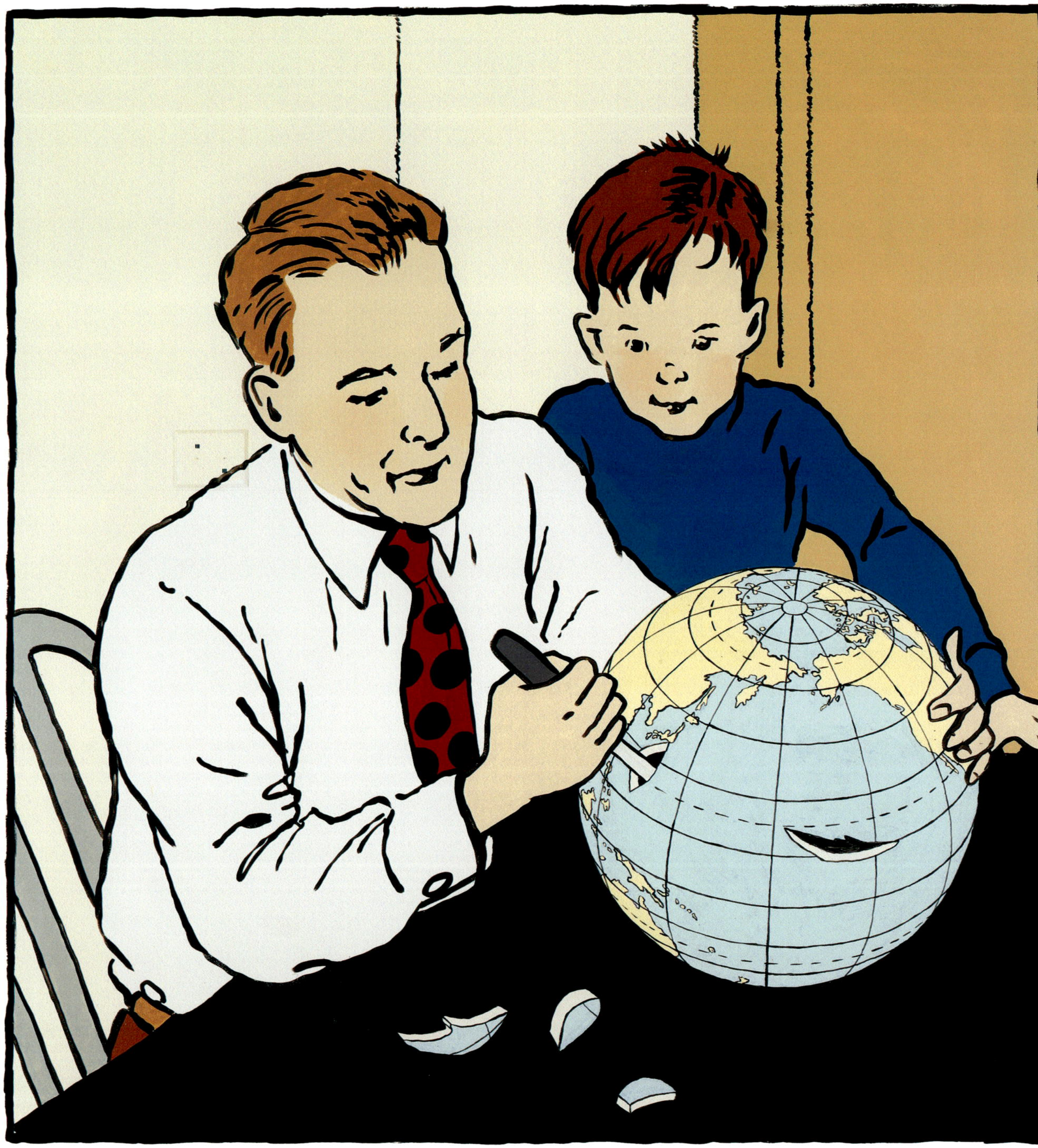

Man Cutting Globe 1988

Pluto 1988

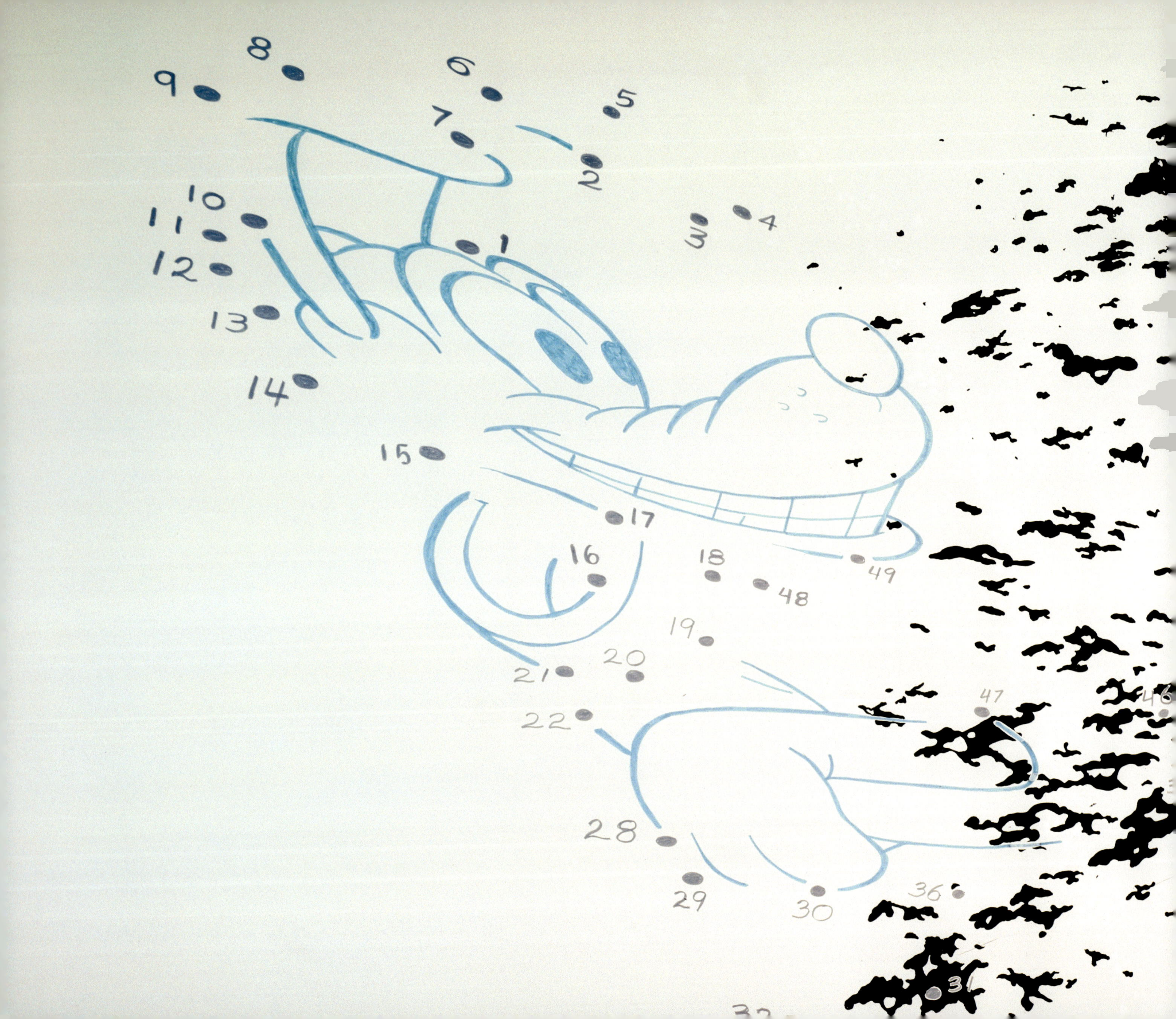

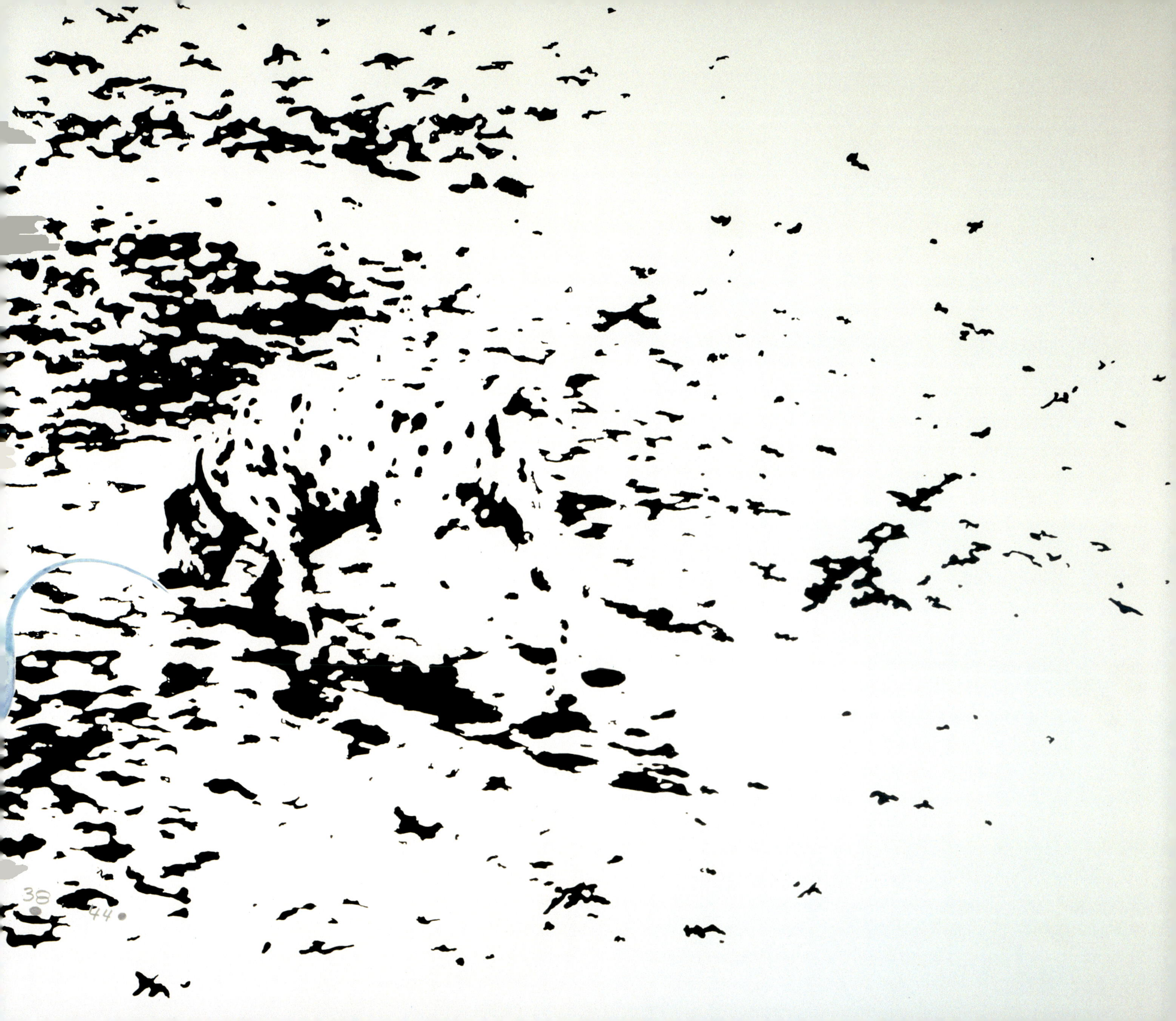

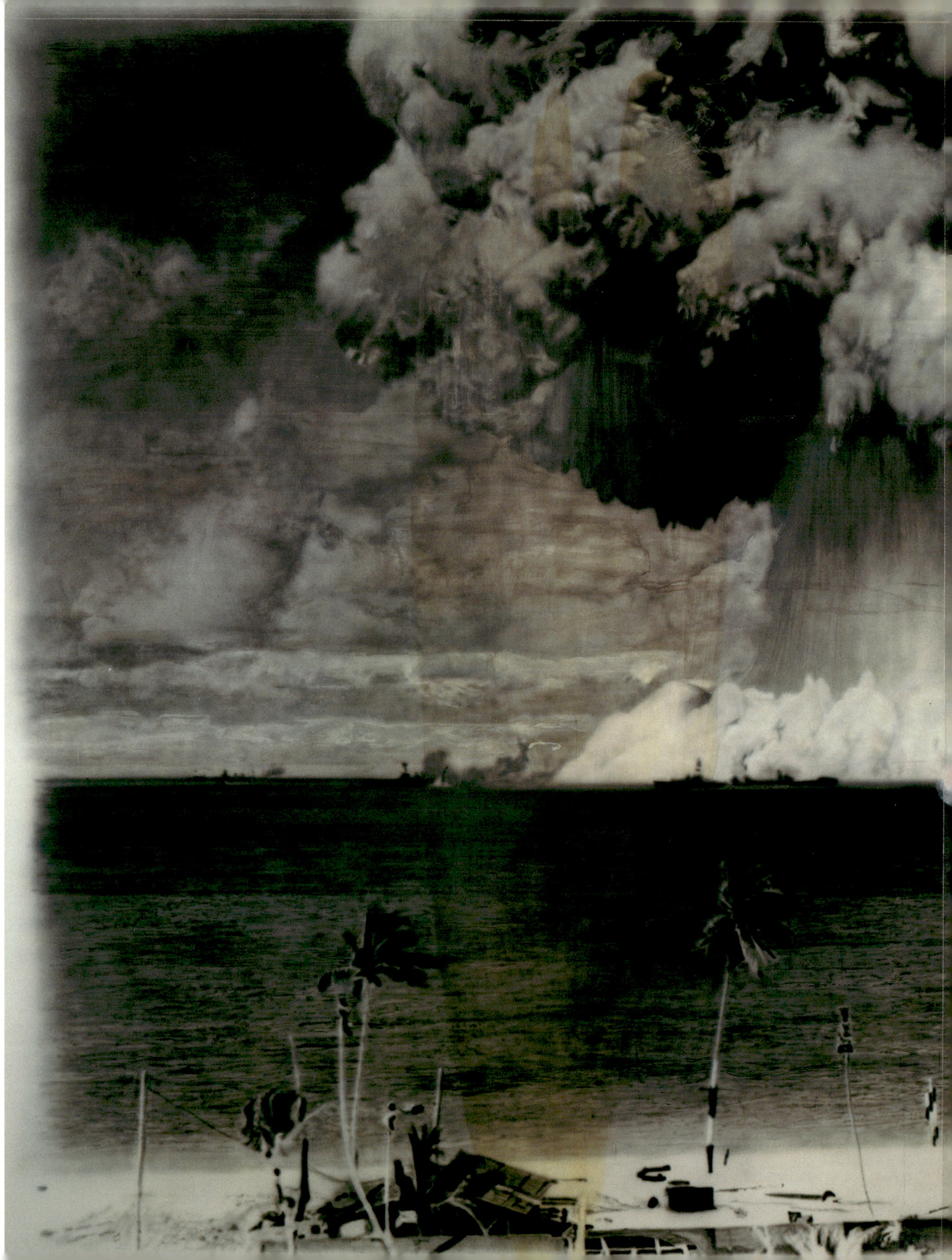

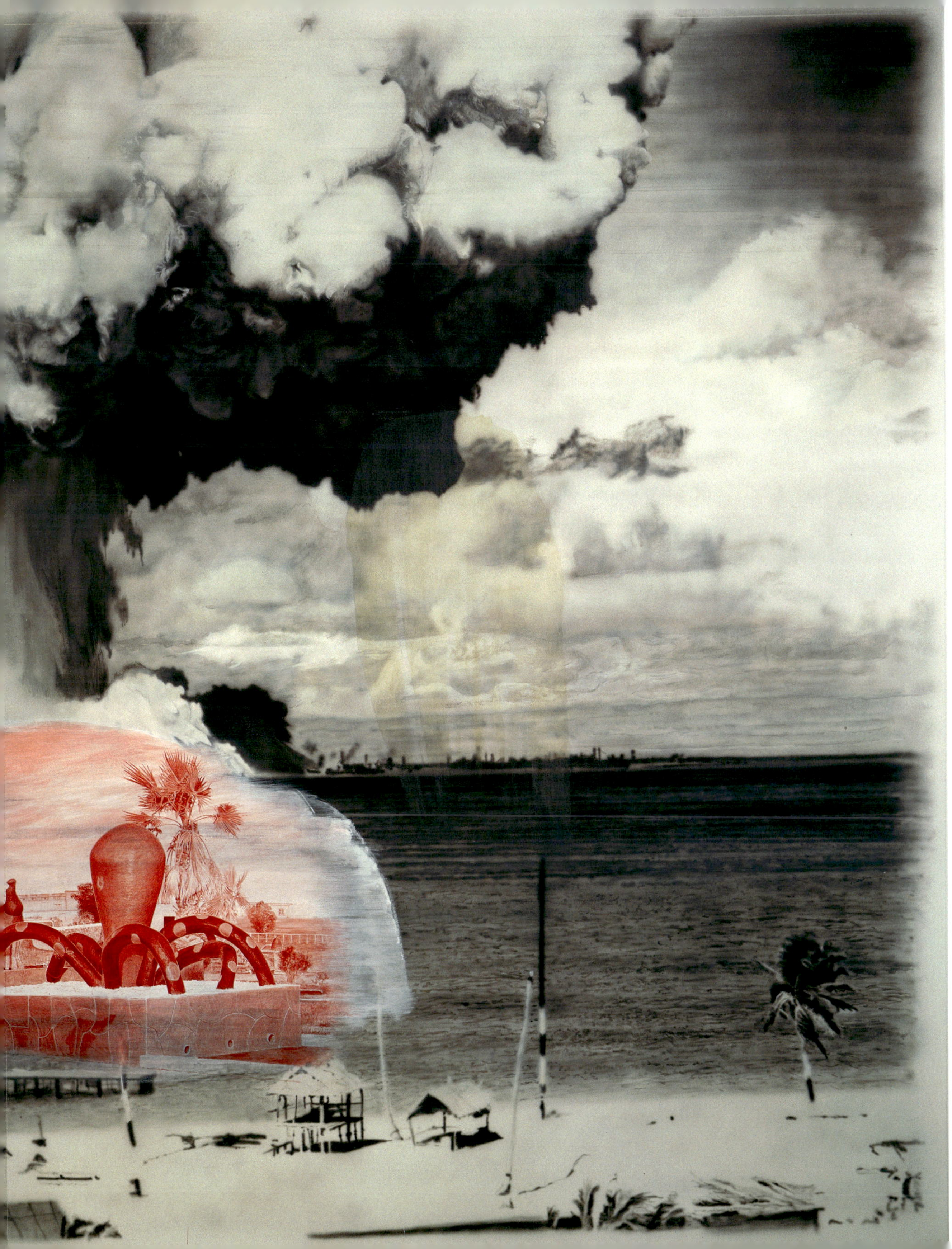

Bikini 1987

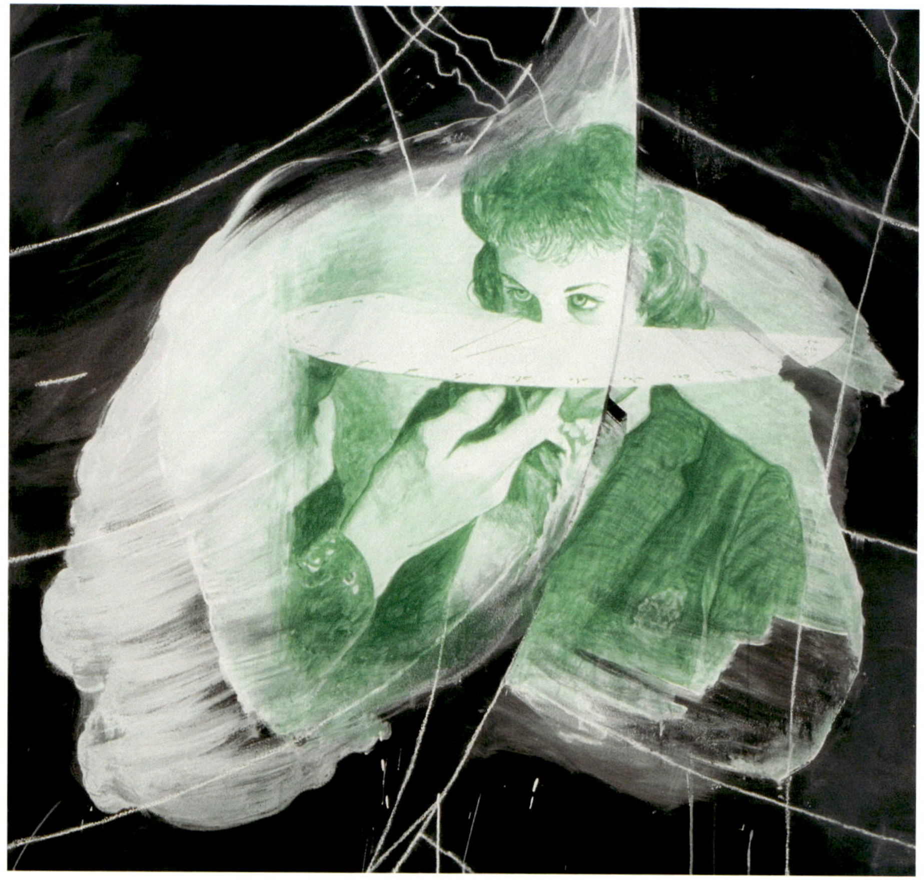

Worlds Collide 1988

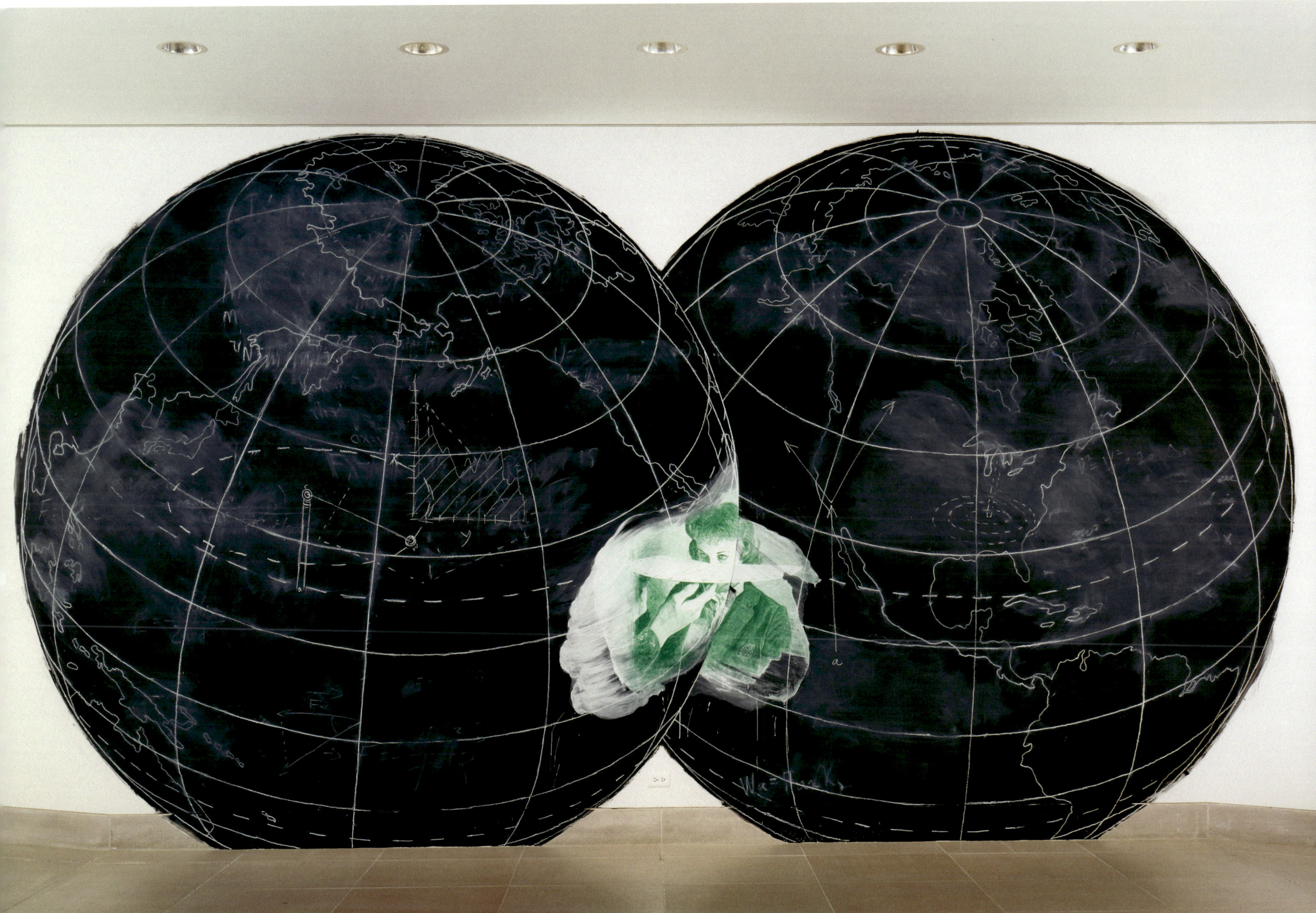

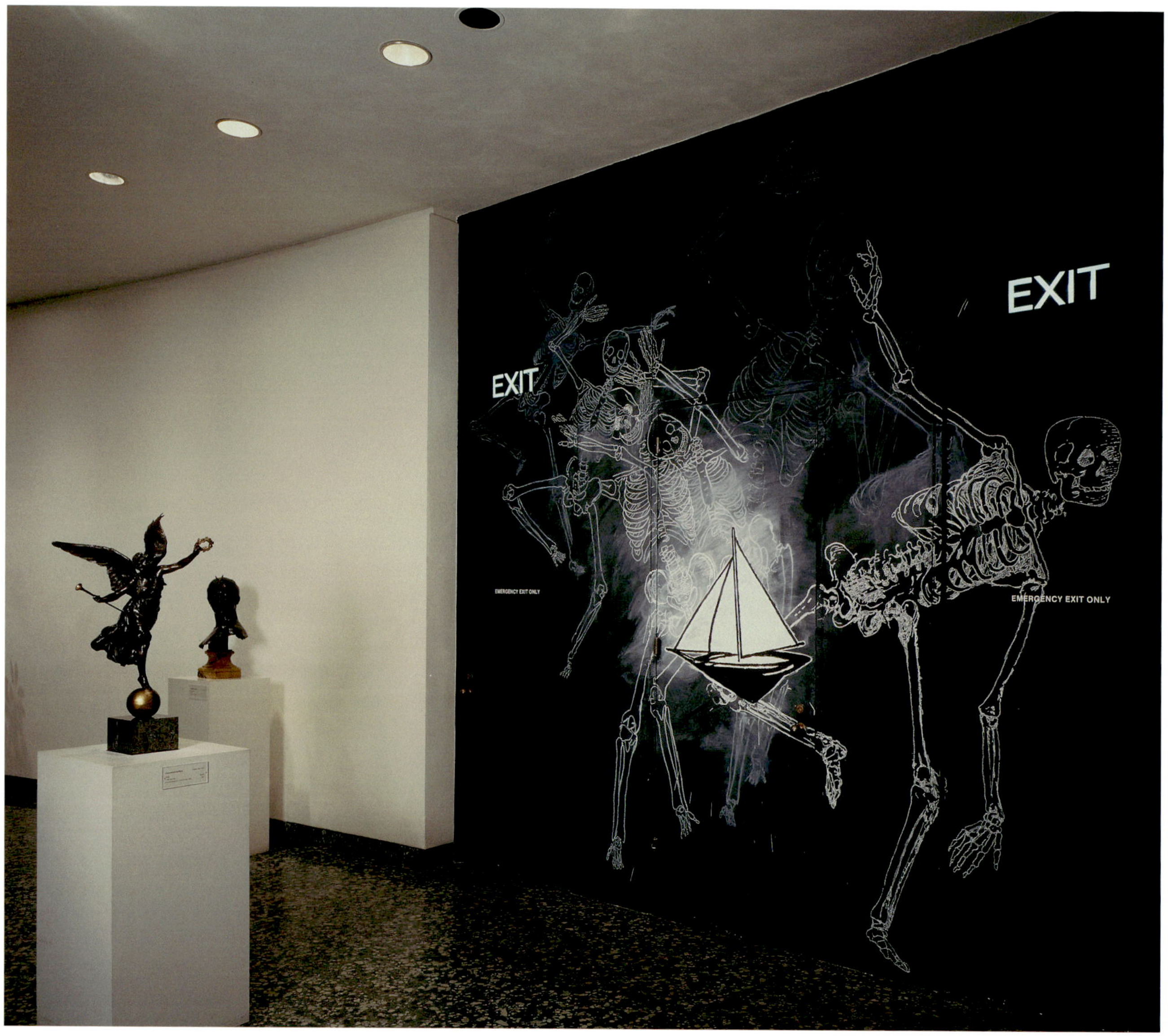
EXIT
EXIT
EMERGENCY EXIT ONLY
EMERGENCY EXIT ONLY

PARALLEL LINES

Hirshhorn Museum and Sculpture Garden, Washington, D.C.
June 22–October 10, 1988

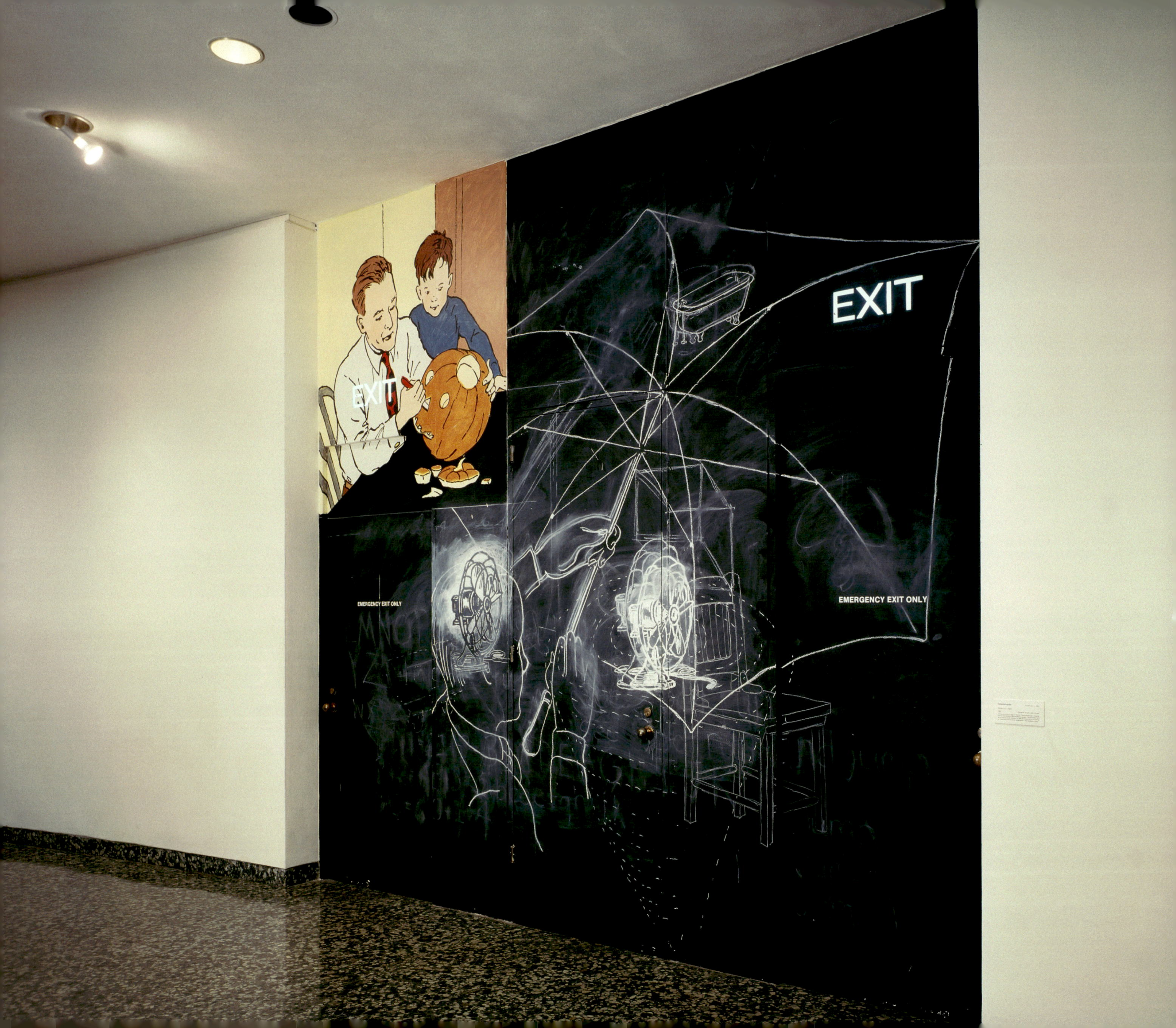
EXIT
EXIT
EMERGENCY EXIT ONLY
EMERGENCY EXIT ONLY

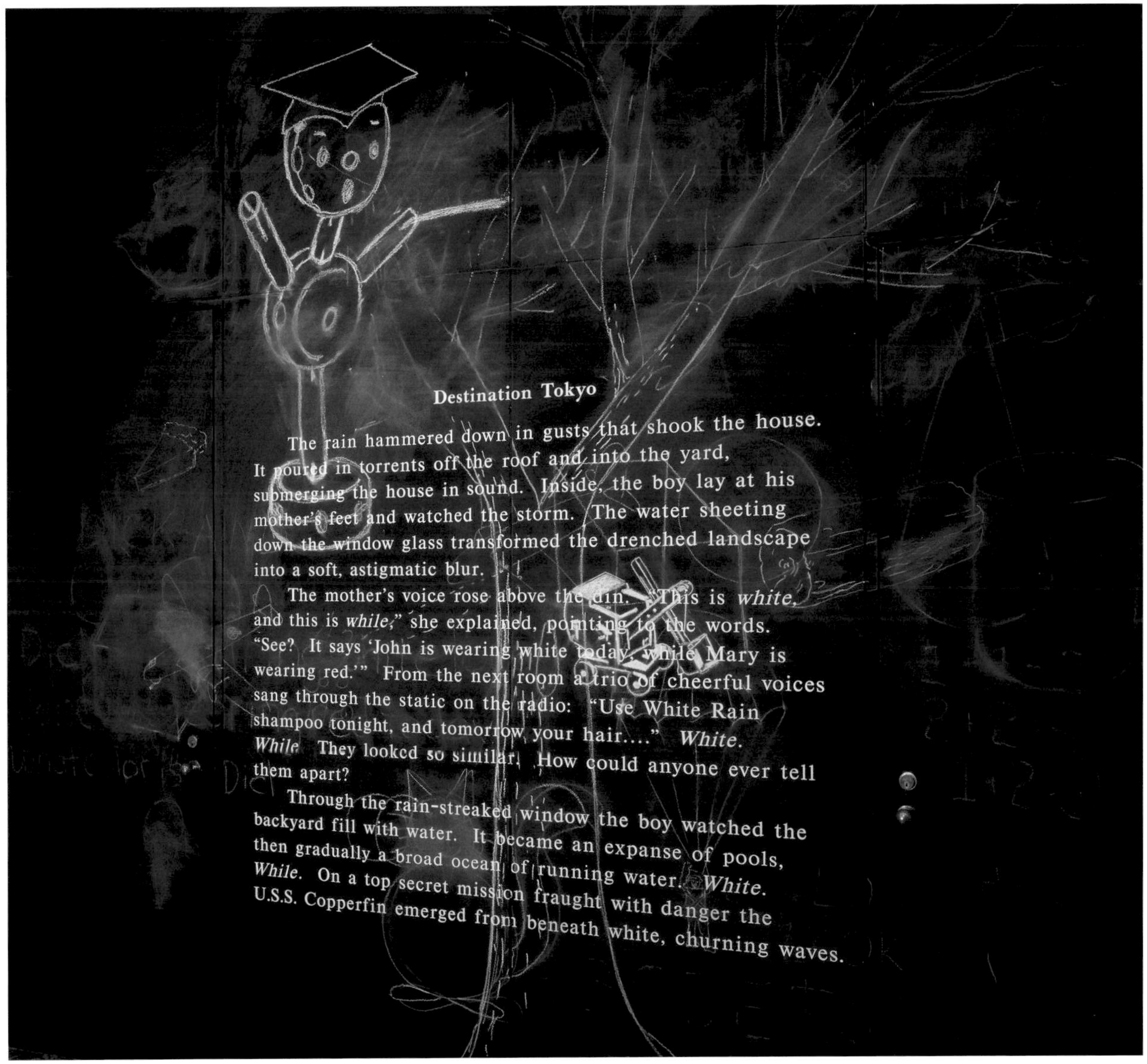

Destination Tokyo

The rain hammered down in gusts that shook the house. It poured in torrents off the roof and into the yard, submerging the house in sound. Inside, the boy lay at his mother's feet and watched the storm. The water sheeting down the window glass transformed the drenched landscape into a soft, astigmatic blur.

The mother's voice rose above the din. "This is *white*, and this is *while*," she explained, pointing to the words. "See? It says 'John is wearing white today, while Mary is wearing red.'" From the next room a trio of cheerful voices sang through the static on the radio: "Use White Rain shampoo tonight, and tomorrow your hair. . . ." *White. While.* They looked so similar. How could anyone ever tell them apart?

Through the rain-streaked window the boy watched the backyard fill with water. It became an expanse of pools, then gradually a broad ocean of running water. *White. While.* On a top secret mission fraught with danger the U.S.S. Copperfin emerged from beneath white, churning waves.

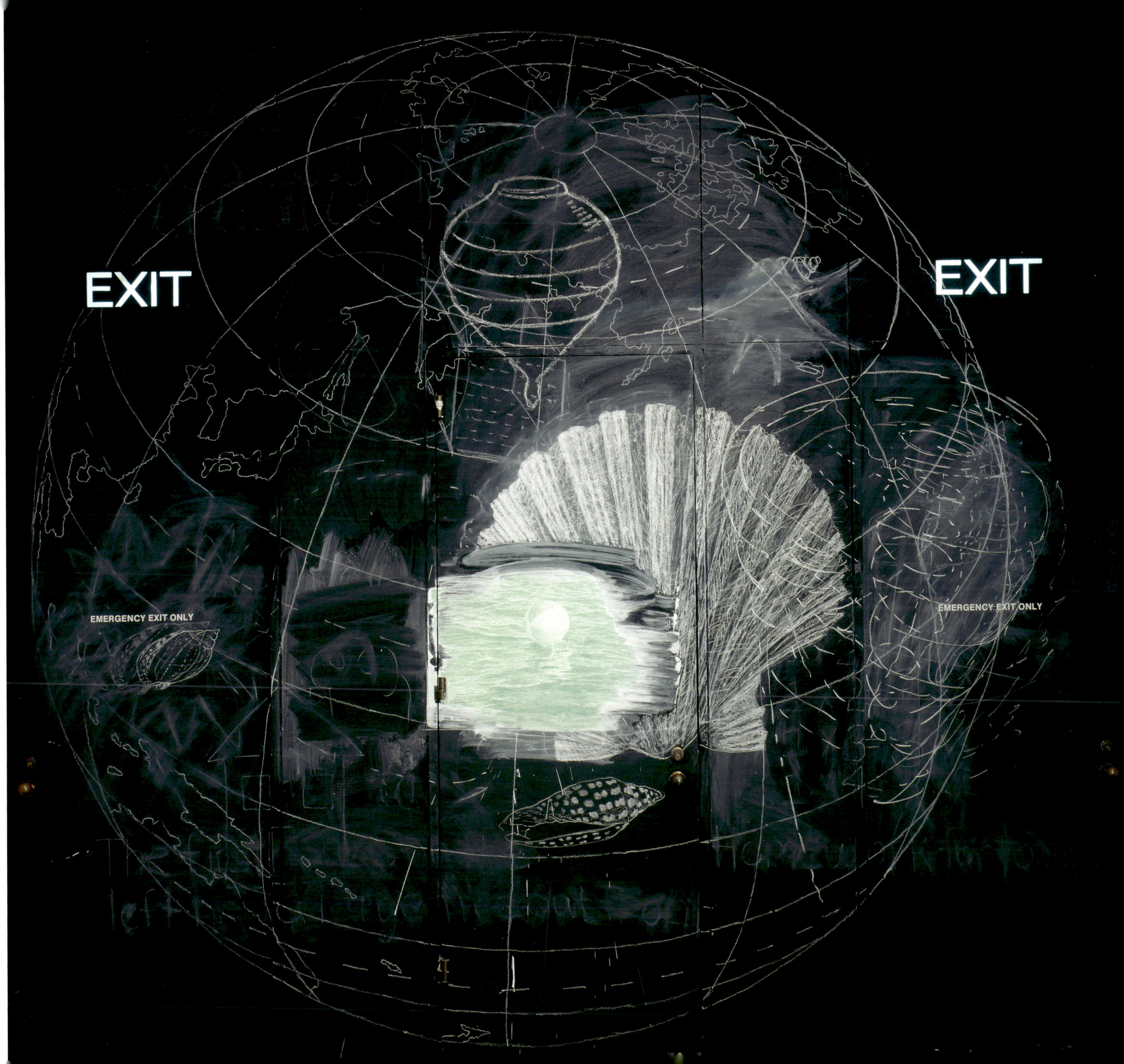
EXIT
EXIT
EMERGENCY EXIT ONLY
EMERGENCY EXIT ONLY

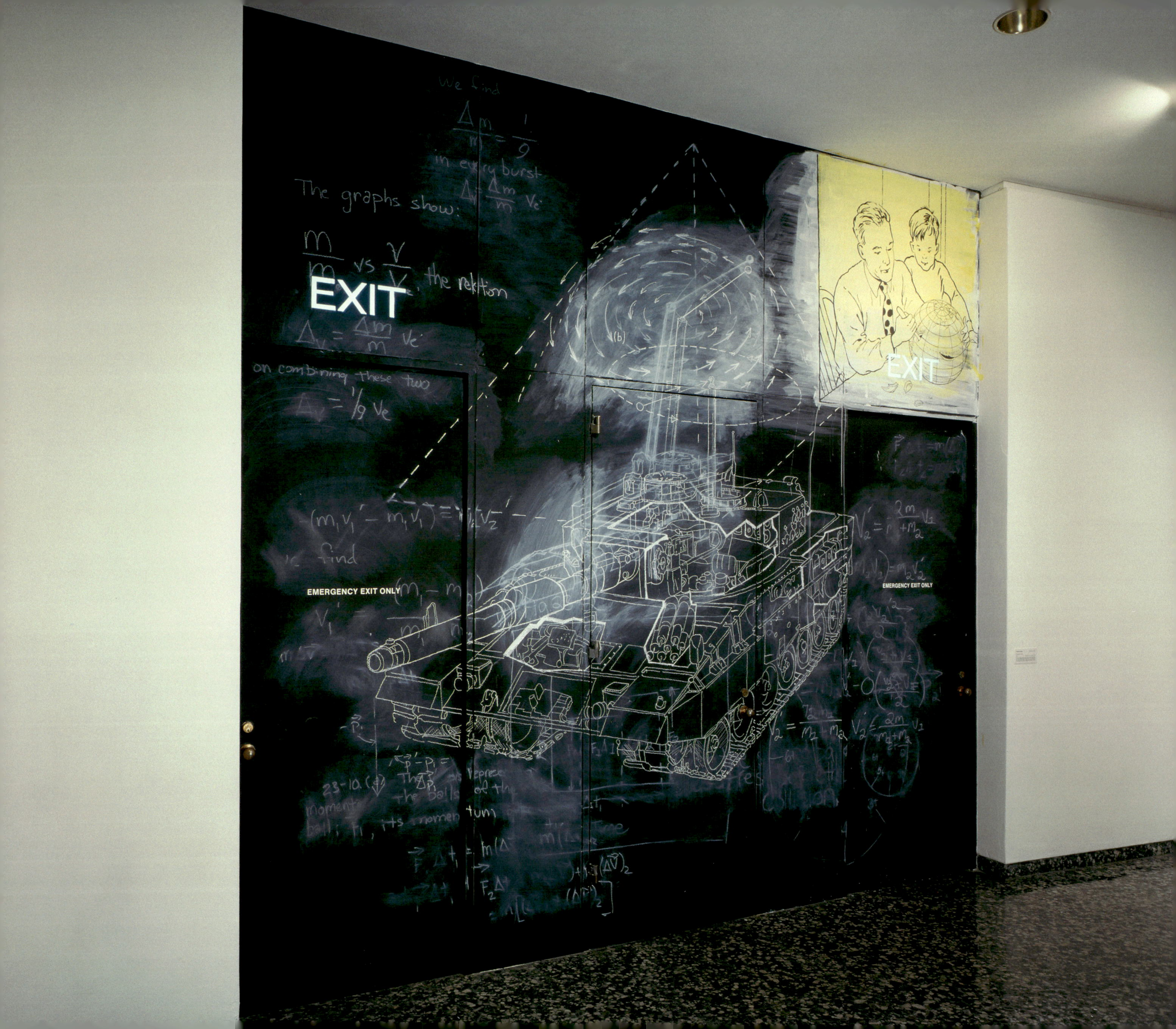
We find
in every burst
The graphs show:
EXIT
the relation
on combining these two
find
EMERGENCY EXIT ONLY
EXIT
EMERGENCY EXIT ONLY

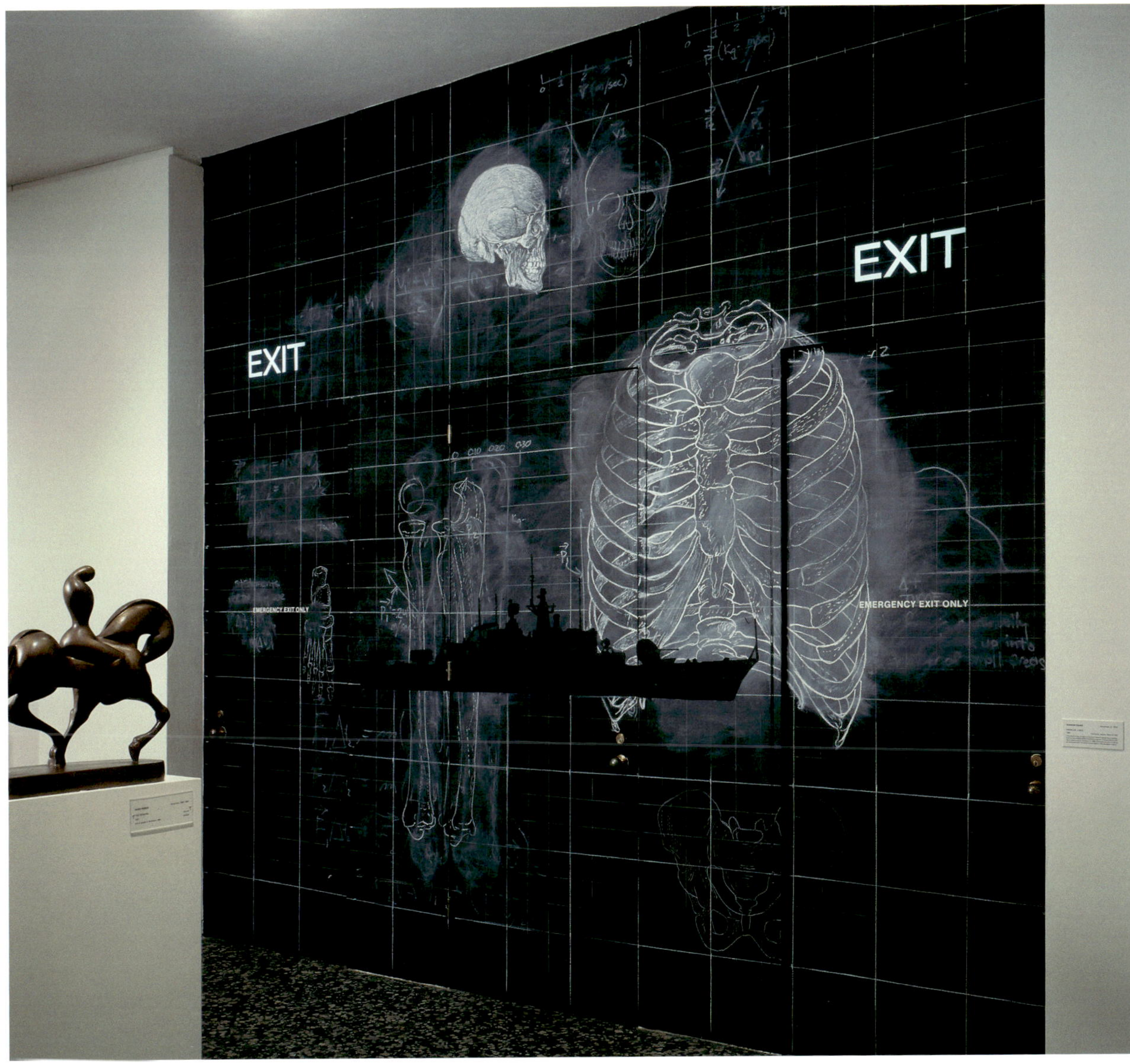
EXIT
EXIT
EMERGENCY EXIT ONLY
EMERGENCY EXIT ONLY

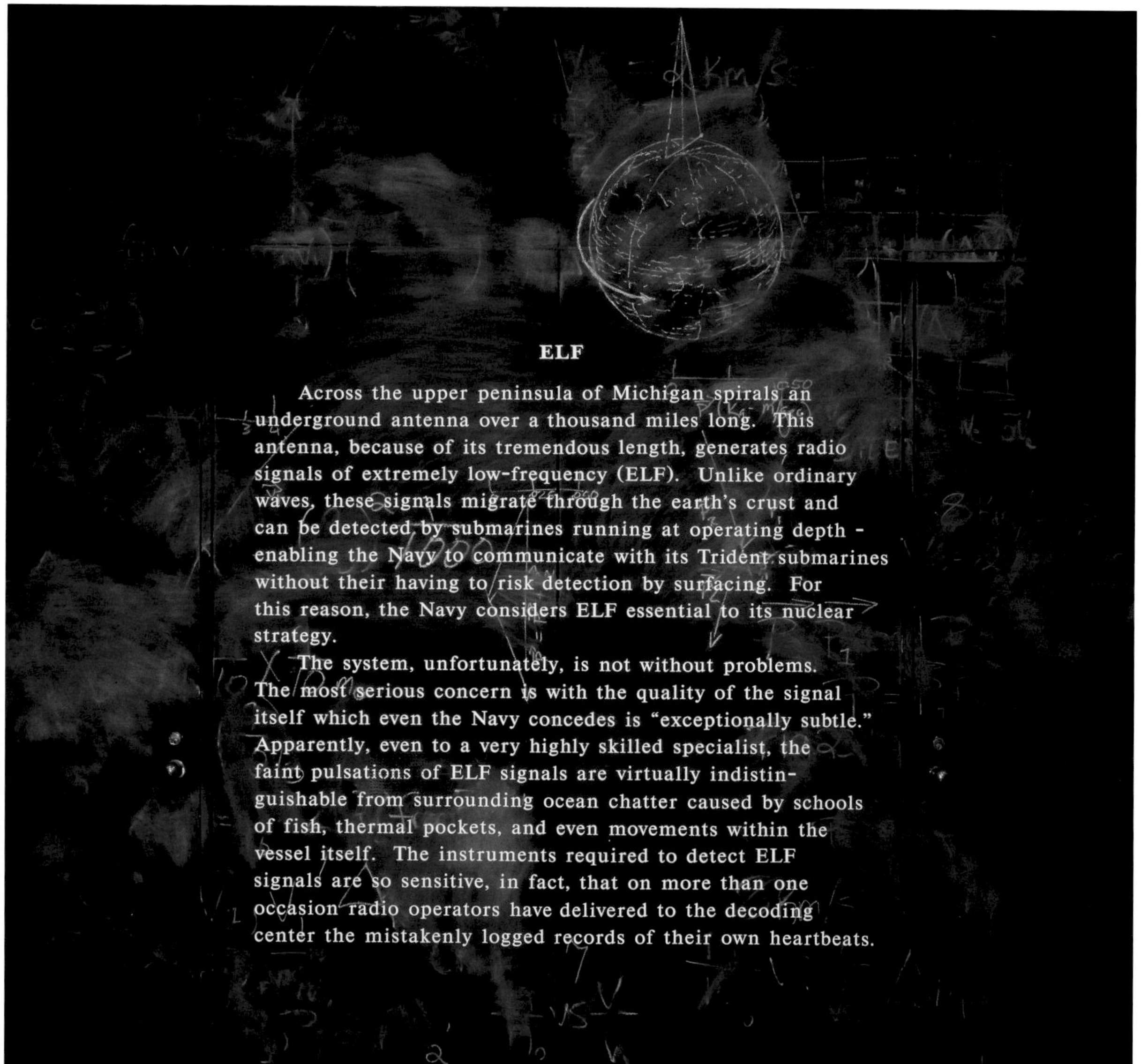

ELF

Across the upper peninsula of Michigan spirals an underground antenna over a thousand miles long. This antenna, because of its tremendous length, generates radio signals of extremely low-frequency (ELF). Unlike ordinary waves, these signals migrate through the earth's crust and can be detected by submarines running at operating depth - enabling the Navy to communicate with its Trident submarines without their having to risk detection by surfacing. For this reason, the Navy considers ELF essential to its nuclear strategy.

The system, unfortunately, is not without problems. The most serious concern is with the quality of the signal itself which even the Navy concedes is "exceptionally subtle." Apparently, even to a very highly skilled specialist, the faint pulsations of ELF signals are virtually indistinguishable from surrounding ocean chatter caused by schools of fish, thermal pockets, and even movements within the vessel itself. The instruments required to detect ELF signals are so sensitive, in fact, that on more than one occasion radio operators have delivered to the decoding center the mistakenly logged records of their own heartbeats.

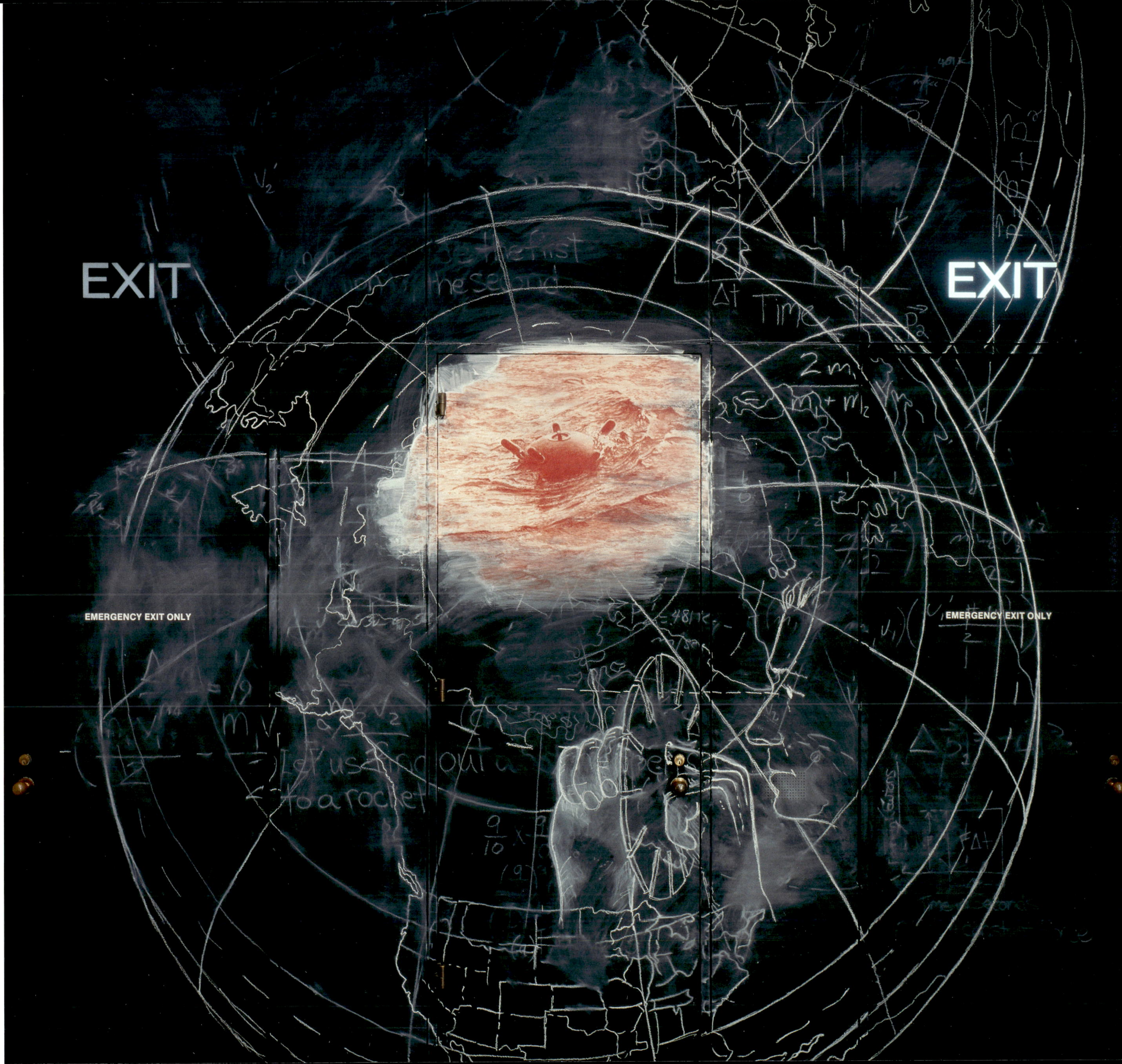
EXIT
EXIT
EMERGENCY EXIT ONLY
EMERGENCY EXIT ONLY

A Twister Forms at Sea 1989

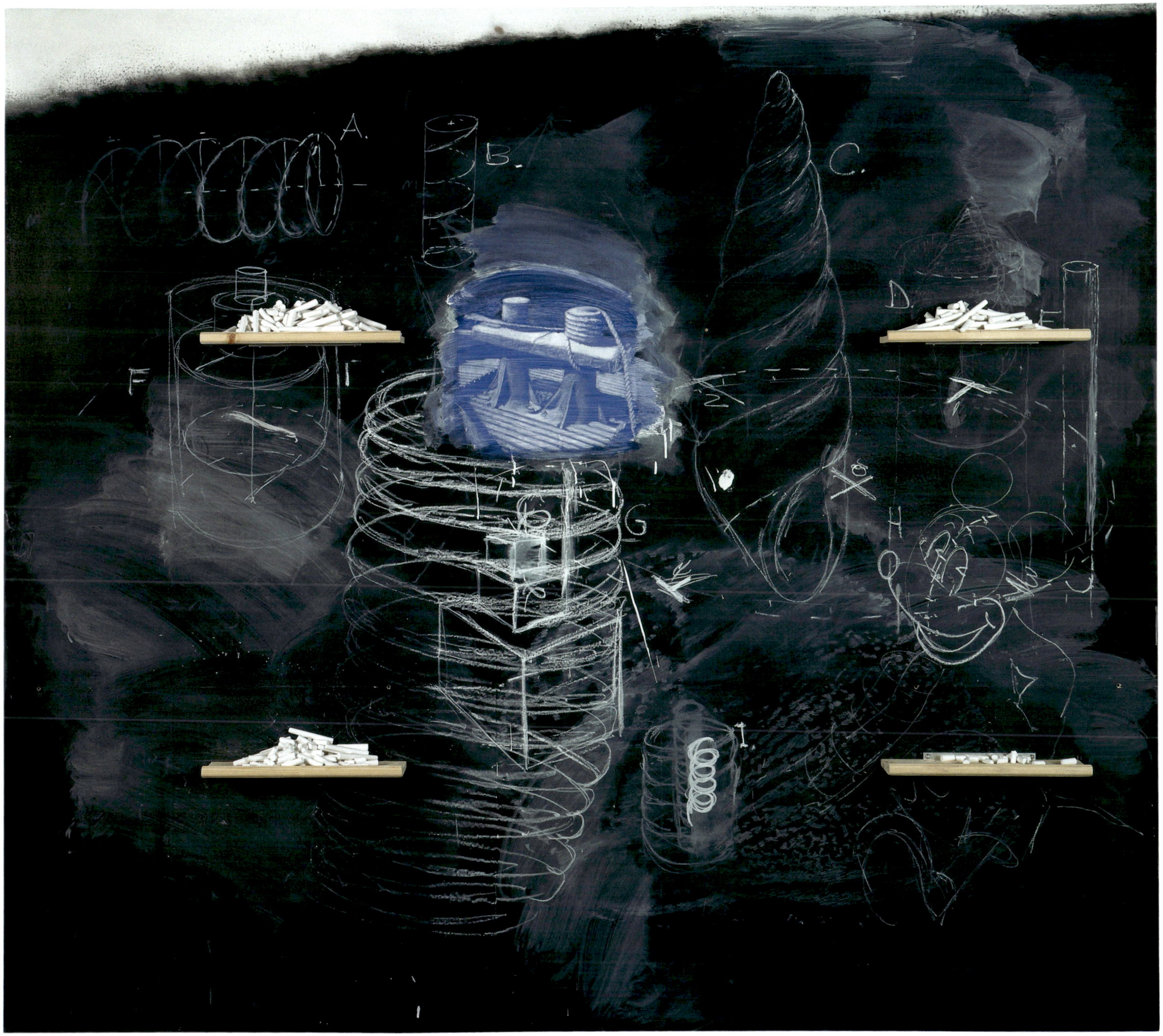
A.
B.
C.
D.
F
G
H

The Time Falling Objects 1989

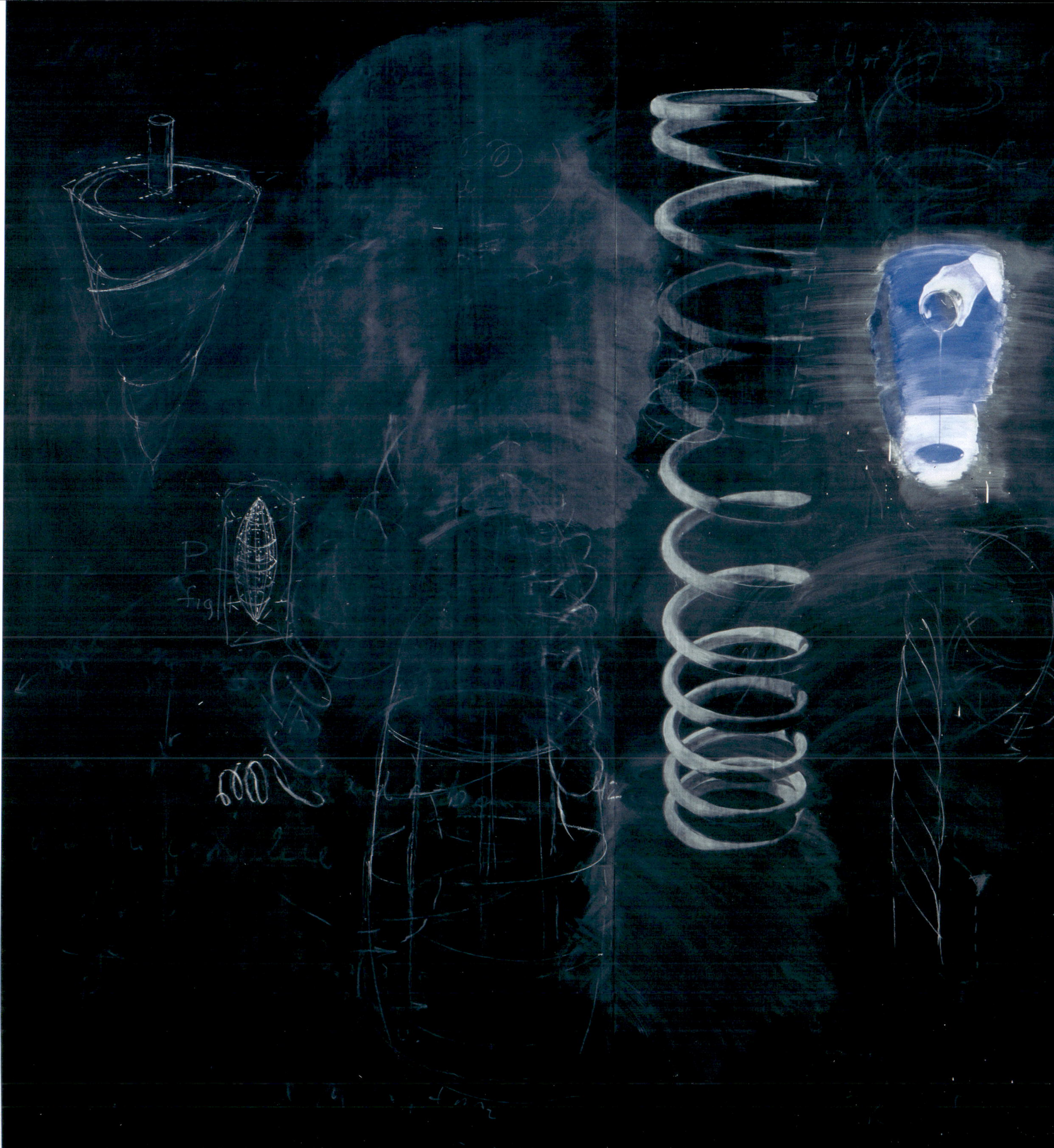

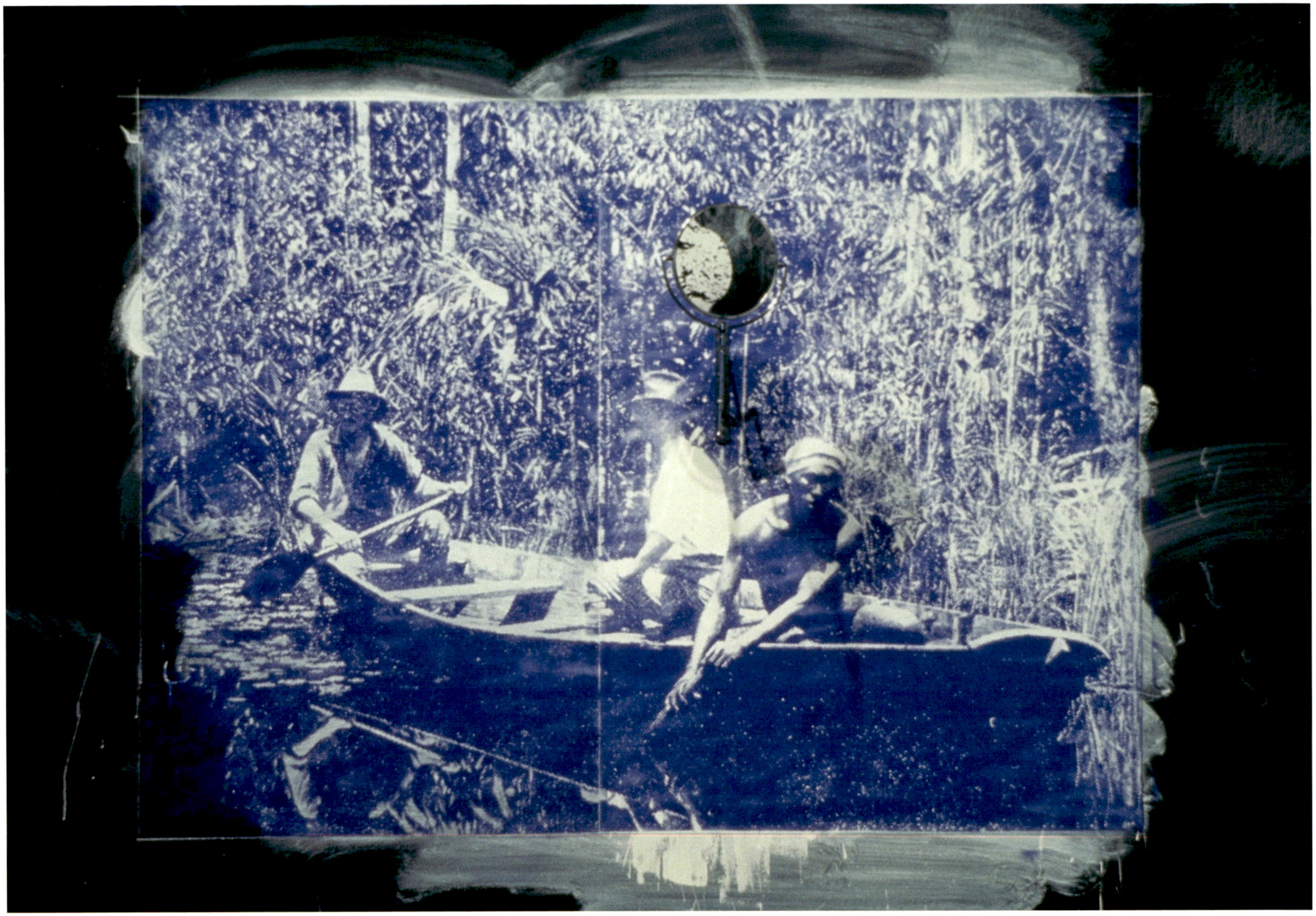

MOVEMENTS AMONG THE DEAD

Museum of Modern Art: Projects 20, New York, New York
January 19–March 6, 1990

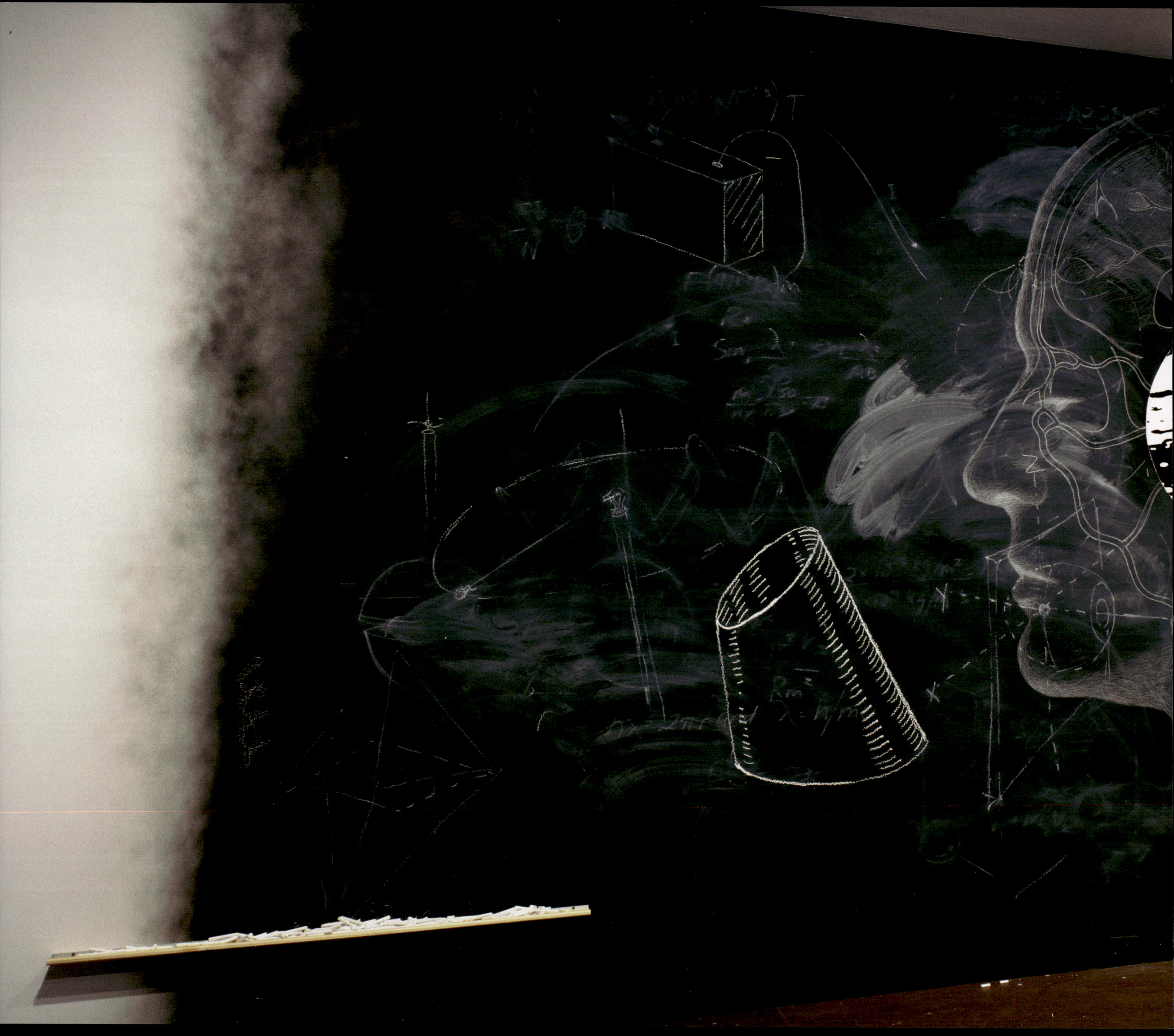

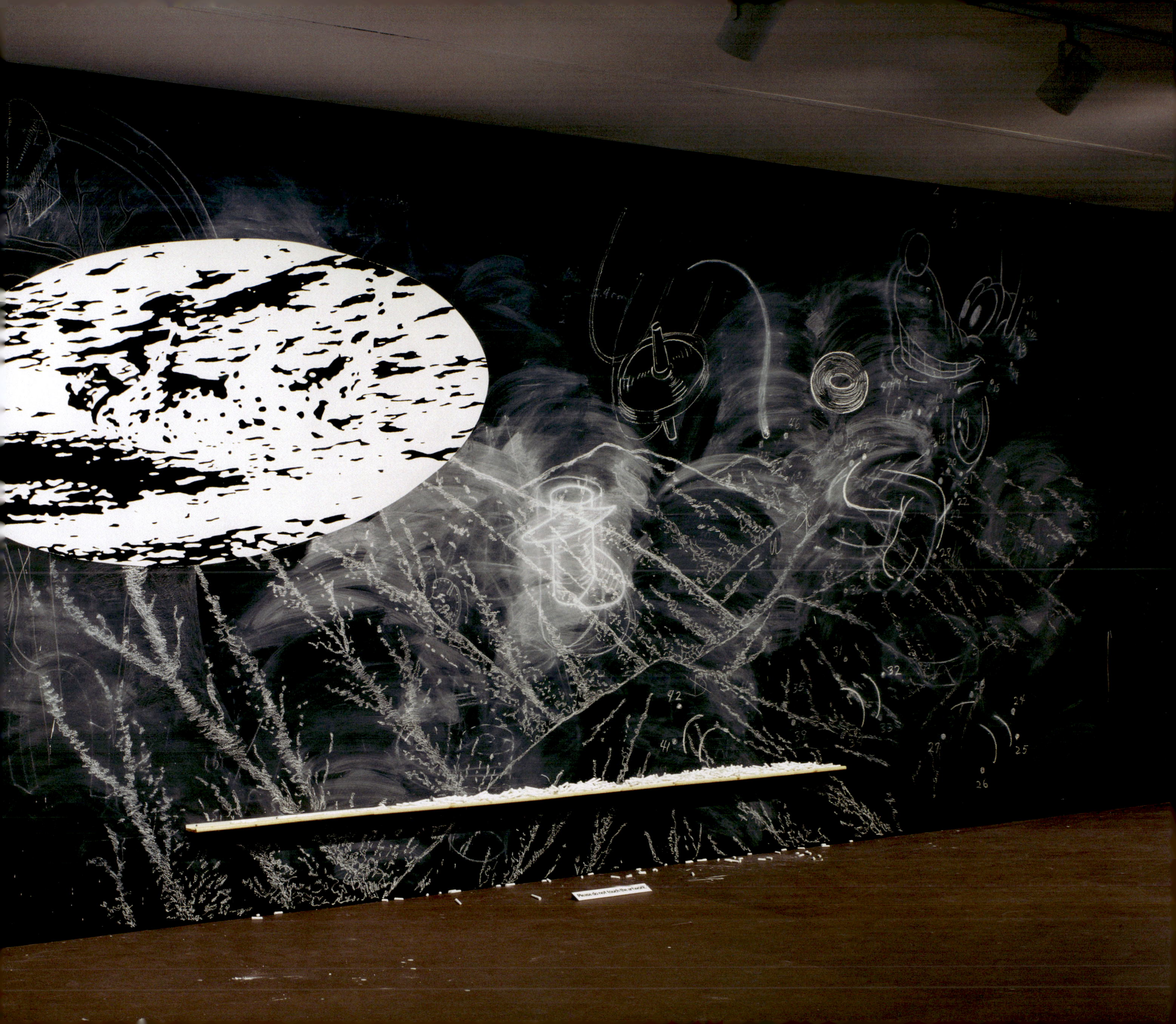
Please do not touch the artwork

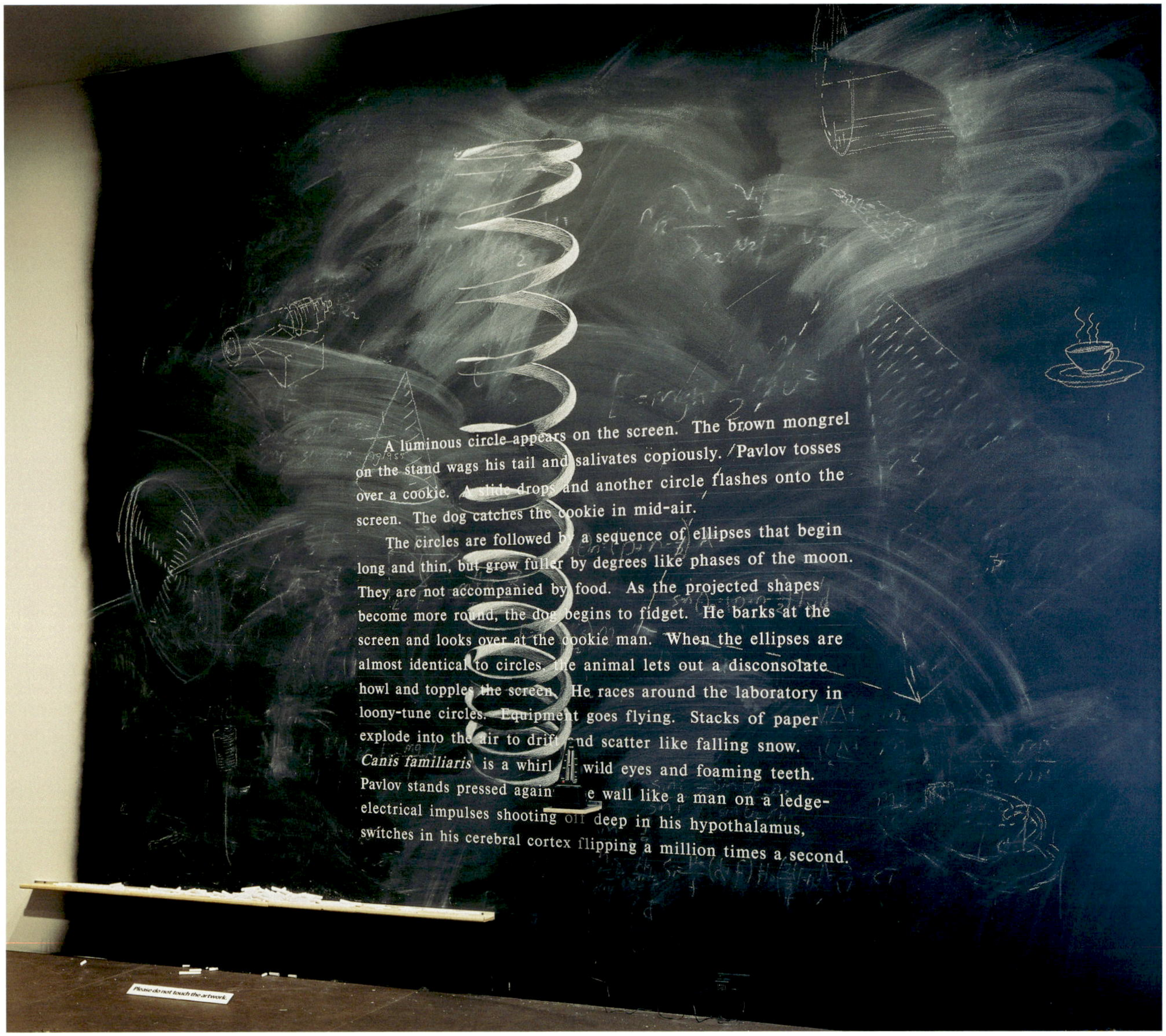
A luminous circle appears on the screen. The brown mongrel
on the stand wags his tail and salivates copiously. Pavlov tosses
over a cookie. A slide drops and another circle flashes onto the
screen. The dog catches the cookie in mid-air.
The circles are followed by a sequence of ellipses that begin
long and thin, but grow fuller by degrees like phases of the moon.
They are not accompanied by food. As the projected shapes
become more round, the dog begins to fidget. He barks at the
screen and looks over at the cookie man. When the ellipses are
almost identical to circles, the animal lets out a disconsolate
howl and topples the screen. He races around the laboratory in
loony-tune circles. Equipment goes flying. Stacks of paper
explode into the air to drift and scatter like falling snow.
Canis familiaris is a whirl wild eyes and foaming teeth.
Pavlov stands pressed again e wall like a man on a ledge-
electrical impulses shooting deep in his hypothalamus,
switches in his cerebral cortex flipping a million times a second.
Please do not touch the artwork.

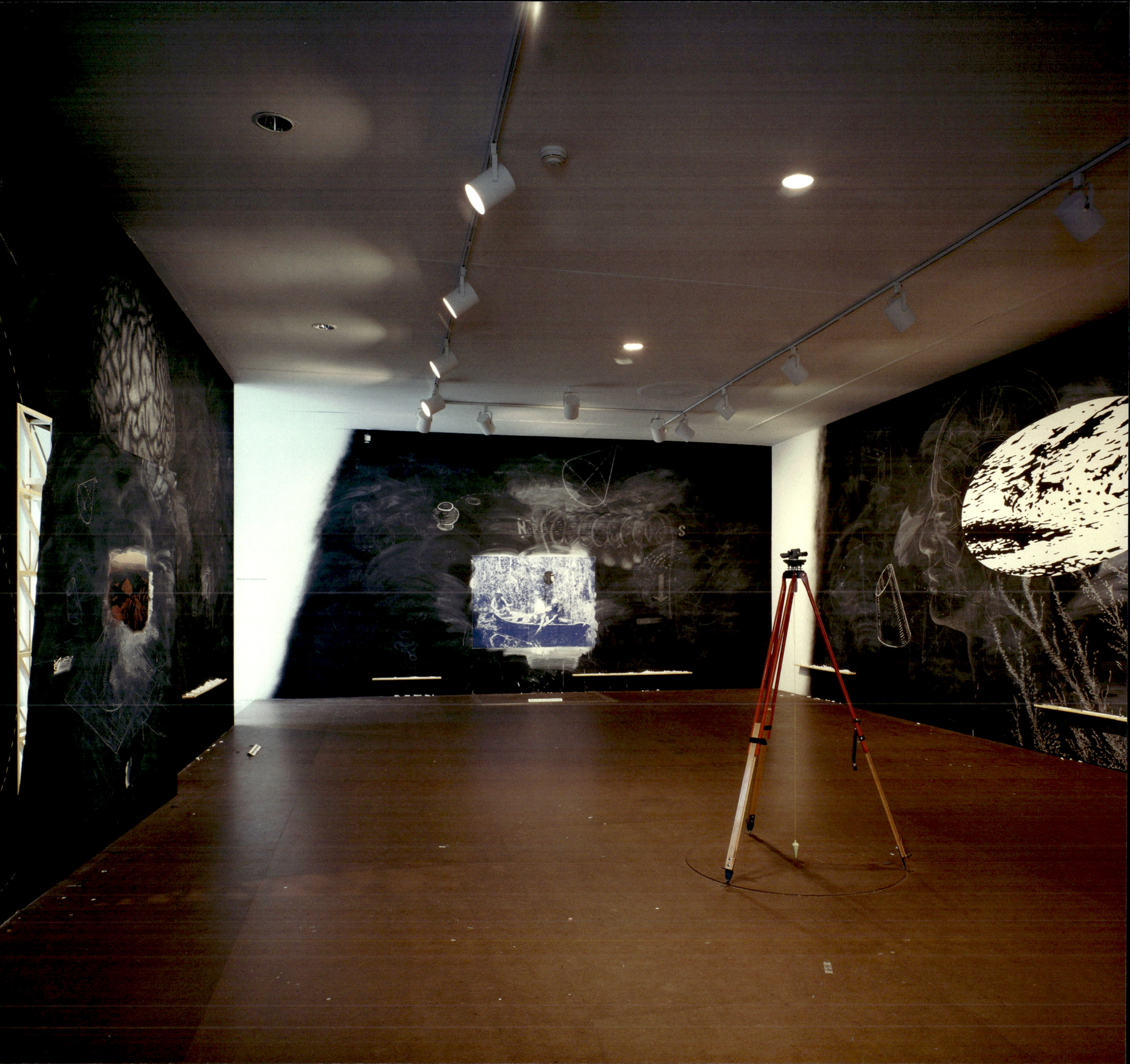
N
S

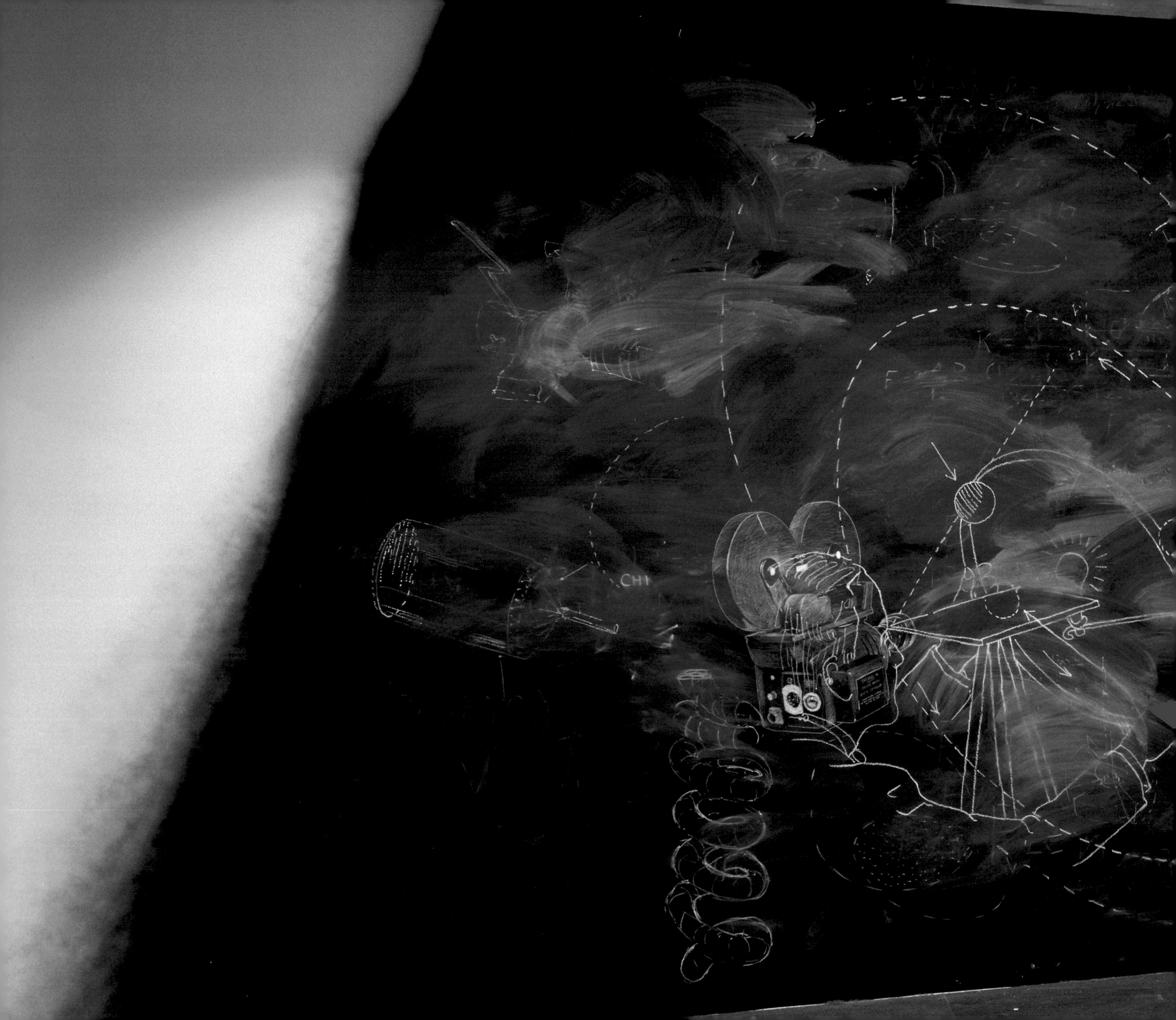
CH1

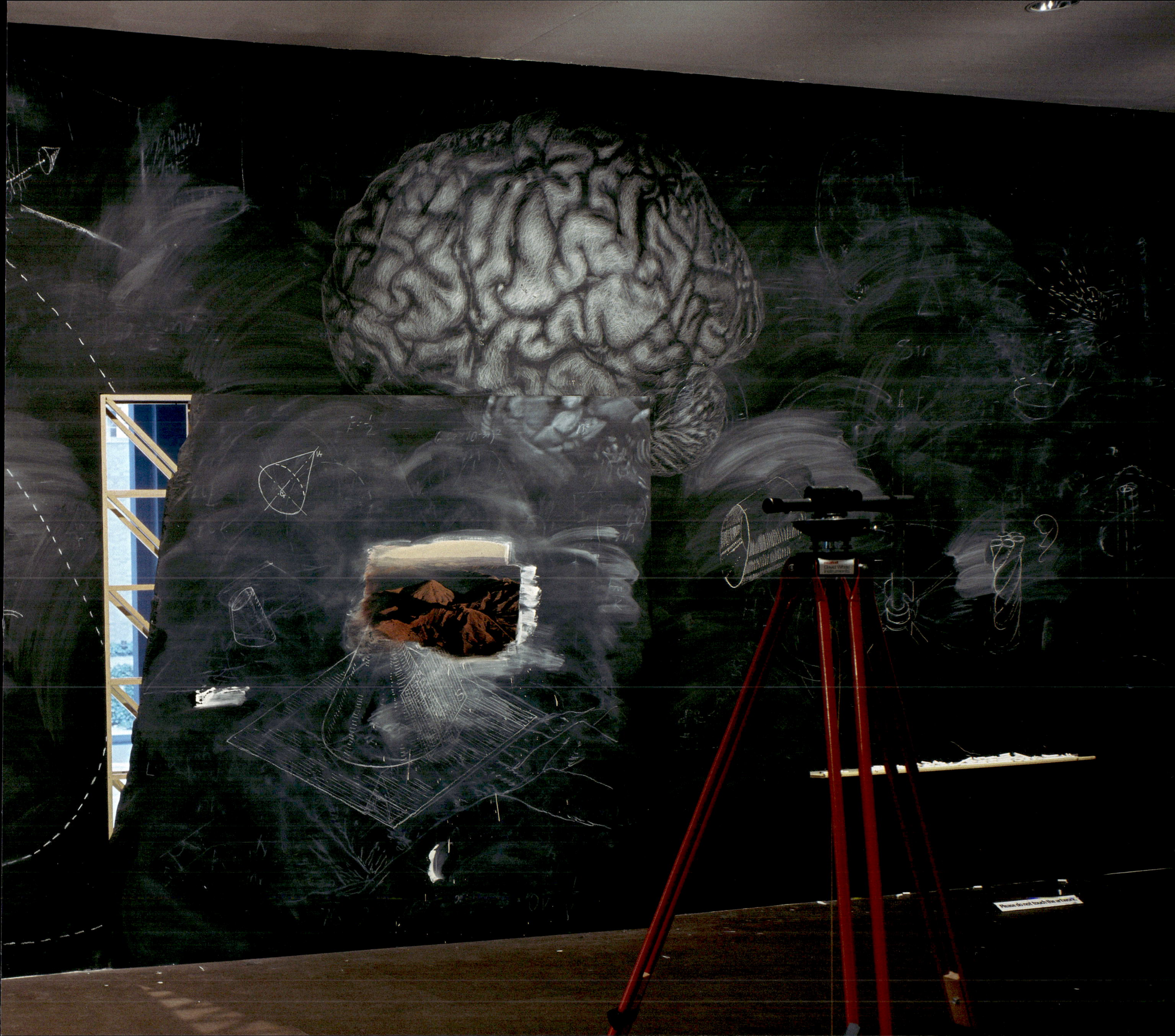
Please do not touch the artwork.

Rules for Bending Circles 1991

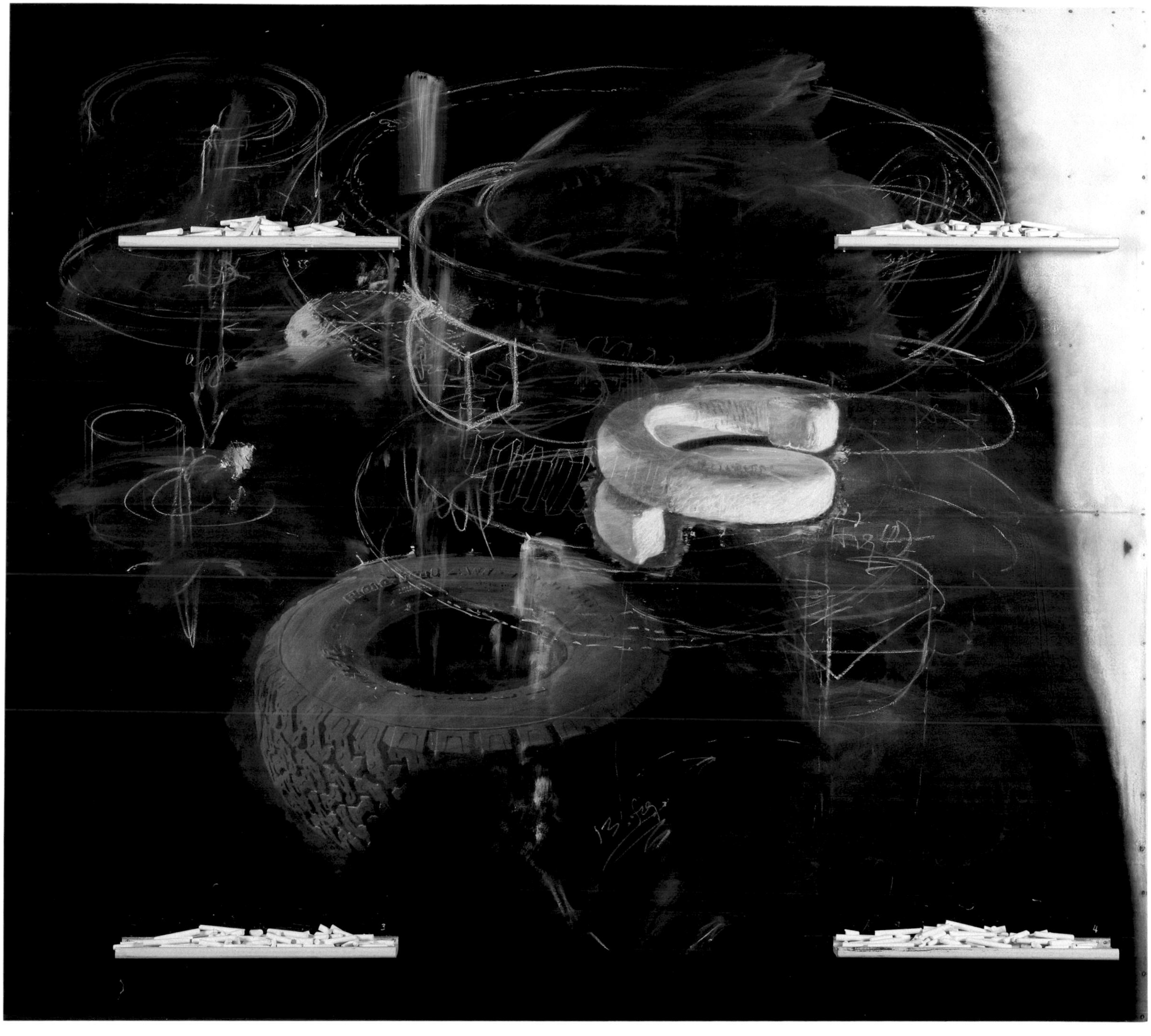

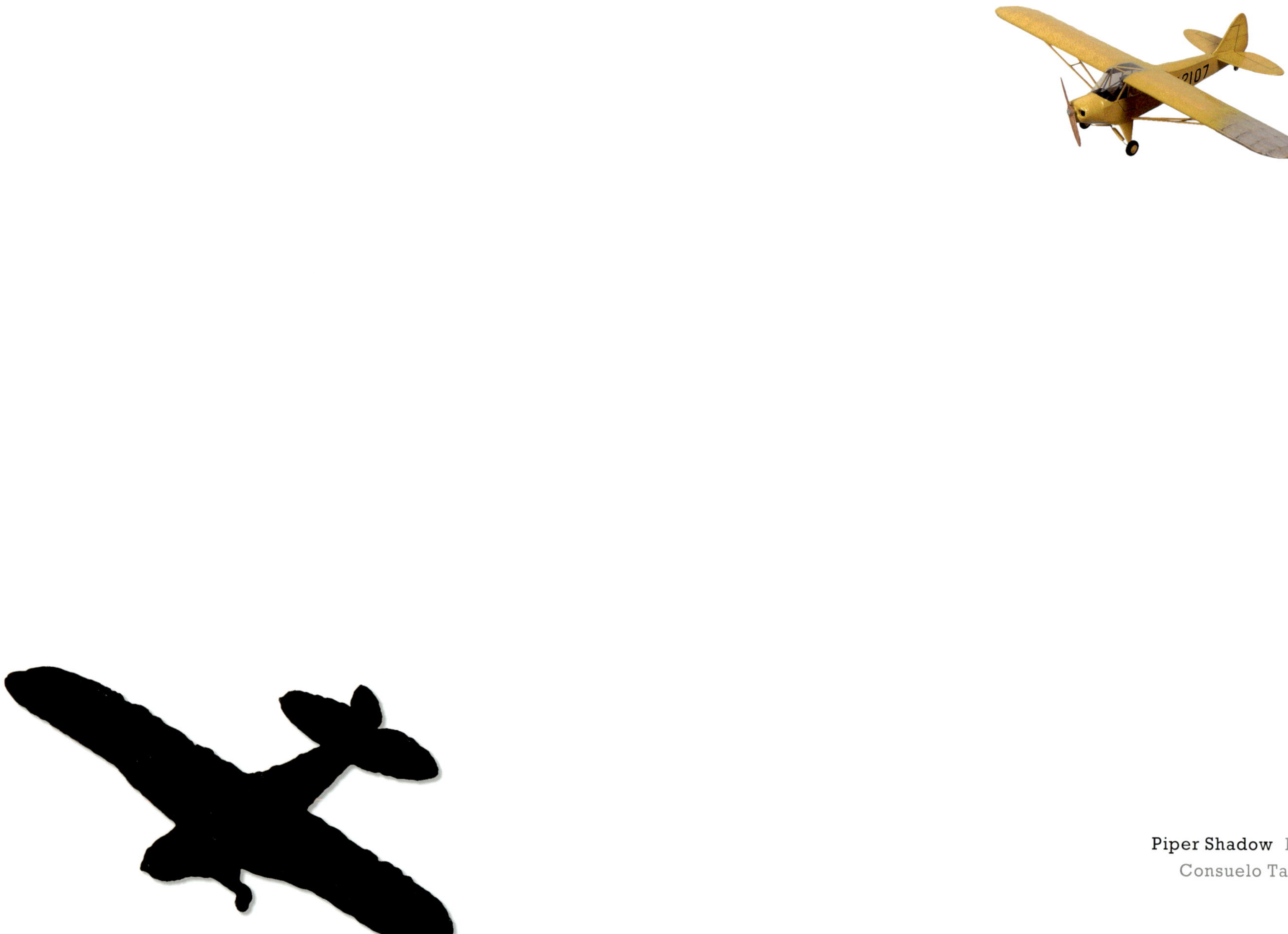

Piper Shadow 1991
Consuelo Tattoo

HILLS LIKE WHITE ELEPHANTS

Center for Contemporary Art, Sacramento, California
December 6, 1991–January 19, 1992

Hills Like White Elephants 1991
Consuelo Tattoo

Boat, Island, Ape 1991
Consuelo Tattoo

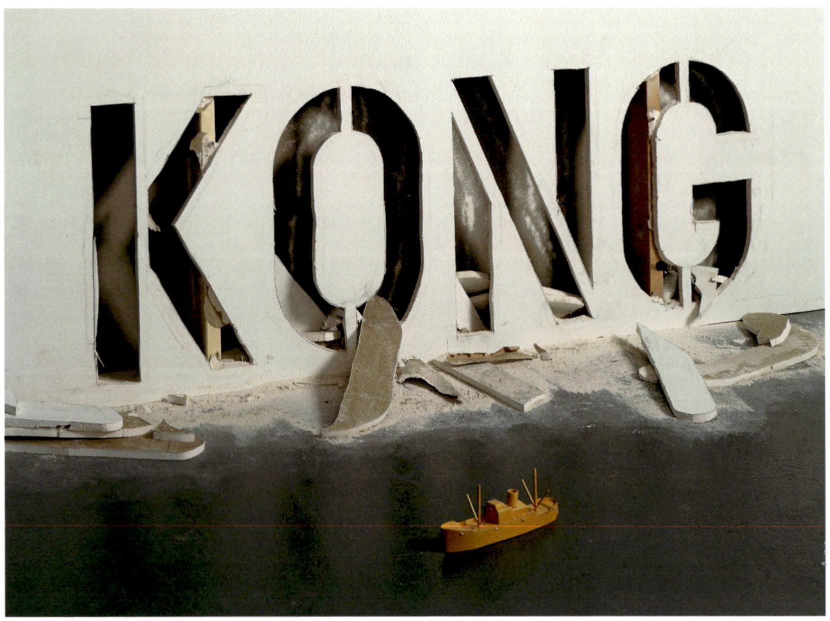

HILLS LIKE WHITE ELEPHANTS

The hills across the valley of the Ebro were long and white. On this side there was no shade and no trees and the station was between two lines of rails in the sun. Close against the side of the station there was the warm shadow of the building and a curtain, made of strings of bamboo beads, hung across the open door into the bar, to keep out the flies. The American and the girl with him sat at a table in the shade, outside the building. It was very hot and the express from Barcelona would come in forty minutes. It stopped at this junction for two minutes and went on to Madrid.

The woman brought two glasses of beer and two felt pads. She put the felt pads and the beer glasses on the table and looked at the man and the girl. The girl was looking off at the line of hills. They were white in the sun and the country was brown and dry.

The girl looked at the bead curtain, then across at the hills. The warm wind blew the
(2) bead curtain against the table. The girl
looked at the ground the table legs rested on. She did not say anything. She looked at the

bead curtain, put her hand out and took hold of two of the string beads.

The girl stood up and walked to the end of the station. Across, on the other side, were fields of grain and trees along the banks of the Ebro. Far away, beyond the river, were mountains. The shadow of a cloud moved across the field of grain and she saw the river through the trees.

They sat down at the table and the girl looked across at the hills on the dry side of the valley and the man looked at her and at the table.

He did not say anything but looked at the bags against the wall of the station. There were labels on them from all the hotels where they had spent nights.

The woman came out through the curtains with two glasses of beer and put them down on the damp felt pads. The girl smiled brightly at the woman, to thank her.

The man picked up the two heavy bags and carried them around the station to the other tracks. He looked up the tracks but could not see the train. Coming back, he walked through the barroom, where people waiting for the train were drinking. He drank an Anis at the bar and looked at the people. They were all waiting reasonably for the train. He went out through the bead curtain. She was sitting at the table and smiled at him.

Aardvark, Shorter History 1991
Vernon Fisher

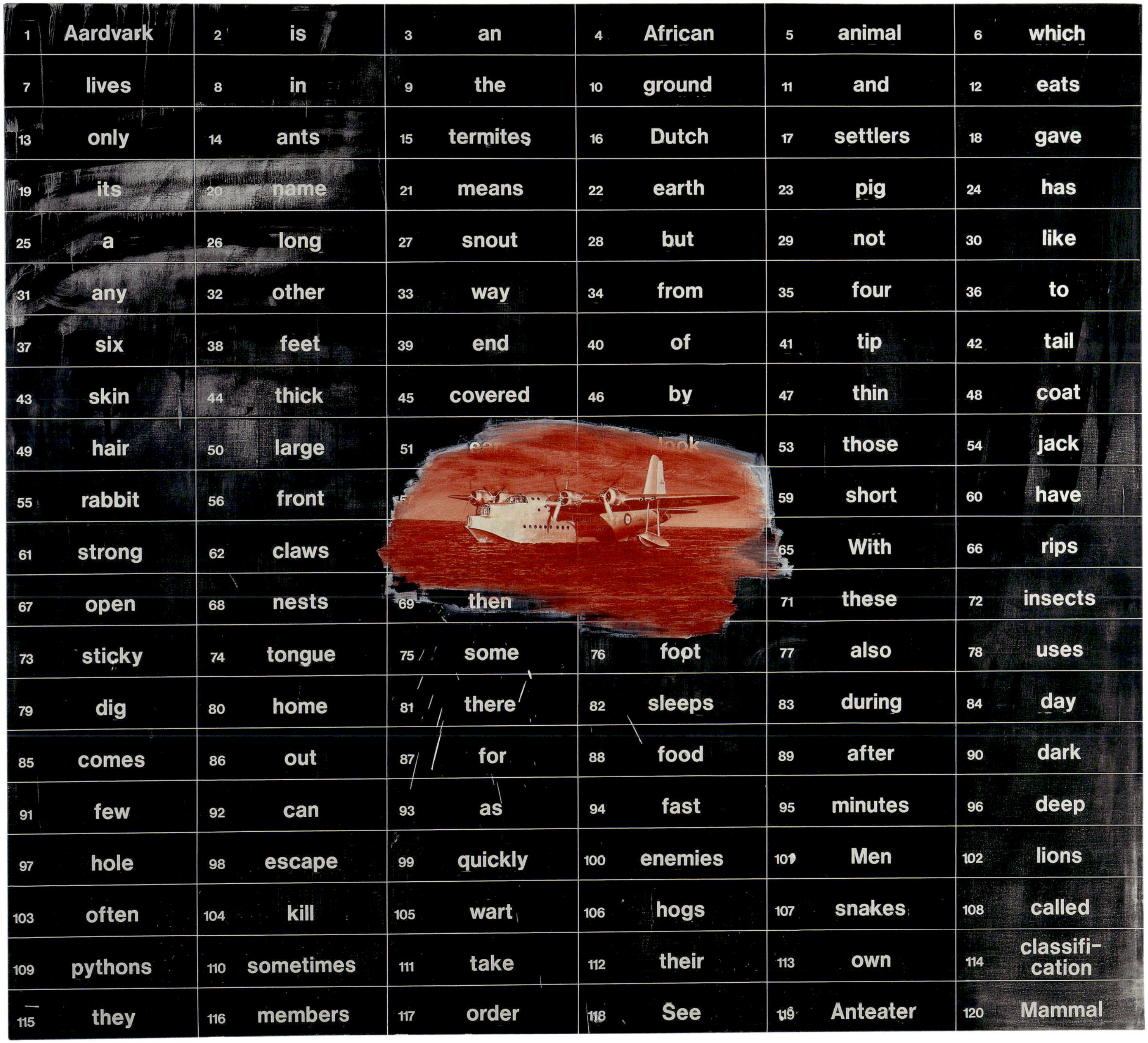
1 Aardvark
2 is
3 an
4 African
5 animal
6 which
7 lives
8 in
9 the
10 ground
11 and
12 eats
13 only
14 ants
15 termites
16 Dutch
17 settlers
18 gave
19 its
20 name
21 means
22 earth
23 pig
24 has
25 a
26 long
27 snout
28 but
29 not
30 like
31 any
32 other
33 way
34 from
35 four
36 to
37 six
38 feet
39 end
40 of
41 tip
42 tail
43 skin
44 thick
45 covered
46 by
47 thin
48 coat
49 hair
50 large
51
53 those
54 jack
55 rabbit
56 front
59 short
60 have
61 strong
62 claws
65 With
66 rips
67 open
68 nests
69 then
71 these
72 insects
73 sticky
74 tongue
75 some
76 foot
77 also
78 uses
79 dig
80 home
81 there
82 sleeps
83 during
84 day
85 comes
86 out
87 for
88 food
89 after
90 dark
91 few
92 can
93 as
94 fast
95 minutes
96 deep
97 hole
98 escape
99 quickly
100 enemies
101 Men
102 lions
103 often
104 kill
105 wart
106 hogs
107 snakes
108 called
109 pythons
110 sometimes
111 take
112 their
113 own
114 classifi-cation
115 they
116 members
117 order
118 See
119 Anteater
120 Mammal

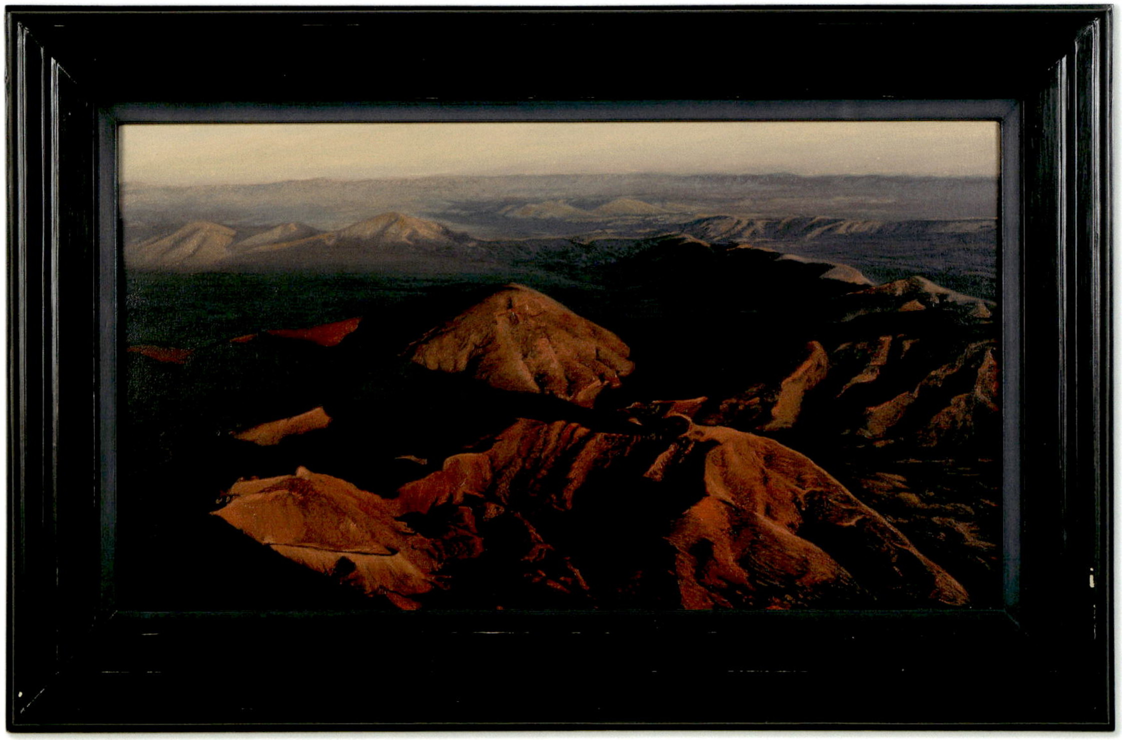

Framed Landscape 1991 ▲
M. Moon

After Malevich 1991 ▶
Consuelo Tattoo

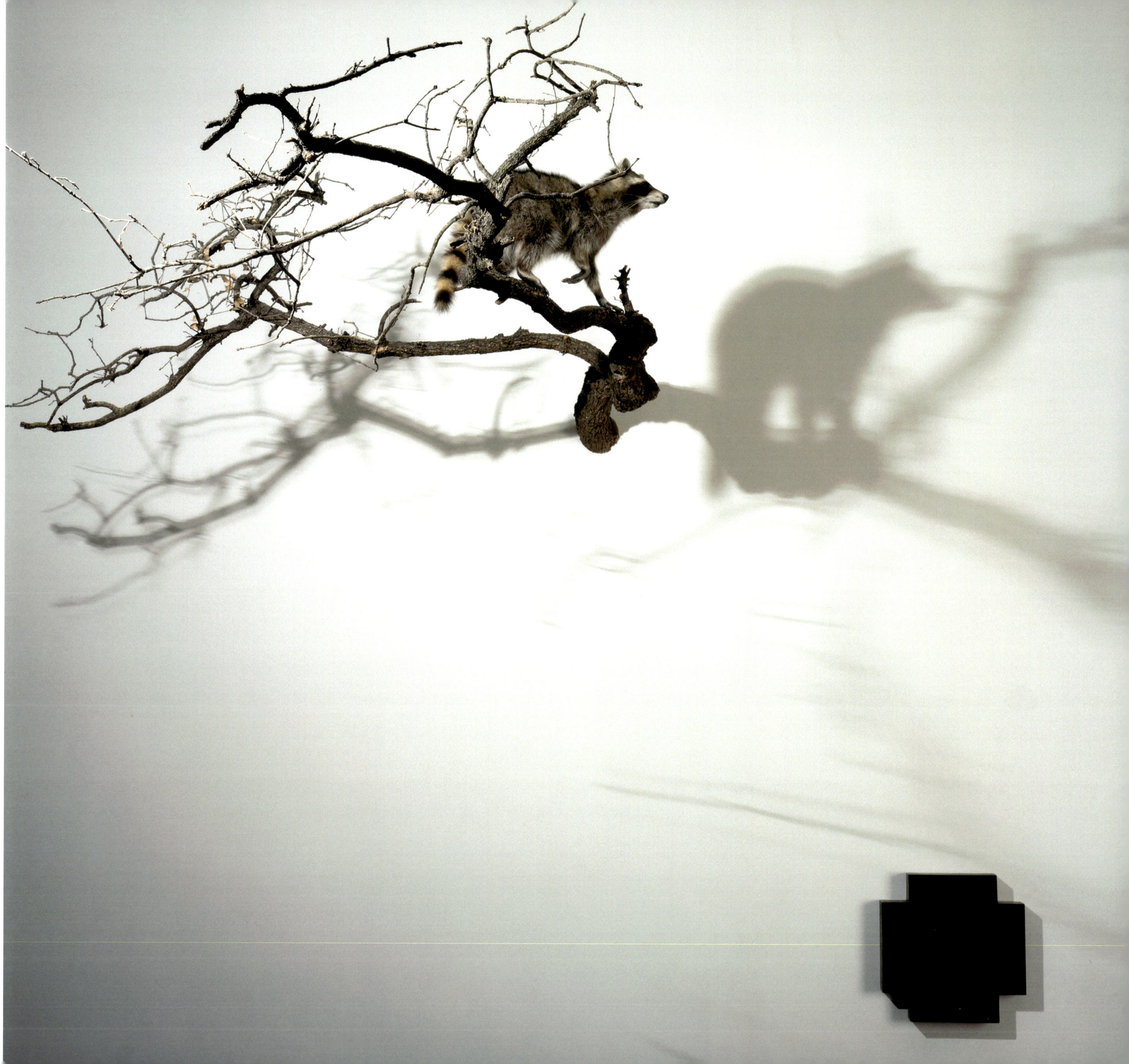

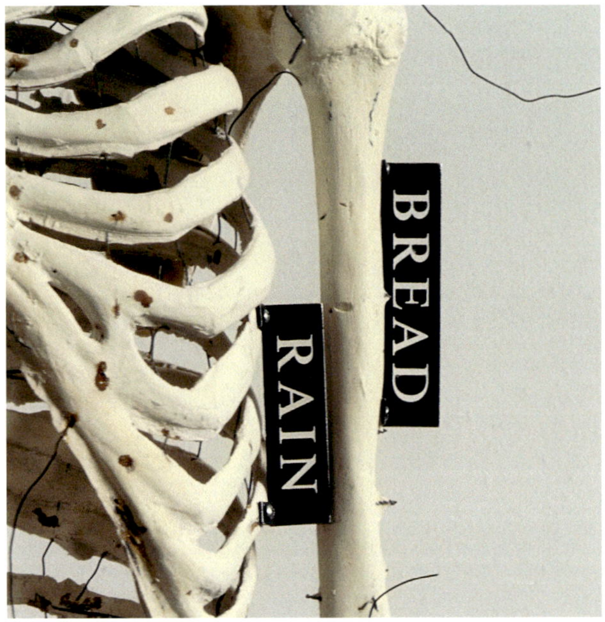

14 Words 1991
Werner Fiche

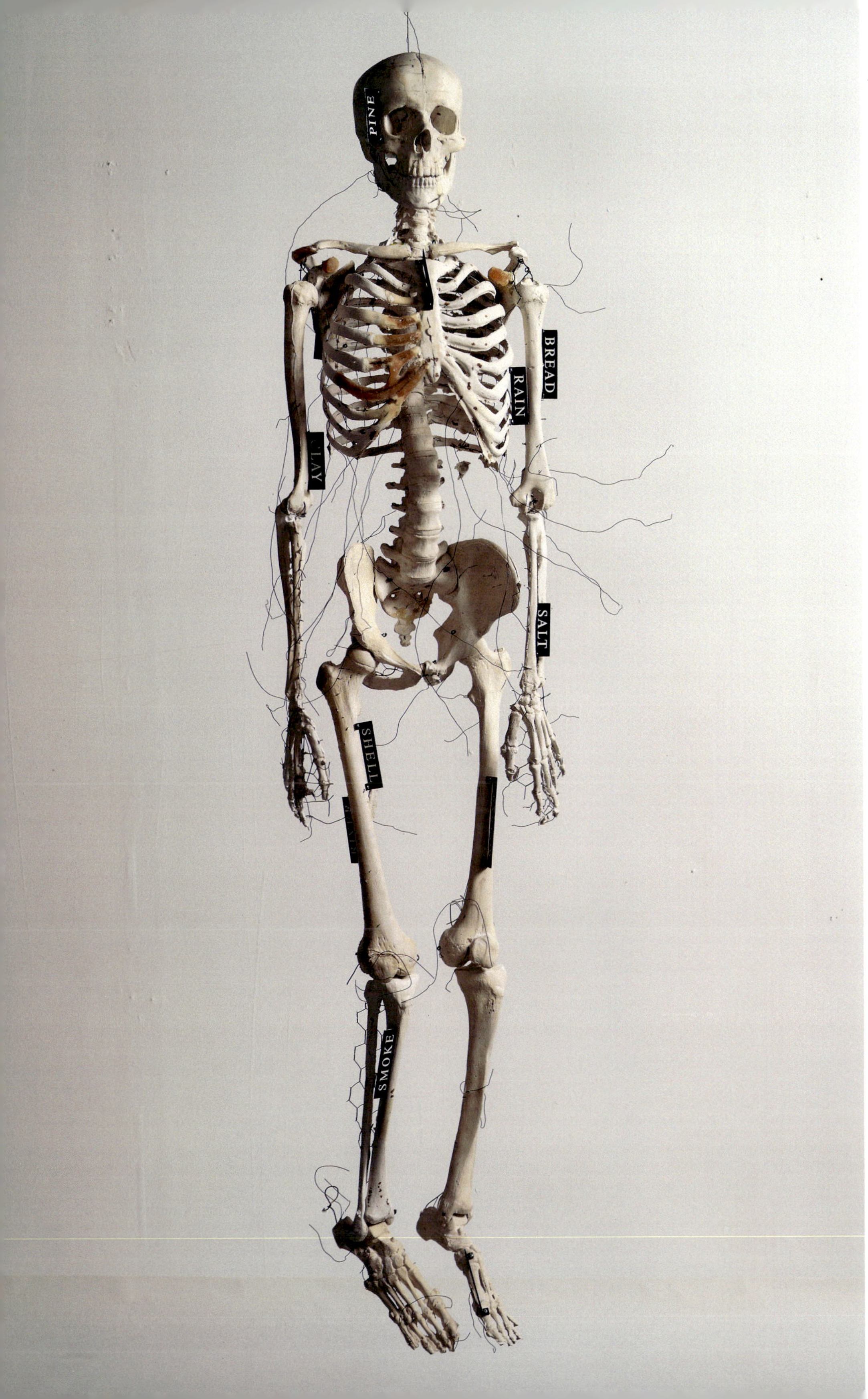

HILLS LIKE WHITE ELEPHANTS

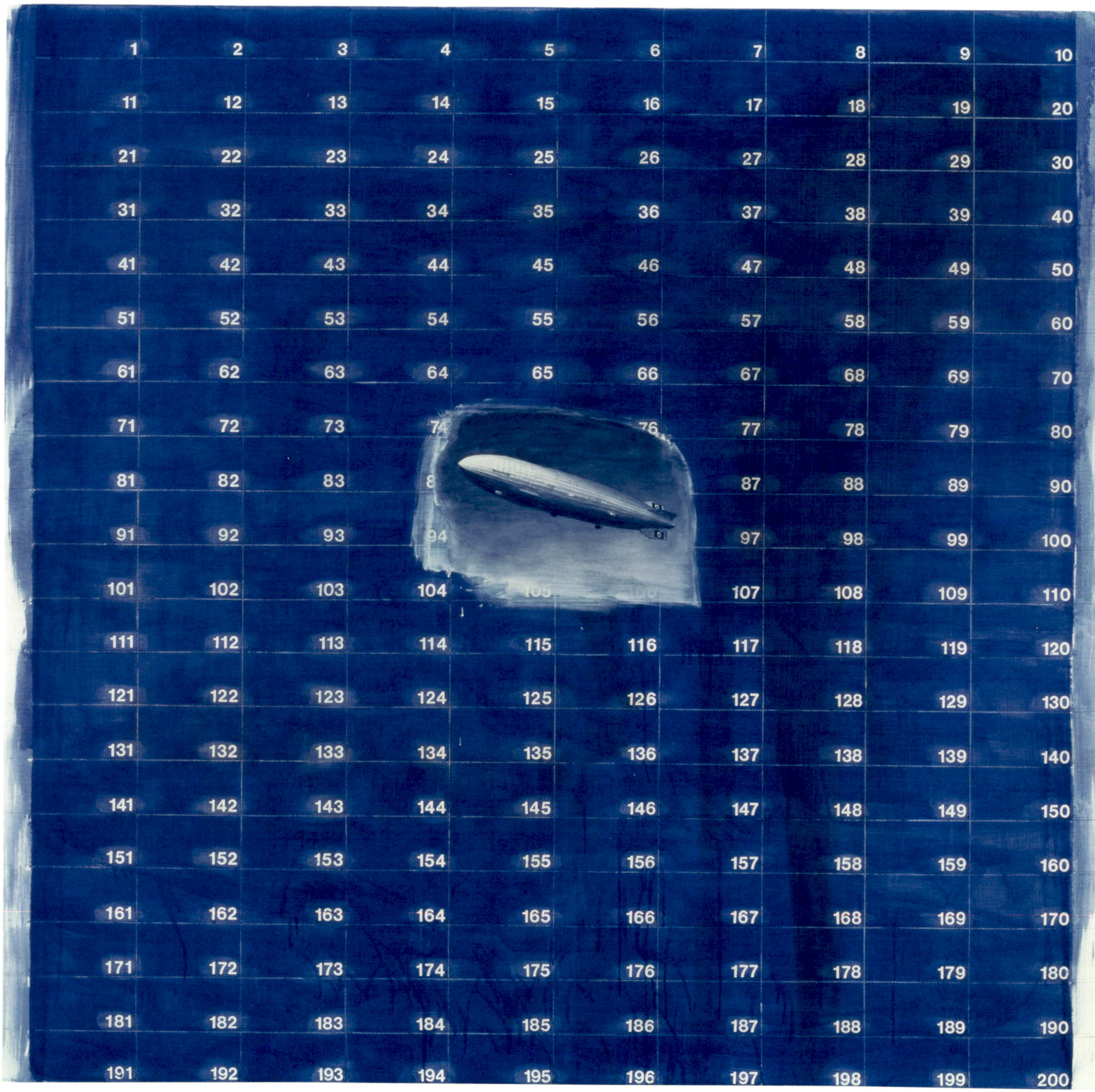
1 2 3 4 5 6 7 8 9 10
11 12 13 14 15 16 17 18 19 20
21 22 23 24 25 26 27 28 29 30
31 32 33 34 35 36 37 38 39 40
41 42 43 44 45 46 47 48 49 50
51 52 53 54 55 56 57 58 59 60
61 62 63 64 65 66 67 68 69 70
71 72 73 74 77 78 79 80
81 82 83 87 88 89 90
91 92 93 94 97 98 99 100
101 102 103 104 107 108 109 110
111 112 113 114 115 116 117 118 119 120
121 122 123 124 125 126 127 128 129 130
131 132 133 134 135 136 137 138 139 140
141 142 143 144 145 146 147 148 149 150
151 152 153 154 155 156 157 158 159 160
161 162 163 164 165 166 167 168 169 170
171 172 173 174 175 176 177 178 179 180
181 182 183 184 185 186 187 188 189 190
191 192 193 194 195 196 197 198 199 200

200 Numbered Rectangles 1989

Vernon Fisher

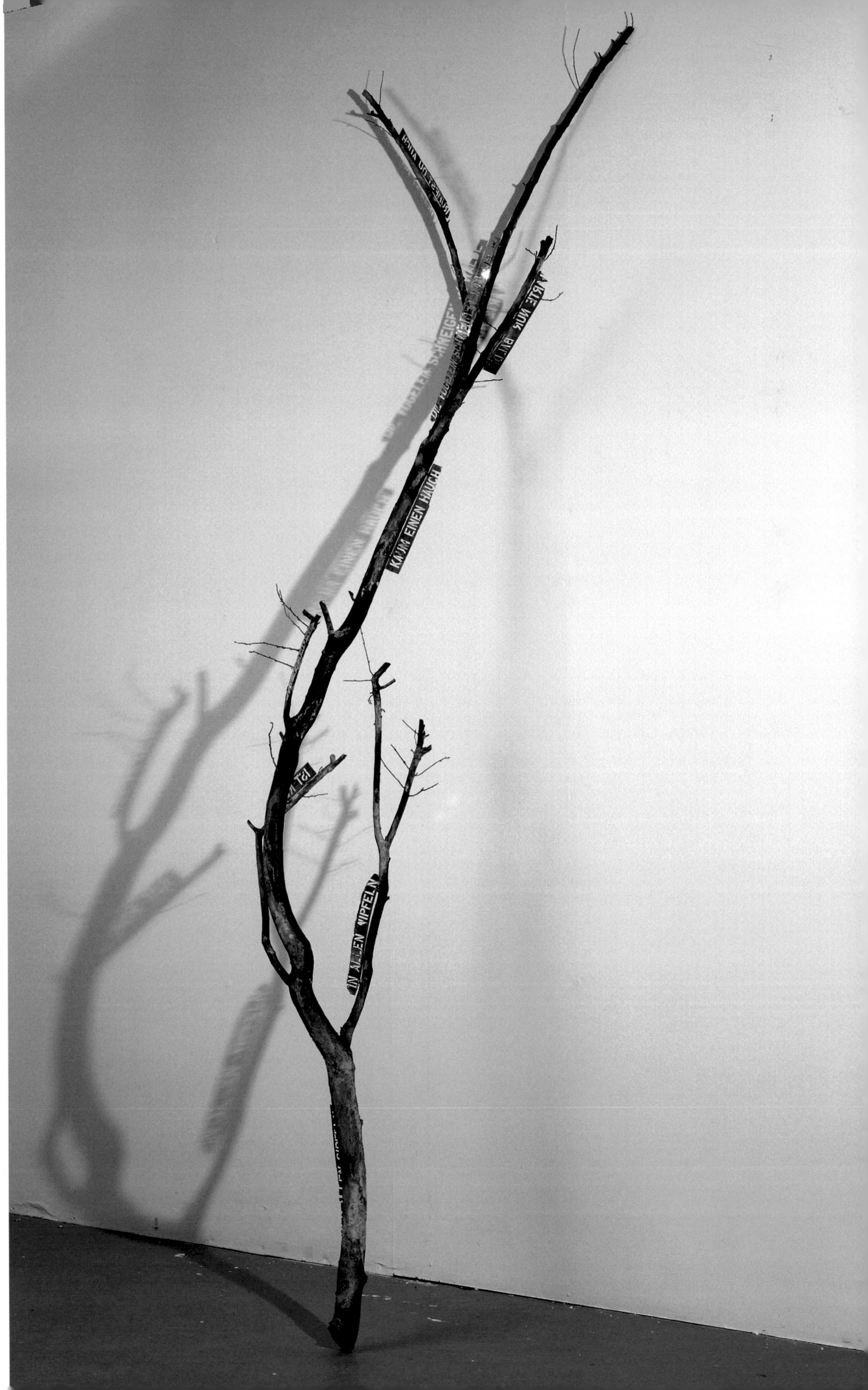
KAUM EINEN HAUCH
IN ALLEN WIPFELN

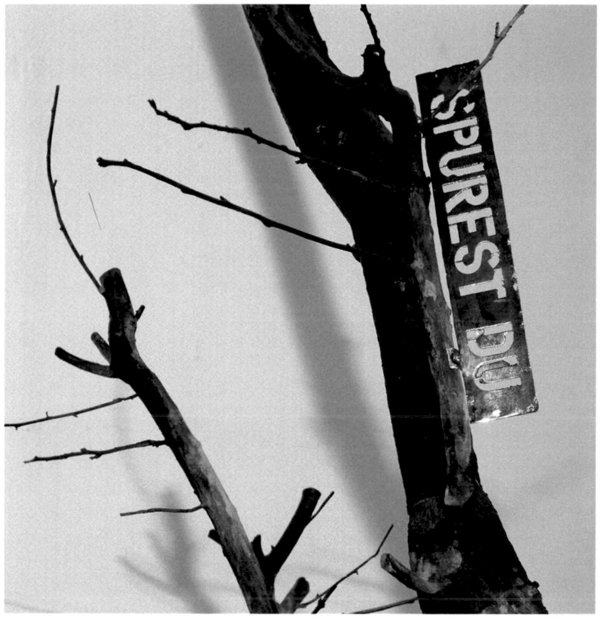

Poison Tree 1991
Werner Fiche

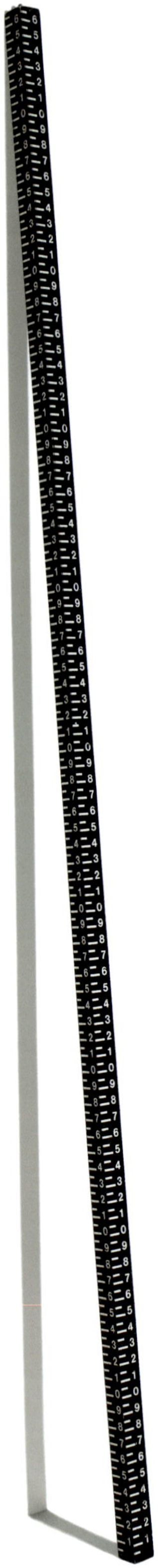

Numbered Pole 1988
M. Moon

That's All Folks 1991
Consuelo Tattoo

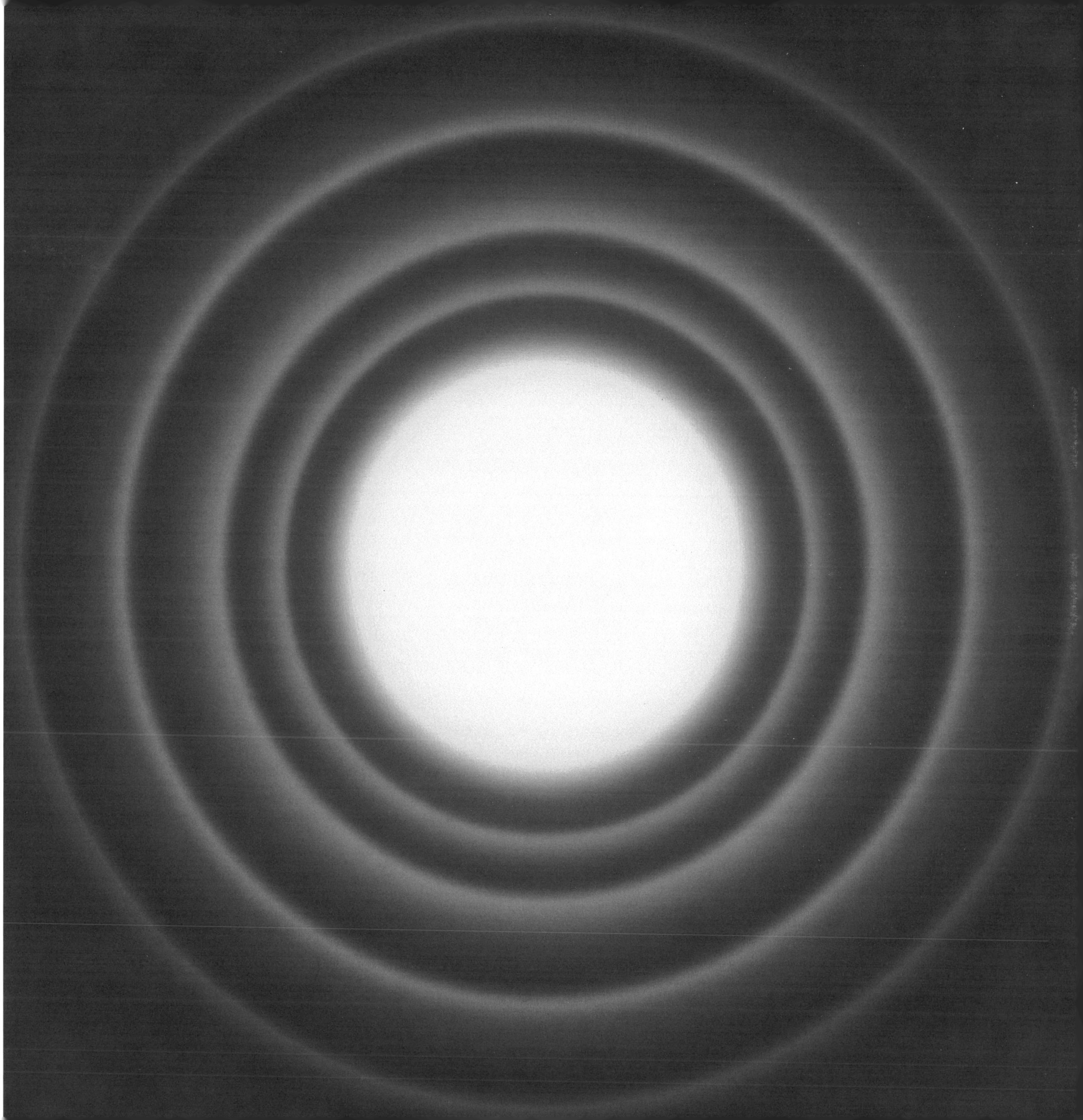

When You Lose Your Mind 1991

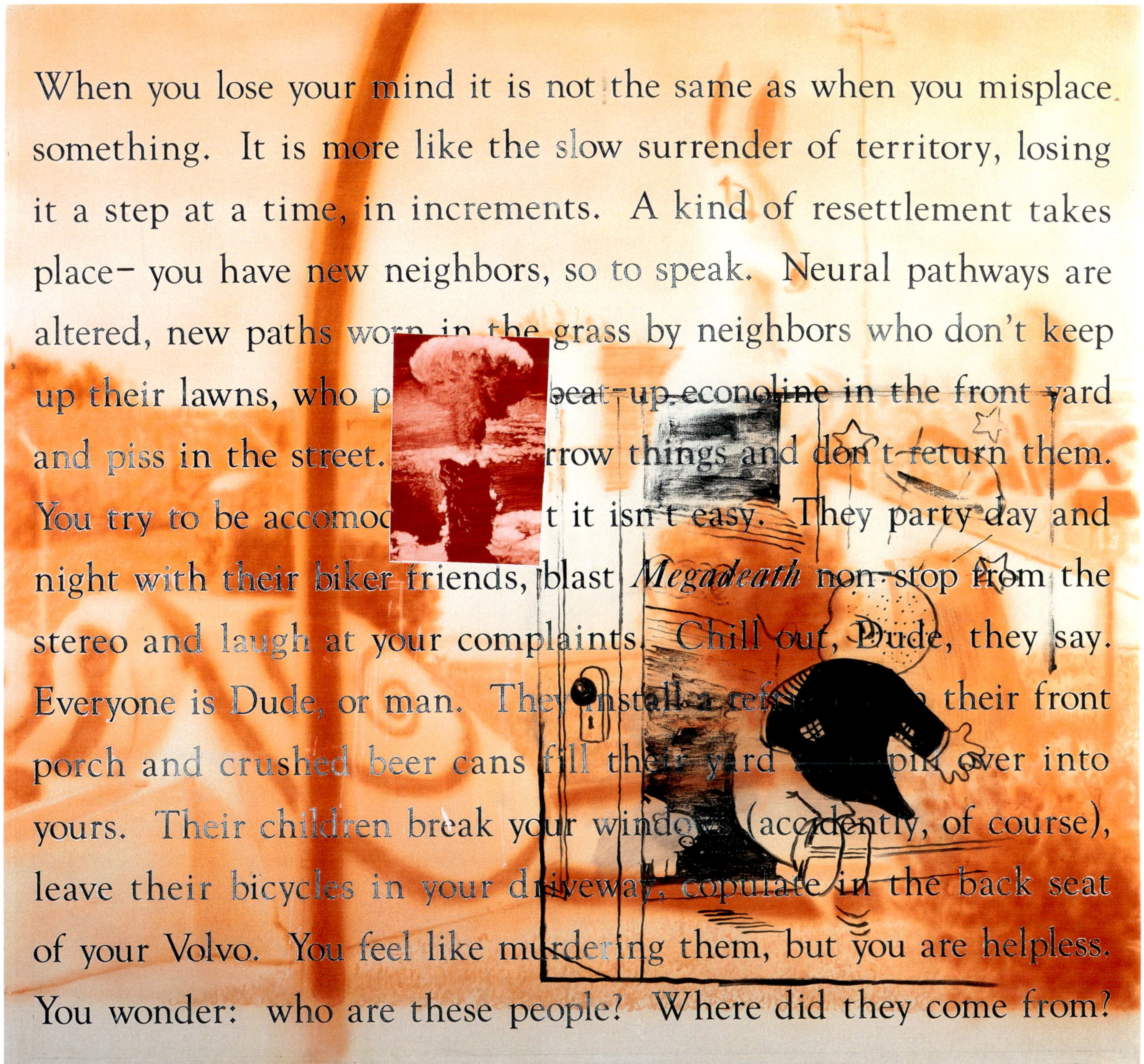
When you lose your mind it is not the same as when you misplace something. It is more like the slow surrender of territory, losing it a step at a time, in increments. A kind of resettlement takes place– you have new neighbors, so to speak. Neural pathways are altered, new paths worn in the grass by neighbors who don't keep up their lawns, who p
beat-up econoline in the front yard and piss in the street.
rrow things and don't return them.
You try to be accomod
t it isn't easy. They party day and night with their biker friends, blast *Megadeath* non-stop from the stereo and laugh at your complaints. Chill out, Dude, they say. Everyone is Dude, or man. They install a ref
their front porch and crushed beer cans fill their yard
over into yours. Their children break your windows (accidently, of course), leave their bicycles in your driveway, copulate in the back seat of your Volvo. You feel like murdering them, but you are helpless. You wonder: who are these people? Where did they come from?

Swimming Between Australia and Japan 1993

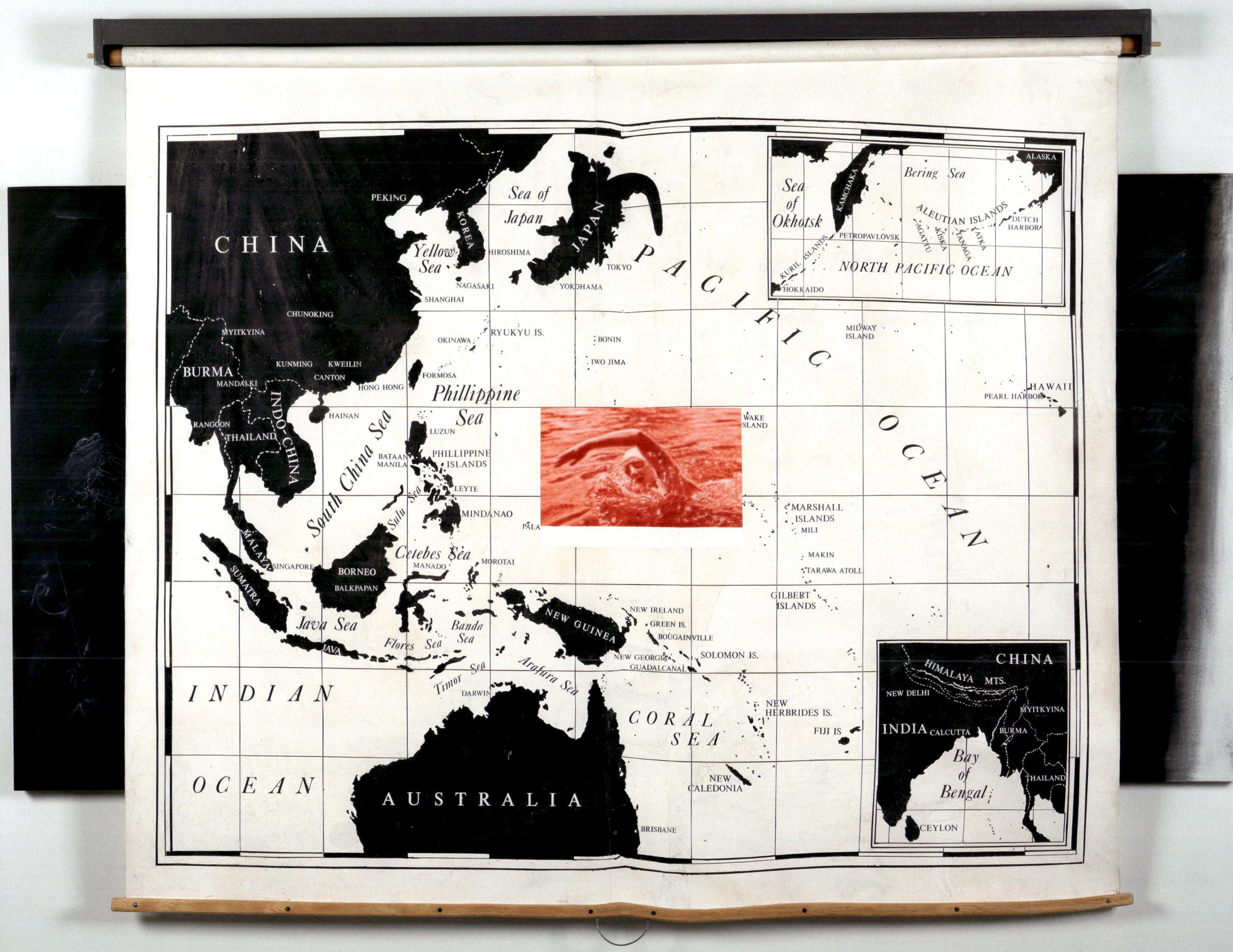

CHINA
PEKING
KOREA
Sea of Japan
JAPAN
Yellow Sea
HIROSHIMA
NAGASAKI
TOKYO
YOKOHAMA
SHANGHAI
PACIFIC OCEAN
Sea of Okhotsk
KAMCHAKA
Bering Sea
ALASKA
ALEUTIAN ISLANDS
DUTCH HARBOR
KURIL ISLANDS
PETROPAVLOVSK
NORTH PACIFIC OCEAN
HOKKAIDO
CHUNOKING
MYITKYINA
KUNMING
KWEILIN
CANTON
BURMA
MANDALKI
INDO-CHINA
HONG HONG
RYUKYU IS.
OKINAWA
BONIN
IWO JIMA
MIDWAY ISLAND
FORMOSA
Phillippine Sea
HAWAII
PEARL HARBOR
HAINAN
RANGOON
THAILAND
LUZUN
WAKE ISLAND
South China Sea
BATAAN
MANILA
PHILLIPPINE ISLANDS
LEYTE
Sulu Sea
MINDANAO
MARSHALL ISLANDS
MILI
MALAYA
SINGAPORE
SUMATRA
BORNEO
BALKPAPAN
Celebes Sea
MANADO
MOROTAI
MAKIN
TARAWA ATOLL
GILBERT ISLANDS
Java Sea
JAVA
Flores Sea
Banda Sea
NEW GUINEA
NEW IRELAND
GREEN IS.
BOUGAINVILLE
SOLOMON IS.
NEW GEORGIA
GUADALCANAL
Timor Sea
Arafura Sea
DARWIN
INDIAN OCEAN
CORAL SEA
NEW HERBRIDES IS.
FIJI IS
NEW CALEDONIA
AUSTRALIA
BRISBANE
CHINA
HIMALAYA MTS.
NEW DELHI
MYITKYINA
INDIA
CALCUTTA
BURMA
Bay of Bengal
THAILAND
CEYLON

Blank Slate Sky 1993

wrong thinking. He recommended cognition therapy, a hundred dollars an hour, more or less. She imagined her brain, rounded and knotty, coursed with rivulets as pictured in encyclopedias. It only looks that way, the psychiatrist said, it actually works much like slate. To remove the pain of memory you have only to erase the surface. She dragged her fingers across the slate and watched the words smear like chalk. She rubbed harder and whole paragraphs disintegrated before her eyes....

Most words, the tedious ones she presumed, powdered down in fragments, accumulating at her feet in desiccated heaps. But others hung in the air like greasy smoke. They gathered over the landscape and blotted out the sun. Swept down canyons and through the branches of junipers. Whistled around the corners of houses where people live.

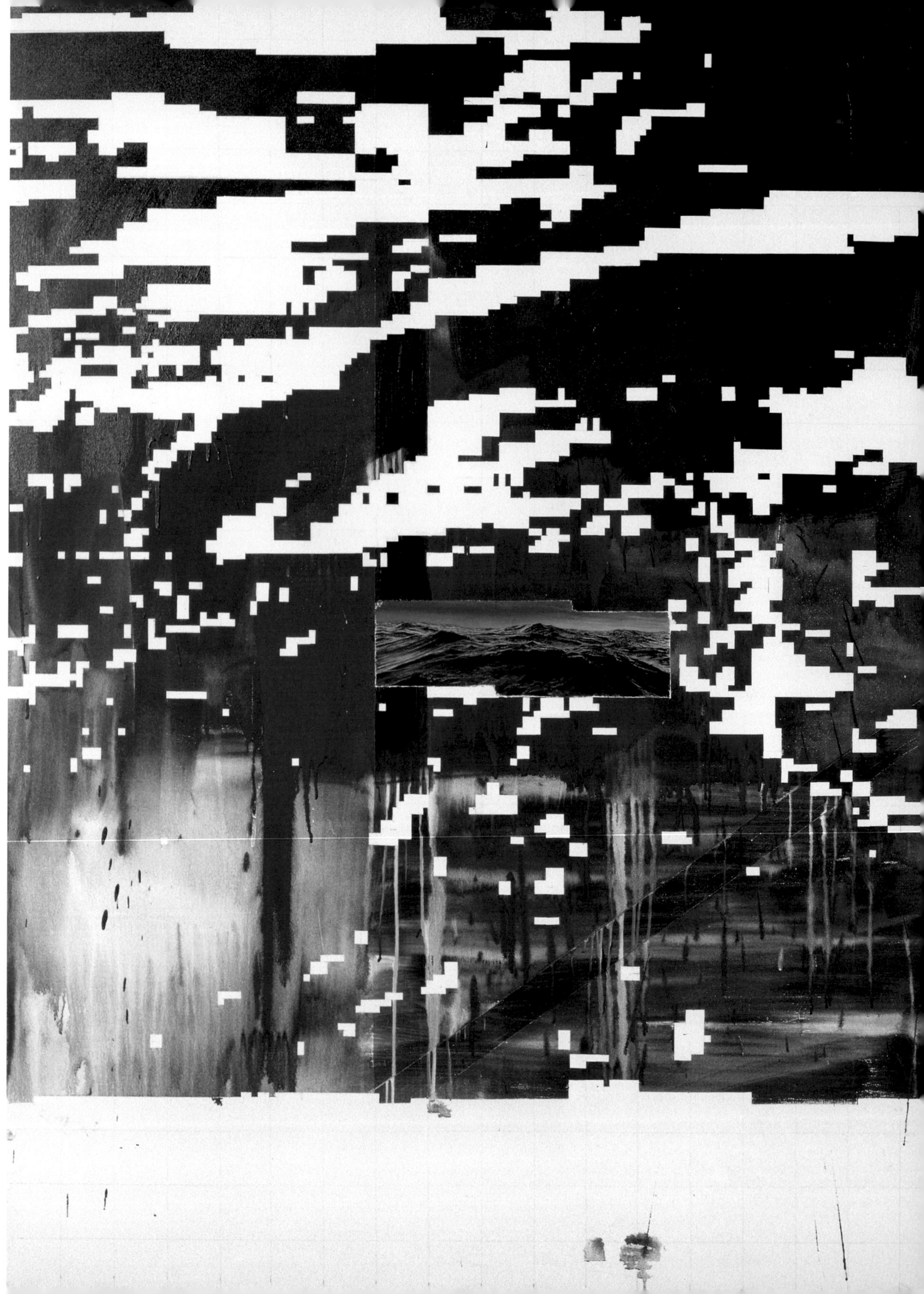

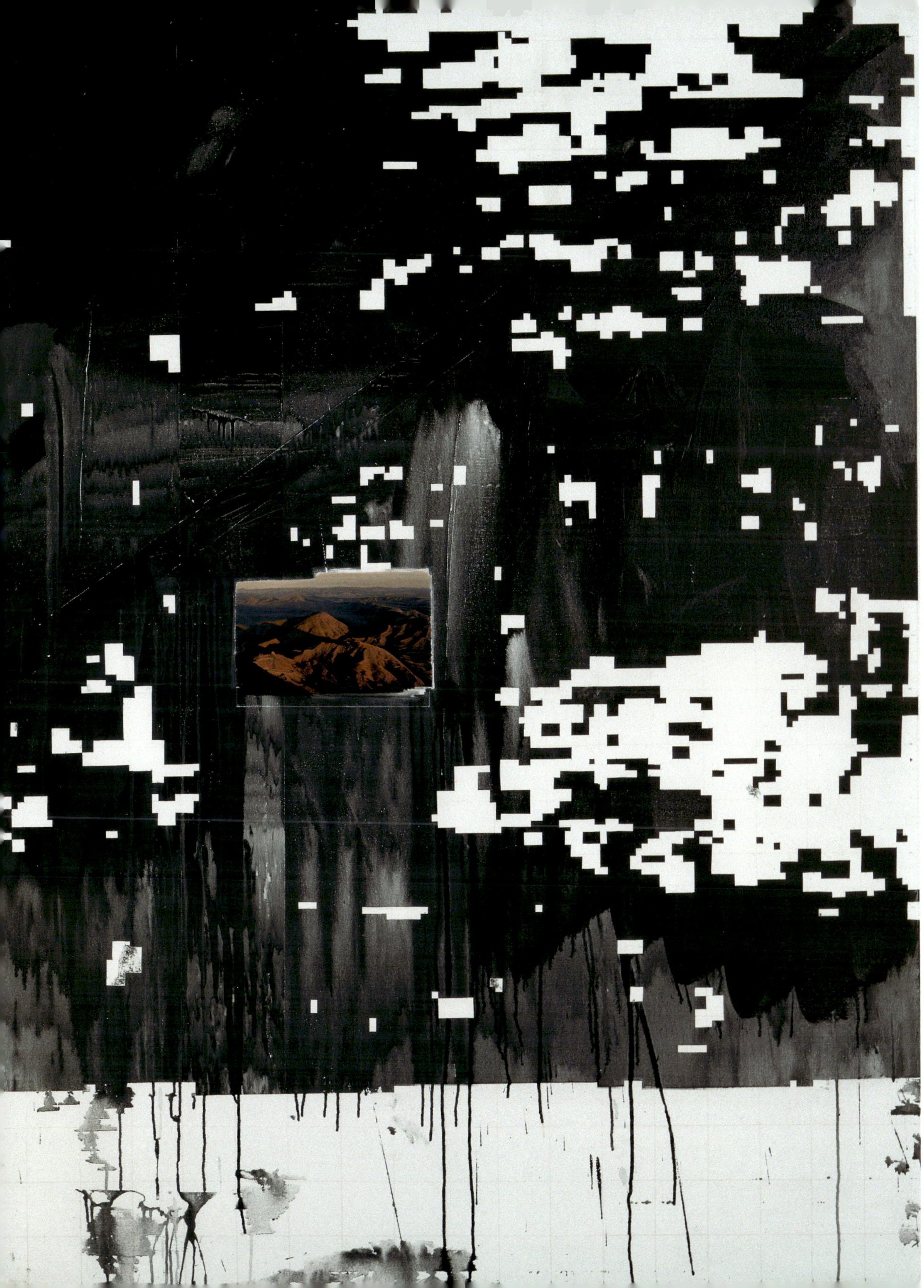

Swimming Against the
Tide for Relaxation
1994

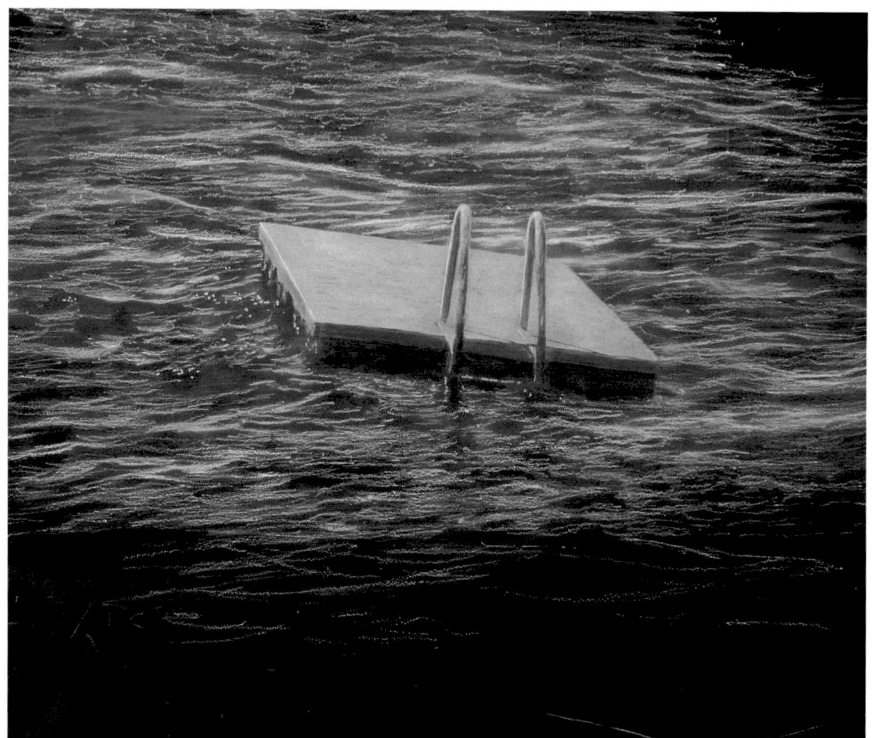

SWIMMING LESIONS

Blue Star Art Space, San Antonio, Texas
December 16, 1994–February 12, 1995

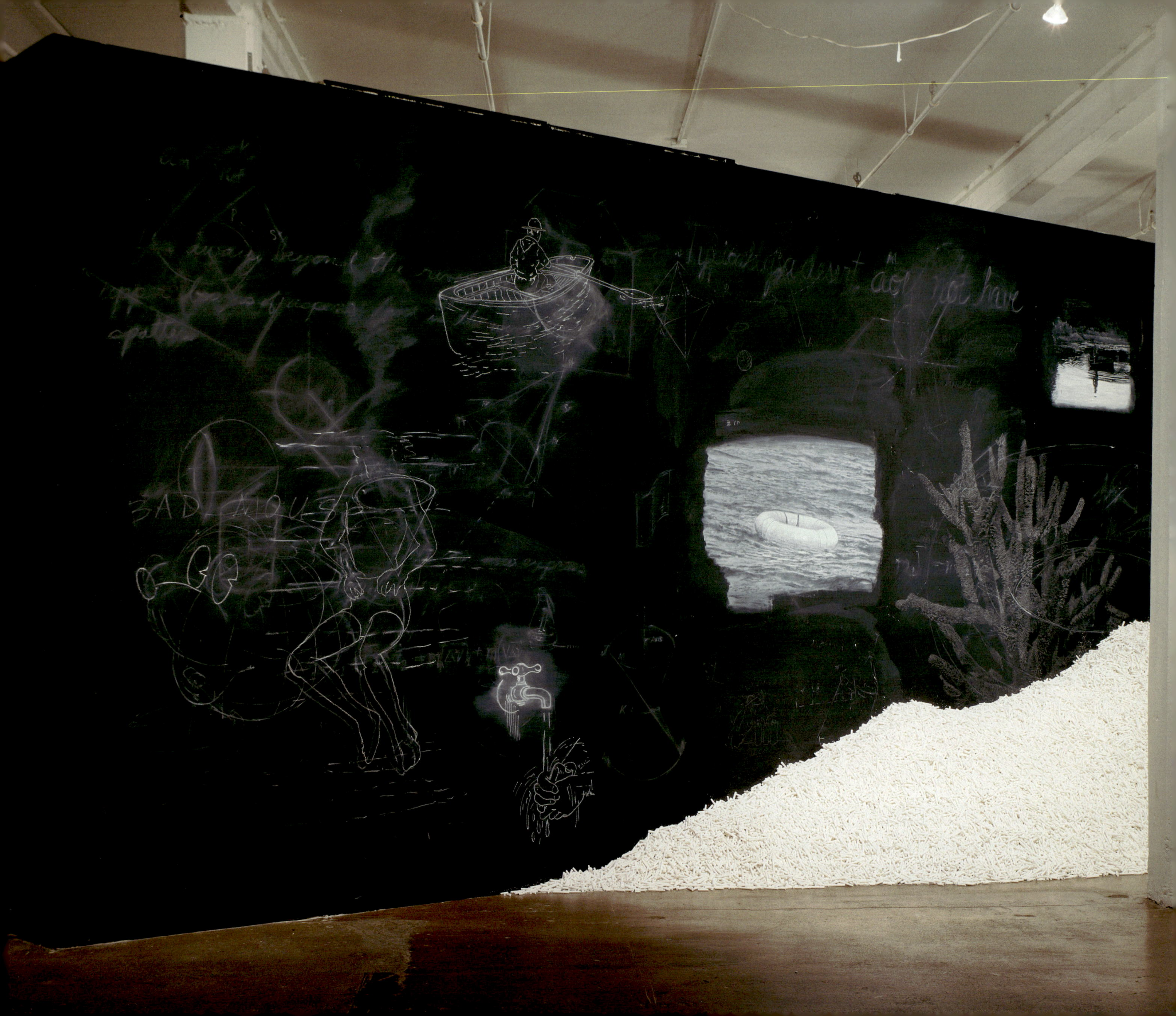

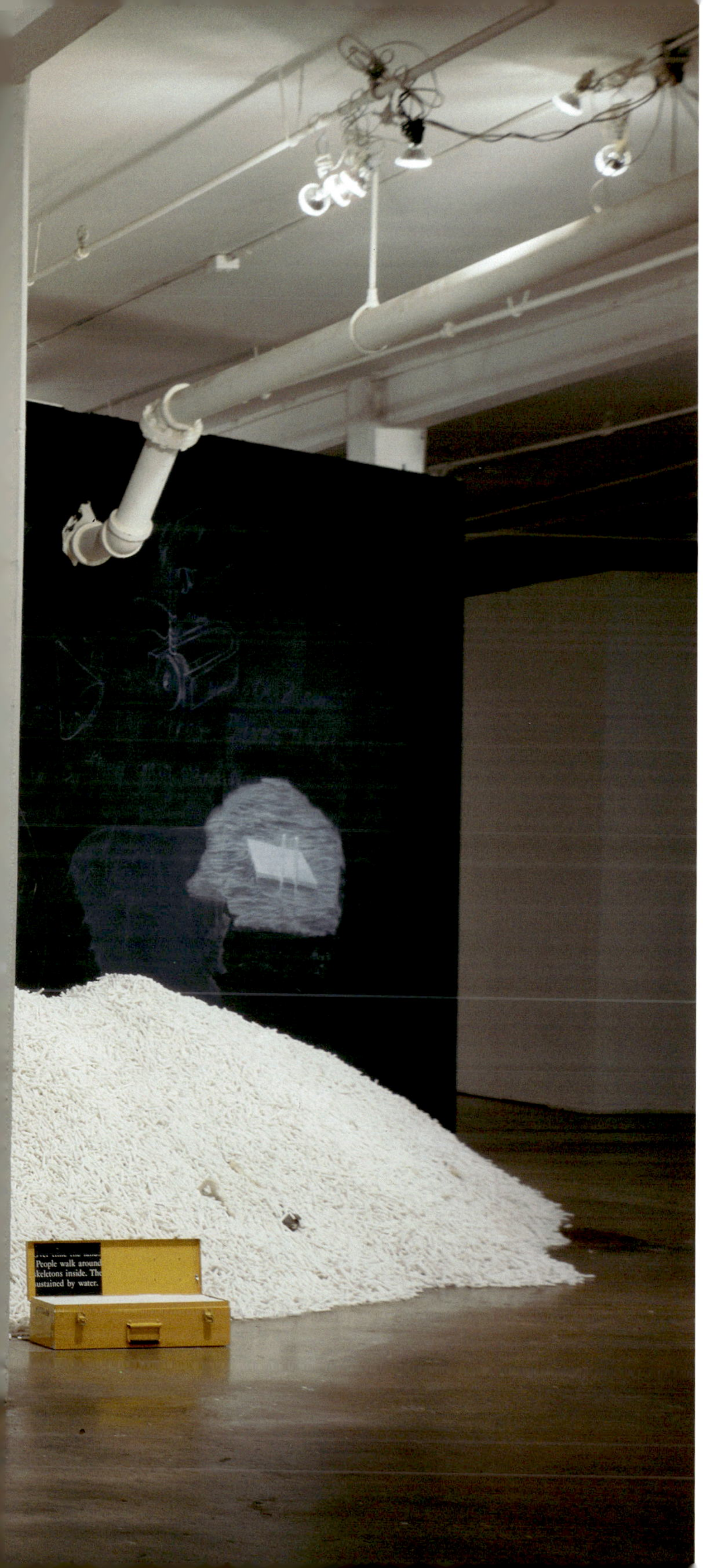

Front Wall

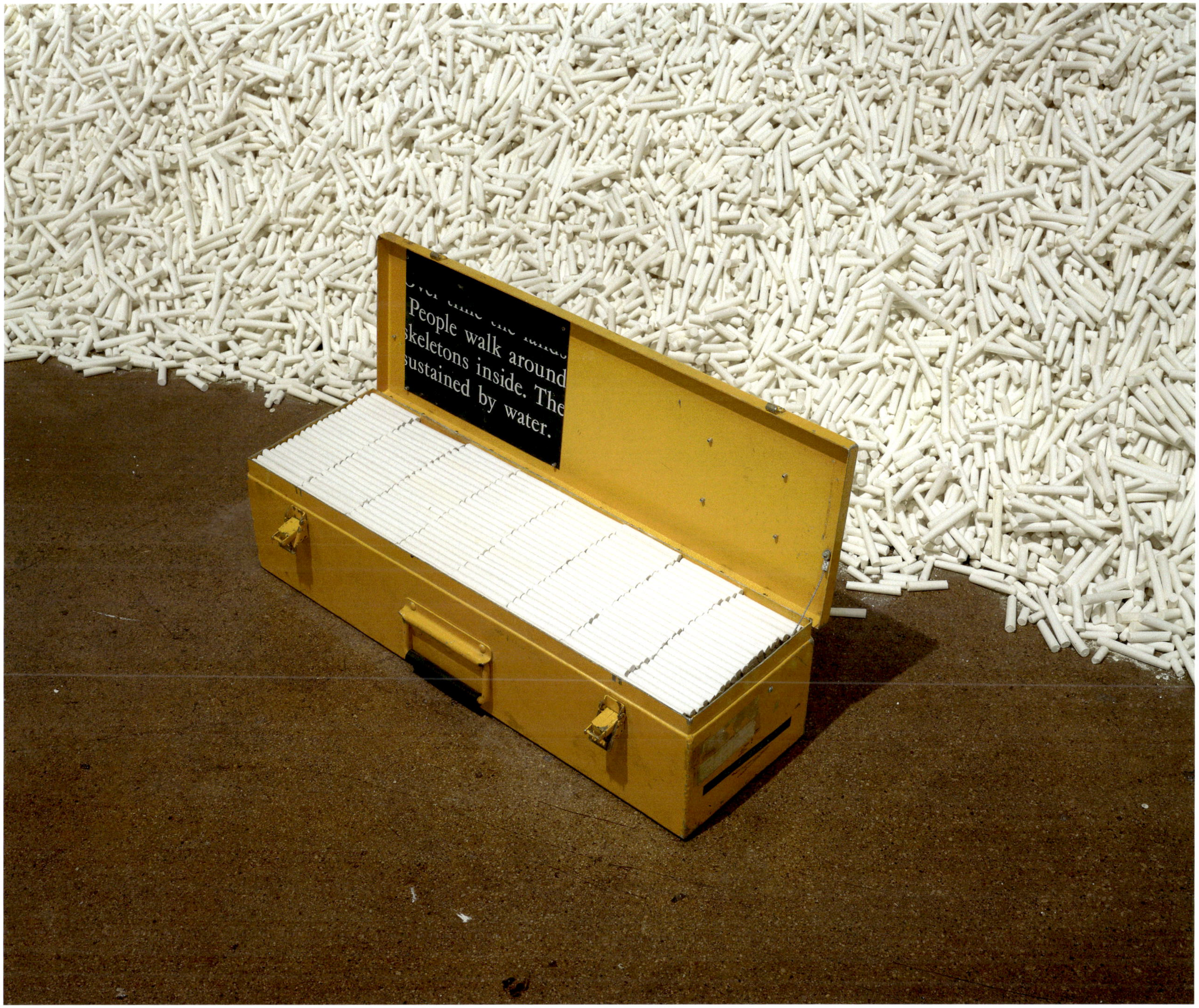
People walk around
skeletons inside. The
sustained by water.

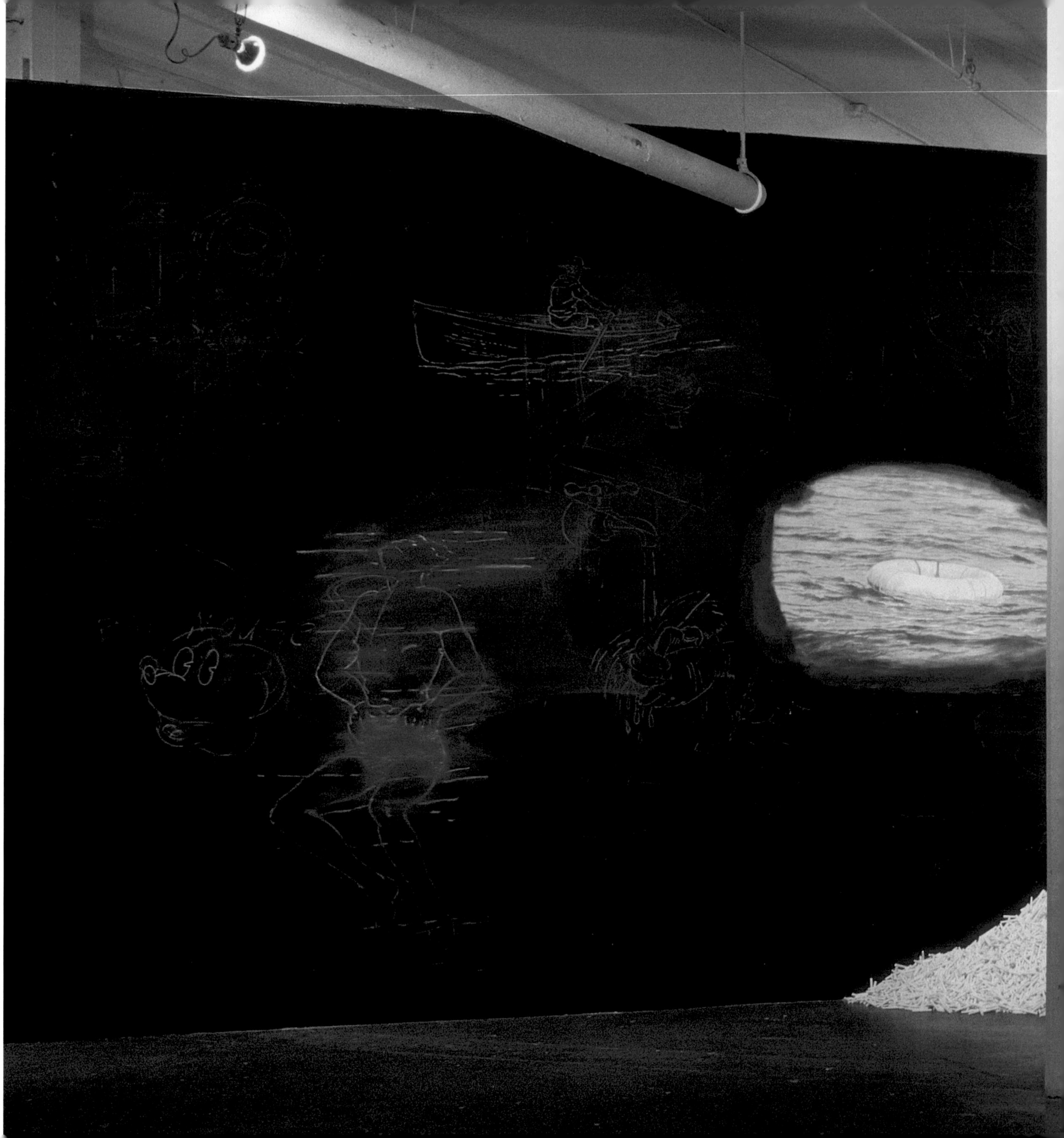

Back Wall

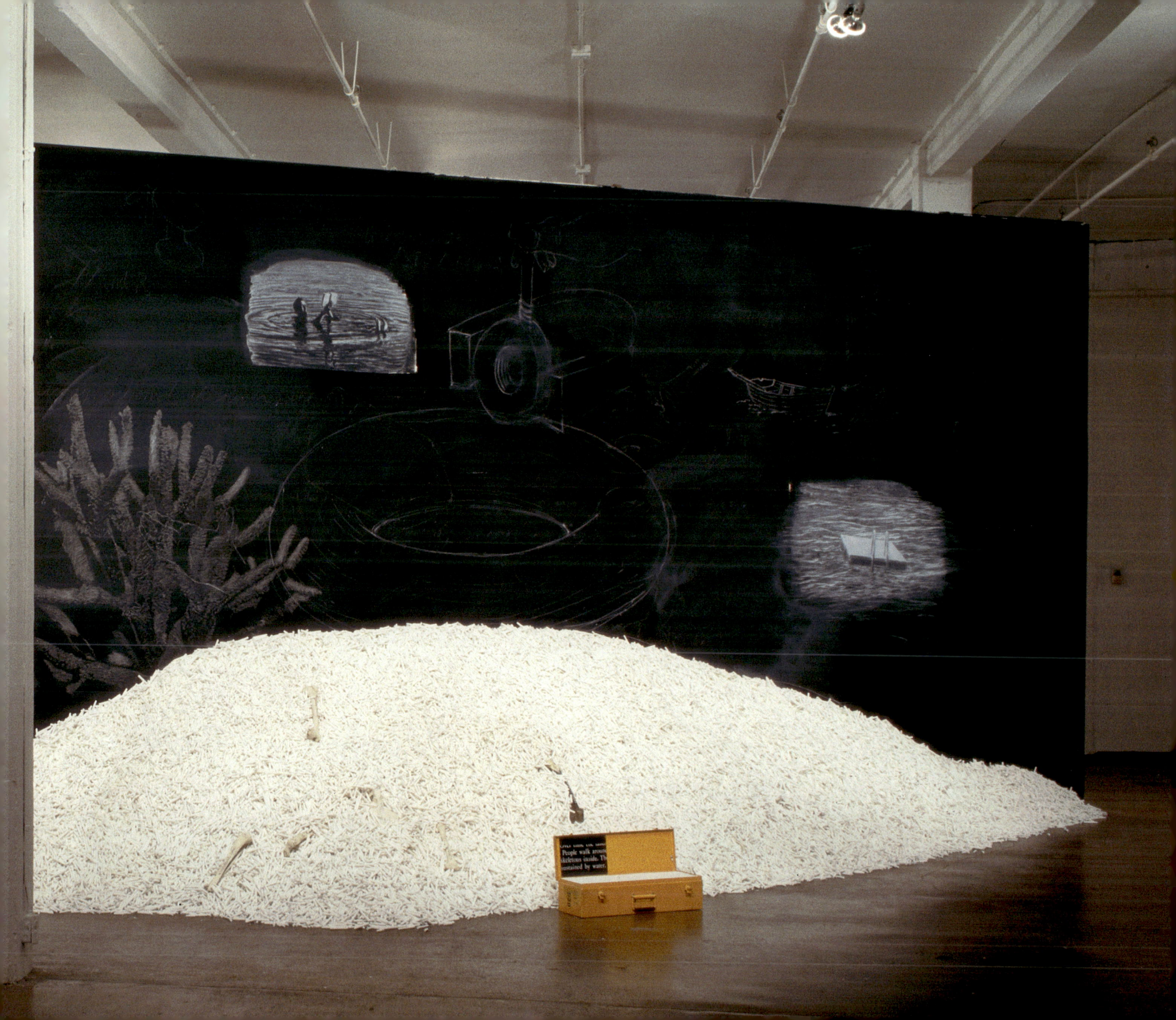
People walk
skeletons inside.
by water.

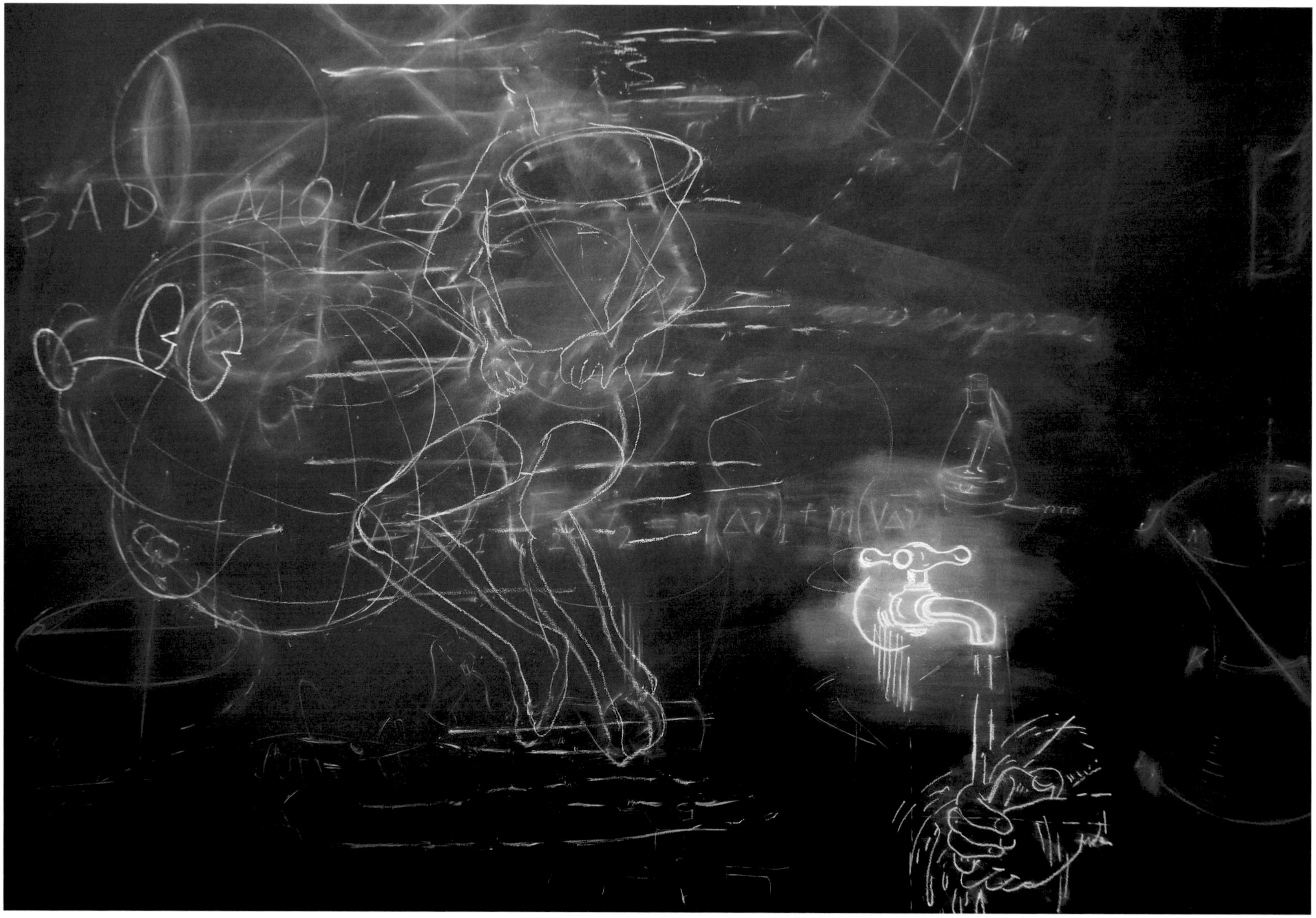

Front Wall Detail

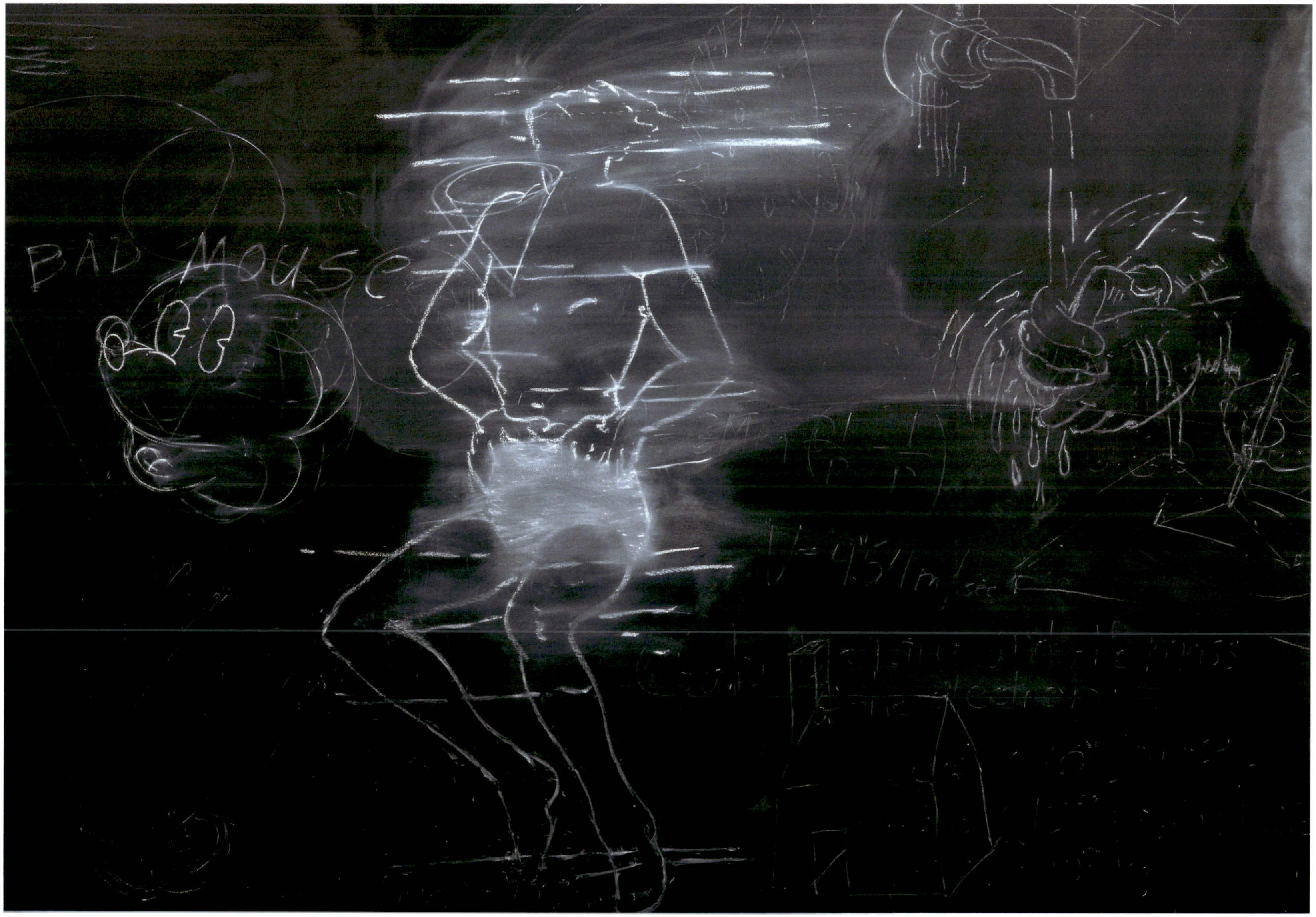

Back Wall Detail

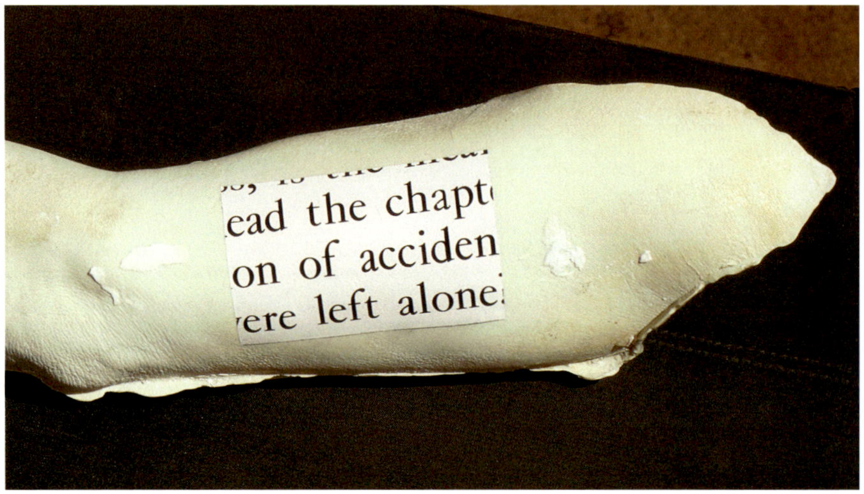

Delirium 1994

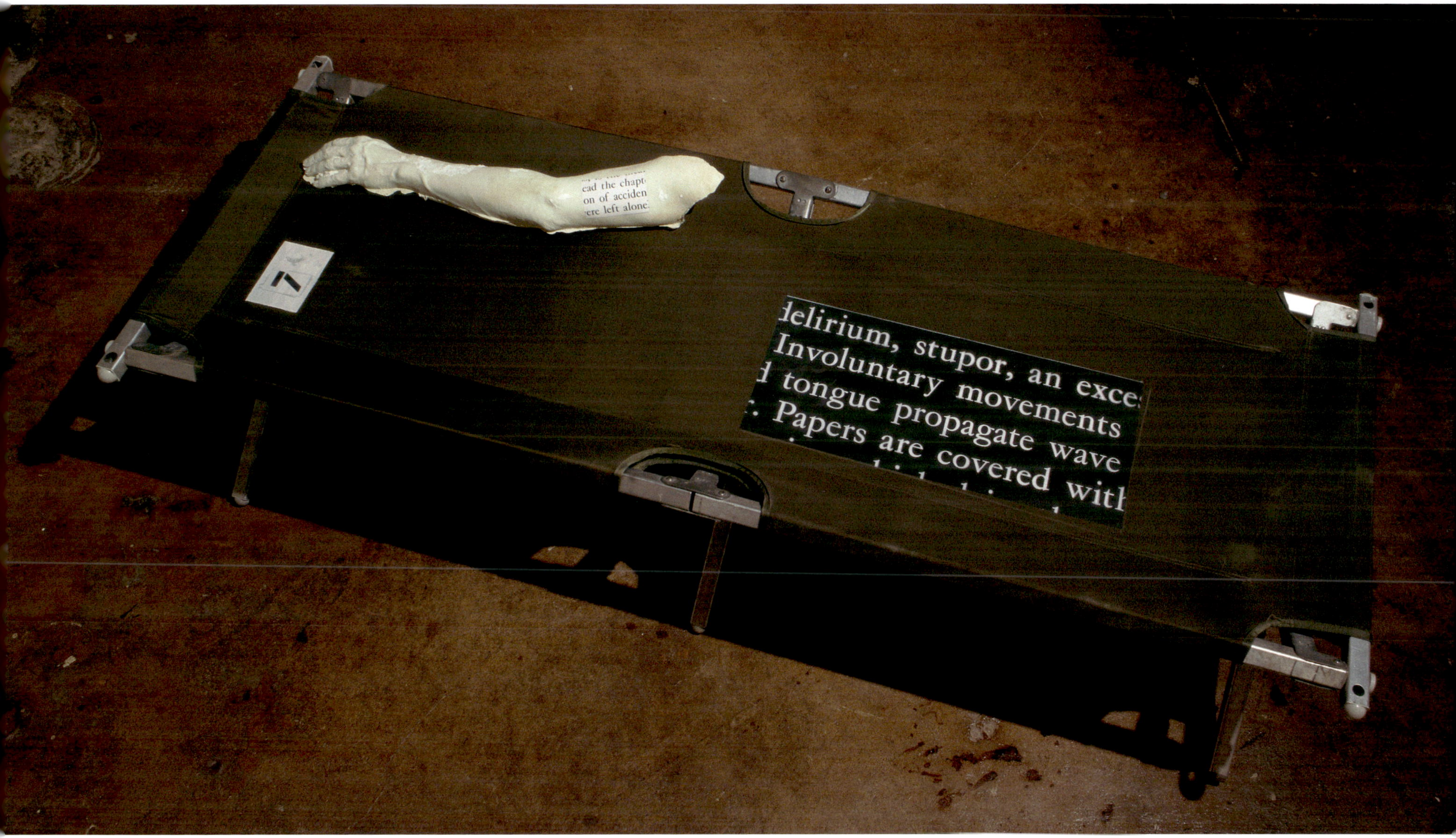
7
left alone.
delirium, stupor, an
Involuntary movements
tongue propagate wave
Papers are covered

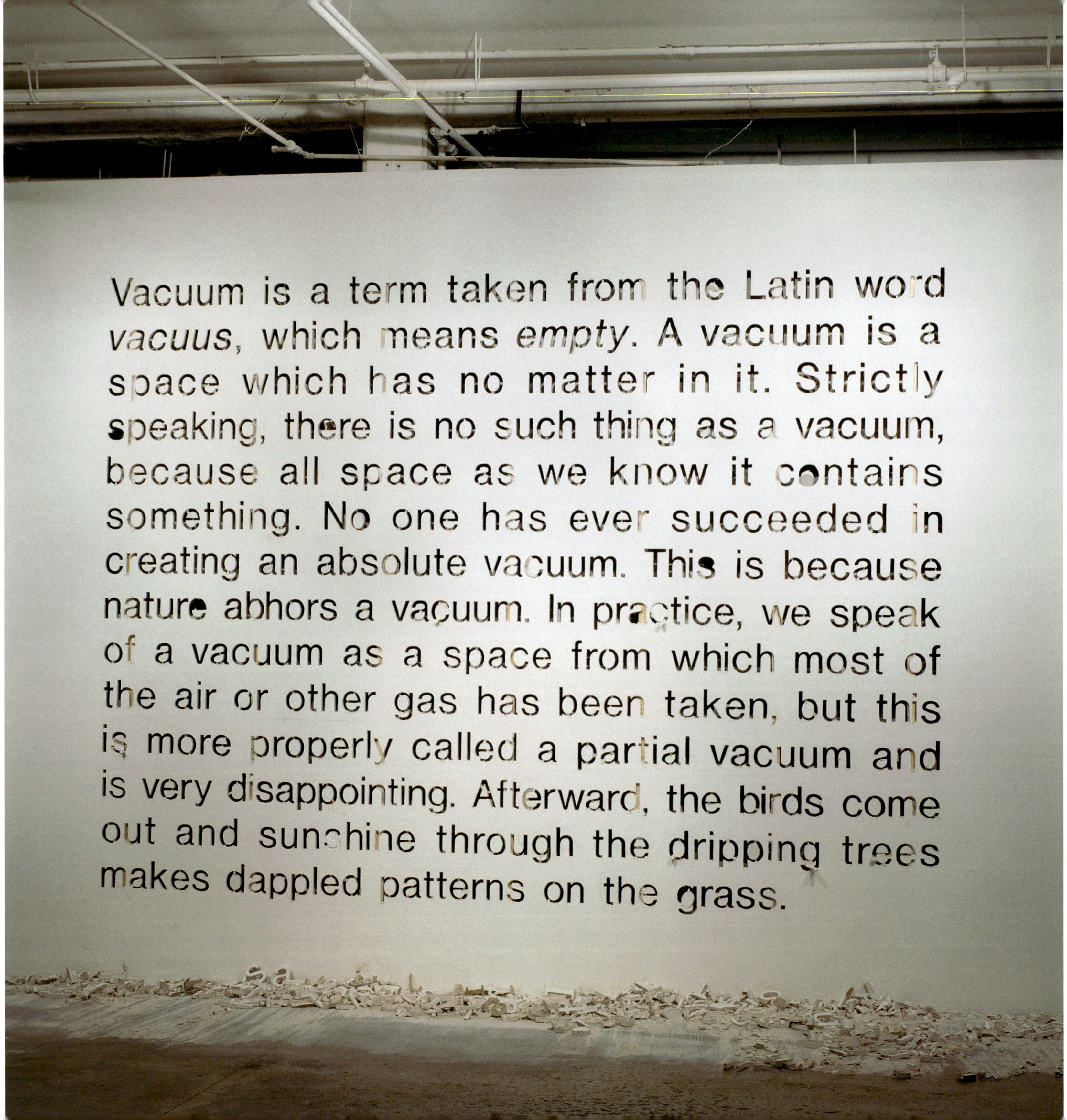
Vacuum is a term taken from the Latin word vacuus, which means empty. A vacuum is a space which has no matter in it. Strictly speaking, there is no such thing as a vacuum, because all space as we know it contains something. No one has ever succeeded in creating an absolute vacuum. This is because nature abhors a vacuum. In practice, we speak of a vacuum as a space from which most of the air or other gas has been taken, but this is more properly called a partial vacuum and is very disappointing. Afterward, the birds come out and sunshine through the dripping trees makes dappled patterns on the grass.

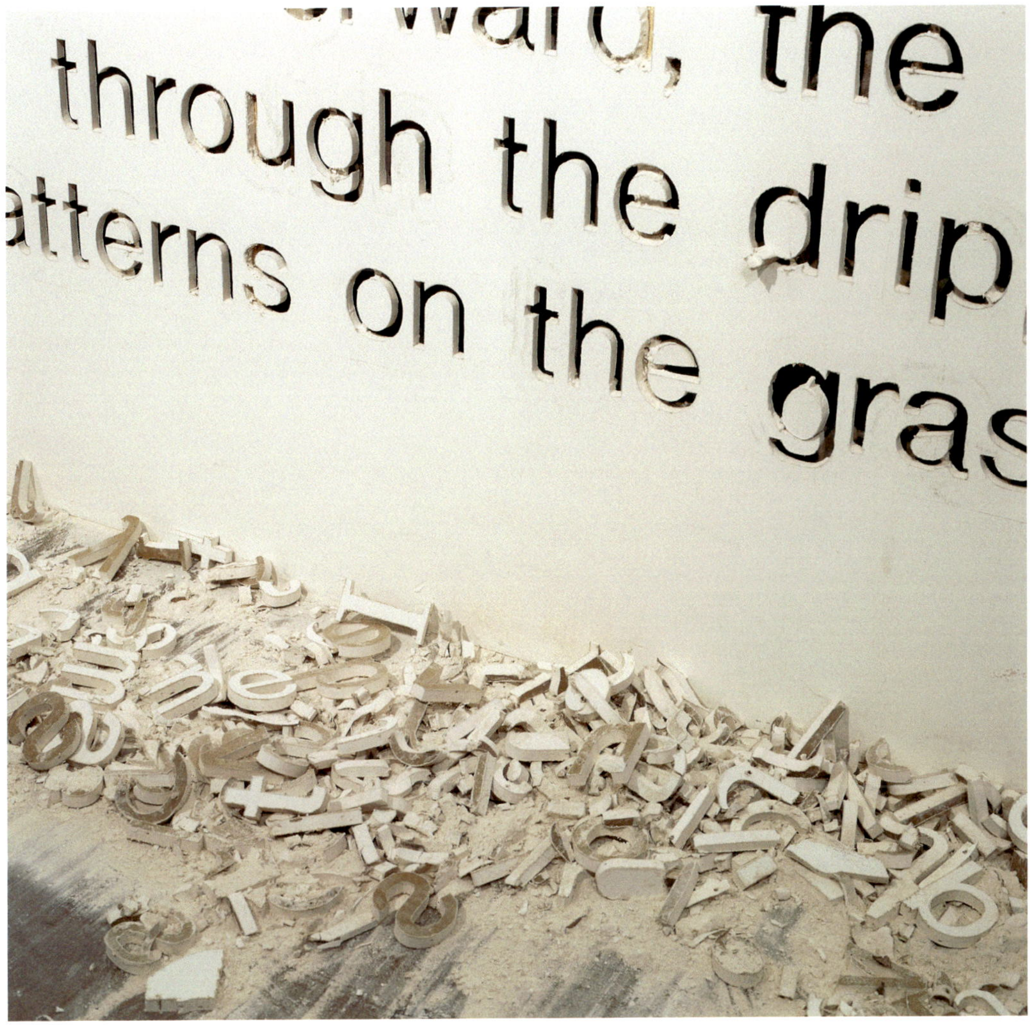

Vacuum 1994

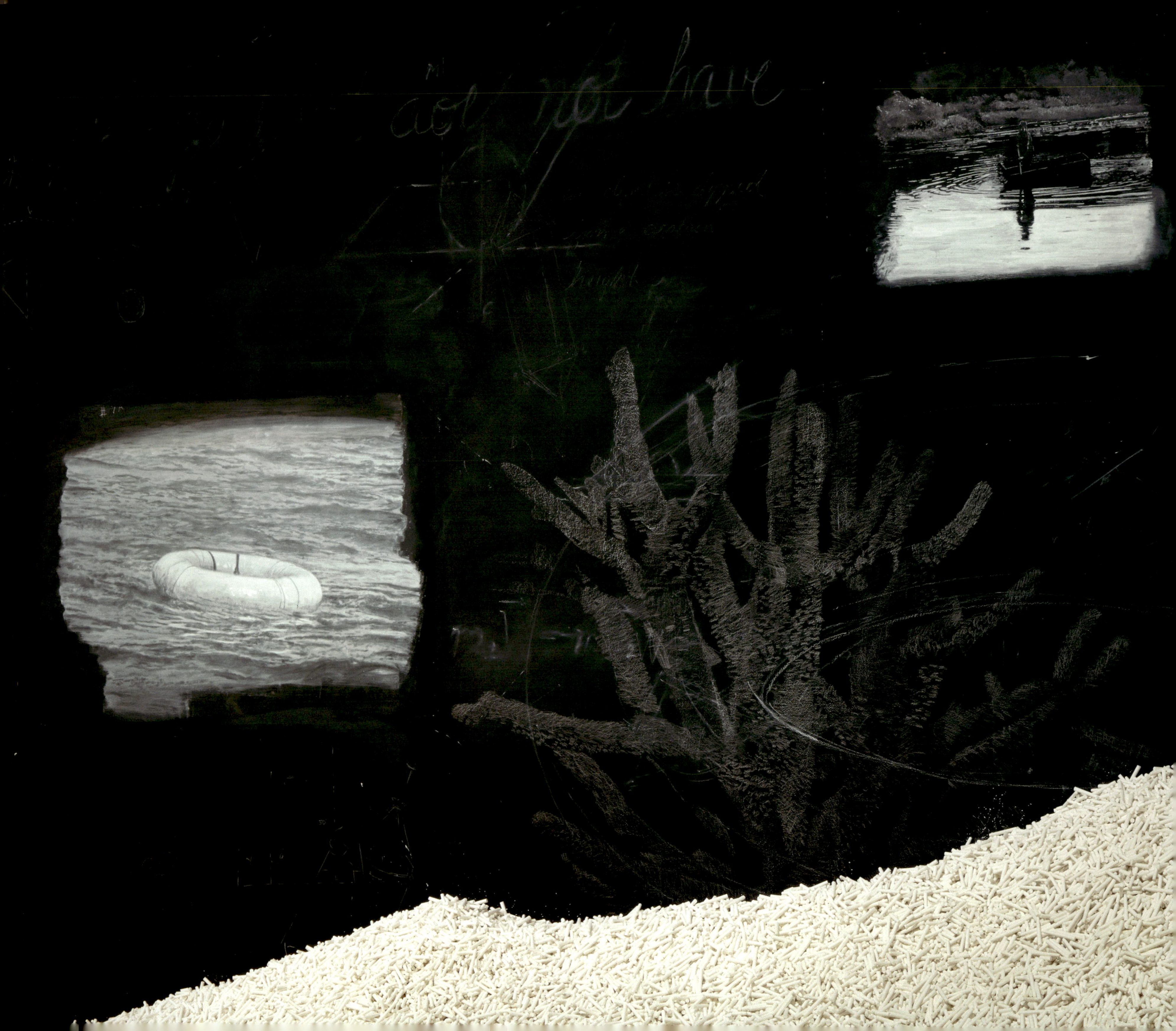
not have

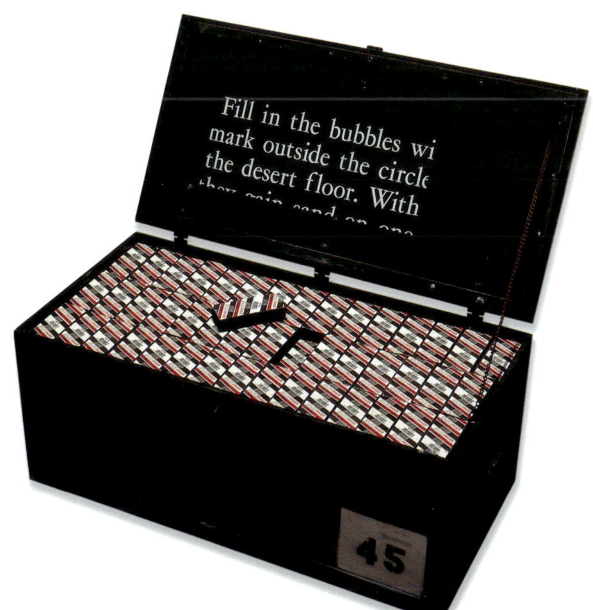
Fill in the bubbles wi
mark outside the circl
the desert floor. With
45

Private Africa 1995

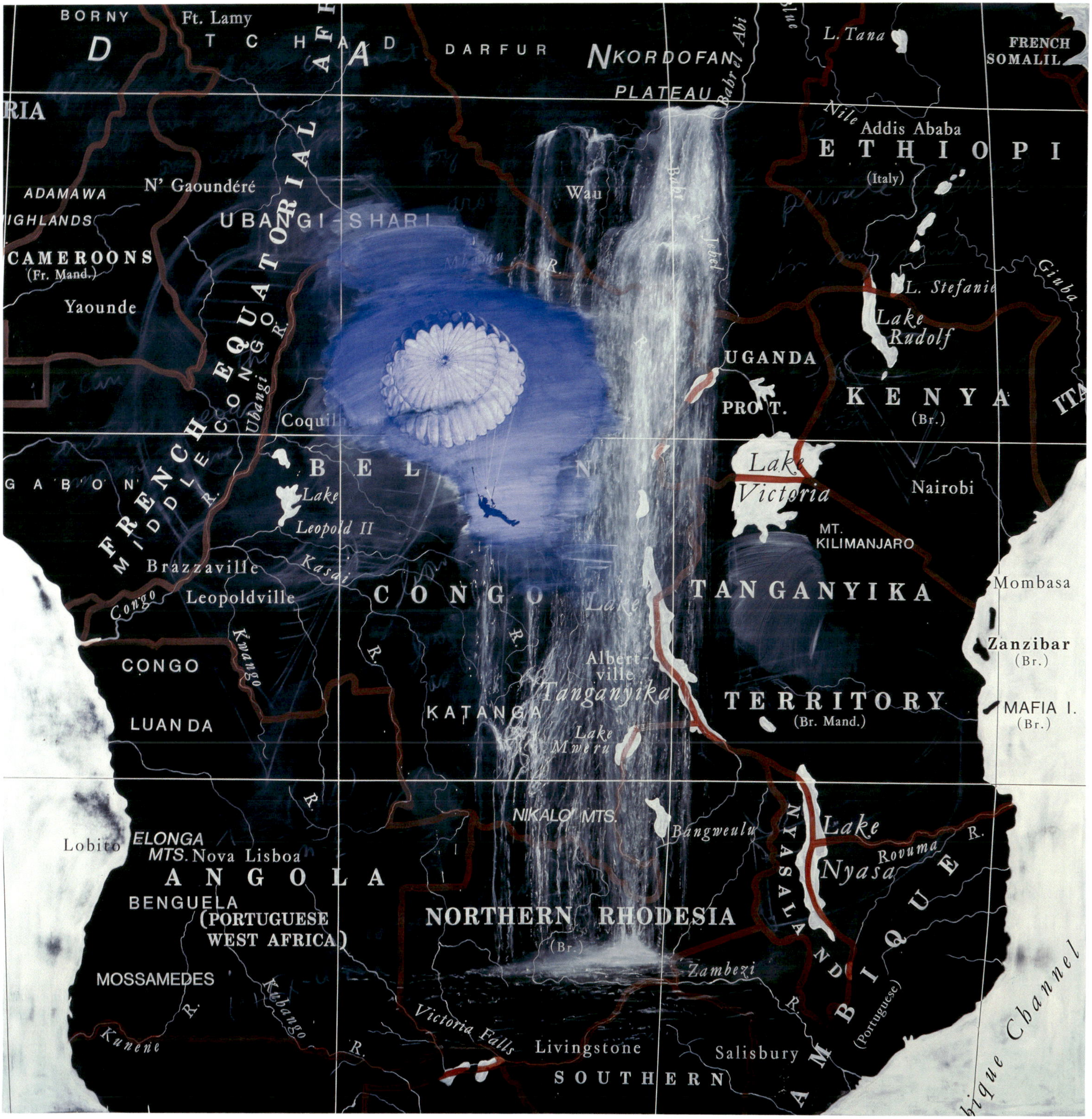
BORNY
Ft. Lamy
T C H A D
DARFUR
KORDOFAN
PLATEAU
L. Tana
FRENCH
SOMALIL
Nile
Addis Ababa
ETHIOPI
(Italy)
ADAMAWA
N' Gaoundéré
UBANGI-SHARI
Wau
CAMEROONS
(Fr. Mand.)
Yaounde
FRENCH EQUATORIAL
MIDDLE CONGO R.
Ubangi
L. Stefanie
Lake
Rudolf
Giuba
UGANDA
PROT.
KENYA
(Br.)
Coquilh
BEL
GABON
Lake
Leopold II
Lake
Victoria
Nairobi
MT.
KILIMANJARO
Brazzaville
Leopoldville
Congo
Kasai
CONGO
TANGANYIKA
Mombasa
Zanzibar
(Br.)
CONGO
LUANDA
Kwango
KATANGA
Albert-
ville
Tanganyika
TERRITORY
(Br. Mand.)
MAFIA I.
(Br.)
Lake
Mweru
NIKALO MTS.
Bangweulu
Lake
Nyasa
Rovuma
NYASALAND
Lobito
ELONGA
MTS.
Nova Lisboa
ANGOLA
BENGUELA
(PORTUGUESE
WEST AFRICA)
NORTHERN RHODESIA
(Br.)
MOZAMBIQUE
(Portuguese)
Zambezi
MOSSAMEDES
Kubango
Kunene
Victoria Falls
Livingstone
Salisbury
SOUTHERN
Channel

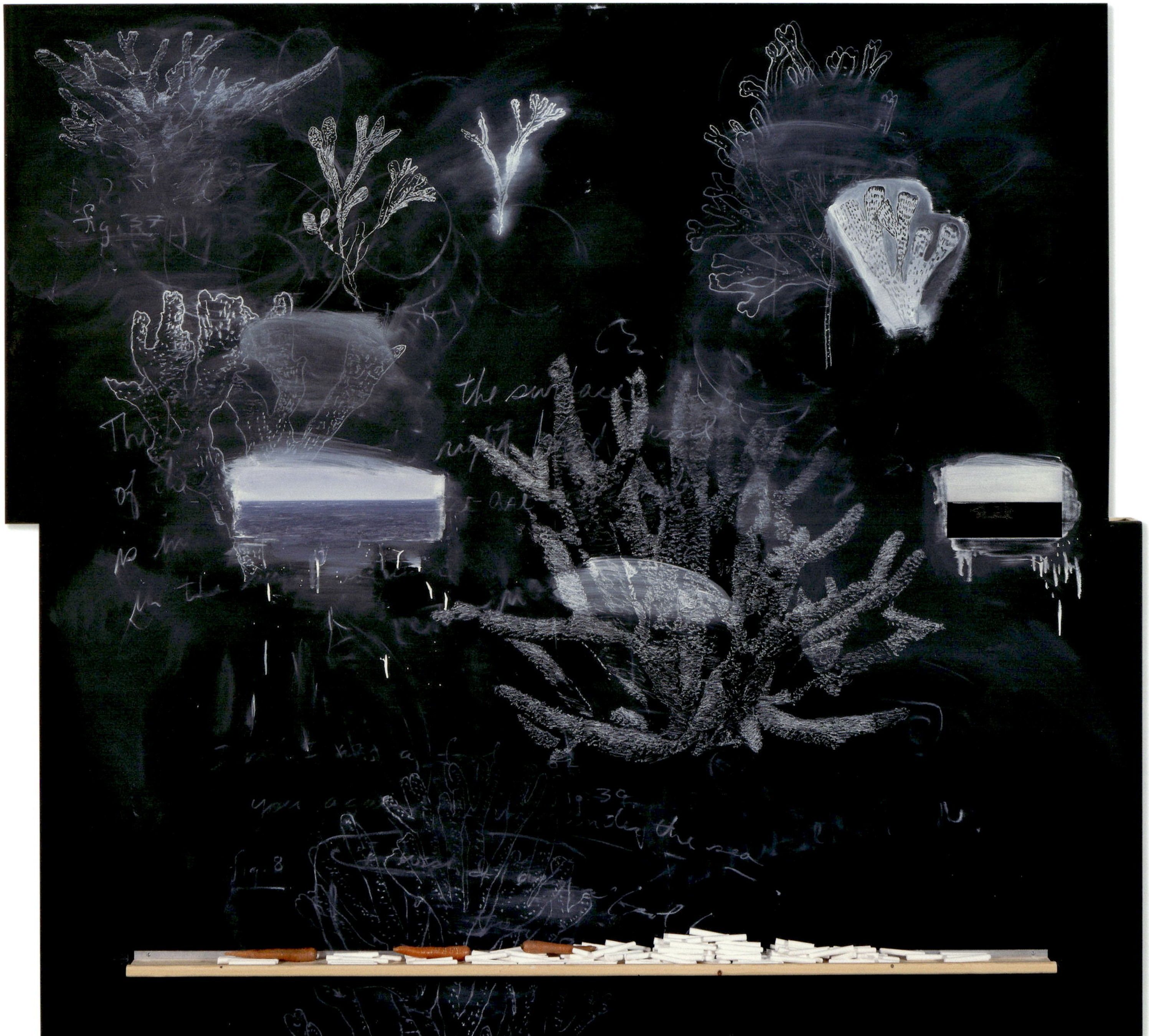

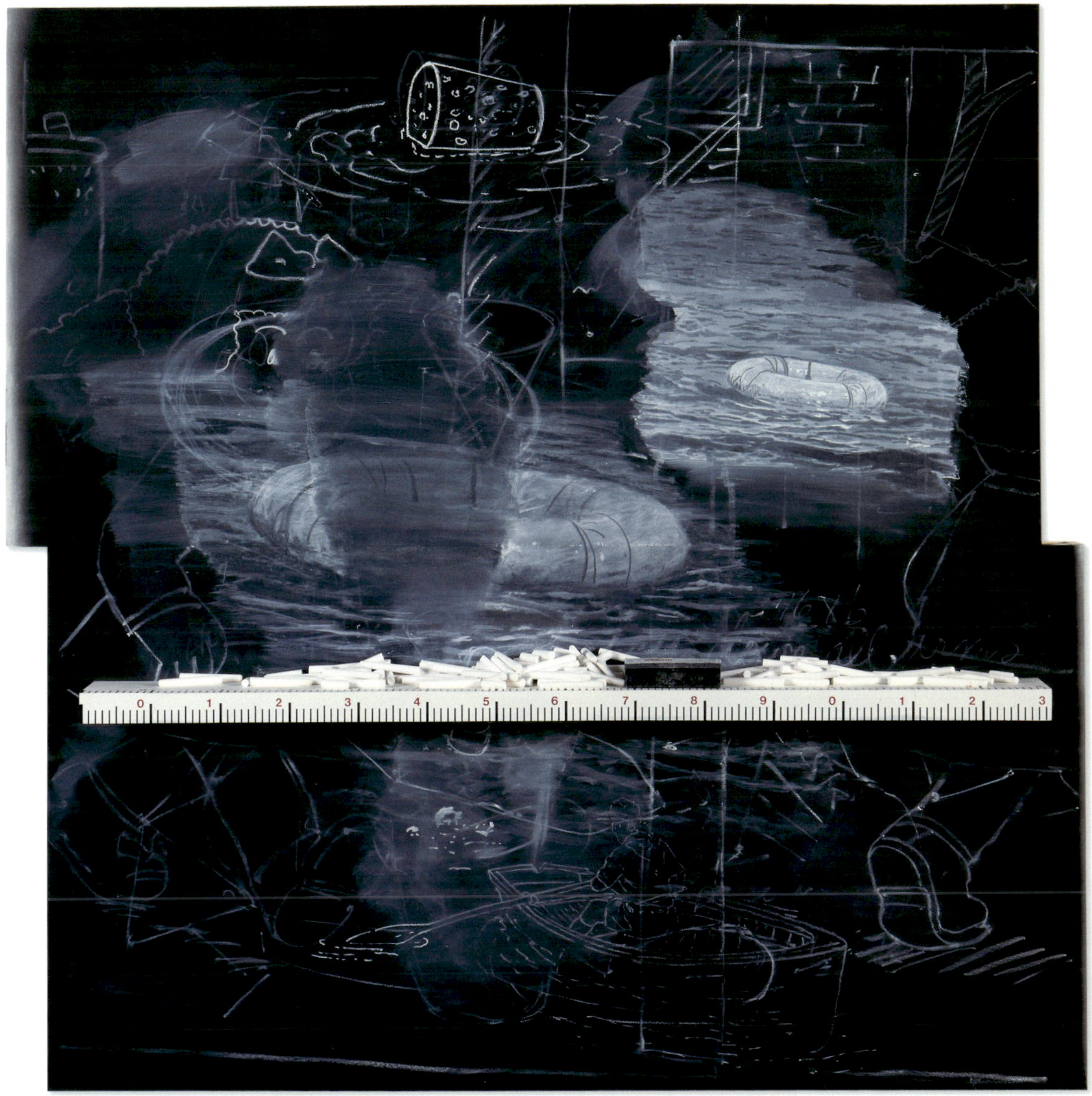

▲ The Skin Between Water and Air 1995

◀ The Value of Water 1995

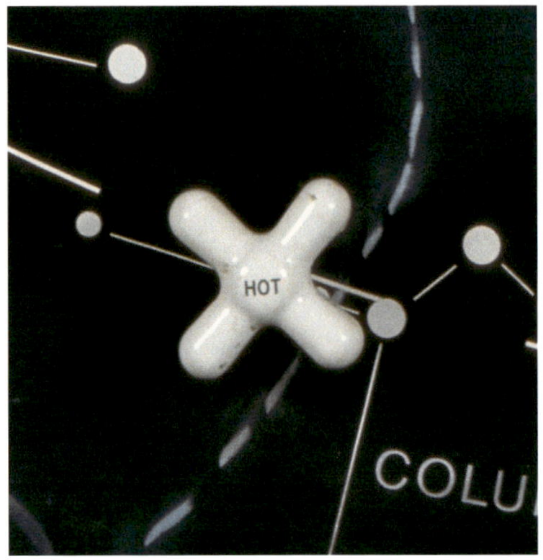

Tutor to a Lunatic 1996

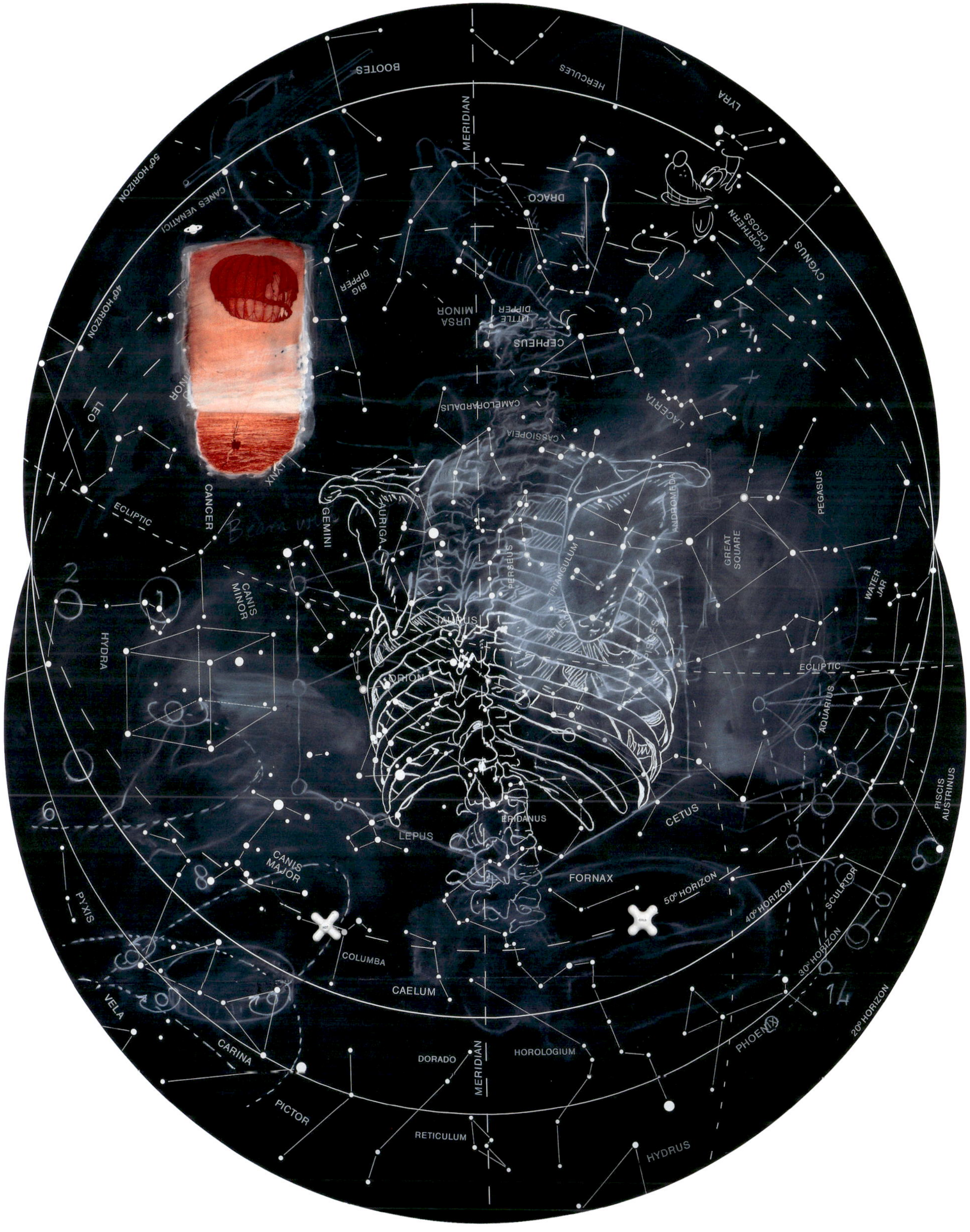

BOOTES
HERCULES
LYRA
MERIDIAN
50° HORIZON
CANES VENATICI
DRACO
NORTHERN CROSS
CYGNUS
BIG DIPPER
URSA MINOR
LITTLE DIPPER
40° HORIZON
CEPHEUS
CAMELOPARDALIS
LACERTA
CASSIOPEIA
LEO
LYNX
ANDROMEDA
PEGASUS
ECLIPTIC
CANCER
GEMINI
AURIGA
PERSEUS
TRIANGULUM
GREAT SQUARE
WATER JAR
CANIS MINOR
HYDRA
TAURUS
ORION
ECLIPTIC
AQUARIUS
PISCIS AUSTRINUS
ERIDANUS
CETUS
LEPUS
CANIS MAJOR
FORNAX
50° HORIZON
40° HORIZON
SCULPTOR
PYXIS
COLUMBA
30° HORIZON
CAELUM
VELA
20° HORIZON
CARINA
DORADO
MERIDIAN
HOROLOGIUM
PHOENIX
PICTOR
RETICULUM
HYDRUS

Good Kid 1997

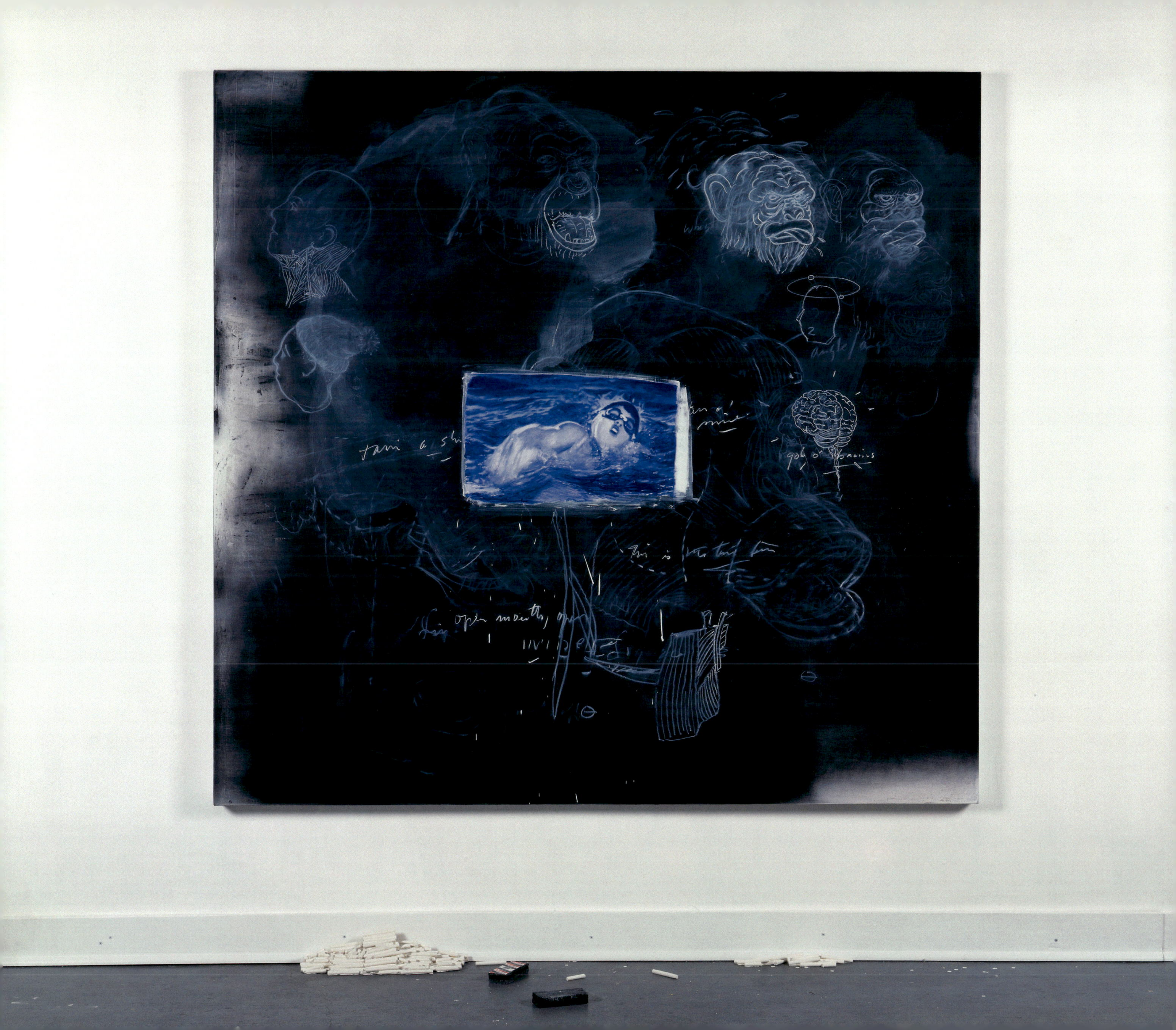

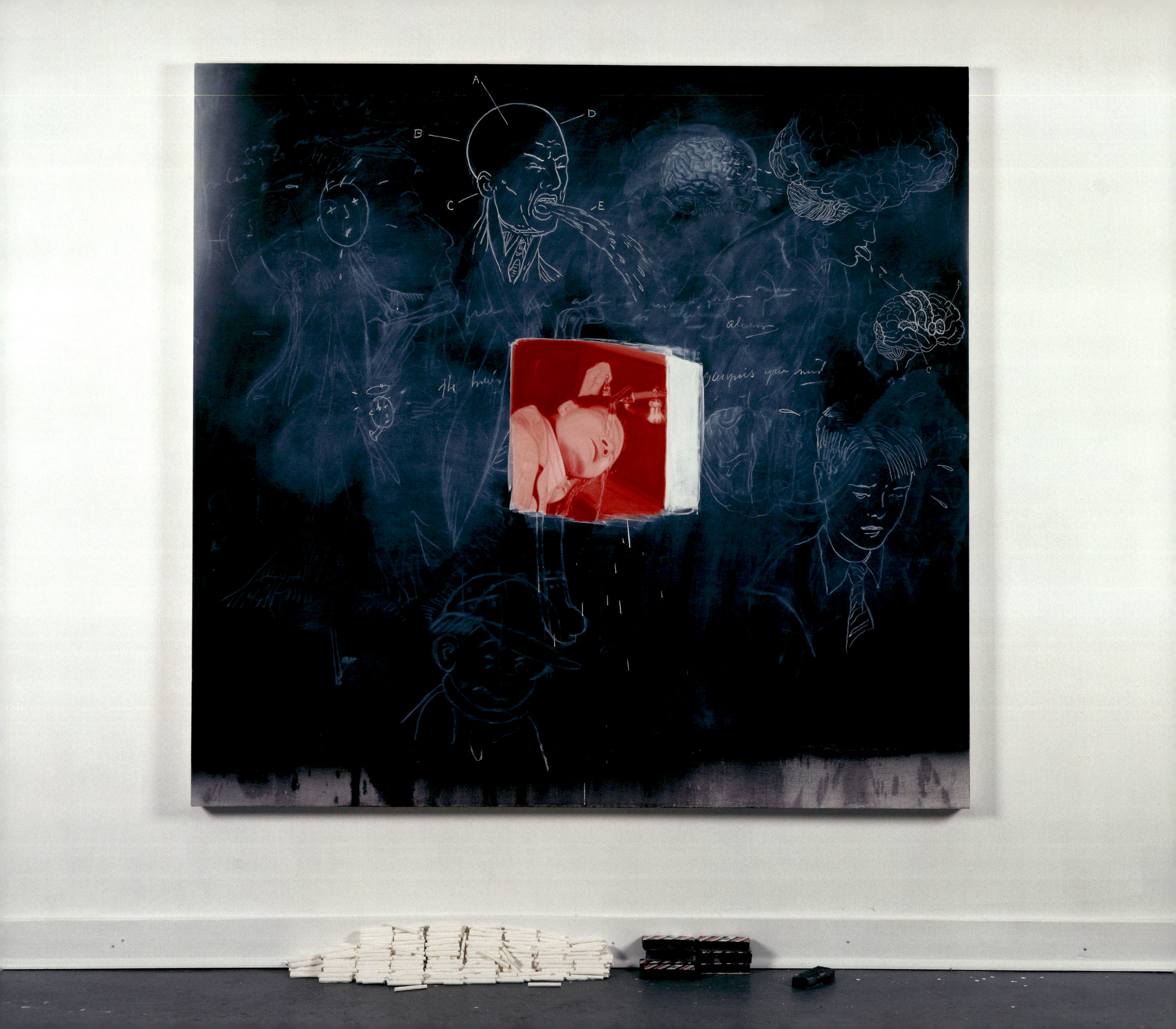
A
B
C
D
E

Streams 1997

"Give me the map," she said.

The man had collapsed to a sitting position on the sand. Sweat dripped off his nose onto the map.

"Give it to me before you fuck it up." She tore the map from his hands.

Spread out across the hood of the truck, the map was a snarl of clotted lines and text. Volcanic peaks, highland deserts, depressed deserts, rugged slopes, rocky plateaus; landforms caused by wind— transverse dunes, parabolic dunes: individually and obsessively illustrated. Dozens of colors for land elevations. Different colors for zones of precipitation (not much), zones of arable land (even less), zones for extremes of temperature. She looked out at the empty horizon. Tried to remain calm.

She found an encouraging blue line, followed it for several inches until it terminated in a small, irregular spot marked: *sometimes water.* Thought of the canteen, half empty, inside the truck. She located a web of meandering lines resembling dry wadis situated in a large, coral-shaded area. "Hey, we're in the pink," she joked. The man clutched his knees, rocked back and forth on the sand.

"Somewhere."

But the layers of information were endless. There were hundreds of intricate drawings depicting the kinds and areas of natural vegetation. Illustrations of animal life from the largest mammal down to insects as small as a fly. Particulars on mineral deposits, surface transport, political divisions, population density, religions, geographical facts, historical facts, something called The Purity of Revolutionary Aspirations. Statistics on crime, on wealth, jobs, job satisfaction. Not everyone liked their job, it turns out. There were celebrity profiles and interviews with the recent dead.

She traced the location of towns and villages along a road—black beads strung along a winding black thread. Beads with names like Abu Bahr, Abu Njaym, Abu Tij. None of the names were familiar and there were no names in the areas of coral.

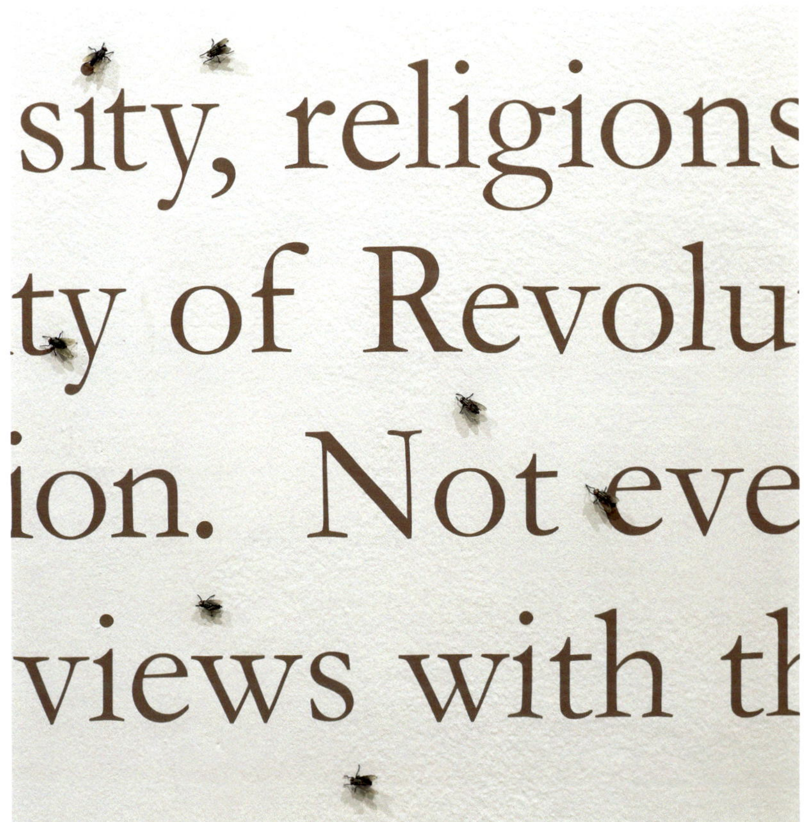

Map 1998

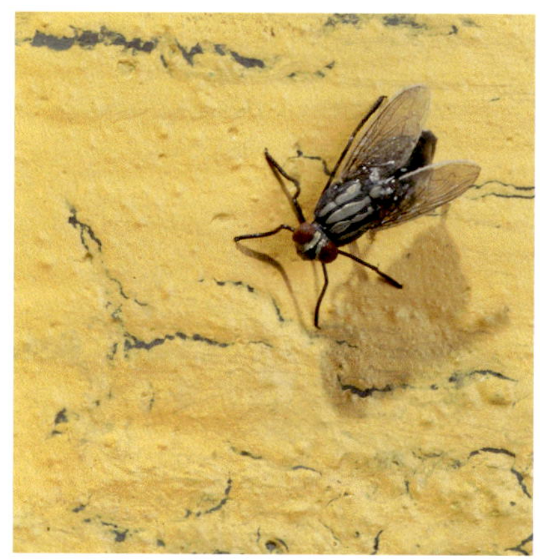

Faya 1998

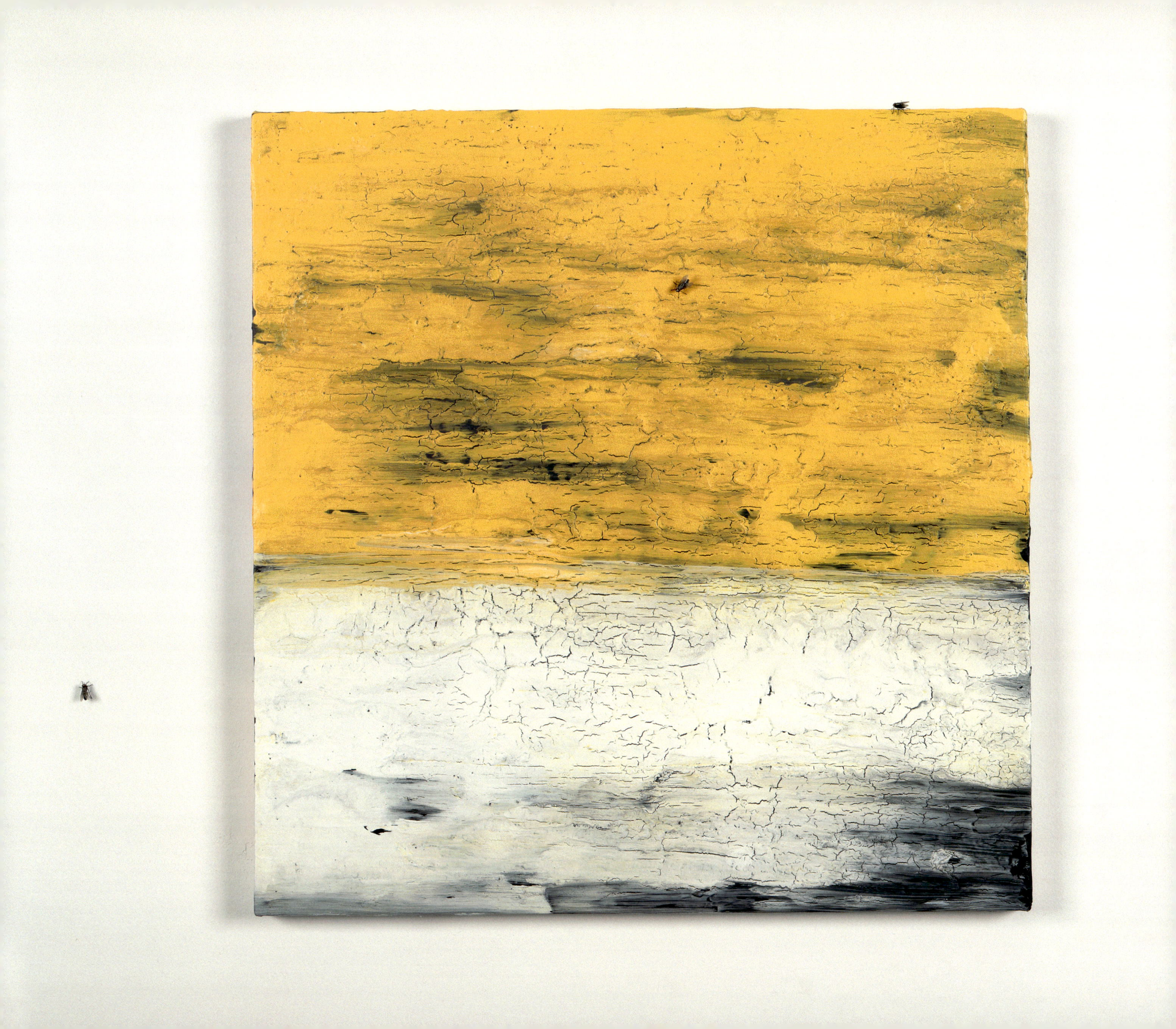

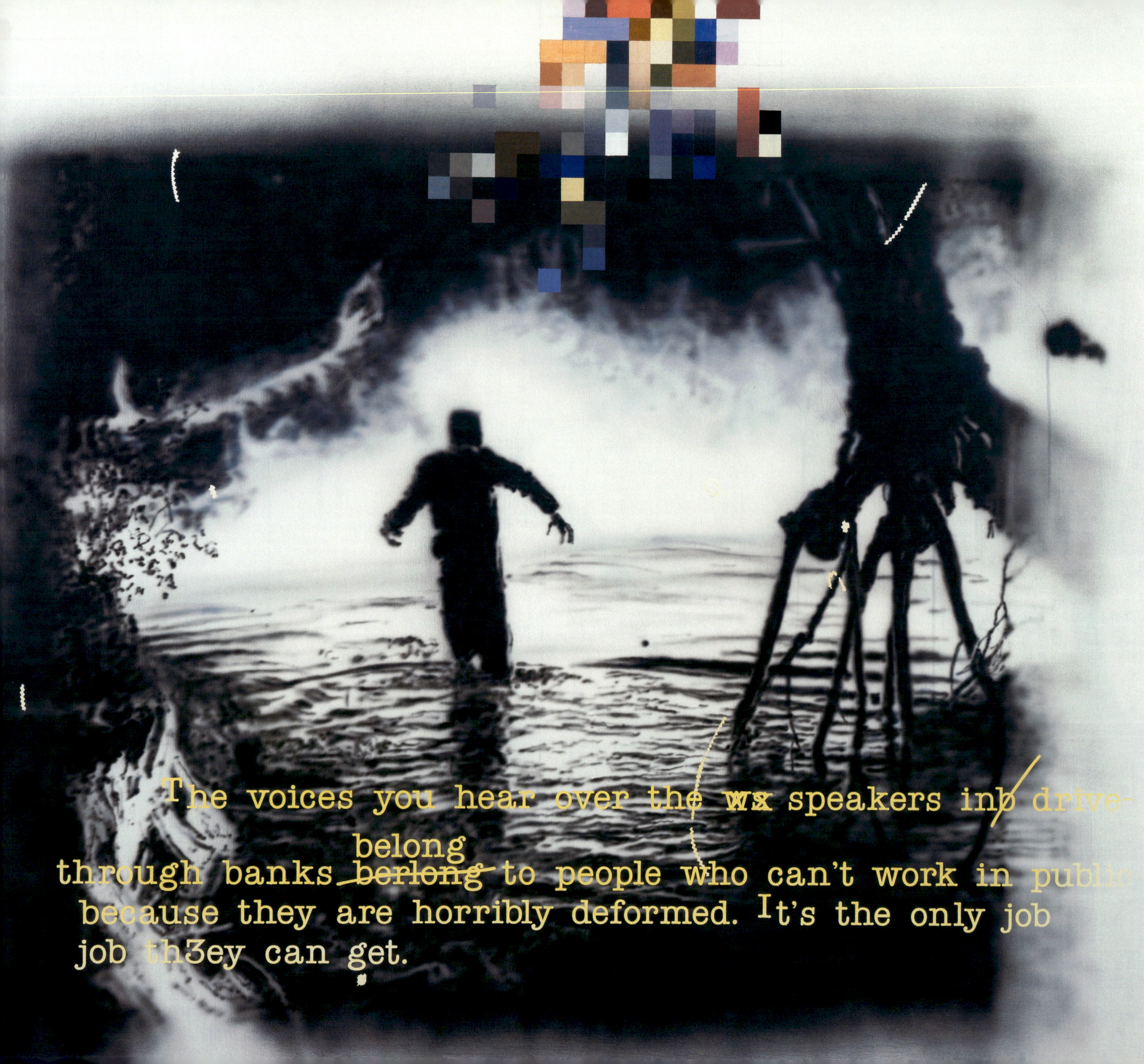
The voices you hear over the wx speakers inb drive-
belong
through banks berlong to people who can't work in public
because they are horribly deformed. It's the only job
job th3ey can get.

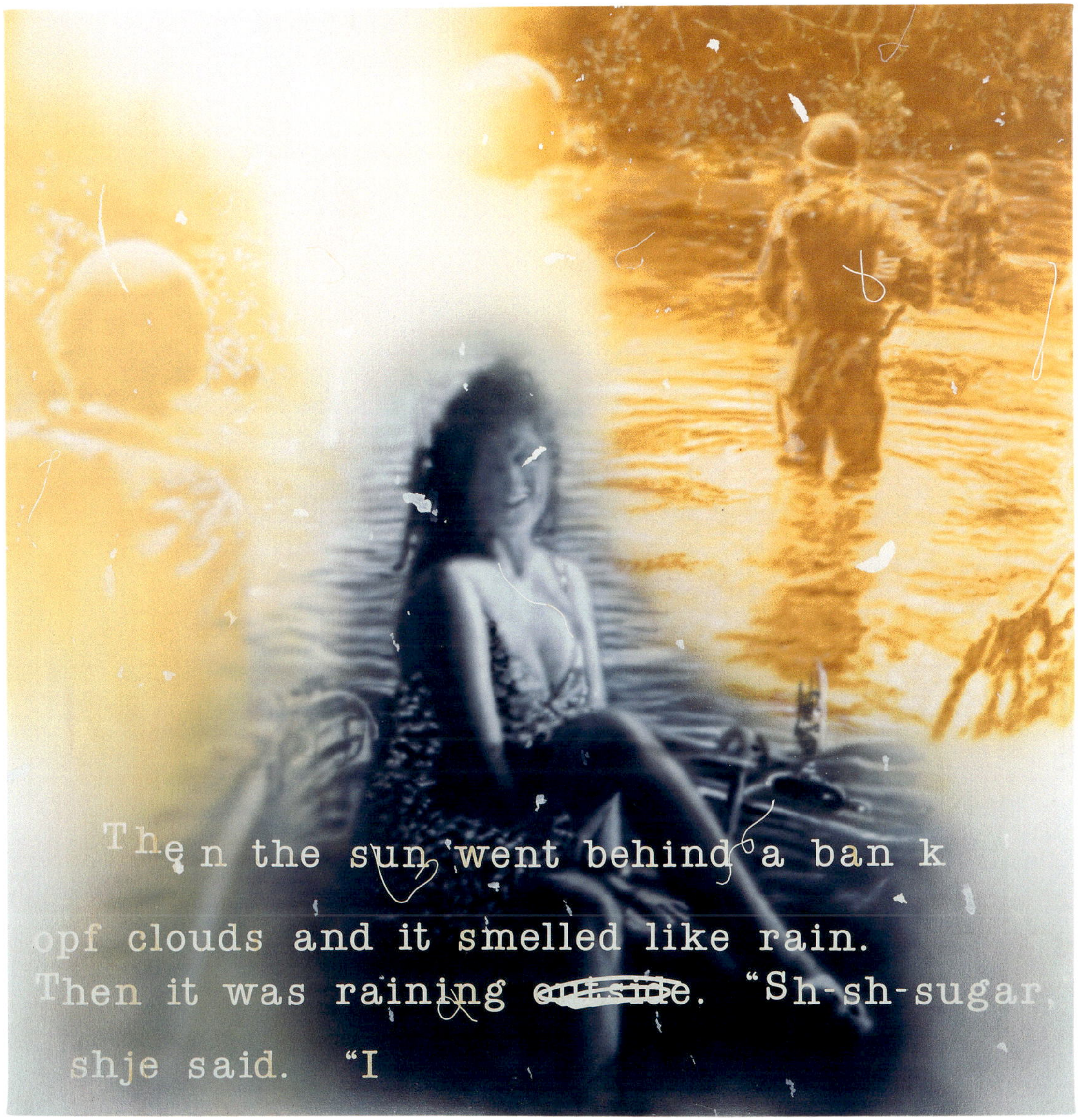

Sh-sh-sugar 2000
Frank 1999

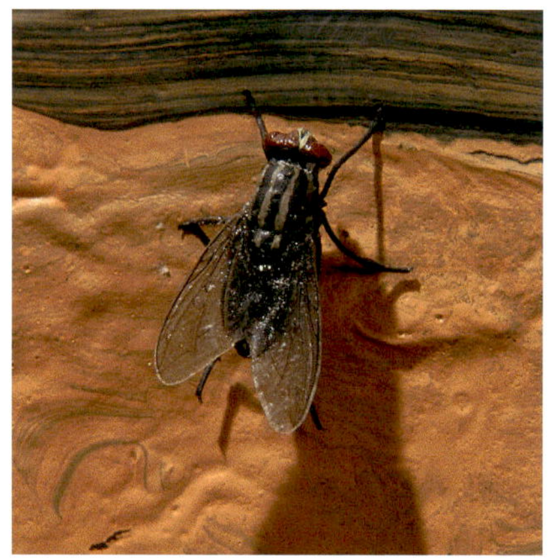

Kinshasa 2000

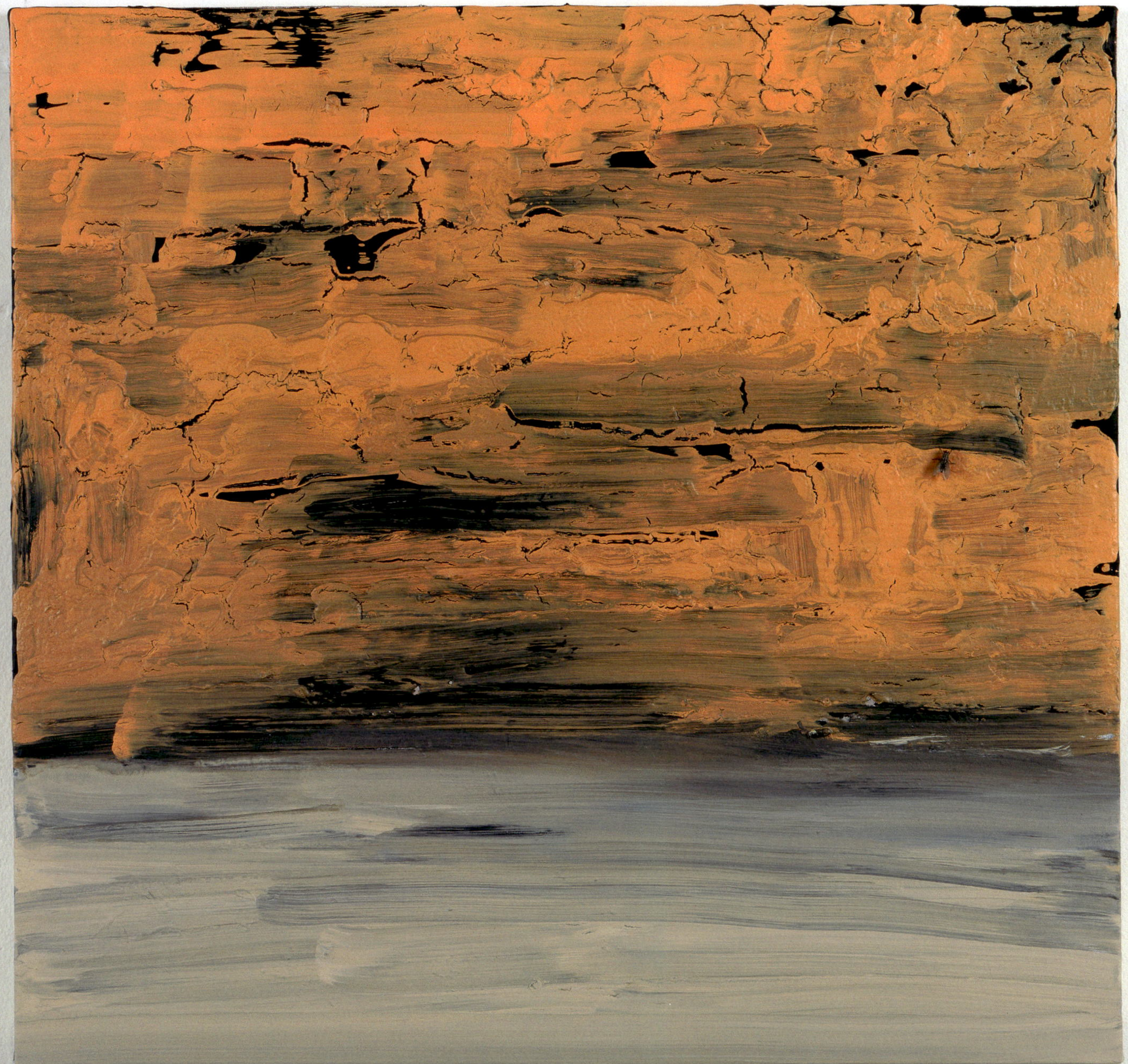

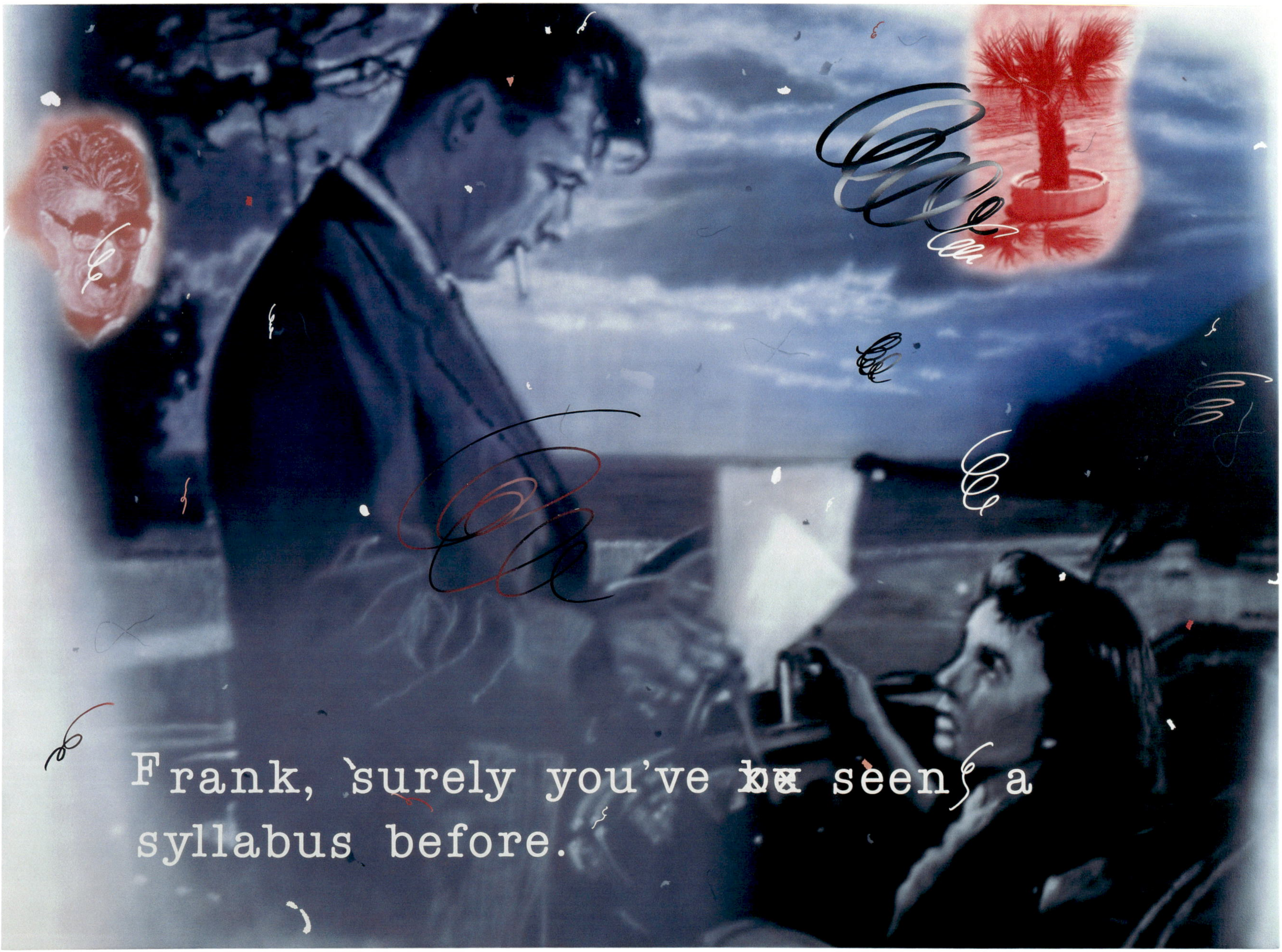
Frank, surely you've seen a
syllabus before.

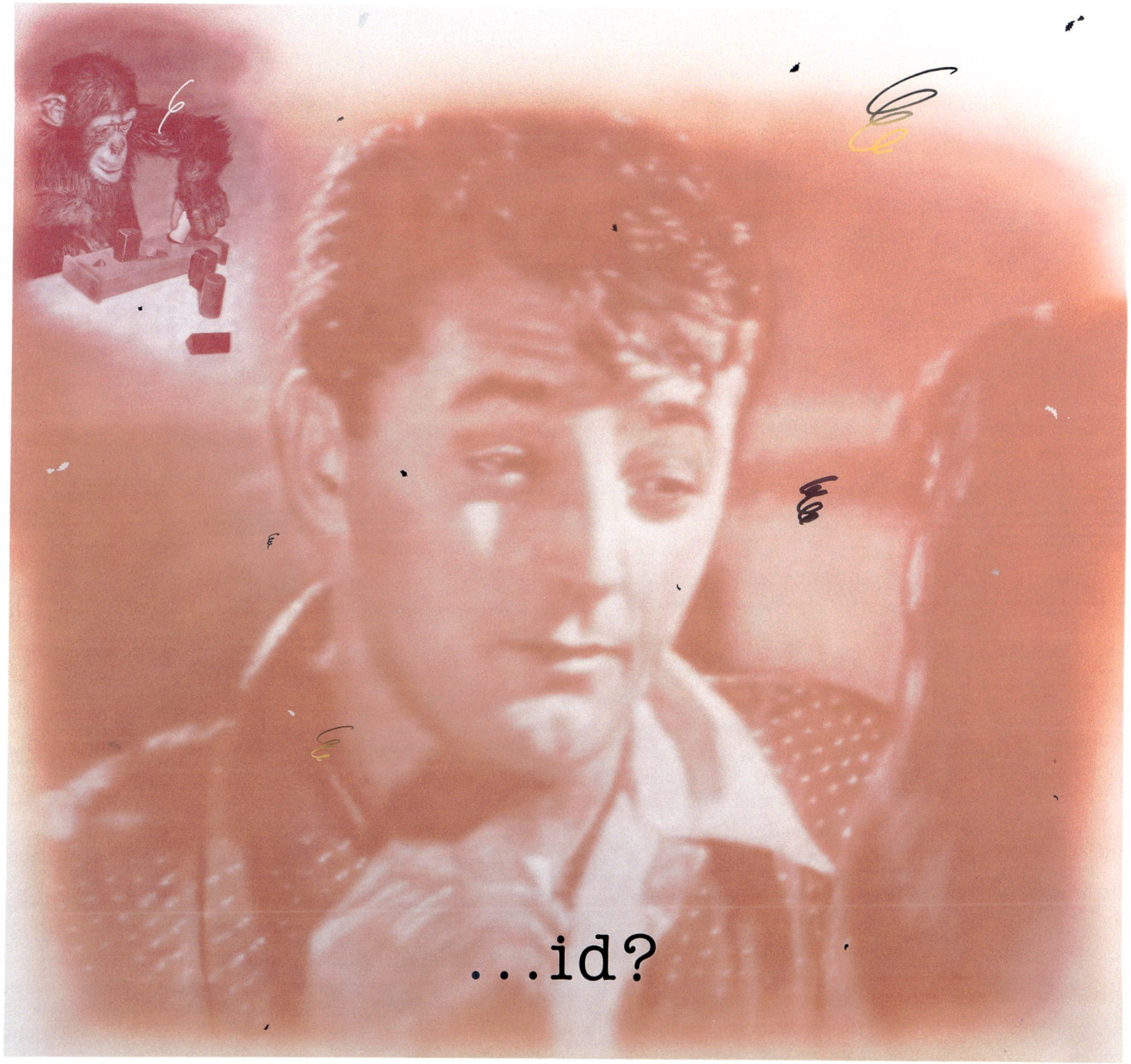

Three-Way Conversation 2000
Syllabus 2000

Scale 2000

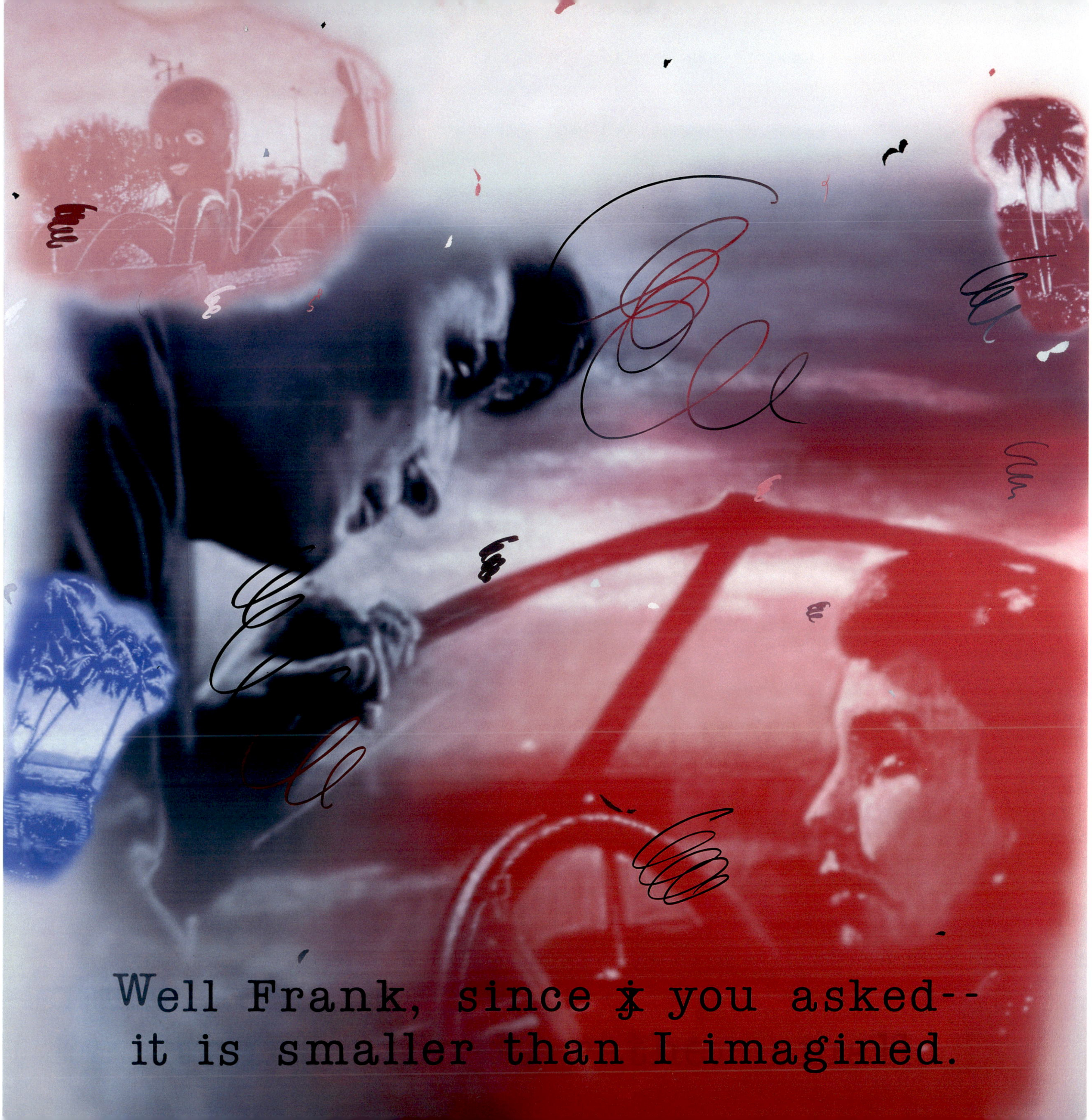
Well Frank, since x you asked--
it is smaller than I imagined.

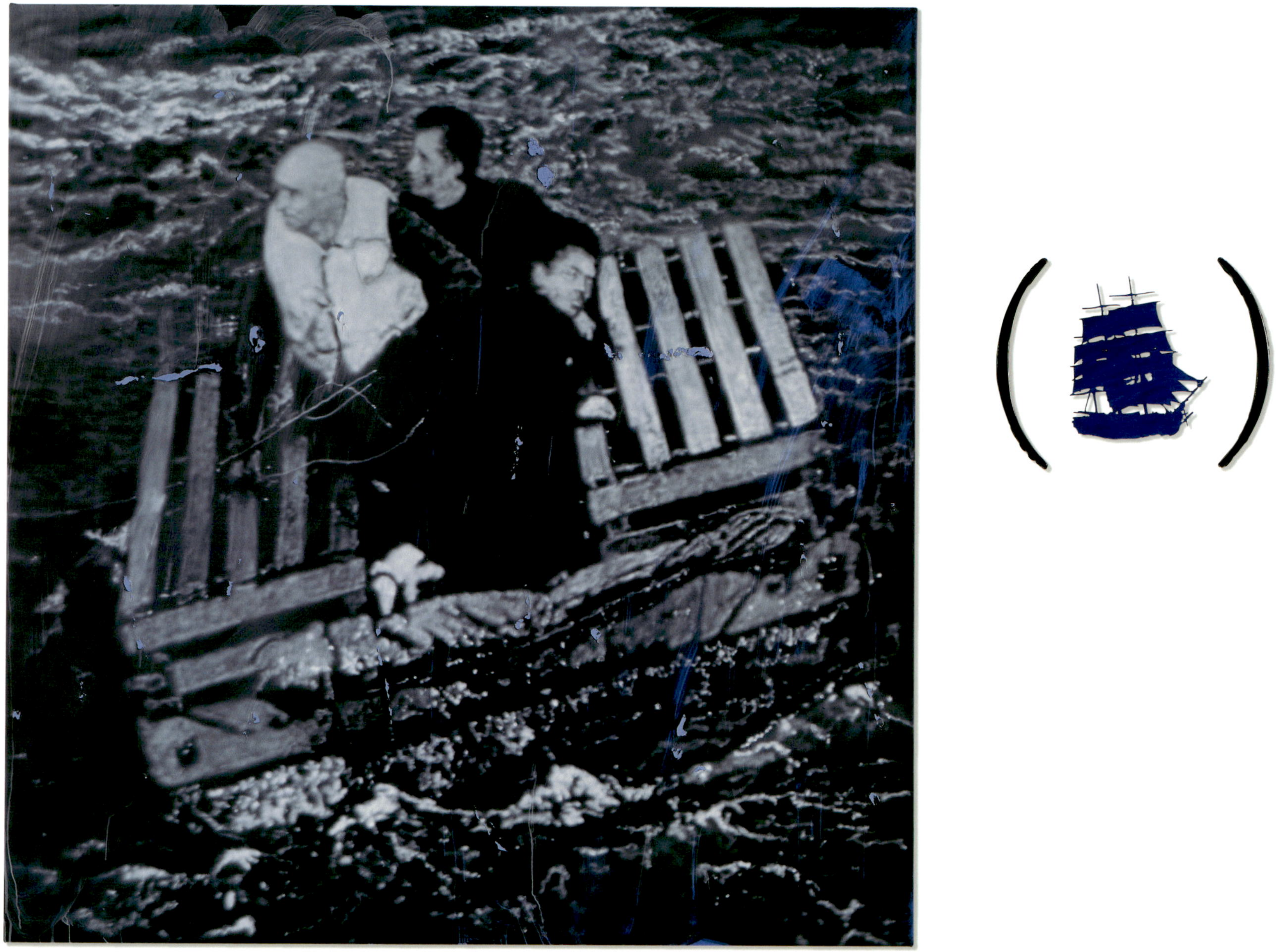

Raft (After Gericault) 2002

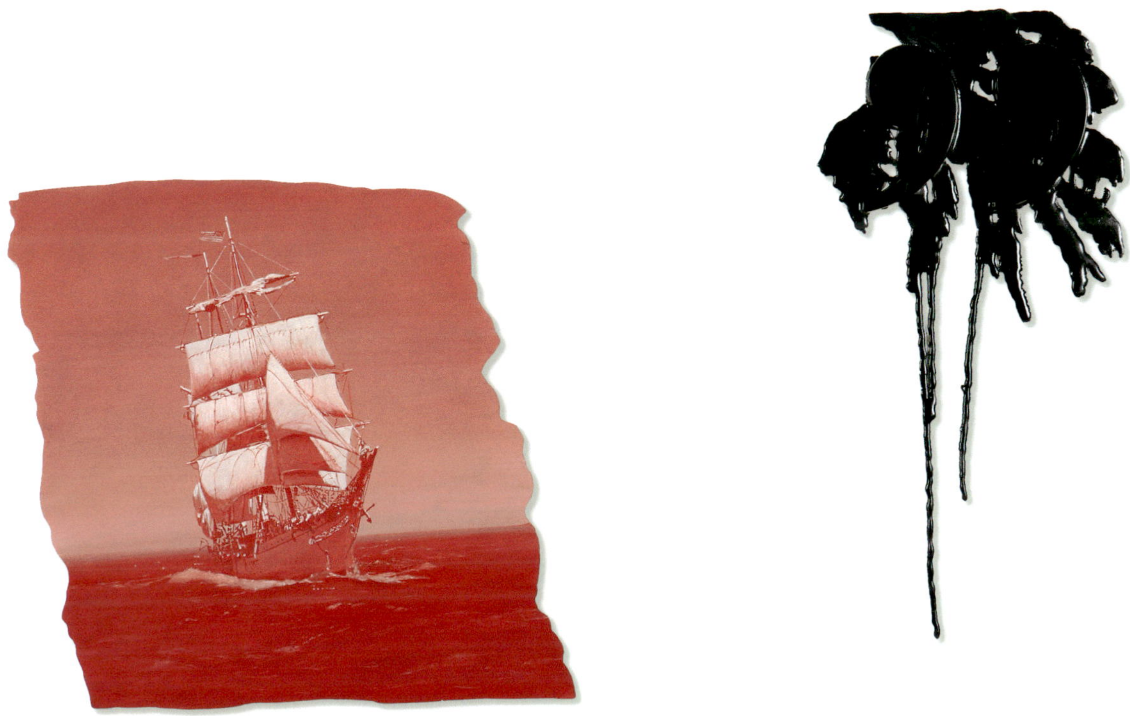

Seascape 2002

Parrot 2002

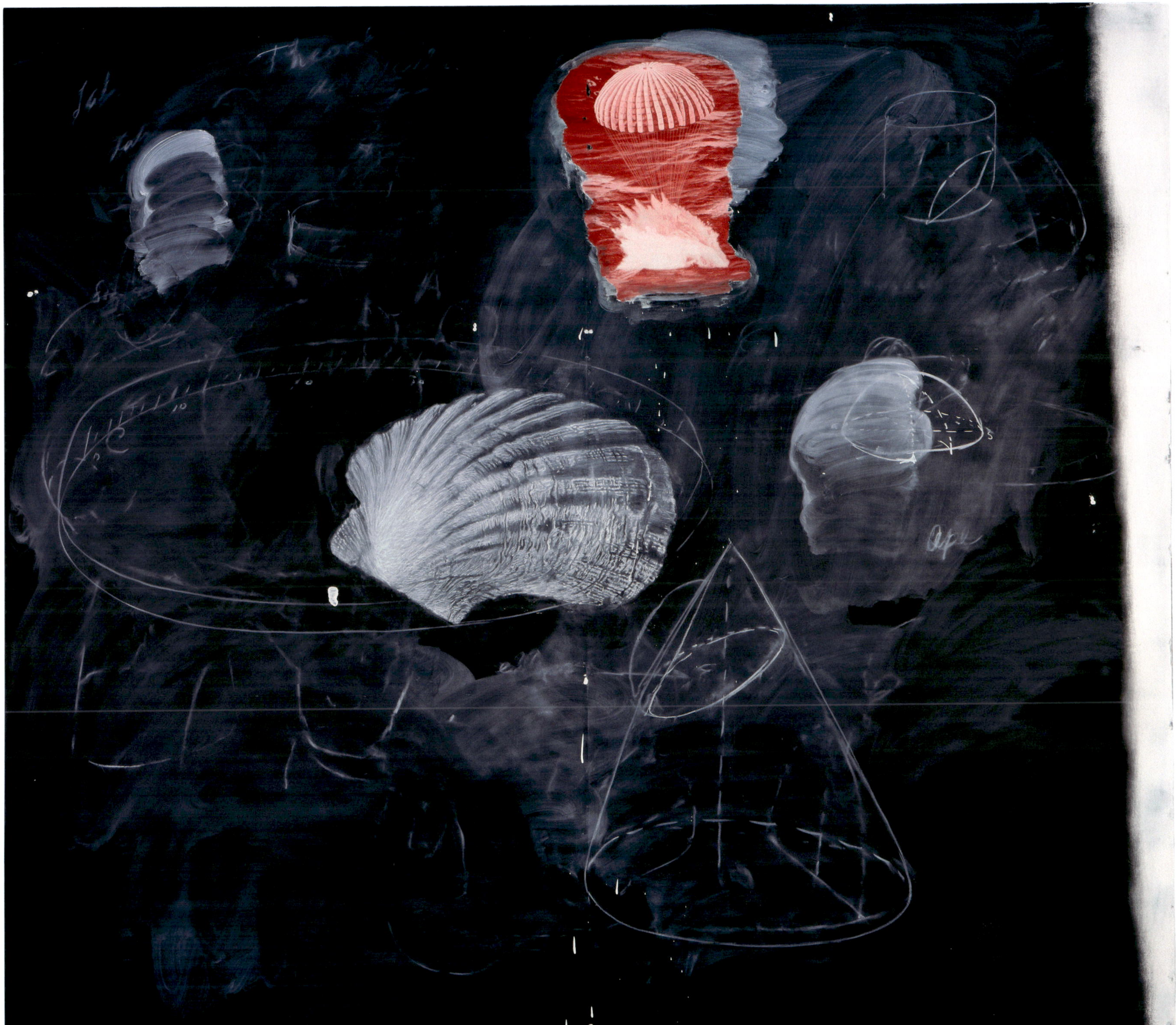

Fold 2002

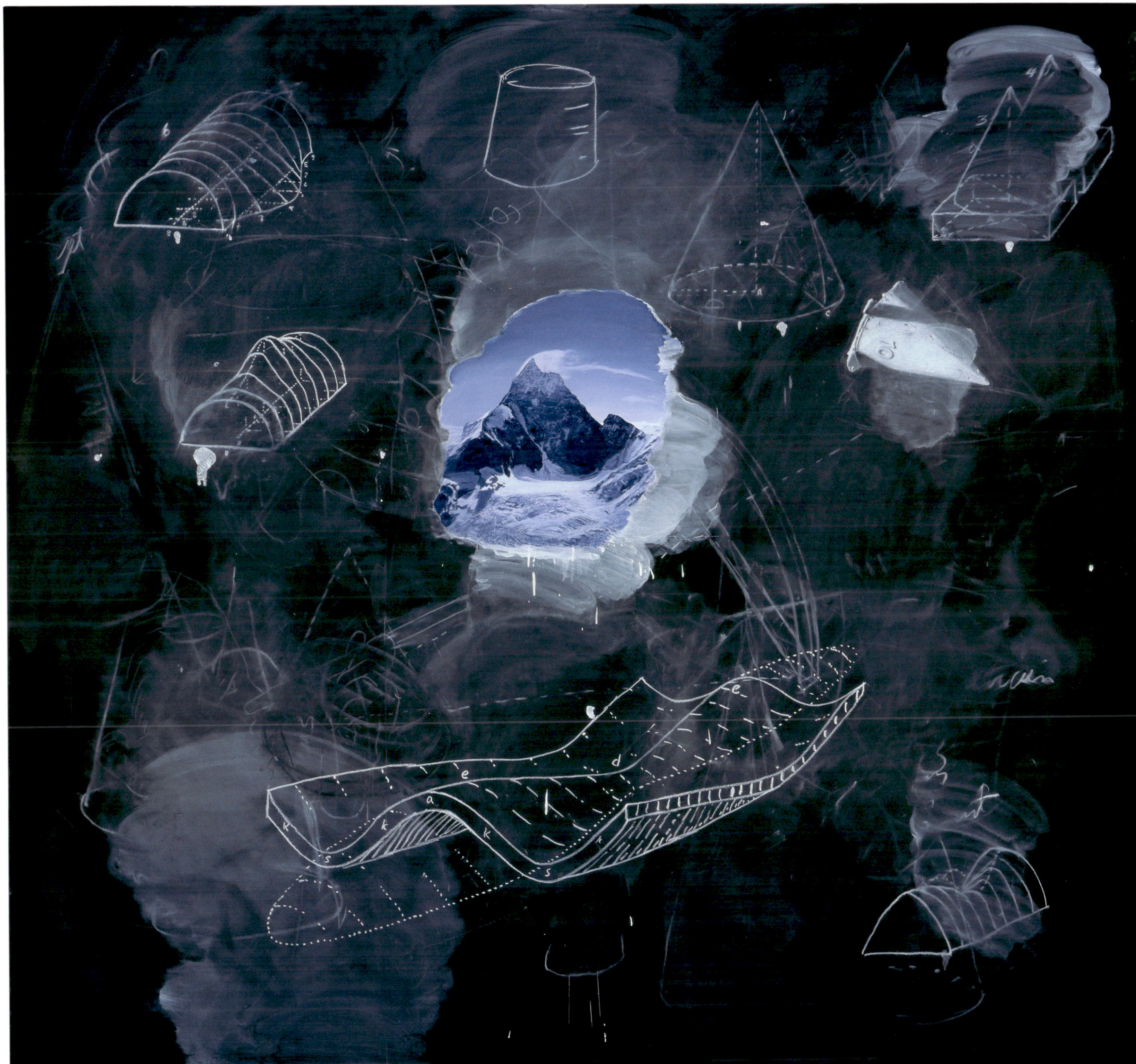

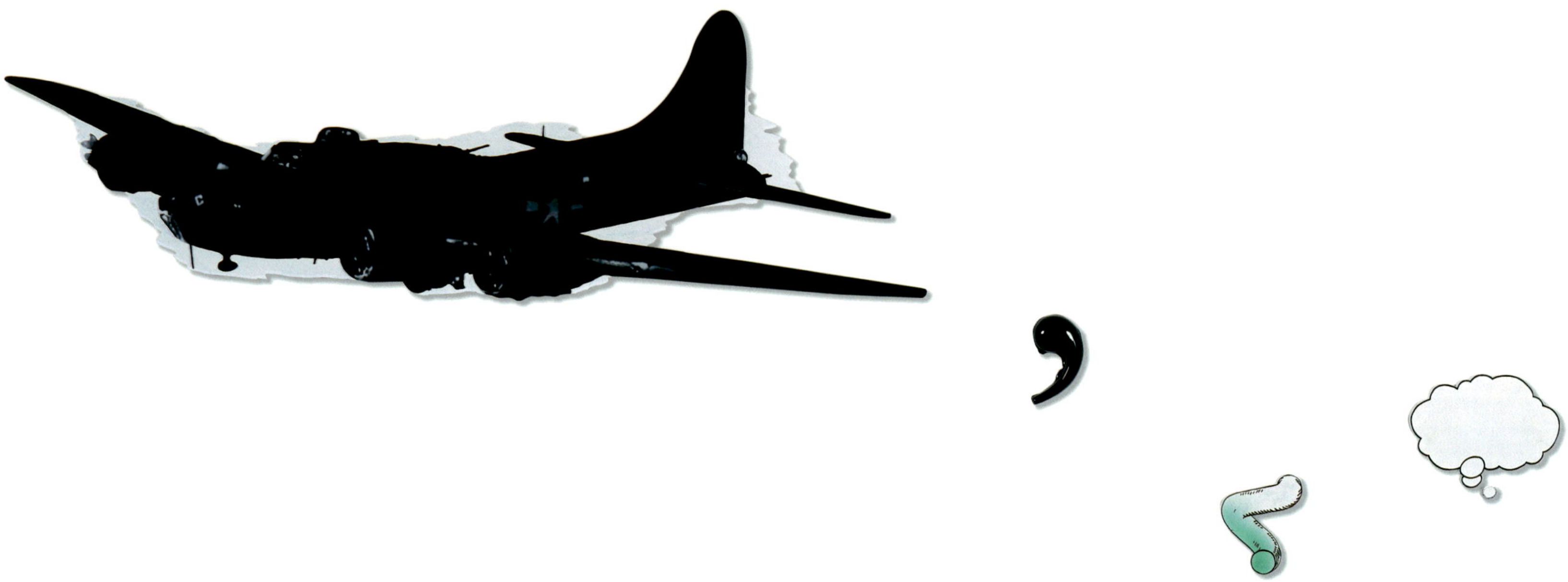

Subject Trailing Debris 2003

B R A I N I A C

Dunn and Brown Contemporary, Dallas, Texas
October 11–November 15, 2003

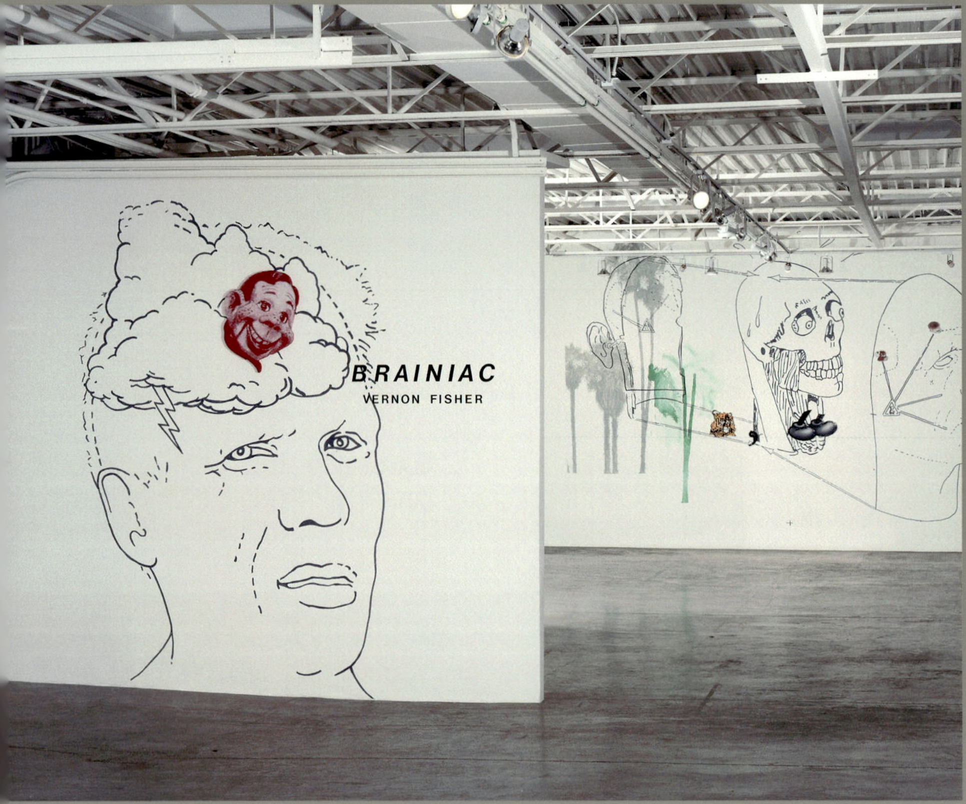

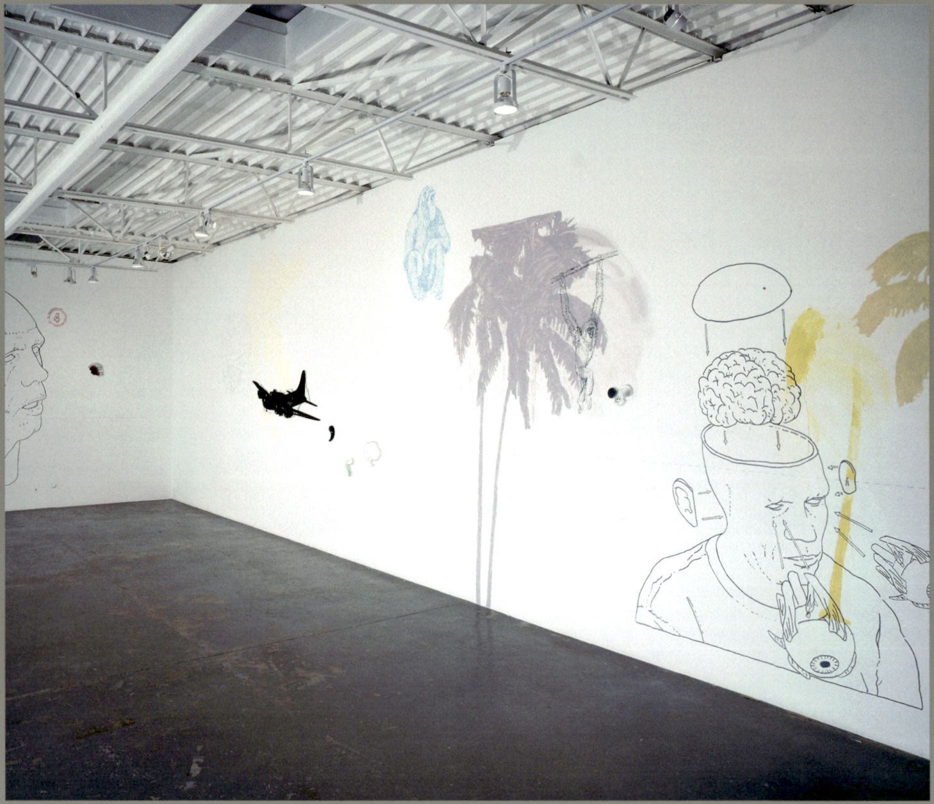

Installation views

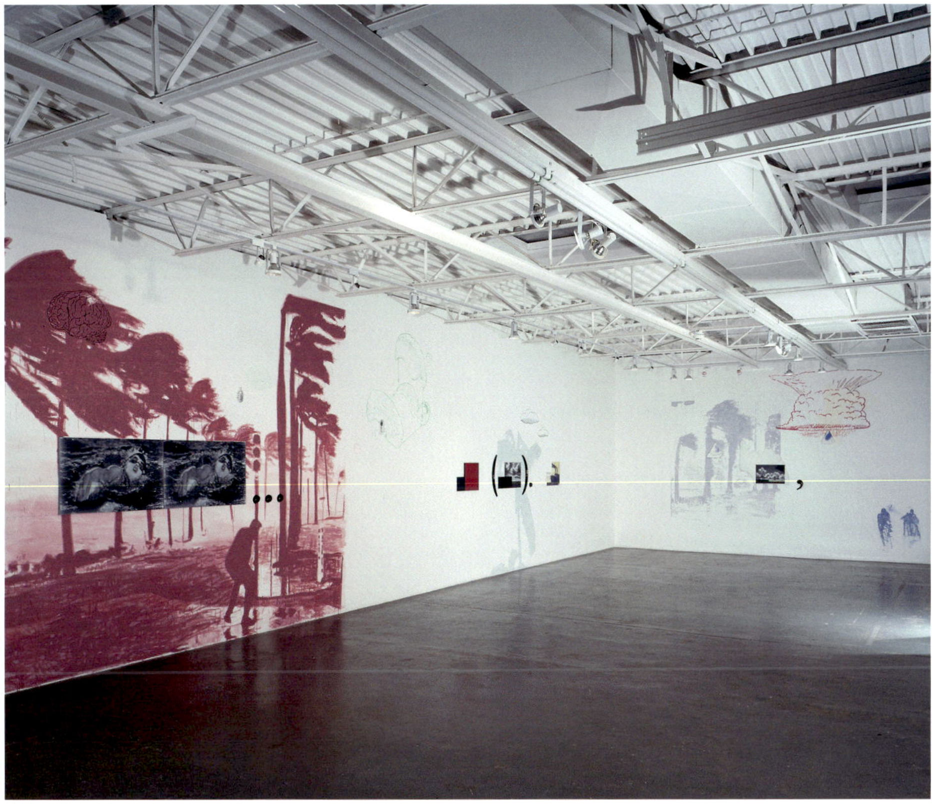

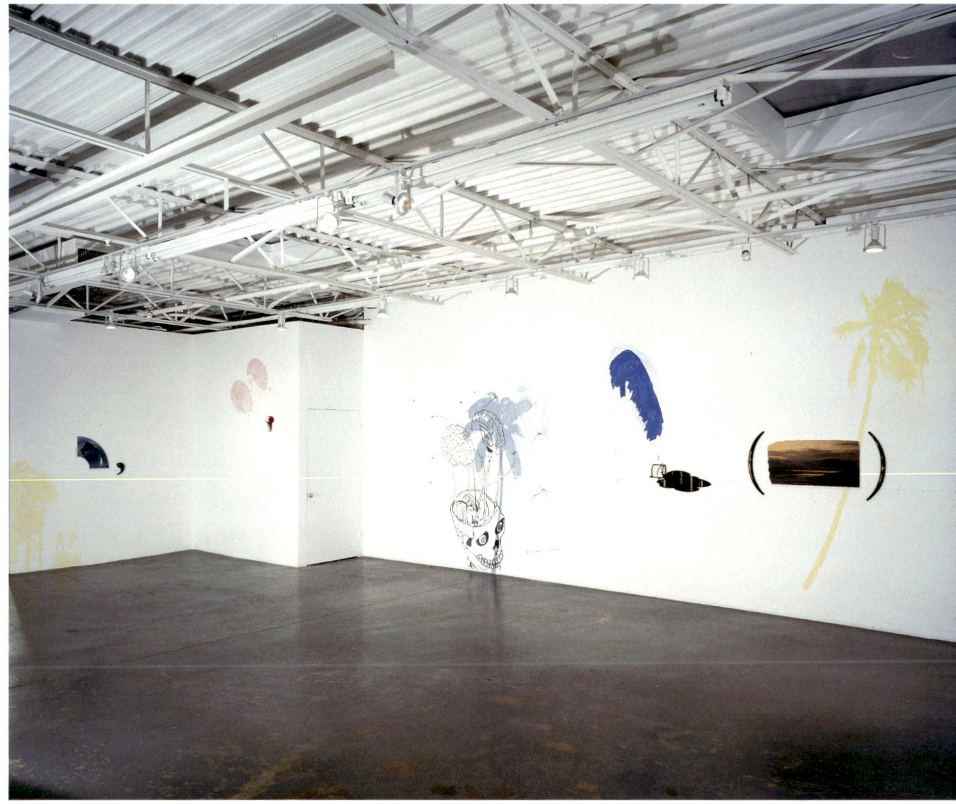

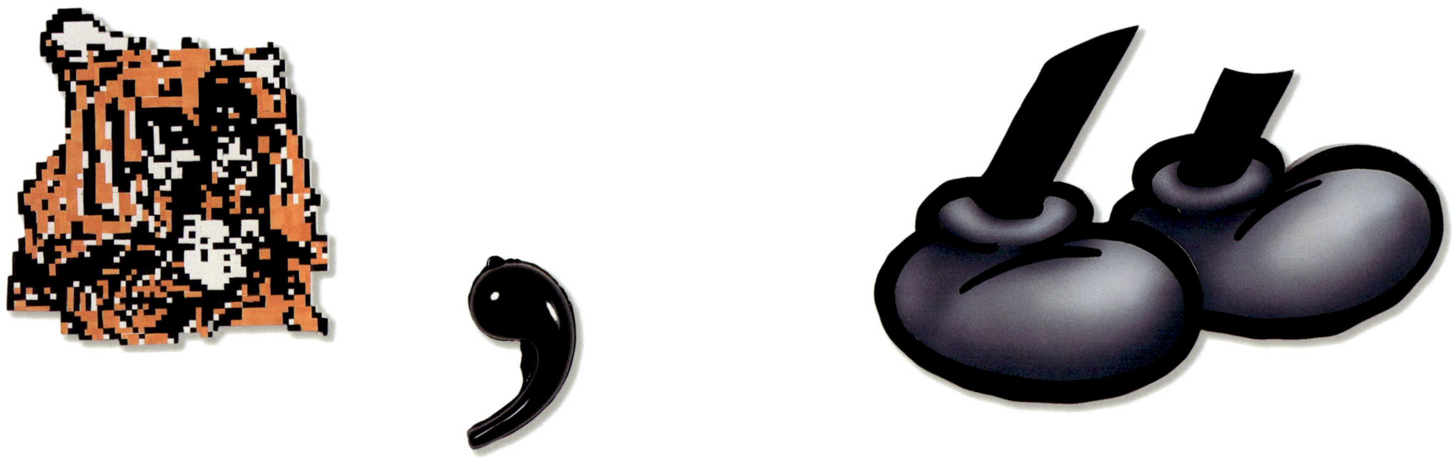

Cat, Mouse 2003

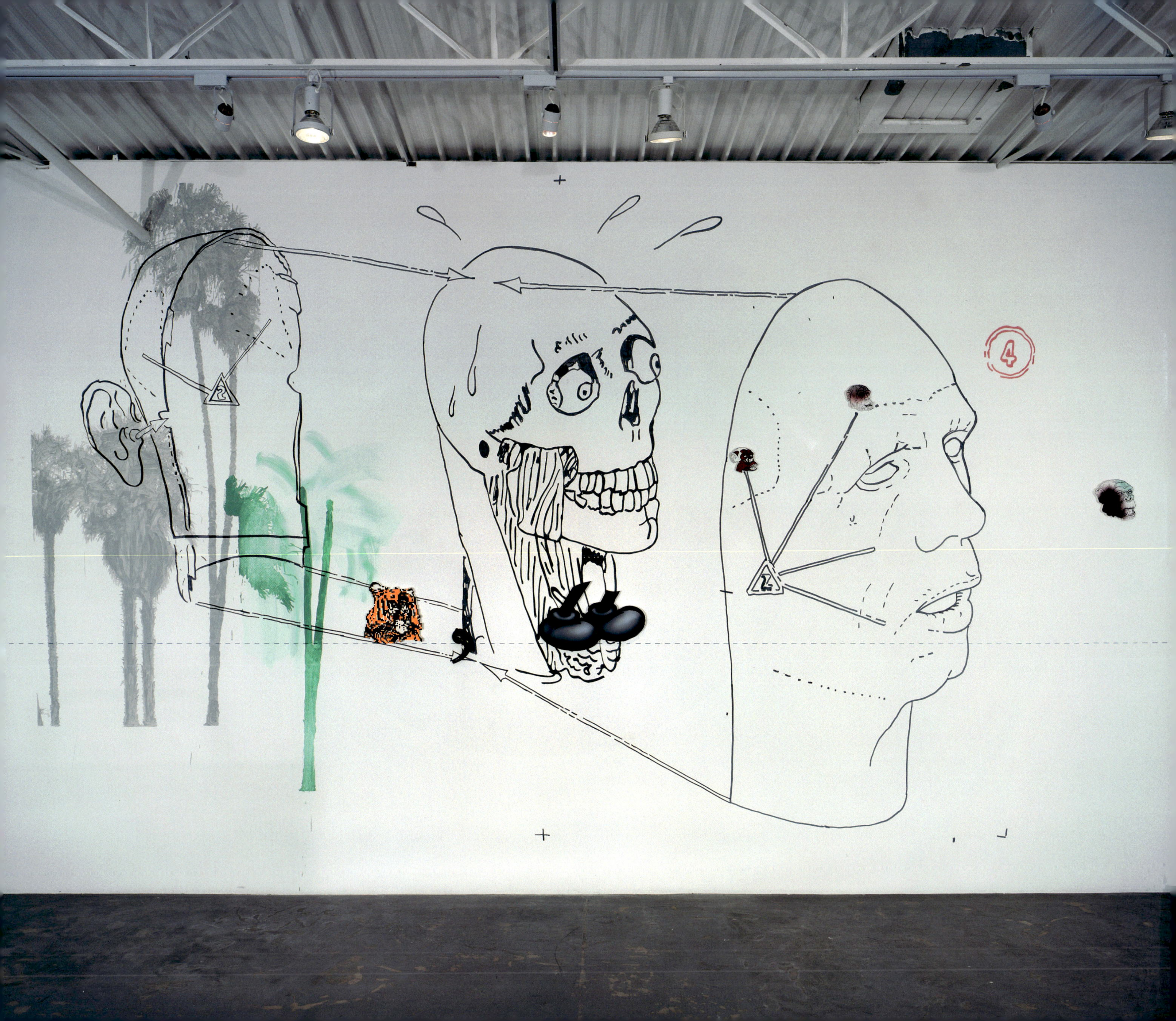

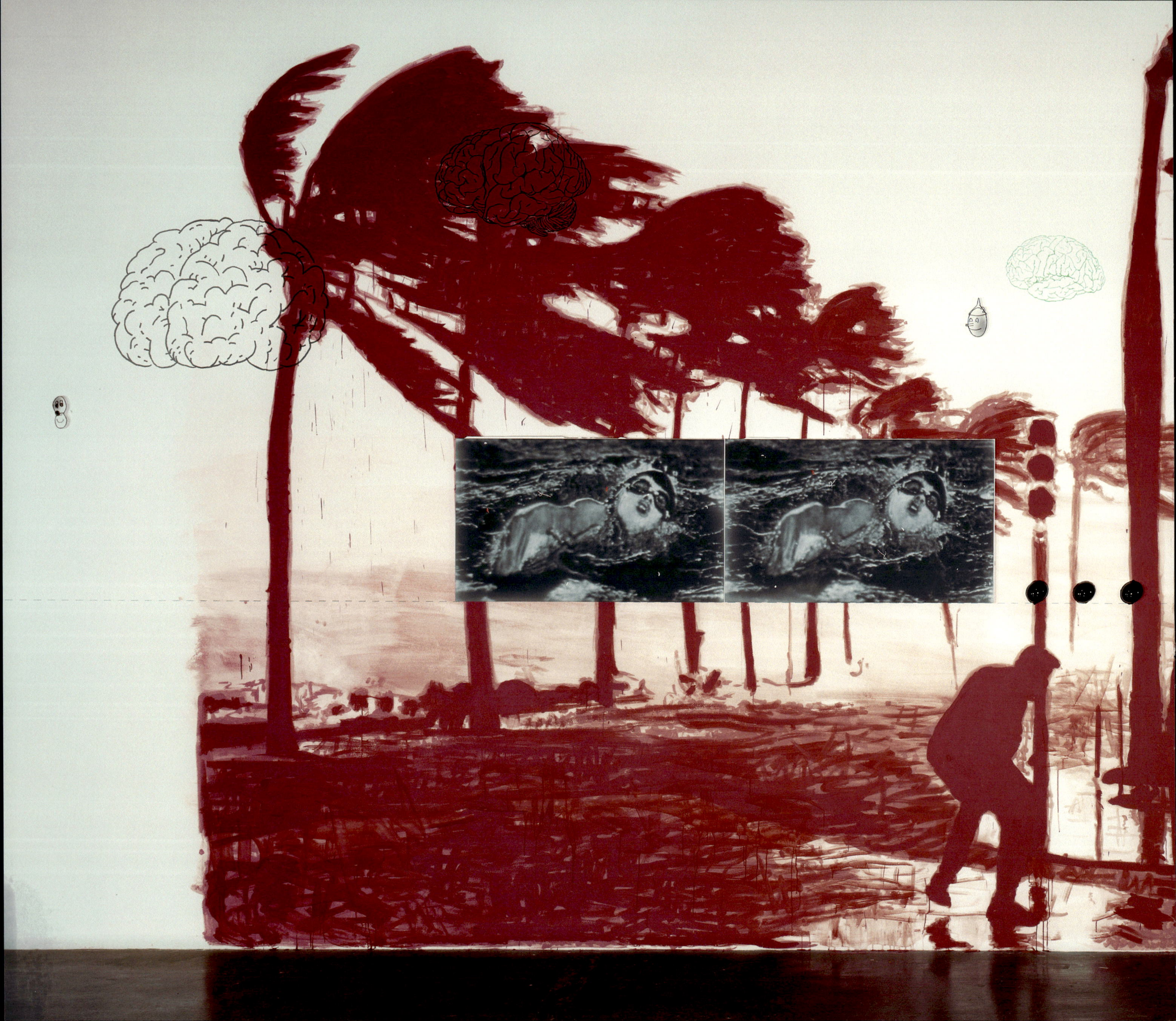

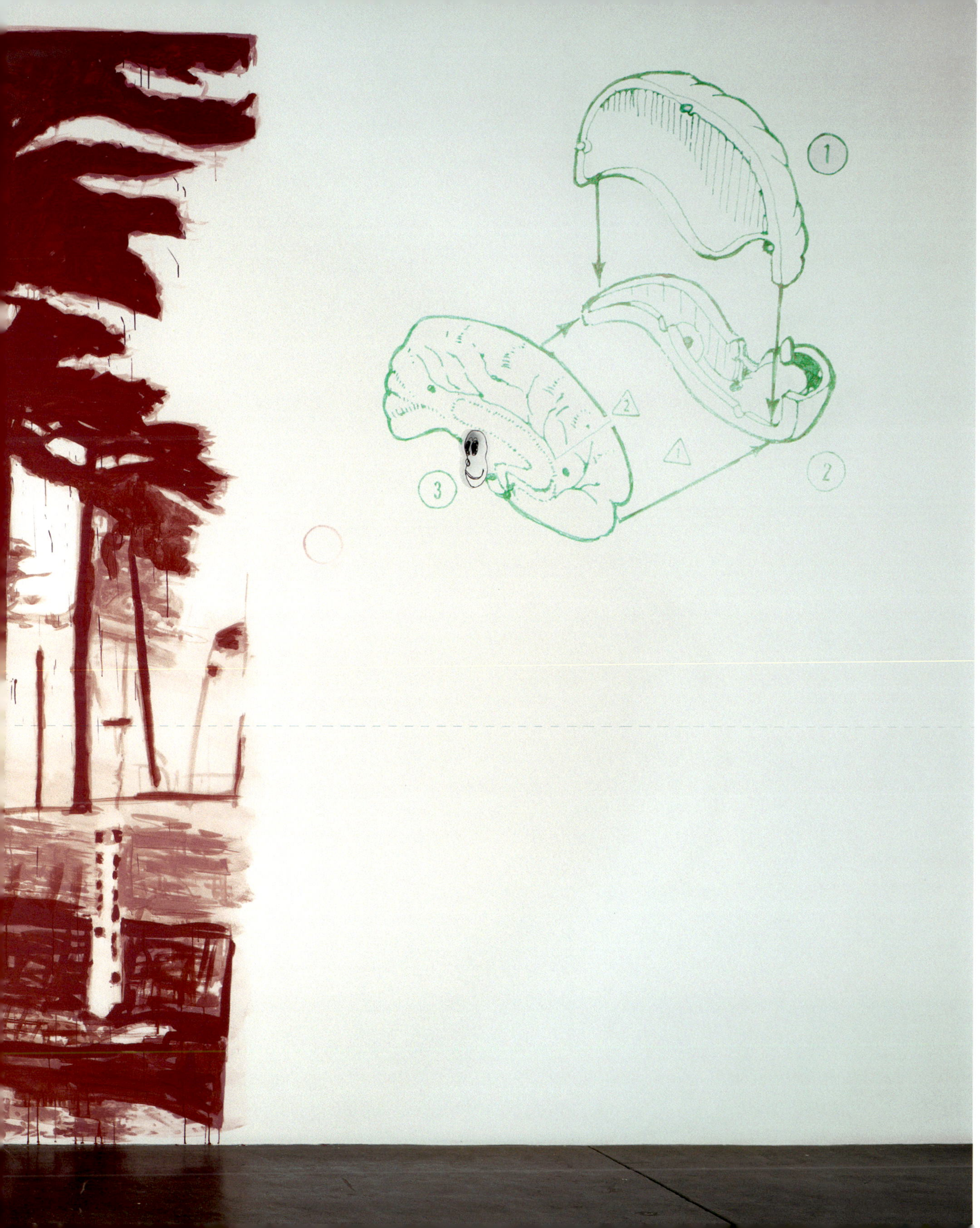

Double Swimmer . . . 2003

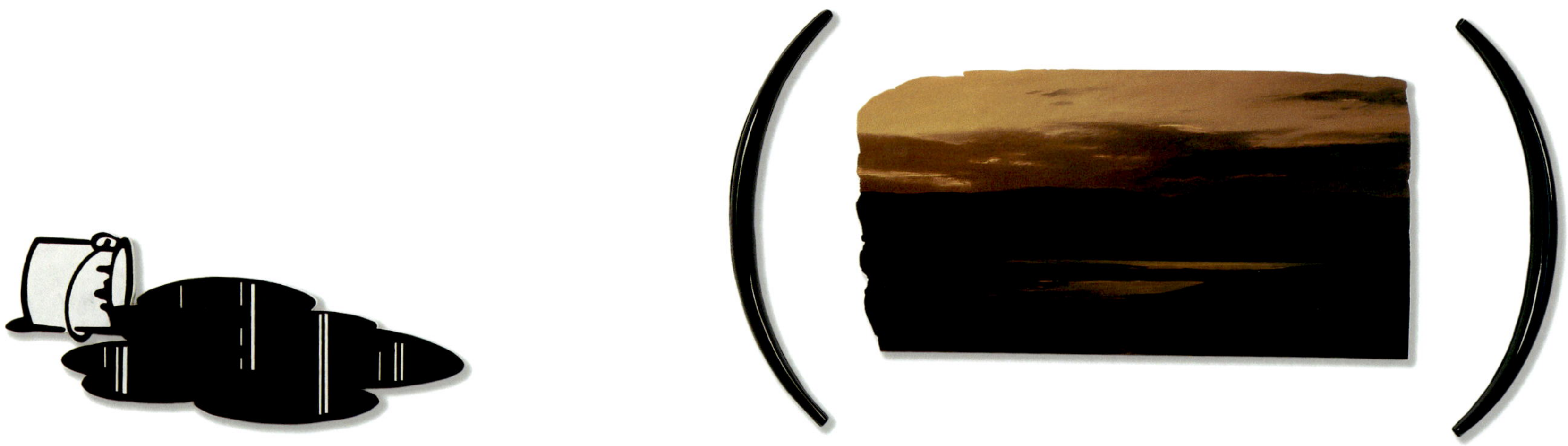

The Death of Marat 2003

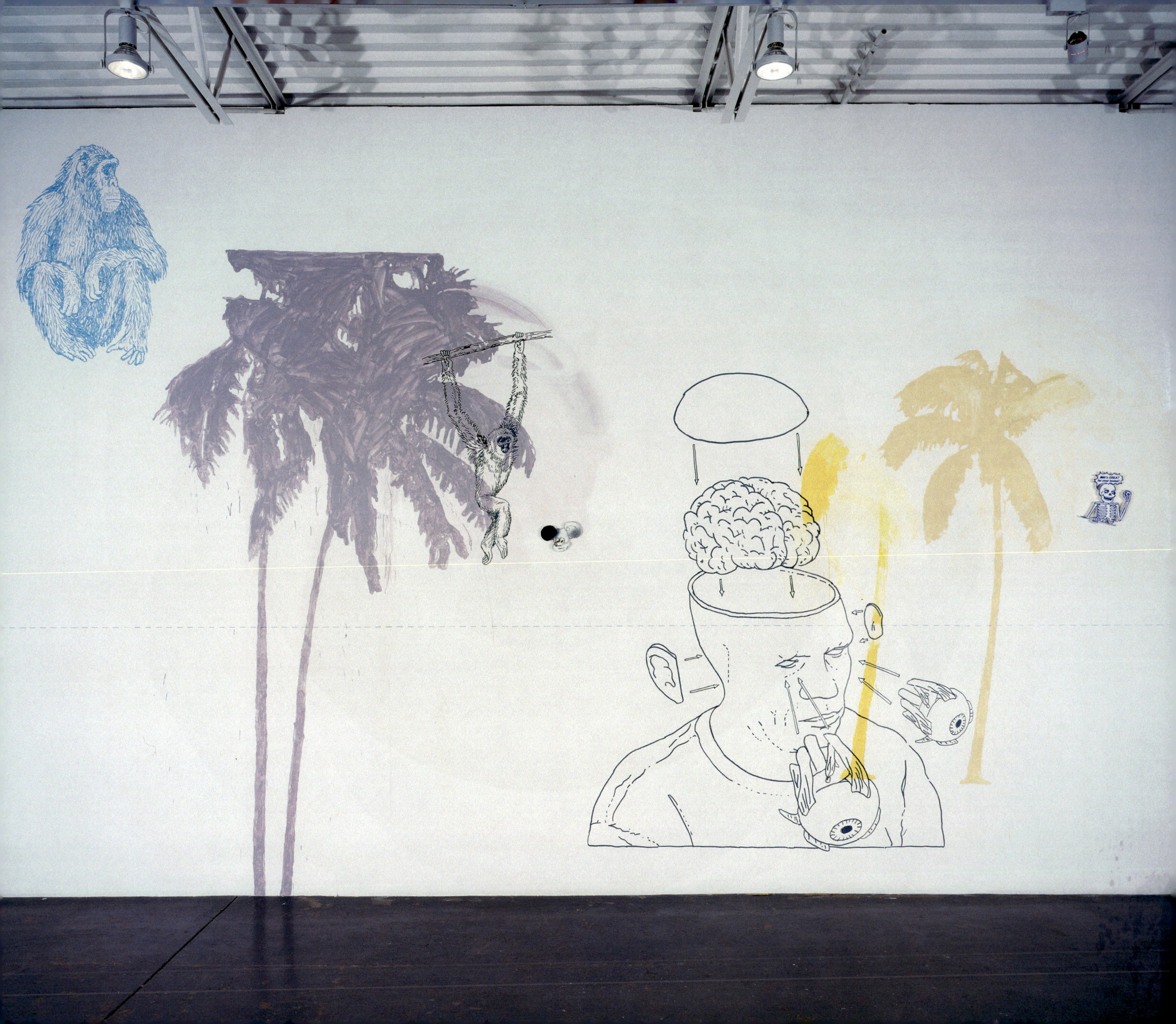

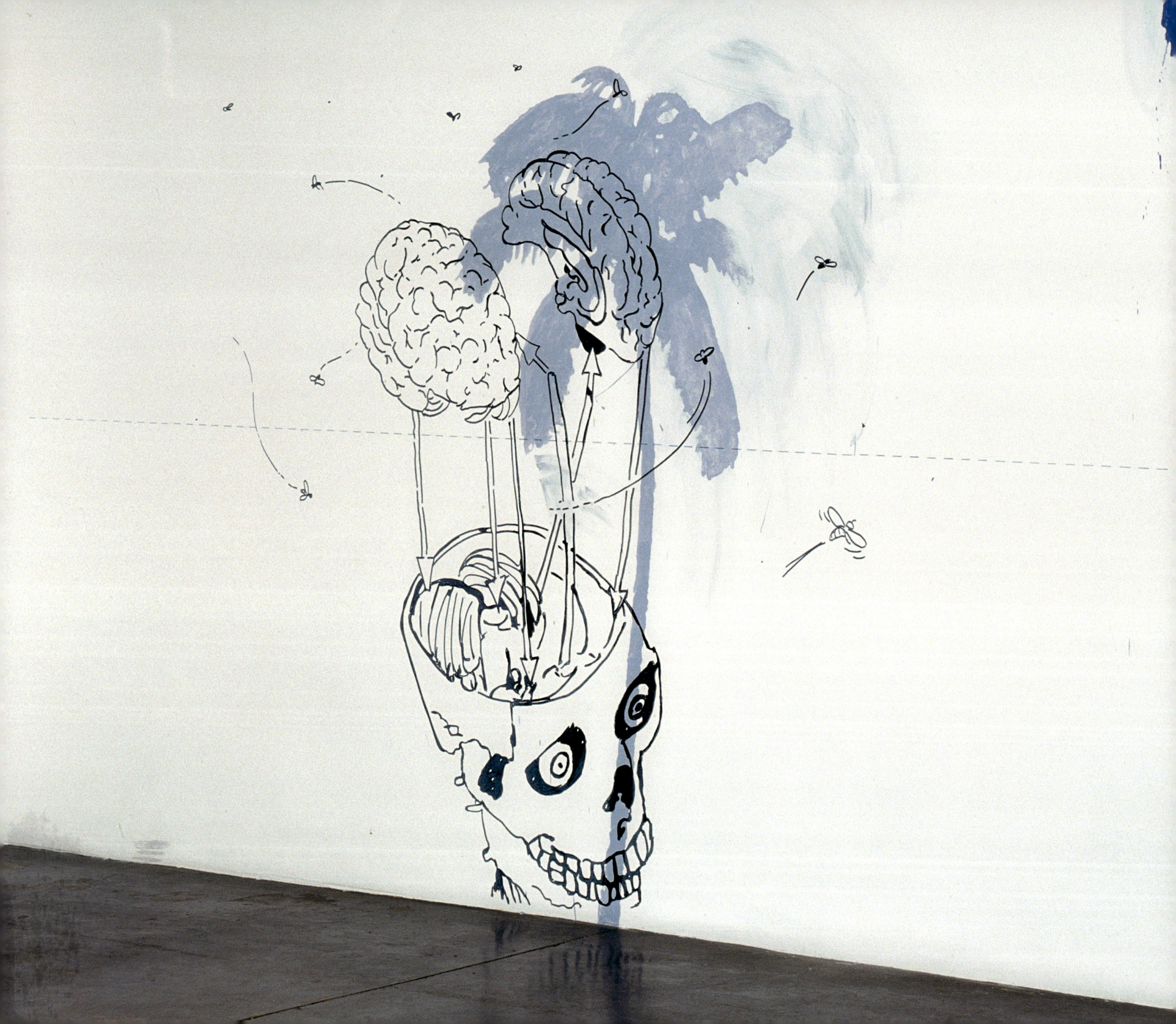

Exploded View Tropics 2003

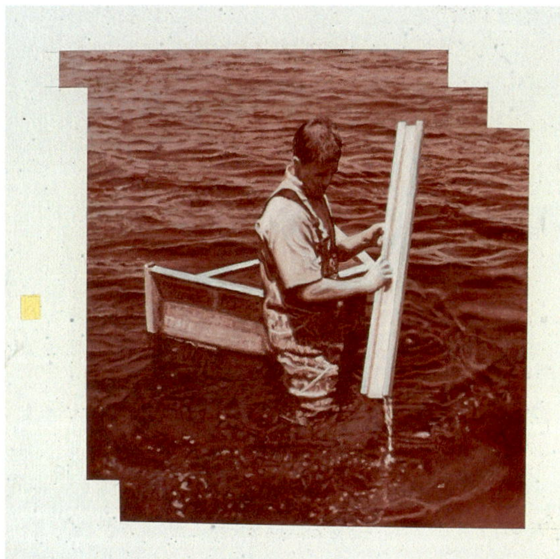

Dead 2005

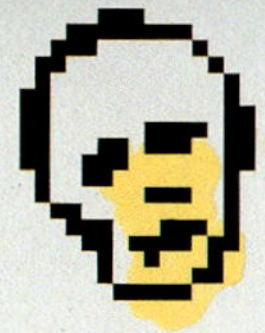

dead (ded), *adj.*, [ME. *deed*, fr. OE *dead*; akin to ON *dauthr* dead, *deyja* to die, OHG *tot* dead 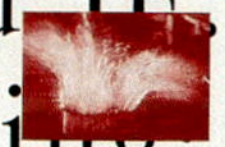 IE. base **dheu-*, to become senseless] **1.** no longer living, 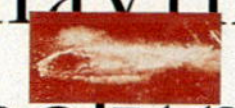 having died. **2.** extinguished: grown cold. **3.** numb: lacking feeling, warmth. **4.** obsolete: *dead* language. **5.** motionless: *dead* 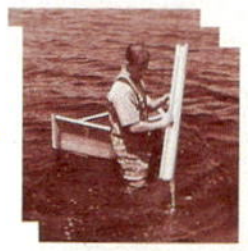 in the water. **6.** inelastic: *dead* tennis ball. **7.** not operating: *dead* microphone. **8.** uncharged: *dead* wire. **9.** [Colloq.], very tired, exhausted. **10.** death as a foregone conclusion: *dead* duck. **11.** unequivocally: *dead* as a doornail. **12.** iconic: cartoon cat with pluses for eyes. **13.** euphemistic: decea 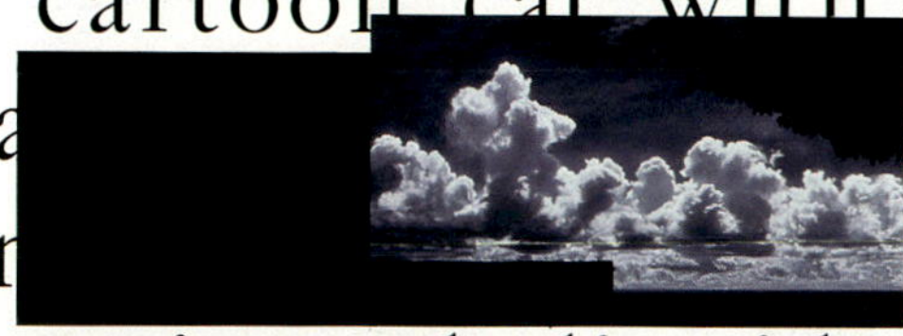 sed away. **14.** jocular: croaked, cashed in d the bucket, bought the farm. **15.** assassinated, liquidated, terminated. **16.** asphyxiated, butchered, crushed, drowned, electrocuted, 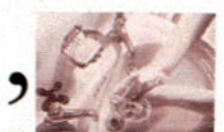 immolated, poisoned, shot, stabbed, strangled. **17.** the ball turret gunner is dead. **18.** poor Michael Furey is dead. **19.** "Mistah Kurtz—he dead." **20.** Butterfly is dead and Bambi's Mom is dead. **21.** Janis and Jimi are dead. **22.** Jim, in Paris, is dead. **23.** and Jerry, gratefully, is among the dead. **24.** oh Marvin, Marvin, Marvin. **25.** bang.

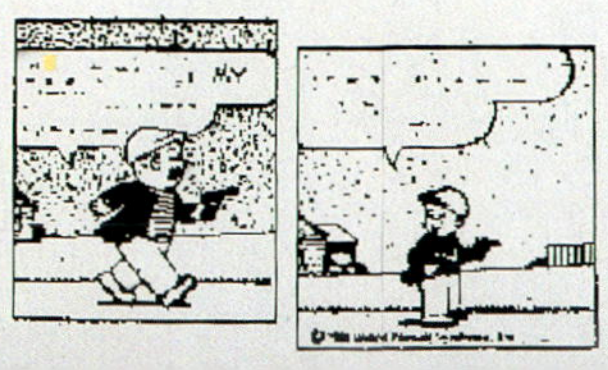

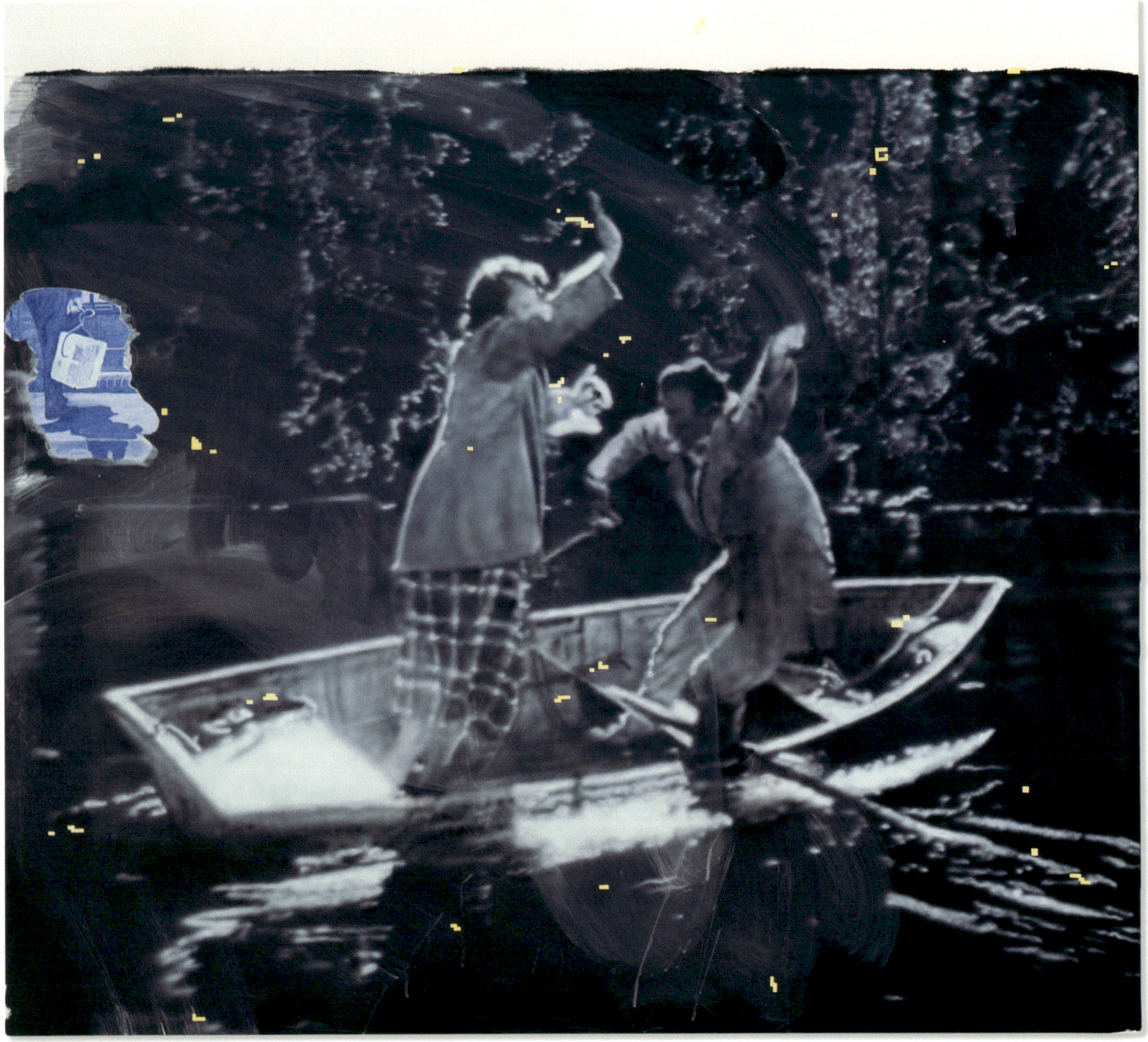

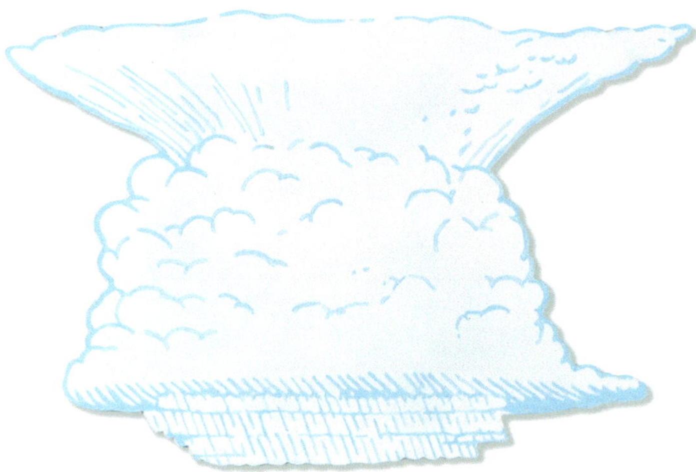

American Tragedy 2005

The Single-State Assumption 2005

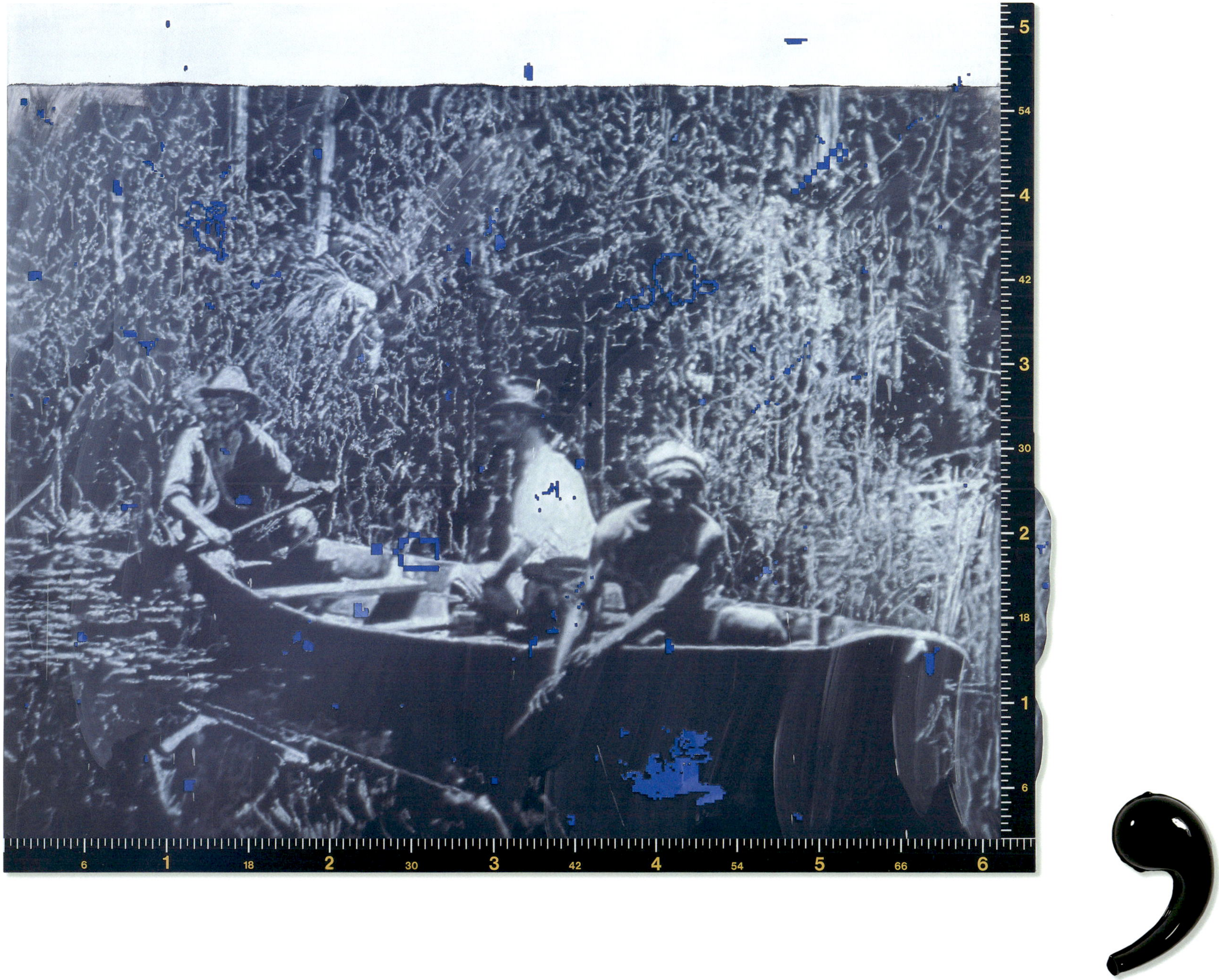

The Raw & the Cooked 2006

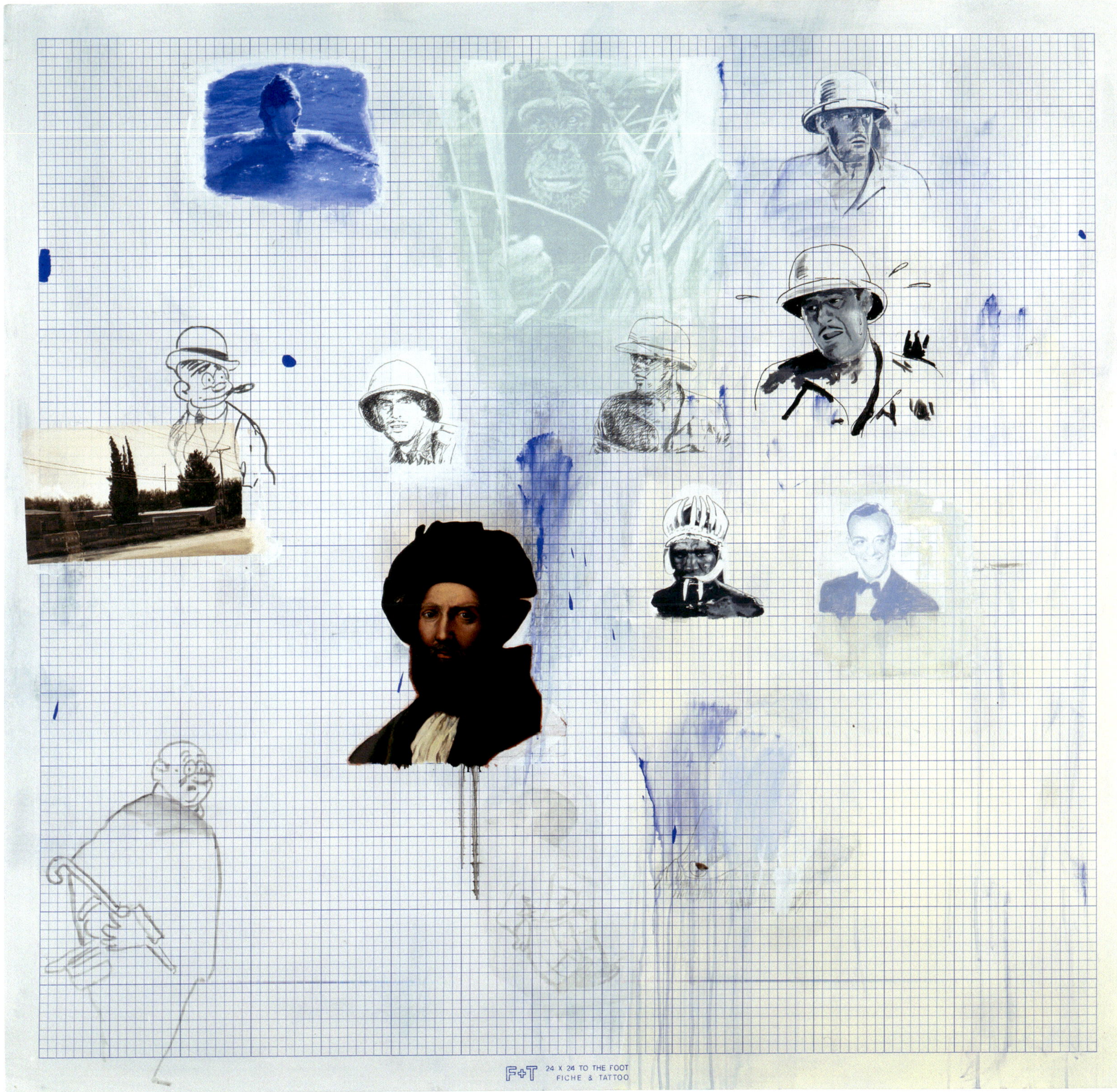
F+T
24 X 24 TO THE FOOT
FICHE & TATTOO

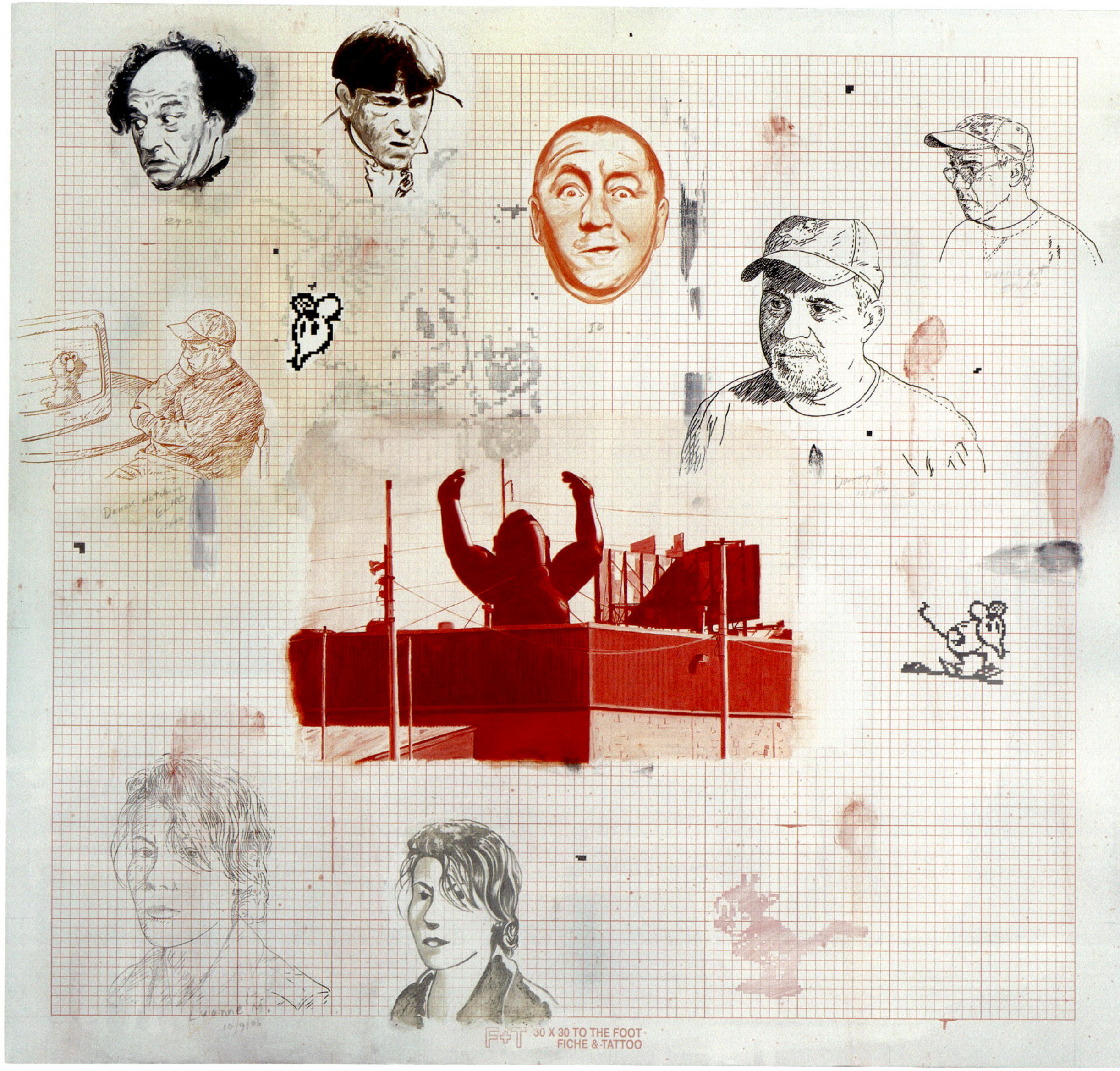

Persona Non-Persona 2006 ▲
Out of Africa 2007 ▶

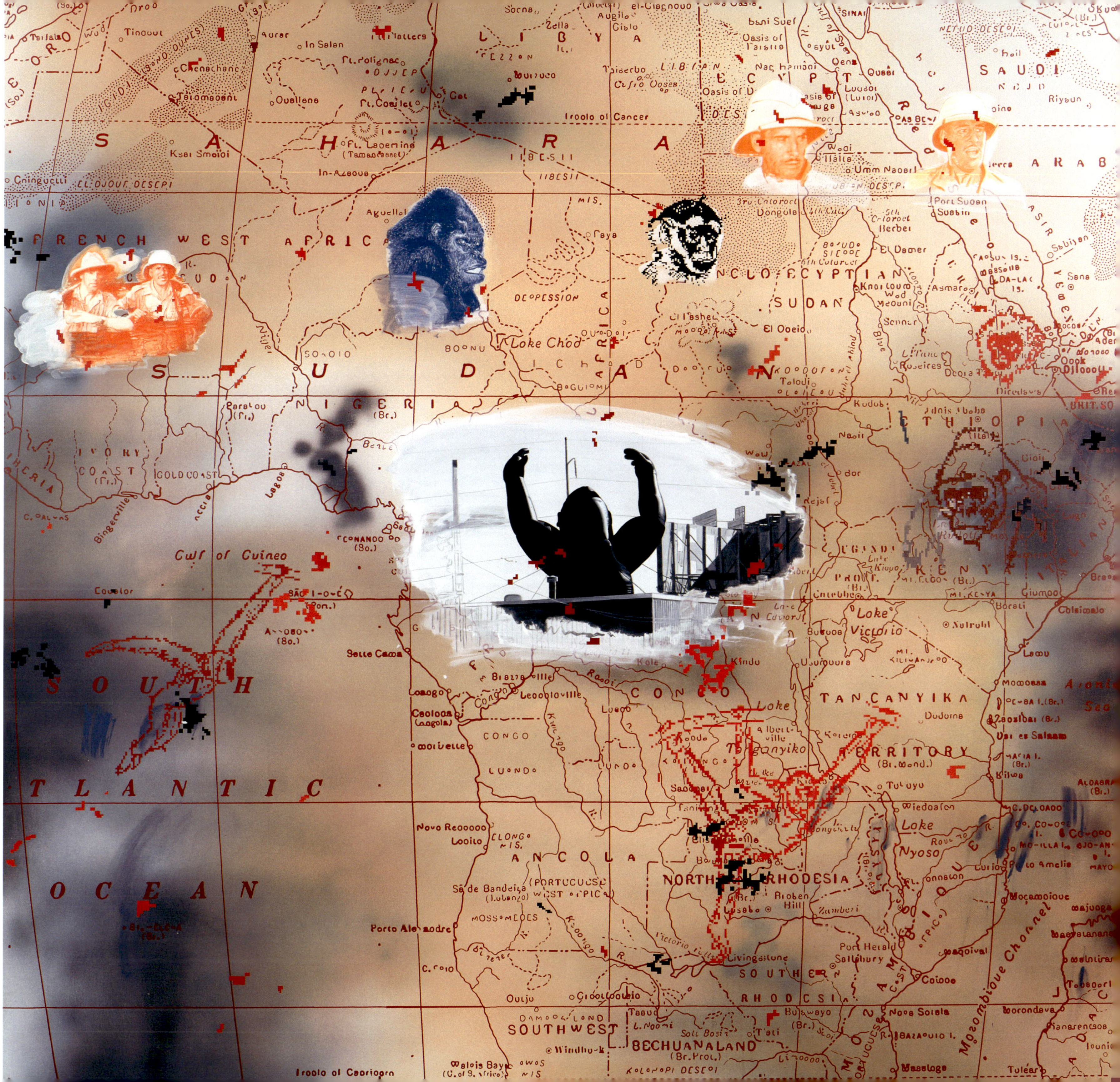
S A H A R A
FRENCH WEST AFRICA
S U D A N
NIGERIA
Loke Chod
SUDAN
ETHIOPIA
UGANDA
KENYA
Loke Victorio
CONGO
TANGANYIKA
TERRITORY
Loke Tonganyiko
ANGOLA
NORTHERN RHODESIA
SOUTHERN RHODESIA
SOUTHWEST
BECHUANALAND
Mozambique Channel
Culf of Cuineo
SOUTH
TLANTIC
OCEAN
SAUDI
ARAB
Livingstone
Tropic of Capricorn

MAYBE I'M NOT ALL I CAN BE

ALL RIGHT, NARCISSISTIC DISASSOCIATIVE PERSONALITY DISORDER WITH SIGNIFICANT FEATURES OF GRANDIOSITY. SO WHAT?

Over time I've tried just about everything. I've been hypnotized, re-birthed, Rolfed like dough. Psychodrama (that was a scene, whacking pillows with a tennis racket while screaming shit at dear ol Mom). In past life regressions I survived the plague, saw St. Joan go up in smoke. Was there when Jerry Lewis learned to sing. I've bonded with my inner child, regressed to a goddamn baby shitting in a diaper. Been locked in a bathroom, curled up on the cold tile, screaming like a wounded beast—spiraling down into darkness with the angel of death.

"Anything approaching the change th

I have never seen before, and hope neve

touched. I was fascinated. It was thoug

on the ivory ~~visage~~ [face] the expression of ~~st~~ [so

of ~~avarice~~ [craven terror], of ~~blood-thirstiness, of cunni~~

intense and hopeless despair. Did he liv

detail of desire, temptation, surrender d

moment? [of complete knowledge] He cried [in a whisper] at some image, at so

cry that was no more than a breath--

"'XX! The horror!' The horror.'

"I blew the ca[ndle]

~~had he been such a m~~

~~earth. The eloquence~~

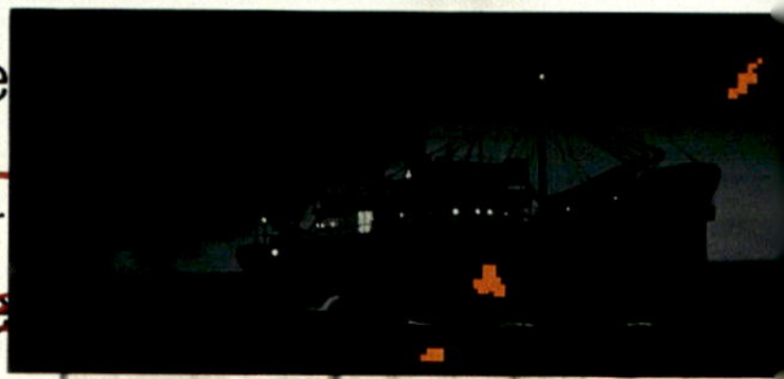

and I took my place opposite the manage

me a questioning glance, which I success

serene, with that peculiar smile of his se

of his meanness. A continuous shower o

the lamp, upon the cloth, upon our hand

manager's boy put his insolent black hea

in a tone of scathing contempt:

"'Mistah Kurtz--he dead.'

X X

"I oughta have my head examined."

"Psychiatrist walks into a bar..."

"guy walks into a psychiatrist's office..."

ame over his features
see again. Oh, I wasn't
veil had been rent. I saw
pride, of ~~mental~~ ruthless power,
f ~~excessive terror,~~ of an
life ~~through~~ again in every
g that ~~short and~~ supreme
ision, he cried but twice with a

~~Never before in his life~~
~~gift as in his last on~~
dining in the mess-room,
ho lifted his eyes to give
y ignored. He leaned back,
g the unexpressed depths
all flies streamed upon
l faces. Suddenly the
the doorway, and said

There, in a grass hut under the shade of a Bodhi Tree, a mystic healer passed her hands over my naked body: "We massage Charkas, you feel pleny good — A-OK."
"Oh my goodness! Oh Mistah Harry! We make mountain out of molehill!"

Heart of Darkness (Revised) 2007

peless despair. Did he live his

e, temptation, surrender during that ~~sho~~

in a whisper

ried at some image, at some vision, ~~he c~~

o more than a breath--

orror!' The horror.'

c le ~~Never bef~~

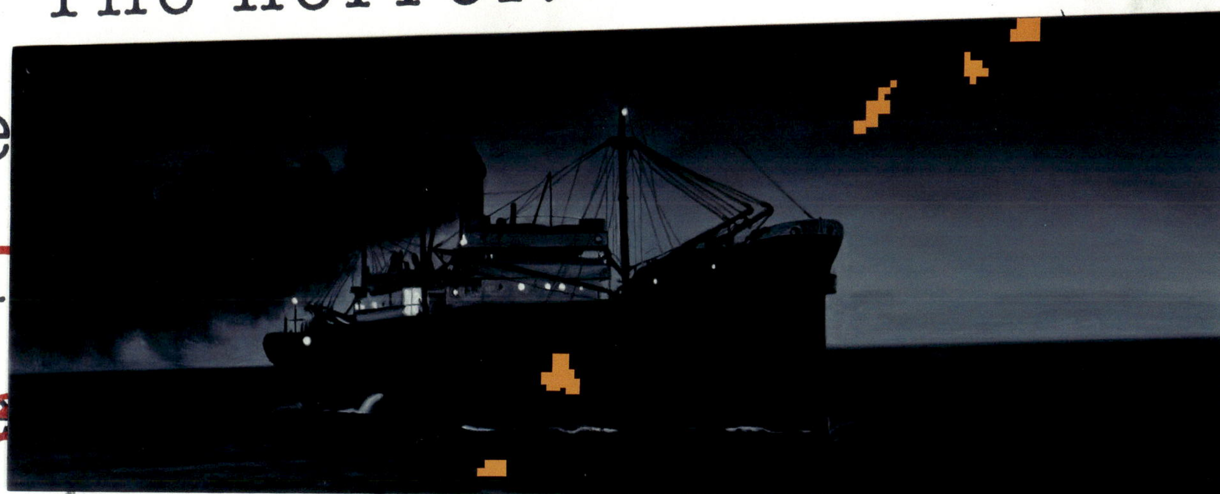

~~ch a m~~ ~~gift as in~~

~~quence~~ dining i

place opposite the manager, who lifted hi

ng glance, which I successfully ignored.

at peculiar smile of his sealing the unex

s. A continuous shower of small flies st

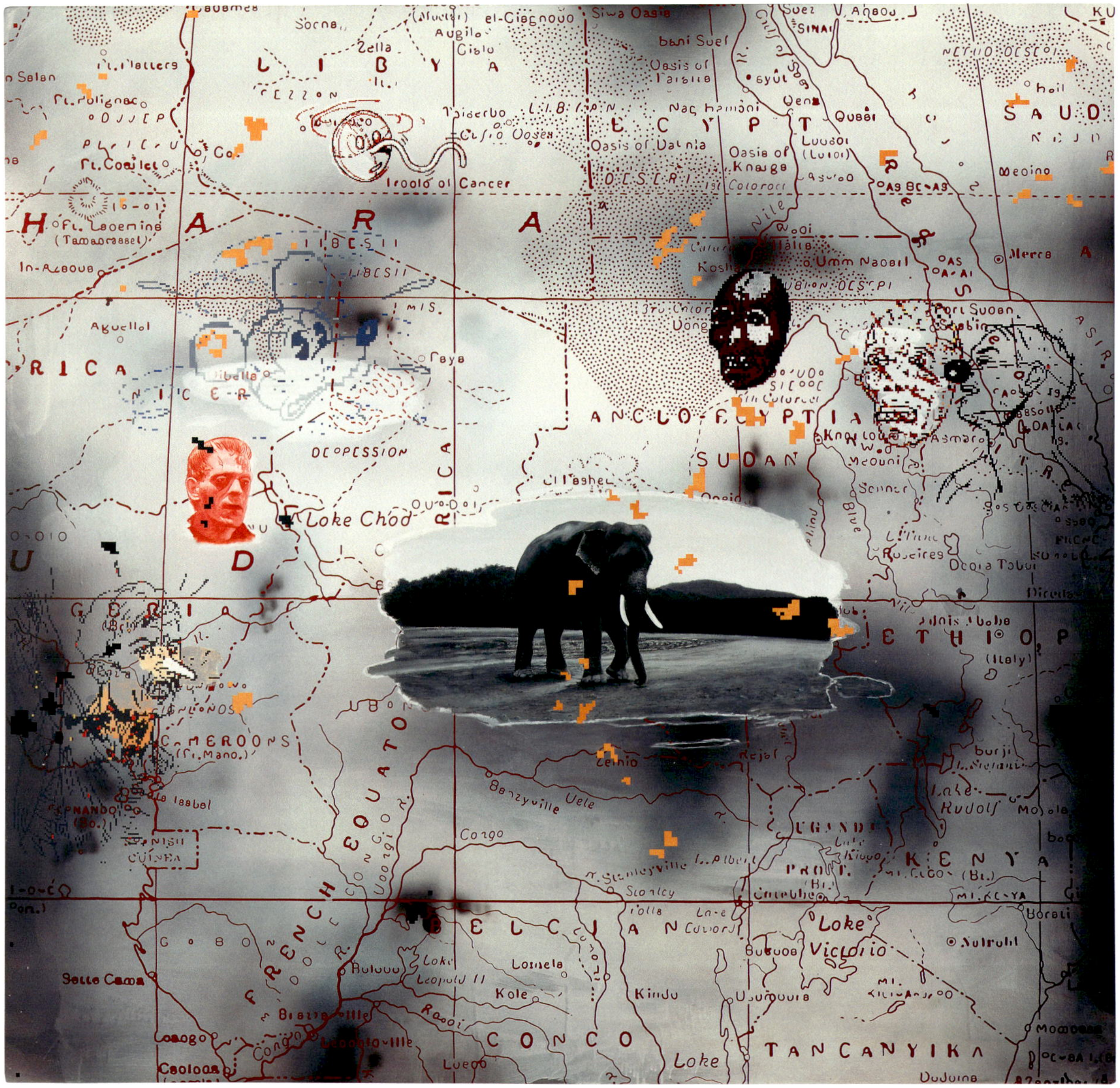

Monster 2007
The Way of Zen 2007

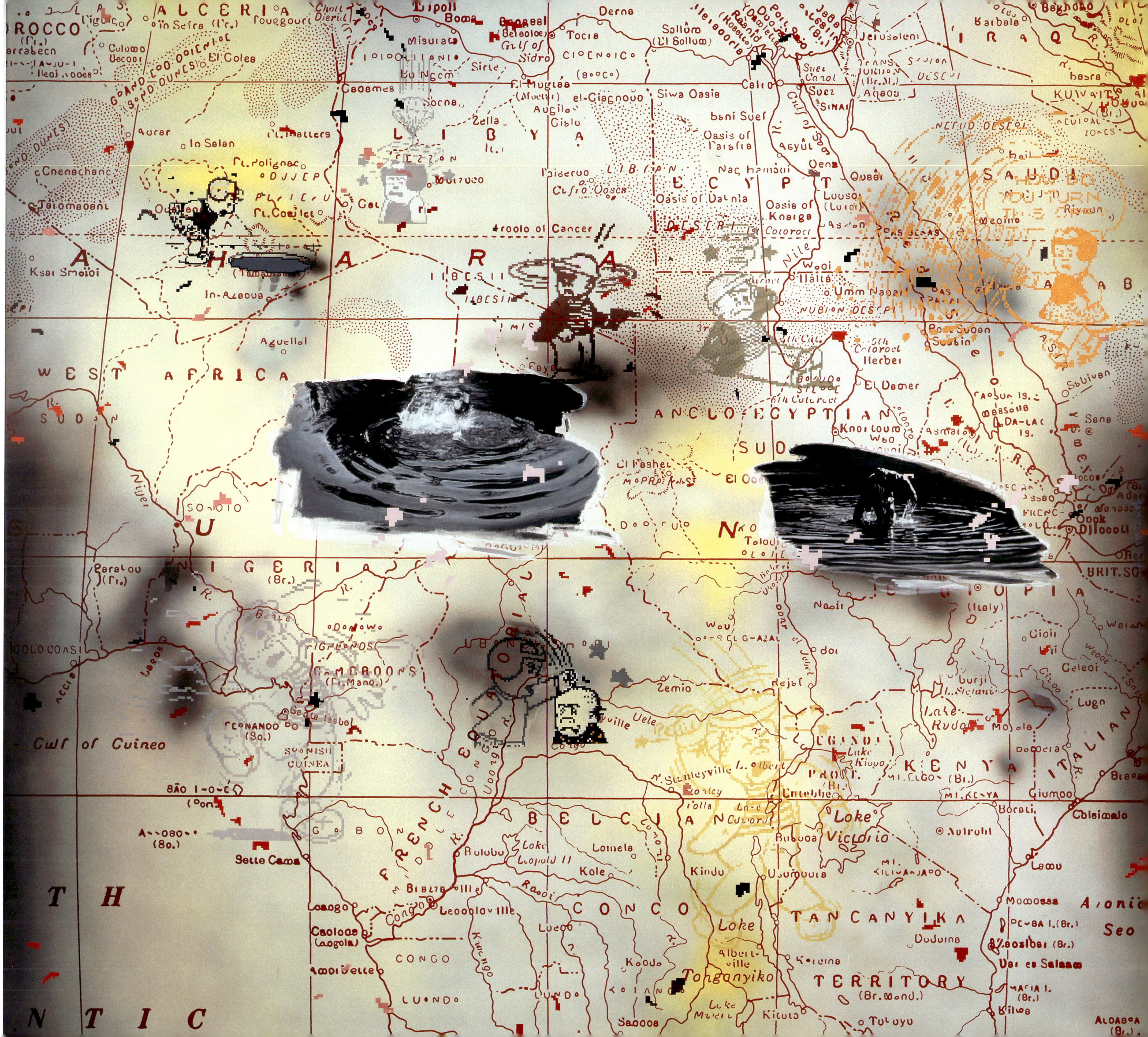

ALGERIA
LIBYA
SAHARA
WEST AFRICA
EGYPT
ANGLO-EGYPTIAN SUDAN
NIGERIA (Br.)
CAMEROONS
Gulf of Guinea
FRENCH EQUATORIAL
BELGIAN CONGO
KENYA
TANGANYIKA TERRITORY (Br. Mand.)
Lake Victoria
Lake Tanganyika
Tropic of Cancer
Siwa Oasis
Cairo
Jerusalem
Nile

Ape Soup 2008

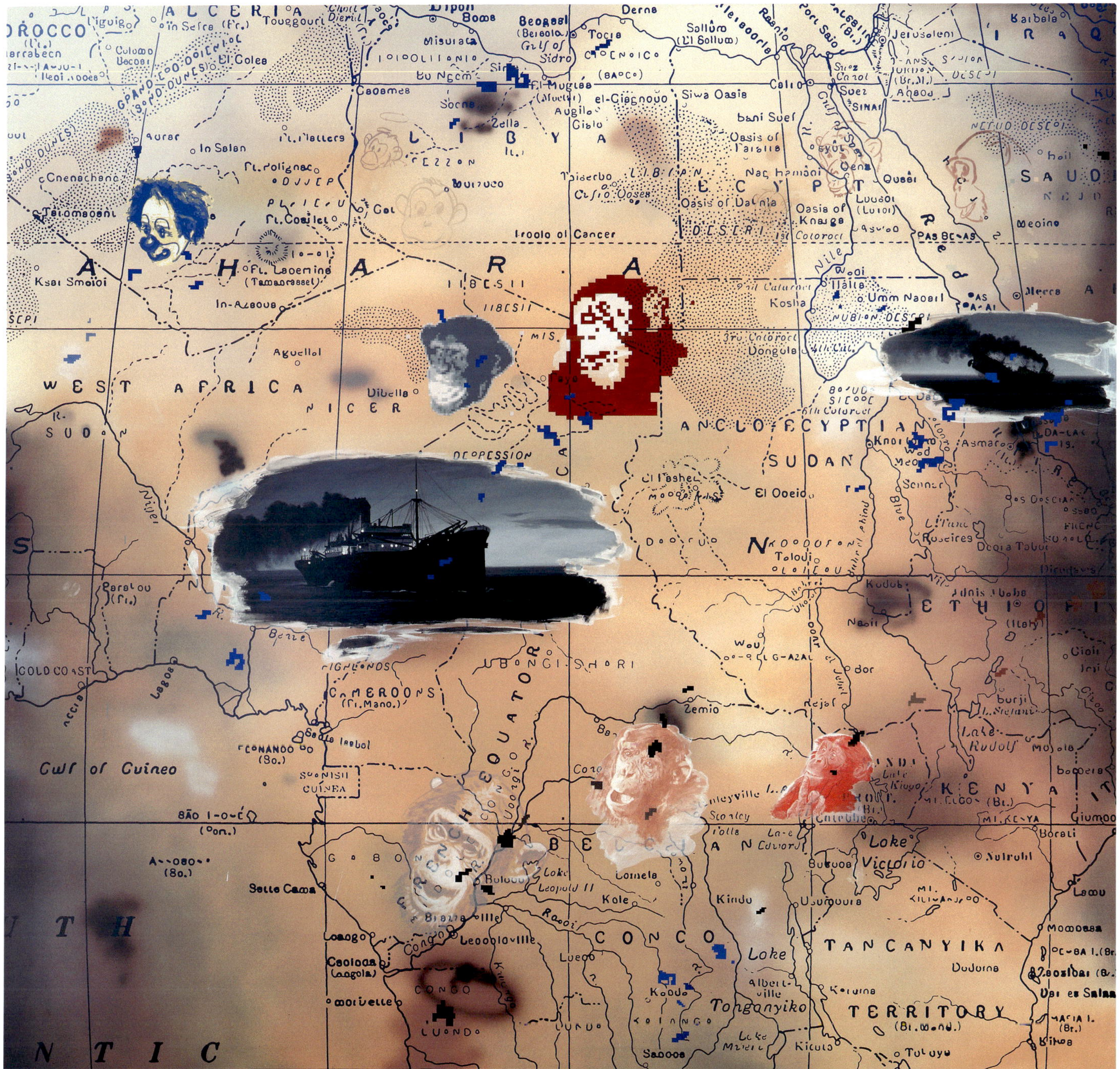
Siwa Oasis
WEST AFRICA
SUDAN
CAMEROONS
KENYA
TERRITORY

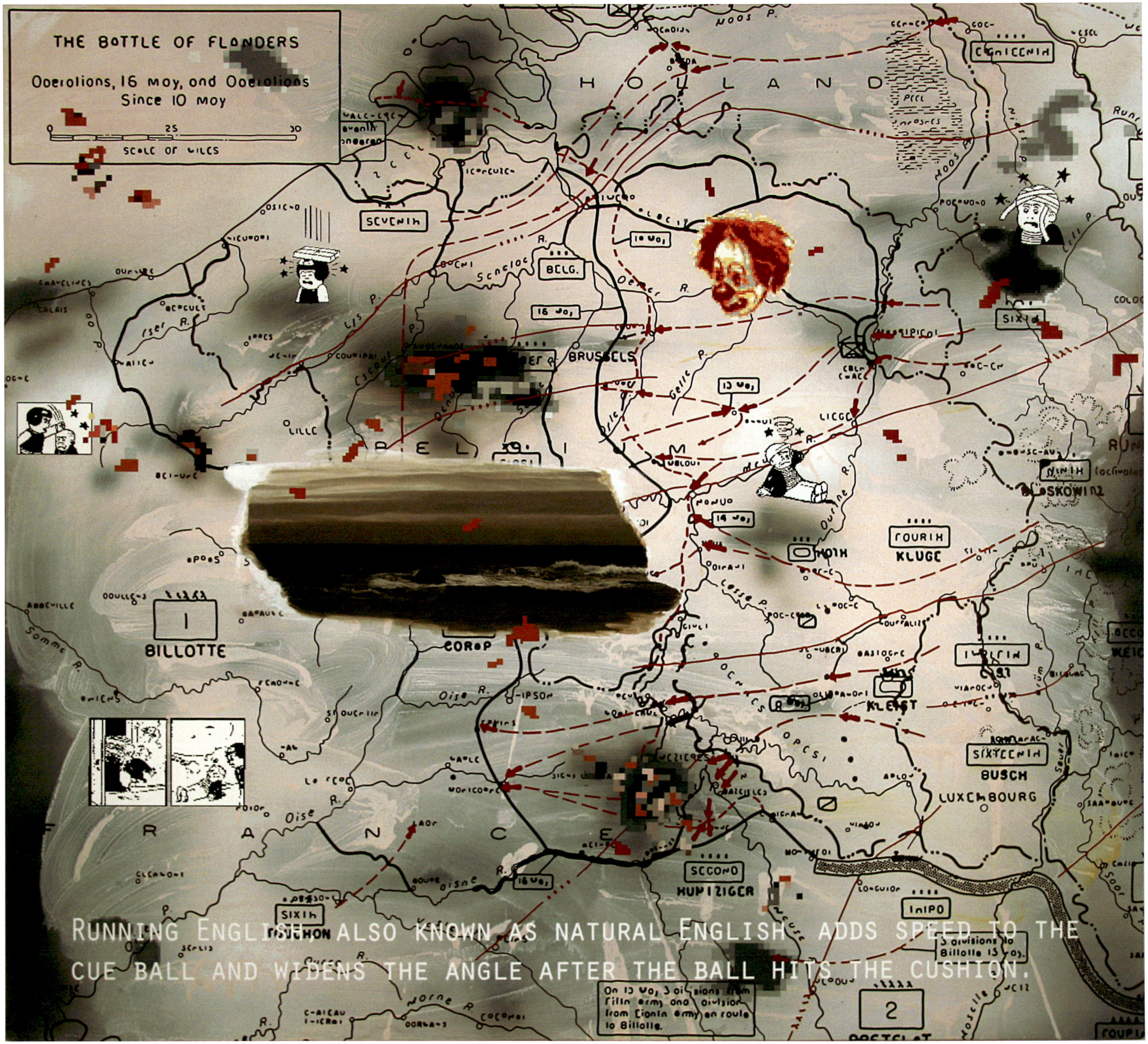
THE BOTTLE OF FLANDERS
HOLLAND
BELG.
BRUSSELS
BILLOTTE
KLUGE
KLEIST
BUSCH
LUXEMBOURG
R A N C E
RUNNING ENGLISH, ALSO KNOWN AS NATURAL ENGLISH, ADDS SPEED TO THE CUE BALL AND WIDENS THE ANGLE AFTER THE BALL HITS THE CUSHION.

Jocko at Dover 2009

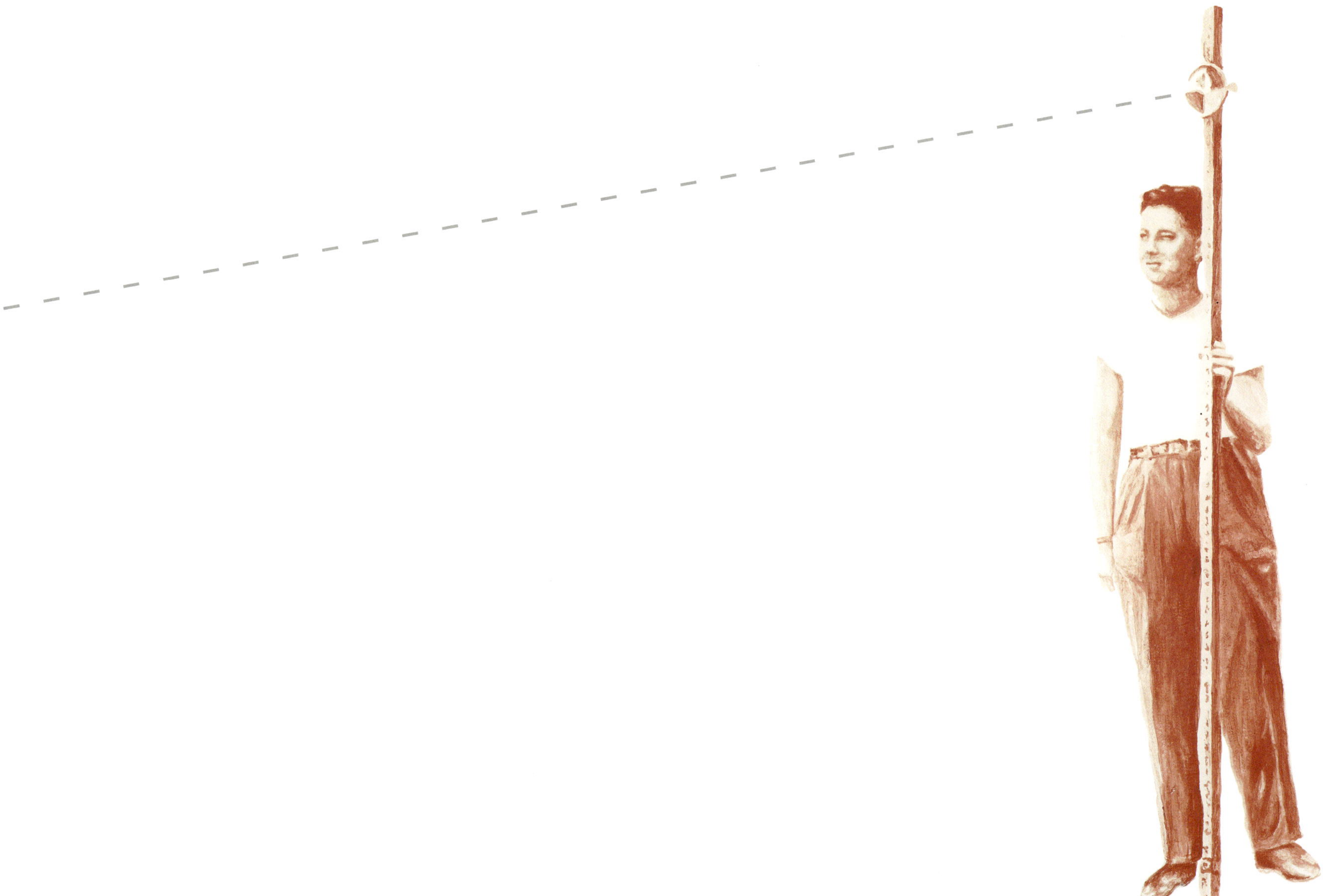

LIST OF PLATES

24 *Visa*, 2000. Acrylic on canvas. 60" × 78". Collection of Nancy and Harold Oelbaum, Bedford Corners, New York.

27 *Tarzan's Adventure Window* (Detail), 1980. Silver gelatin photograph, acrylic on laminated paper, enamel on wood. 37" × 144". Private Collection, Düsseldorf, Germany.

29 *Disconsolate Pairs*, 2006. Oil and acrylic on canvas. 60" × 64".

32 *Jack,* 1994. Oil and blackboard slating on wood. 56" × 57½" × 6½". Collection of Vicki and Kent Logan, fractional and promised gift to the San Francisco Museum of Modern Art, Logan Collection, Vail, Colorado.

34 *Animal*, 2006. Oil and acrylic on canvas. 48" × 48". Collection of Carol and Peter York, Dallas, Texas.

37 *Annette*, 1977. Silver gelatin photograph. 21" × 25½". Collection of Bob and Ann Myers, Orange, California.

38 *Junction 54*, 1977. Acrylic on laminated paper. 90" × 94". Private Collection, Düsseldorf, Germany.

40–41 *84 Sparrows*, 1979. Acrylic, graphite, and laminated paper. 10' x 29'. Collection of the Modern Art Museum of Fort Worth, Fort Worth, Texas.

42–43 *Wasp Killer,* 1979. Acrylic on laminated paper, wooden yardstick. 38" x 144". Collection of Bob and Ann Myers, Orange, California.

44–45 *Tarzan's Adventure Window*, 1980. Silver gelatin photo, acrylic on paper, enamel on wood. 37" × 144". Private Collection, Düsseldorf, Germany.

46–47 *I Try to Be Objective*, 1980. Acrylic on laminated paper, slating on wood, acrylic on wall. 58" × 172". Private Collection, Düsseldorf, Germany.

49 *Pollock*, 1981. Oil on wood, acrylic on laminated paper, porcelain urinal. 75" x 160". Collection of Contemporary Art Consortium, Mineola, New York.

50–51 *Tarzan's Adventure I*, 1981. Enamel on wood, silkscreen on wall, acrylic on wood. 40" × 144" × 1". Collection of Mary Dohne, Brooklyn, New York.

53–55 *Red and Yellow, Black and White*, 1982. Cast polyester resin and wood, acrylic on laminated paper, slating on wood. 7' × 20'1" × 8" overall. Collection of the Dallas Museum of Art, Dallas, Texas.

56–57 *Bridge*, 1983. Acrylic on laminated paper, acrylic on canvas. 72" × 138". Collection of Dr. and Mrs. Edmund P. Pillsbury, Dallas, Texas.

59 *White Clouds/Black Sky*, 1984. Steel, acrylic on laminated paper, wood. 76" × 108". Collection of the Walker Art Center, Minneapolis, Minnesota.

60–61 *Stickchart Navigation*, 1983. Enamel and acrylic on wood, acrylic on laminated paper, seashells. 6'10" x 22'8" x 4". Collection of the Corcoran Gallery of Art, Washington, D.C.

63 *Basutoland*, 1986. Acrylic on umbrella, neon, and text. 120" x 120" x 36". Collection of the Arizona State University Art Museum, Tempe, Arizona.

64–65 *Spider*, 1986. Oil on slating on wood, porcelain sink, metal fixtures. 94" × 94" × 19". Collection of the Museum of Contemporary Art, San Diego, California.

66–67 *Heart of Darkness*, 1986. Oil, blackboard slating, canvas. 1.1 × 1 × 1 meter. Collection of the Virginia Museum of Fine Arts, Richmond.

69 *Objects in a Field*, 1986. Oil and charcoal on canvas. 96" × 96". Collection of Michael Krichman, San Diego, California.

70 *Scenes from the American West*, 1986. Oil and blackboard slating on wood. 70" × 77½" × 3½". Private collection.

73 *Pumpkin Field*, 1986. Oil on cast fiberglass. 72" × 72" × 12" overall. Collection of Toni and Jeffery Beauchamp, Houston, Texas.

74–77 *Complementary Pairs*, June 25–August 29, 1987. Chalk on latex on wall with teeth casts. 12' × 25'. Installation at Hiram Butler Gallery, Houston, Texas. Private collection, Basel, Switzerland.

78–79 *The Coriolis Effect*, April 23–July 12, 1987. Green neon, text on wall with sculptural elements. 17' x 15' x 5'. Installation at Los Angeles Country Museum of Art.

80–83 *Perdido en el Mar*, October 8, 1987–October 22, 1988. Acrylic on wall. 9' × 16' and 10' × 16'. Installation at the Lannan Museum, Lake Worth, Florida.

84–95 *Lost for Words*, January 23–April 17, 1988. Installation at the Dallas Museum of Art, Dallas, Texas.

84 *Surveyors* (Detail), 1988. Acrylic wall painting. Collection of Rosalie Taubman, Dallas, Texas.

86 Installation views (left to right): *Bikini*, *Heart of Darkness*, *Pluto*, *Man Cutting Globe*.

87 *ELF*, 1988. Acrylic on wall. Dimensions variable.

88 *Man Cutting Globe*, 1988. Acrylic on wall. 6'6" × 6'2½".

90–91 *Pluto*, 1988. Acrylic on wall. 12' x 30'.

92–93 *Bikini*, 1987. Acrylic on canvas. 11'6" x 18'6". Collection of the Krannert Art Museum, Champaign, Illinois.

94–95 *Worlds Collide*, 1988. Paintstick, acrylic, and latex on wall. 12' × 22'.

96–105 *Parallel Lines*, June 22–October 10, 1988. Acrylic and paintstick wall drawing. Each of eight emergency exit doors, 12' × 13'. Installation at the Hirshhorn Museum and Sculpture Garden, Washington, D.C.

107 *A Twister Forms at Sea*, 1989. Oil, paintstick, blackboard slating on wood, and chalk trays with chalk. 71" × 83" × 8". Collection of Kelli and Allen Questrom, Dallas, Texas.

109 *The Time Falling Objects*, 1989. Oil and blackboard slating on wood. 110½" × 119½" × 5½". Private collection, Los Angeles, California.

110–117 *Movements Among the Dead*, January 19–March 6, 1990. Oil and acrylic on wall. 11'3" × 42'6" × 22'6". Installation at the Modern Museum of Art: Projects 20, New York, New York.

119 *Rules for Bending Circles*, 1991. Oil, blackboard slating on wood, chalk. 71½" × 83" × 8". Collection of Ms. Carolyn Farb, Houston, Texas.

120–135 *Hills Like White Elephants*, December 6, 1991–January 19, 1992. Installation at the Center for Contemporary Art, Sacramento, California.

120 *Piper Shadow*, 1991, Consuelo Tattoo. Balsawood and cast rubber. Dimensions variable. Collection of Tom Patchett, Los Angeles, California.

122 *Boat, Island, Ape*, 1991, Consuelo Tattoo. Enamel on steel and dry wall. Ship length, 11"; overall, variable.

123 *Hills Like White Elephants*, 1991, Consuelo Tattoo. Acrylic on wall. 87" × 88½". Collection of Rosalie Taubman, Dallas, Texas.

125 *Aardvark, Shorter History*, 1991, Vernon Fisher. Oil and acrylic on canvas. 84" × 96".

126 *Framed Landscape*, 1991, M. Moon. Oil on canvas and frame. 21" × 33¼". Private Collection, Los Angeles, California.

127 *After Malevich*, 1991, Consuelo Tattoo. Mounted raccoon on an oak limb with a blackboard cross. Limb length, 9' × 5"; overall, variable.

128–129 *14 Words*, 1991, Werner Fiche. Hydrostone, steel, and enamel on aluminum. 68" × 15" × 9".

130 *200 Numbered Rectangles*, 1989, Vernon Fisher. Acrylic and oil on canvas. 90" x 95".

132–133 *Poison Tree*, 1991, Werner Fiche. Bronze, nickel-plated copper. Limb length, 11'.

134 *Numbered Pole*, 1988, M. Moon. Enamel and blackboard slating on wood. 97" × 1½" × 1½".

135 *That's All Folks* (first version), 1991, Consuelo Tattoo. Acrylic on canvas. 42½" × 42½".

137 *When You Lose Your Mind*, 1991. Oil and acrylic on canvas. 58" x 63". Collection of Michael Caddell and Cynthia Chapman, Houston, Texas.

139 *Swimming Between Australia and Japan*, 1993. Acrylic on laminated paper; blackboard slating on wood. 72" × 100" × 5".

141 *Blank Slate Sky*, 1993. Acrylic on canvas, chalk tray, chalk, and felt eraser. 72" × 72" × 5". Private Collection, Beverly Hills, California.

142–143 *Swimming Against the Tide for Relaxation*, 1994. Oil and acrylic on canvas. 72" × 108".

144–159 *Swimming Lesions*, December 16, 1994–February 12, 1995. Installation at Blue Star Art Space, San Antonio, Texas.

146–153 Two-sided blackboard wall, 1994. Acrylic on wallboard, chalk, plaster. Each side 12' x 40' x 6'.

154–155 *Delirium*, 1994. Enamel on polyester resin arm on cot. 20" × 78" × 30".

156–157 *Vacuum*, 1994. Cut drywall. 12' x 25'.

161 *Private Africa*, 1995. Oil and blackboard slating on wood. 92½" × 93½" × 4". Collection of the Modern Art Museum of Fort Worth, Fort Worth, Texas.

162 *The Value of Water*, 1995. Oil and blackboard slating on wood, enamel on cast resin, chalk, and wooden chalk tray. 72" × 79" × 7". Private collection, La Jolla, California.

163 *The Skin Between Water and Air*, 1995. Oil and blackboard slating on wood, chalk, and felt eraser. 56" × 58" × 7". Collection of Irv and Marge Weiser, Minneapolis, Minnesota.

164–165 *Tutor to a Lunatic*, 1996. Oil and blackboard slating on wood, porcelain knobs. 102" × 84" x 8". Collection of the High Museum of Art, Atlanta, Georgia.

167 *Good Kid*, 1997. Oil and acrylic on canvas, cast epoxy, and felt erasers. Canvas, 72" × 78"; overall, variable. Collection of Guillermo C. Nicolas, San Antonio, Texas.

168 *Streams*, 1997. Oil and acrylic on canvas, cast epoxy, and felt erasers. Canvas, 72" × 78"; overall, variable. Private collection, Dallas, Texas.

170–171 *Map*, May 1–July 5, 1998. Wall text and oil on cast epoxy and steel. 12' x 30'. Installation at Miami Art Museum, Miami, Florida.

172–173 *Faya*, 1998. Acrylic on canvas, oil on cast epoxy and steel. Canvas, 24" × 24"; overall, variable. Museum of Contemporary Art, San Diego, California.

174 *Frank*, 1999. Acrylic on canvas. 46½" × 52½". Karol Howard and George Morton, Plano, Texas.

175 Sh-sh-sugar, 2000. Acrylic on canvas. 42" × 42".

176–177 *Kinshasa*, 2000. Acrylic on canvas, oil on cast epoxy and steel. 24" × 26"; overall, variable. Collection of Nona and Richard Barrett, Dallas, Texas.

178 *Syllabus*, 2000. Acrylic on canvas. 60" × 84". Collection of Edwina von Gal, East Hampton, New York.

179 *Three-Way Conversation*, 2000. Acrylic on canvas. 60" × 66".

181 *Scale*, 2000. Acrylic on canvas. 84" × 84". Collection of Cara and Larry Lichtenstein, Highland Park, Illinois.

182 *Raft (After Gericault)*, 2002. Acrylic on canvas, enamel on cast polyurethane, enamel on copper. 64" × 89" overall. Collection of Stephen and Ellen Susman, Houston, Texas.

183 *Seascape*, 2002. Oil on wood and enamel on epoxy. 17" × 27½". Collection of Michael Paselk, Corona del Mar, California.

185 *Parrot*, 2002. Oil and blackboard slating on wood. 72" × 84".

187 *Fold*, 2002. Oil and blackboard slating on wood. 75" × 83". Private collection, Seoul, South Korea.

188 *Subject Trailing Debris*, 2003. Acrylic on masonite over aluminum, enamel on cast polyurethane and MDF. Plane, 73"; overall length, 120". Collection of Dean and Dana Anderson, Chicago, Illinois.

189–198 *Brainiac*, October 11–November 15, 2003. Installation at the Dunn and Brown Contemporary, Dallas, Texas.

192 *Cat, Mouse*, 2003. Acrylic on panel, acrylic and enamel on panel, cast polyurethane, fiberglass, and enamel. 16" x 53".

194–195 *Double Swimmer . . .* (Installation view), 2003. Acrylic on canvas and enamel on cast polyurethane. 23½" × 102". Collection of Ms. Driek Zirinsky, Boise, Idaho.

196 *The Death of Marat*, 2002–2005. Oil and blackboard slating on MDF, enamel on cast polyurethane, oil on MDF. 27½" × 91". Collection of Ned Rifkin, Austin, Texas.

198 *Exploded View Tropics* (Installation view), 2003. Markers and acrylic on wall, acrylic on MDF. 12' x 20', dimensions variable.

200–201 *Dead*, 2005. Oil and acrylic on canvas. 90" × 96". Collection of Nancy and Rick Rome, Dallas.

202–203 *American Tragedy*, 2005. Oil and acrylic on canvas, enamel on cast polyurethane, acrylic on panel. 51" × 101". Pamela and Robert Goergen, Greenwich, Connecticut.

205 *The Single-State Assumption*, 2005. Acrylic on canvas and enamel on cast polyurethane. Panel, 61½" × 77"; 69" × 89" × 2½" overall.

207 *The Raw & the Cooked*, 2006. Oil and acrylic on canvas. 60" × 64". Collection of the artist.

208 *Persona Non-Persona*, 2006. Ink, oil, and acrylic on canvas. 44" × 48".

209 *Out of Africa*, 2007. Oil and acrylic on canvas. 83" × 89". Collection of Bryan Lipinski, Dallas.

210–213 *Heart of Darkness (Revised)*, 2007. Acrylic and graphite on wall, enamel on cast polyurethane. 12' × 30'. Installation at the Dunn and Brown Contemporary, Dallas, Texas.

214 *Monster*, 2007. Acrylic and oil on canvas. 60" × 64". Collection of June Lee, Newport Beach, California.

215 *The Way of Zen*, 2007. Acrylic and oil on canvas. 84" × 96".

217 *Ape Soup*, 2008. Oil and acrylic on canvas. 84" × 90".

218 *Jocko at Dover*, 2009. Oil and acrylic on canvas. 58" × 66".

220 *The Surveyors* (Detail), from *Lost for Words*, 1988. Acrylic wall painting. Collection of Rosalie Taubman, Dallas, Texas.

244 Descent of Man (Detail), 2007. Acrylic and oil on canvas.

BIOGRAPHY AND AWARDS

Born in Fort Worth, Texas, 1943
Lives and works in Fort Worth, Texas

EDUCATION

1967 BA, Hardin-Simmons University

1969 MFA, University of Illinois

TEACHING

1978–2006 Regents Professor of Art Emeritus, University of North Texas, Denton, Texas

1969–1978 Associate Professor of Art, Austin College, Sherman, Texas

GRANTS AND AWARDS

1995 John Simon Guggenheim Fellowship

1992 Distinguished Teaching of Art Award, College Art Association

1988 Awards in the Visual Arts, Southeastern Center for Contemporary Art

1984 Louis Comfort Tiffany Foundation

1981–1982 National Endowment for the Arts Individual Artist's Fellowship

1980–1981 National Endowment for the Arts Individual Artist's Fellowship

1974–1975 National Endowment for the Arts Individual Artist's Fellowship

1968–1969 University Fellow in Art, University of Illinois

1967–1968 University Fellow in Art, University of Illinois

EXHIBITIONS AND INSTALLATIONS

SELECTED SOLO EXHIBITIONS AND INSTALLATIONS

2009 "Dead Reckoning," Dallas Contemporary, Dallas, Texas

2008 "Descent of Man," Charles Cowles Gallery, New York, New York

2007 "Heart of Darkness," Dunn and Brown Contemporary, Dallas, Texas

"Two Decades of Prints and Drawings," Landfall Press Gallery, Santa Fe, New Mexico

2006 "North American Birds," Mark Moore Gallery, Santa Monica, California

2005 "Notes for a New Novel," Sarah Moody Gallery of Art, University of Alabama, Tuscaloosa, Alabama

"American Tragedy," Charles Cowles Gallery, New York, New York

2004 "Vernon Fisher 1977–1982," Mark Moore Gallery, Santa Monica, California

2003 "New Work," Devin Borden Hiram Butler Gallery, Houston, Texas

"Brainiac," Dunn and Brown Contemporary, Dallas, Texas

2002 Mark Moore Gallery, Santa Monica, California

Charles Cowles Gallery, New York, New York

2001 "Angel Face," Charles Cowles Gallery, New York, New York

"Vernon Fisher," Herter Art Gallery, University of Massachusetts, Amherst, Massachusetts

"Vernon Fisher," Bentley Gallery, Scottsdale, Arizona

2000 "Vernon Fisher's File 00," Glassell School of Art, Museum of Fine Arts, Houston, Texas

"Zulu," Dunn and Brown Contemporary, Dallas, Texas

1999 "Vernon Fisher," Devin Borden Hiram Butler Gallery, Houston, Texas

1998 "Hills Like White Elephants," Charles Cowles Gallery, New York, New York

"Zombies," Mark Moore Gallery, Santa Monica, California

"Vernon Fisher," Zolla/Lieberman Gallery, Chicago, Illinois

1997 "Vernon Fisher," Gerald Peters Gallery, Dallas, Texas

"Vernon Fisher," Jan Weiner Gallery, Kansas City, Missouri

"Four Ways to Enter a Story," Museum of Modern Art, Fort Worth, Texas

1996 "Vernon Fisher," Charles Cowles Gallery, New York, New York

"Vernon Fisher: Works on Paper 1977–1995" Barry Whistler Gallery, Dallas, Texas

Mark Moore Gallery, Santa Monica, California

Hiram Butler Gallery, Houston, Texas

1995 Hiram Butler Gallery, Houston, Texas

"Heart of Darkness," Mark Moore Gallery, Santa Monica, California

"Vernon Fisher," Gallery Seomi, Seoul, Korea

"Vernon Fisher," Milagros, San Antonio, Texas

1994 "Swimming Lesions," Blue Star Art Space, San Antonio, Texas (Installation)

"Vernon Fisher," Mark Moore Gallery, Santa Monica, California

"Vernon Fisher," Gallery Seomi, Seoul, South Korea

"Vernon Fisher," I-Space, Chicago, Illinois. Traveled to Krannert Art Museum, Champaign, Illinois

Zolla/Lieberman Gallery, Chicago, Illinois

1993 "Vernon Fisher at Landfall Press: 1983–1993," Landfall Press, Chicago, Illinois

"Vernon Fisher," Hiram Butler Gallery, Houston, Texas

"Framing Water," Modernism, San Francisco, California

"Vernon Fisher Graphic Work 1983–1993," Quartet Editions, New York, New York

1992 "Drawings," Hiram Butler Gallery, Houston, Texas

"Moonrise, Hernandez, New Mexico, 1951," The Center for Creative Photography, The University of Arizona, Tucson, Arizona (Installation)

Works Gallery, Long Beach, California

"Art in the Armory: Occupied Territory," Museum of Contemporary Art, Chicago, Illinois ("Pac. War Diary," Installation)

1991 "Blank Slate Sky," Yellowstone Art Center, Billings, Montana (Installation)

"Hills Like White Elephants," Barry Whistler Gallery, Dallas, Texas (Installation)

"Hills Like White Elephants," Fred Hoffman Gallery, Los Angeles, California (Installation)

"Hills Like White Elephants," The Center for Contemporary Art, Sacramento, California (Installation)

1990 "Movements Among the Dead," Museum of Modern Art, New York, New York (Installation)

University of Texas at Arlington, Center for Research in Contemporary Art, Arlington, Texas (Installation)

Hiram Butler Gallery, Houston, Texas

"Dead Reckoning," Smith College Museum of Art, Northampton, Massachusetts (Installation)

1989 "Vernon Fisher," La Jolla Museum of Contemporary Art, La Jolla, California. Traveled to Albright Knox Art Gallery, Buffalo, New York; Contemporary Arts Museum, Houston, Texas; Modern Art Museum of Fort Worth, Fort Worth, Texas; Center for the Fine Arts, Miami, Florida

"Vernon Fisher," Interim Art, London, England

Fred Hoffman Gallery, Santa Monica, California

"Niagara: Welcome to US," Albright-Knox Art Gallery, Buffalo, New York (Installation)

"Alpha," Res Nova Gallery, New Orleans, Louisiana

"Vernon Fisher Prints," Landfall Press, New York, New York

1988 "Lost for Words," Dallas Museum of Art, Dallas, Texas (Installation)

"Screaming: Installation of Recent Work," Barry Whistler Gallery, Dallas, Texas

"Parallel Lines," Hirshhorn Museum and Sculpture Garden, Washington, D.C. (Installation)

1987 Barbara Gladstone Gallery, New York, New York

"Contemporary Pairs," Hiram Butler Gallery, Houston, Texas (Installation)

"Perdido en el Mar," Lannan Museum, Lake Worth, Florida (Installation)

1986 "The Knight's Move: An Installation of Recent Work," Asher-Faure Gallery, Los Angeles, California

1985 Hiram Butler Gallery, Houston, Texas

1984 Barbara Gladstone Gallery, New York, New York

1983 Barbara Gladstone Gallery, New York, New York

"Bridge," Madison Art Center, Madison, Wisconsin (Installation)

1982 Galerie T'Venster, Rotterdam, Holland

"Vernon Fisher New Work," Delahunty Gallery, Dallas, Texas

1981 "Breaking the Code," Franklin Furnace, New York, New York

"Vernon Fisher New York," Barbara Gladstone Gallery, New York, New York

"Vernon Fisher Drawings," Delahunty Gallery, Dallas, Texas

1980 Denise Rene/Hans Mayer Gallery, Düsseldorf, Germany

"Vernon Fisher: Story Paintings and Drawings," Contemporary Arts Museum, Houston, Texas

1979 Delahunty Gallery, Dallas, Texas

1977 "Paintings, Drawings, and Photographs," Delahunty Gallery, Dallas, Texas

1976 William Sawyer Gallery, San Francisco, California

1975 Delahunty Gallery, Dallas, Texas

1973 Smither Gallery, Dallas, Texas

SELECTED GROUP EXHIBITIONS

2009 "Sight Mapping," Herter Gallery, University of Massachusetts, Amherst, Massachusetts

"Trouble in Paradise: Examining Discord Between Nature and Society," Tucson Museum of Art, Tucson, Arizona

"Masculine: Interpretations of Manhood," Charles Cowles Gallery, New York, New York

"American Concepts and Global Visions/Selections from the AT&T Collection," The Marion Koogler McNay Art Museum, San Antonio, Texas

"Death of a Propane Salesman: Anxiety and the Texas Artist," Fort Worth Contemporary Arts, Texas Christian University, Fort Worth, Texas

2008 "Lone Star Legacy II: The Barrett Collection of Contemporary Art," Dallas Museum of Art, Dallas, Texas

2007 "Fast Forward: Contemporary Collections for the Dallas Museum of Art," Dallas Museum of Art, Dallas, Texas

"Sheldon Survey: An Invitational, New Works from Twenty Contemporary Artists," Sheldon Memorial Art Gallery, University of Nebraska, Lincoln, Nebraska

2006 "MMoCA Collects," Madison Museum of Contemporary Art, Madison, Wisconsin

"Collectors × 3," Art League of Houston, Houston, Texas

2005 "Masters of Illusion: 150 Years of Trompe l'Oeil in America," Kresge Art Museum, Michigan State University, East Lansing, Michigan

"Land," Dunn and Brown Contemporary, Dallas, Texas

"Summer Paper," Devin Borden Hiram Butler Gallery, Houston, Texas

"A Summer Group," Charles Cowles Gallery, New York, New York

"Christmas in July," Gerald Peters Gallery, Dallas, Texas

"Artists Interrogate: Race and Identity," Milwaukee Art Museum, Milwaukee, Wisconsin

"Revising Arcadia, Cornell Fine Arts Museum," Rollins College, Winter Park, Florida. Traveled 2005–2007

2004 "A Sharp Eye: An Art Dealer's 40-Year Journey," Evanston Art Center, Evanston, Illinois

"Water World," South Bend Regional Museum of Art, South Bend, Indiana

"Misleading Trails," China Art Archives and Warehouse, Beijing, China. Traveled to various art museums in the United States

"Perspectives@25: A Quarter-Century of New Art in Houston," Contemporary Arts Museum, Houston, Texas

"5th Anniversary Exhibition," Dunn and Brown Contemporary, Dallas, Texas

"Texas Vision: The Barrett Collection," Meadows Art Museum, Southern Methodist University, Dallas, Texas

2003 "Beyond the Academy: Encouraging New Talent from Texas," Arthouse, Austin, Texas

"Pairings: Artists' Selections from the Dallas Museum of Art Collection," Dallas Center for Contemporary Art, Dallas, Texas

"Selections from the Permanent Collection," Modern Art Museum of Fort Worth, Fort Worth, Texas

2002 "The Cultural Desert: Inside Contemporary Sculpture," Scottsdale Museum of Contemporary Art, Scottsdale, Arizona

"Time/Frame," Jack S. Blanton Museum of Art at the University of Texas at Austin, Austin, Texas

"Labyrinth," Devin Borden Hiram Butler Gallery, Houston, Texas

"Lateral Thinking, Art of the 1990's," Museum of Contemporary Art, San Diego, California. Traveled to Colorado Springs Fine Arts Center, Colorado Springs, Colorado; Hood Museum, Dartmouth University, Hanover, New Hampshire; Dayton Art Institute, Dayton, Ohio

"Text/Tile," Deutsche Bank, New York, New York

"Next," Dunn and Brown Contemporary, Dallas, Texas

"Summarize/Summer Eyes," Jan Weiner Gallery, Kansas City, Kansas

"Made in USA," Devin Borden Hiram Butler Gallery, Houston, Texas

"Systems Order Nature," Devin Borden Hiram Butler Gallery, Houston, Texas

"110 Years: The Permanent Collection of the Modern Art Museum of Fort Worth," Modern Art Museum of Fort Worth, Fort Worth, Texas

2001 "On the Edge," El Paso Museum of Art, El Paso, Texas

"Rembrandt to Rauschenberg," Jack S. Blanton Museum of Art at the University of Texas at Austin, Austin, Texas

"Texas," Museum of Fine Arts, Houston, Texas

"Kinds of Drawings," Herter Art Gallery, University of Massachusetts, Amherst, Massachusetts

2000 "2000 Biennial Exhibition," Whitney Museum of American Art, New York, New York

"Reconstructions: The Imprint of Nature/ The Impact of Science," Sidney Mishkin Gallery, Baruch College, New York, New York

"Paint, American Style," Mark Moore Gallery, Santa Monica, California

"Natural Deceits," Modern Art Museum of Fort Worth, Fort Worth, Texas

Devin Borden Hiram Butler Gallery, Houston, Texas

"Almost Warm and Fuzzy," Des Moines Art Center and Independent Curators International, Des Moines, Iowa. Traveled to P.S. 1 Contemporary Art Center, New York, New York; Fundacio la Caixa, Barcelona, Spain; Art Gallery of Hamilton, Ontario, Canada, among others

Tyler Museum of Art, Tyler, Texas

"Arthur Rogers Gallery," New Orleans, Louisiana

"Dealer's Choice: New New York," Robert Kidd Gallery, Birmingham, Michigan

"A Lasting Legacy: Recent Additions to the Collection," Orange County Museum of Art, Newport Beach, California

"Crossing State Lines," Museum of Fine Arts, Houston, Texas

1999 "Texas Draws," Contemporary Arts Museum, Houston, Texas

"Altered States," Charles Cowles Gallery, New York, New York

1998 "New Works: Words & Images II," Miami Art Museum, Miami, Florida (Installation)

"Double Trouble: The Patchett Collection," Museum of Contemporary Art, San Diego, California

"Works on Paper," Charles Cowles Gallery, New York, New York

"Link," Gerald Peters Gallery, Dallas, Texas

1997 "A Singular Vision: Prints from Landfall Press," Museum of Modern Art, New York, New York

"Private Landscapes," Modern at Sundance Square, Fort Worth, Texas

"Continuity & Contraction," Miami Art Museum, Miami, Florida

"Finders Keepers," Contemporary Arts Museum, Houston, Texas

"Drawings: A Bi-Coastal Invitational," Meyerson & Nowinski Gallery, Seattle, Washington

"In the Beginning Was the Word," Charles A. Watson Museum of Fine Arts, Racine, Wisconsin

"Dis/Functional," Arizona State University Art Museum, Tempe, Arizona

"Link," Gerald Peters Gallery, Dallas, Texas

"Robert Kidd Gallery," Birmingham, Michigan

1996 "48th Annual Purchase Exhibition," American Academy of Arts and Letters, New York, New York

"Under Glass," Sarah Moody Gallery, University of Alabama, Tuscaloosa, Alabama

"Maps, Charts & Routes," Irvine Arts Center, Irvine, California

"Black and White," Gallery Seomi, Seoul, South Korea

"New Talent, New Ideas," Charles Cowles Gallery, New York, New York

"Jennifer Bartlett, Vernon Fisher, and Martin Mull," Bentley Gallery, Scottsdale, Arizona

"Landfall Press: Twenty-five Years of Printmaking," Milwaukee Art Museum, Milwaukee, Wisconsin. Traveled to Chicago Cultural Center, Chicago, Illinois; Davenport Museum of Art, Davenport, Iowa; Springfield Museum of Art, Springfield, Ohio

"Decathalon," Fay Gold Gallery, Atlanta, Georgia

Zolla/Lieberman Gallery, Chicago, Illinois

Microsoft Art Walk 12: Print Exhibition," Microsoft Corporation, Redmond, Washington

"Establishment Exposed," Dallas Visual Art Center, Dallas, Texas

"Trans-Positions," University of South Florida, Tampa, Florida

1995 "Previews," Charles Cowles Gallery, New York, New York

"Color in Space: Pictorialism in Contemporary Sculpture," List Art Center, Brown University, Providence, Rhode Island

"In the Black," Irvine Fine Arts Center, Irvine, California

"10th Anniversary Show," Barry Whistler Gallery, Dallas, Texas

"Genesis in Fire," Glassell School of Art, Museum of Fine Arts, Houston, Texas

"Under Glass," Charles Cowles Gallery, New York, New York

1994 "The Big Picture," Barry Whistler Gallery, Dallas, Texas

"Out of This World," Contemporary Arts Museum, Houston, Texas

"Mapping," University of Texas at San Antonio, San Antonio, Texas

"Art on the Map," Chicago Cultural Center, Chicago, Illinois

"Uncommon Objects," Barry Whistler Gallery, Dallas, Texas

"Altered Egos," Santa Monica Museum of Art, Santa Monica, California

"Year 1: A Survey," Mark Moore Gallery, Santa Monica, California

"Transtextualism," Mark Moore Gallery, Santa Monica, California

"Fictions," Center for Creative Photography, Tucson, Arizona

"Where Have You Gone, Joe DiMaggio?" Galveston Arts Center, Galveston, Texas

1993 "Darkness + Light, Twentieth-Century Works from Texas Collections," Blaffer Gallery, University of Houston, Houston, Texas

"Reading Print," Museum of Modern Art, New York, New York

"Landscapes: Left to Right," Landfall Press, Chicago, Illinois

"Idols and Icons," University Art Museum, Arizona State University, Tempe, Arizona

"Texas Contemporary: Acquisitions of the '90s," Museum of Fine Arts, Houston, Texas

"Sculptors & Paper," Hiram Butler Gallery, Houston, Texas

1992 "Art and Nature," Hiram Butler Gallery, Houston, Texas

"Printmaking in Texas: The 1980s," Laguna Gloria Art Museum, Austin, Texas

"Summer Invitational '92," Jan Weiner Gallery, Kansas City, Missouri

"Thirty Prints," Barry Whistler Gallery, Dallas, Texas

"Paint/Print," Rena Bransten Gallery, San Francisco, California

"Island Inspired," Galveston Art Center, Galveston, Texas

"Beyond Just Words: I," Modernism, San Francisco, California

"Out of Bounds: Contemporary Sculpture Takes Shape," Museum of Fine Arts, Houston, Texas

"The Artist's Eye," Kimbell Museum of Art, Fort Worth, Texas

"Painting/Sculpture/Drawing: Vernon Fisher, Joseph Havel, Douglas MacWithey," Barry Whistler Gallery, Dallas, Texas

"100th Anniversary Exhibition: Master Works from Fort Worth Collections," Modern Art Museum of Fort Worth, Fort Worth, Texas

1991 "Not on Canvas," Asher-Faure Gallery, Los Angeles, California

"The Eyes of Texas," Jan Weiner Gallery, Kansas City, Missouri

"Little Things (Slice It Down to Size) Mean a Lot," Momentary Modern, Amsterdam, Holland

"The State I'm In: Texas Art at the Dallas Museum of Art," Dallas Museum of Art, Dallas, Texas

"The Perfect World," San Antonio Museum of Art, San Antonio, Texas

1990 "Northwest × Southwest: Painted Fictions," Palm Springs Desert Museum, Palm Springs, California

"Tradition & Innovation: A Museum Collection of Texas Art," Museum of Fine Arts, Houston, Texas

"Word as Image: American Art 1960–1990," Milwaukee Art Museum, Milwaukee, Wisconsin

"1990 Triennial," Phoenix Art Museum, Phoenix, Arizona

"The Common Wealth: Twentieth-Century American Masterpieces from Virginia Collections," Roanoke Museum of Fine Arts, Roanoke, Virginia

"Direct References: Drawings by Texas Artists," Glassell School of Art, Museum of Fine Arts, Houston, Texas

"Forty Texas Printmakers," Modern Art Museum of Fort Worth, Fort Worth, Texas

1989 "A Brave New World," Karsten Schubert Ltd., London, England

"Unstable Universe," Asher-Faure Gallery, Los Angeles, California

"Modern Myths and Narratives," Pensacola Museum of Art, Pensacola, Florida

"A Century of Sculpture in Texas, 1889–1989," Archer M. Huntington Art Gallery, University of Texas at Austin, Austin, Texas

"The New American Landscape," Museum of Fine Arts, Houston, Texas

"Coming of Age: Twenty-one Years of Collecting by the Madison Art Center," Madison Art Center, Madison, Wisconsin

"Painting Beyond the Death of Painting," Kuznetsky Most Exhibition Hall, Moscow, USSR

"Water," Hiram Butler Gallery, Houston, Texas

1988 "Texas Art," Richmond Hall, Menil Collection, Houston, Texas

"Not for the Living Room 'Lecture on Photography,'" DiverseWorks, Houston, Texas (Installation)

"Awards in the Visual Arts 7," Los Angeles County Museum of Art, Los Angeles, California. Traveled to Carnegie Mellon University Art Gallery, Pittsburgh, Pennsylvania; Virginia Museum of Fine Arts, Richmond, Virginia

"New York, New York," Spencer Museum of Art, University of Kansas, Lawrence, Kansas. Traveled to Seattle Art Museum, Seattle, Washington

"Looking South: A Different Dixie," Birmingham Museum of Art, Birmingham, Alabama

"Words in Print," Landfall Press, Chicago, Illinois, and New York, New York

"Traveling," Althea Viafora Gallery, New York, New York

1987 Tilden-Foley Gallery, New Orleans, Louisiana

"Works on Paper," Barry Whistler Gallery, Dallas, Texas

"Avant-garde in the Eighties, 'Walking on Air: The Coriolis Effect,'" Los Angeles County Museum of Art, Los Angeles, California (Installation)

"Past Imperfect: Eric Fischl/Vernon Fisher/Laurie Simmons," Walker Art Center, Minneapolis, Minnesota. Traveled to Knight Gallery/Spirit Square for the Arts, Charlotte, North Carolina; Contemporary Arts Center, Cincinnati, Ohio; Institute of Contemporary Art, University of Pennsylvania, Philadelphia, Pennsylvania

"Comic Iconoclasm," Institute of Contemporary Arts, London, England. Traveled to Douglas Hyde Gallery, Dublin, Ireland; Cornerhouse Gallery, Manchester, England; Círculo de Bellas Artes, Madrid, Spain; Kunstmuseum Bern, Bern, Switzerland

"Diamonds Are Forever: Artists and Writers on Baseball," New York State Museum, Albany, New York

"At Conception: Small Drawings for Big Ideas," School of Art & Design, University of Illinois, Champaign, Illinois

"Works on Paper," Nina Freudenheim Gallery, Buffalo, New York

1986 "National Print Exhibition, 24th Biennial: Public and Private: American Prints Today," Brooklyn Museum, Brooklyn, New York

"New Orleans Triennial: The Centennial Exhibition," New Orleans Museum, New Orleans, Louisiana

"Seventy-fifth American Exhibition," Art Institute of Chicago, Chicago, Illinois

"Texas," Tilden-Foley Gallery, New Orleans, Louisiana

"Five Texas Artists," McIntosh-Drysdale Gallery, Washington, D.C.

"Contemporary Prints," Lawrence Monk Gallery, New York, New York

"The Texas Landscape, 1900–1986," Museum of Fine Arts, Houston, Texas

"Wallworks," John Weber Gallery, New York, New York (Installation)

"A Sense of Place: Contemporary Southern Art," MCAD Gallery, Minneapolis, Minnesota

"Memento Mori," Centro Cultural Arte Contemporáneo, Mexico City, Mexico

"Text and Image: The Wording of American Art," Holly Solomon Gallery, New York, New York

1985 "Crescent Collection," Crescent Gallery, Dallas, Texas

"Psychodramas," Philadelphia Art Alliance, Philadelphia, Pennsylvania

"Comic Relief," Barry Whistler Gallery, Dallas, Texas

"Drawings," Barbara Toll Gallery, New York, New York; Knight Gallery, Spirit Square Center, Charlotte, North Carolina

Barbara Toll Gallery, New York, New York

1984 "Words Pictures," Bronx Museum of the Arts, New York, New York

"New American Painting," Archer M. Huntington Art Gallery, University of Texas, Austin, Texas

"Verbally Challenged Images," Independent Curators International

"The Shadow of the Bomb," Mount Holyoke College Art Museum and University Gallery, University of Massachusetts, South Hadley, Massachusetts

"Content: A Contemporary Focus, 1974–1984," Hirshhorn Museum and Sculpture Garden, Washington, D.C.

"Narrative Forms," Museo Rufino Tamayo, Mexico City, Mexico

"Word Images," San Antonio Art Institute, San Antonio, Texas

"Contemporary Works on Paper," University Art Museum, University of Southwest Louisiana, Lafayette, Louisiana

1983 "1984," Ronald Feldman Gallery, New York, New York, Sponsored by Ronald Feldman and the *Village Voice*

"Fact and Fiction: James Surls, Roy Fridge, Vernon Fisher," Aspen Center for the Visual Arts, Aspen, Colorado

"Images of Texas," Archer M. Huntington Art Gallery, University of Texas, Austin, Texas

"Stroke, Line and Figure," Gimpel Fils Gallery, London, England

"38th Corcoran Biennial Exhibition of American Paintings," Corcoran Gallery of Art, Washington, D.C.

"Comment," Long Beach Museum of Art, Long Beach, California

"Perspectives of Landscape," Fuller Goldeen Gallery, San Francisco, California

"Southern Fictions," Contemporary Arts Museum, Houston, Texas

"The Comic Art Show," Whitney Museum of American Art, Downtown Branch, New York, New York

"Language, Drama, Source, and Vision," New Museum, New York, New York

"The White Wall Papers," Swen Parson Gallery, Northern Illinois University, DeKalb, Illinois

"3rd Annual Artists' Books," Kathryn Markel Gallery, New York, New York

"Contemporary Works on Paper," Frumkin & Struve Gallery, Chicago, Illinois

"Fragment/Fragmentary/Fragmentation," New Britain Museum of American Art, New Britain, Connecticut

1982 "Fifth India Triennial," New Delhi, India

"Painting and Sculpture Today, 1982," Indianapolis Museum of Art, Indianapolis, Indiana

"Post-Romance: Artists' Valentines, Windows on White," New York, New York

"Texas on Paper," Contemporary Arts Museum, Houston, Texas. Traveled to University of Colorado, Boulder, Colorado; Tyler Museum of Art, Tyler, Texas; Hallwalls Contemporary Arts Center, Buffalo, New York; University of Arizona, Tucson, Arizona; and Amarillo Art Center, Amarillo, Texas

"The Americans: The Collage," Contemporary Arts Museum, Houston, Texas

"Still Modern after All These Years," Chrysler Museum, Norfolk, Virginia

"The Erotic Impulse," Roger Litz Gallery, New York, New York

"Mediums of Language," Hayden Gallery, M.I.T., Cambridge, Massachusetts. Installations by Vernon Fisher, Paul Sharits, and Myrel Chernick

1981 "19 Artists: Emergent Americans," 1981 Exxon National Exhibition, Guggenheim Museum, New York, New York

"1981 Biennial Exhibition," Whitney Museum of American Art, New York, New York

"Directions 1981," Hirshhorn Museum and Sculpture Garden, Smithsonian Institution, Washington, D.C.

"Words as Images," Bergman Gallery, The Renaissance Society at the University of Chicago, Chicago, Illinois

"A Texas Group Show, 1981," Charles Cowles Gallery, New York, New York

"Summer Pleasures," Barbara Gladstone Gallery, New York, New York

"Basel Art II '81," International Art Fair, Basel, Switzerland

"The Southern Voice: Terry Allen, Vernon Fisher, Ed McGowin," Fort Worth Art Museum, Fort Worth, Texas

"Selections from the Chase Manhattan Bank Art Collection," University Gallery, University of Massachusetts at Amherst, Amherst, Massachusetts

"Currents: The New Mannerism," Jacksonville Art Museum, Jacksonville, Florida

1980 "Response," Tyler Museum of Art, Tyler, Texas

"Basel Art II '80," International Art Fair, Basel, Switzerland

"Investigations: Probe, Structure, Analysis," New Museum, New York, New York

1979 "Fire," Contemporary Arts Museum, Houston, Texas

"Made in Texas," University Art Museum, University of Texas at Austin, Austin, Texas

"Paperworks: An Exhibition of Texas Artists," Witte Museum, San Antonio, Texas

"New York/New Media," Marianne Deson Gallery, Chicago, Illinois

1978 "Corsicana Panorama," Warehouse Living Arts Center, Corsicana, Texas (Multimedia installation produced with Main Street Image Company, Fort Worth, Texas)

"Chandelier," Delahunty Gallery, Dallas, Texas (Installation produced with Main Street Image Company, Fort Worth, Texas)

"Texas in Chicago: Green, Fisher, Surls, Wade," Marianne Deson Gallery, Chicago, Illinois

"Art of Texas," The Renaissance Society at the University of Chicago, Chicago, Illinois

1977 William Sawyer Gallery, San Francisco, California

"Recent Works on Paper by Contemporary American Artists," Madison Art Center, Madison, Wisconsin

"American Narrative/Story Art, 1967–1977," Contemporary Arts Museum, Houston, Texas. Traveled to Contemporary Art Center, New Orleans, Louisiana; University Art Museum, Santa Barbara, California; University Art Museum, Berkeley, California; and Winnipeg, Ontario, Canada

1976 D. W. Gallery, Dallas, Texas

1975 "Exchange DFW/SFO," Fort Worth Art Museum, Fort Worth, Texas, 1975; San Francisco Museum of Modern Art, San Francisco, California, 1976

"Texas Drawing Show," Delahunty Gallery, Dallas, Texas

1974 Henri Gallery, Washington D.C.

1973 "Texas Drawing Exhibition," Smither Gallery, Dallas, Texas

1972 "Exhibition of Ten Painters," Art Museum of South Texas, Corpus Christi, Texas

Smither Gallery, Dallas, Texas

1971 "Ten Texas Painters," Skidmore, Owens & Merrill, Houston, Texas (Invitational exhibition organized by Henry Hopkins for Bank of Texas).

"Tarrant County 34th Exhibition," Fort Worth Art Center, Fort Worth, Texas

1970 "Project South/Southwest: Younger American Artists," Fort Worth Art Center, Fort Worth, Texas

"SIU Invitational Drawing Show," Southern Illinois University, Carbondale, Illinois

PUBLIC COLLECTIONS

Albright-Knox Museum, Buffalo, New York
Art Institute of Chicago, Chicago, Illinois
Baltimore Museum of Art, Baltimore, Maryland
Birmingham Museum of Art, Birmingham, Alabama
Blanton Museum of Art, University of Texas, Austin
Cantor Center for Visual Arts, Stanford University, Palo Alto, California
Castellani Art Museum, Niagara University, New York
Center for Creative Photography, Tucson, Arizona
Chase Manhattan Bank, New York, New York
The Contemporary Museum, Honolulu, Hawaii
Corcoran Gallery of Art, Washington, D.C.
Dallas Museum of Art, Dallas, Texas
Denver Art Museum, Denver, Colorado
Des Moines Art Center, Des Moines, Iowa
El Paso Art Museum, El Paso, Texas
High Museum of Art, Atlanta, Georgia
Hirshhorn Museum and Sculpture Garden, Washington, D.C.
Hunter Museum of American Art, Chattanooga, Tennessee
Kansas City Art Institute, Kansas City, Kansas
Krannert Art Museum, University of Illinois at Urbana-Champaign, Champaign, Illionis
Los Angeles County Museum of Art, Los Angeles, California
Madison Museum of Contemporary Art, Madison, Wisconsin
Milwaukee Art Museum, Milwaukee, Wisconsin
Modern Art Museum of Fort Worth, Fort Worth, Texas
Museum of Contemporary Art Chicago, Chicago, Illinois
Museum of Fine Arts, Houston, Texas
Museum of Modern Art, New York, New York
Museum of Texas Tech University, Lubbock, Texas
Newcomb Hall, University of Virginia, Charlottesville, Virginia
New Orleans Museum of Art, New Orleans, Louisiana
Nora Eccles Harrison Museum of Art, Utah State University, Logan, Utah
Orange County Museum of Art, Newport Beach, California
Phoenix Art Museum, Phoenix, Arizona
San Angelo Museum of Fine Arts, San Angelo, Texas
San Antonio Museum of Art, San Antonio, Texas
San Diego Art Museum, San Diego, California
San Francisco Museum of Modern Art, San Francisco, California
Solomon R. Guggenheim Museum, New York, New York
Tucson Museum of Art, Tucson, Arizona
Tyler Museum of Art, Tyler, Texas
Ulrich Museum of Art, Wichita, Kansas
University Art Museum, Arizona State University, Tempe, Arizona
University of Virginia Art Museum, Charlottesville, Virginia
Virginia Museum of Fine Arts, Richmond, Virginia
Weisman Art Museum, Minneapolis, Minnesota
Whitney Museum of American Art, New York, New York

SELECTED BIBLIOGRAPHY

PUBLICATIONS BY VERNON FISHER

2000 "Moonrise Hernandez, New Mexico, 1951." *Art Lies*, no. 27 (Summer 2000): 4–5.

1992 "From 'Navigating by the Stars.'" *Neon* (Summer 1992).

1989 *Navigating by the Stars*. Chicago: Landfall Press, 1989.

"Navigating by the Stars." *American Way* (August 1, 1989).

1981 "Four Stories: 'Deaf Mute,' 'Desert Malevich,' 'Lecture on Photography,' 'President's Golf Lesson.'" *Paris Review* 23, no. 80 (Summer 1981): 15–21.

1980 "A Childhood Friend." *Whitewalls*, no. 4 (Summer 1980): 17–18.

1979 "Five Stories." Whitewalls, no. 2 (Winter–Spring 1979).

CATALOGUES

2009 Harmon, Katharine. *The Map as Art*. New York: Princeton Architectural Press.

Trouble in Paradise: Examining Discord Between Nature and Society. Tucson, AZ: Tucson Museum of Art.

2008 Arntzen, Etta, et al. *Krannert Art Museum: Selected Works*. Seattle: Washington University Press.

2007 Chen, Yuwen. *Alternative and Caricature Maps*. Taiwan: Acorn Press.

de Corral, Maria, and John R. Lane, eds. *Fast Forward: Contemporary Collections for the Dallas Museum of Art*. New Haven: Yale University Press.

2006 Carlozzi, Annette DiMeo, and Kelly Baum, eds. *American Art since 1900*. Blanton Museum of Art, Austin, TX: University of Texas Press.

Reese, Becky Duval. *Texas 100: Selections from the El Paso Museum of Art*. El Paso, TX: El Paso Museum of Art.

2005 *American Tragedy*. New York: Charles Cowles Gallery.

2004 *Texas Vision: The Barrett Collection*. Dallas, TX: Meadows Art Museum, Southern Methodist University.

2003 *Beyond the Academy: Encouraging New Talent from Texas*. Austin, TX: Arthouse at the Jones Center.

Brainiac. Dallas, TX: Dunn and Brown Contemporary.

Heartney, Eleanor, and Jacquelyn Serwer. *A Capital Collection: Masterworks from the Corcoran Gallery of Art*. Washington, D.C.: The Corcoran Museum of Art.

2002 Auping, Michael, ed. *Modern Art Museum of Fort Worth: 110*. Fort Worth, TX: Modern Art Museum.

Kamps, Toby. *Lateral Thinking: Art of the 1990s*. San Diego, CA: Museum of Contemporary Art. Introduction by Hugh M. Davies.

2001 Ivey, Bill. *A Creative Legacy: A History of the National Endowment for the Arts, 1966–1995*. New York: Henry N. Abrams.

Kinds of Drawing. Amherst, MA: Herter Art Gallery.

2000 Auping, Michael. *Natural Deceits*. Fort Worth, TX: Modern Art Museum of Fort Worth.

Greene, Alison de Lima. *Texas: 150 Works from the Museum of Fine Arts, Houston*. New York: Henry N. Abrams.

Olsen, Valerie Loupe. *Vernon Fisher's File 00*. Houston, TX: Glassell School of Art, Museum of Fine Arts.

2000 Biennial Exhibition. New York: Whitney Museum of American Art.

1999 *Texas Draws*. Houston, TX: Contemporary Arts Museum.

1997 Davies, Hugh M. *Blurring the Boundaries: Installation Art 1969–1996*. San Diego, CA: Museum of Contemporary Art, Distributed Art Publishers.

Finders Keepers. Houston, TX: Contemporary Arts Museum.

Vernon Fisher. Dallas, TX: Gerald Peters Gallery.

1996 Ruzicka, Joseph. *Landfall Press: Twenty-five Years of Printmaking*. Milwaukee, WI: Milwaukee Art Museum.

1995 *Color in Space: Pictorialism in Contemporary Sculpture*. Providence, RI: List Art Center, Brown University.

1994 Colpitt, Frances. *Mapping*. San Antonio, TX: University of Texas at San Antonio.

———. *Swimming Lesions*. San Antonio, TX: Blue Star Art Space.

Moss, Karen, and Scott Boberg. *Altered Egos*. Santa Monica, CA: Santa Monica Museum of Art.

Vernon Fisher. Champaign, IL: Krannert Art Museum.

1993 *Darkness + Light: Twentieth-Century Works from Texas Collections*. Houston, TX: Sarah Campbell Blaffer Gallery, University of Houston.

1992 *Art at the Armory: Occupied Territory*. Chicago, IL: Museum of Contemporary Art Chicago.

Island Inspired. Galveston, TX: Galveston Art Center.

New Texas Art. Spokane, WA: Cheney Cowles Museum.

1991 Edwards, Jim. *The Perfect World*. San Antonio, TX: San Antonio Museum of Art.

Hickey, Dave. *Hills Like White Elephants*. Sacramento, CA: Center for Contemporary Art.

1990 *1990 Triennial*. Phoenix, AZ: Phoenix Art Museum.

Northwest × Southwest: Painted Fictions. Palm Springs, CA: Palm Springs Desert Museum.

Word as Image: American Art 1960–1990. Milwaukee, WI: Milwaukee Art Museum.

1989 *A Brave New World*. London: Karsten Schubert LTD.

Davies, Hugh M. *Vernon Fisher*. La Jolla, CA: La Jolla Museum of Contemporary Art.

Looking South: A Different Dixie. Birmingham, AL: Birmingham Museum of Art.

Niagara: Welcome to US. Buffalo, NY: Albright-Knox Gallery.

1988 Los Angeles County Museum of Art, et al. *Awards in the Visual Arts 7*. Winston-Salem, NC: Southeastern Center for Contemporary Art.

New Work New York. Lawrence, KS: Spencer Museum of Art.

1987 Fox, Howard N. *Avant-Garde in the Eighties*. Los Angeles, CA: Los Angeles County Museum of Art.

Past-Imperfect: Eric Fischl, Vernon Fisher, Laurie Simmons. Minneapolis, MN: Walker Art Center.

Wagstaff, Sheena. *Comic Iconoclasm*. London: Institute of Contemporary Arts.

1986 Kalil, Susie. *The Texas Landscape, 1900–1986*. Houston, TX: Museum of Fine Arts.

Speyer, A. James. *Seventy-Fifth American Exhibition: The Art Institute of Chicago*. Chicago, IL: The Art Institute.

1984 *El Arte Narrativo*. Mexico City: Museo Rufino Tamayo.

Fox, Howard N. *Content: A Contemporary Focus 1974–1984*. Washington, D.C.: Hirshhorn Museum and Sculpture Garden, Smithsonian Institution.

McReady, Eric. *New American Painting: A Tribute to James and Mari Michener*. Austin, TX: Archer M. Huntington Art Gallery.

1983 Carlin, John, and Sheena Wagstaff. *The Comic Art Show*. New York: Whitney Museum of American Art.

Comment. Long Beach, CA: Long Beach Museum of Art.

Southern Fictions. Houston, TX: Contemporary Arts Museum.

The 38th Corcoran Biennial Exhibition of American Painting. Washington, D.C.: Corcoran Gallery of Art.

1982 *The Americans: The Collage*. Houston, TX: Contemporary Arts Museum.

Currents: A New Mannerism. Jacksonville, FL: Jacksonville Art Museum.

Halbreien, Kathy. *Mediums of Language: Vernon Fisher, Myrel Chernick, Paul Sharits*. Cambridge, MA: MIT List Visual Arts Center.

Painting and Sculpture Today 1982. Indianapolis, IN: Indianapolis Museum of Art. Essays by Helen Ferrulli and Robert Yassin.

Rotterdam Arts Council. *Vernon Fisher—Keith Haring*. Rotterdam, Holland: Galerie T'Venster. Essay by Richard Flood.

1981 Chase Manhattan Bank. *Selections from the Chase Manhattan Bank Art Collection*. Amherst, MA: University Gallery, University of Massachusetts at Amherst.

Frank, Peter. *19 Artists, Emergent Americans: 1981 Exxon National Exhibition*. New York: Solomon R. Guggenheim Foundation.

Freudenheim, Susan, and Marge Goldwater. *The Southern Voice: Terry Allen, Vernon Fisher, Ed McGowin*. Fort Worth, TX: Modern Art Museum of Fort Worth. Essay by Dave Hickey.

McClintic, Miranda. *Directions 1981*. Washington, D.C.: Hirshhorn Museum and Sculpture Garden, Smithsonian Institution.

1981 Biennial Exhibition. New York: Whitney Museum of American Art. Organized by Barbara Haskell.

Vernon Fisher: Story Paintings and Drawings. Houston, TX: Contemporary Arts Museum. Essay by Marti Mayo.

1980 Gumpert, Lynn. *Investigations: Probe-Structure-Analysis*. New York: The New Museum. Introduction by Allen Schwartzman and Lynn Gumpert.

Rifkin, Ned. *Response*. Tyler, TX: Tyler Museum of Art.

1979 San Antonio Museum Association. *Paperworks: An Exhibition of Texas Artists*. San Antonio, TX: Witte Museum.

1973 *123456*. Tyler, TX: Tyler Museum of Art. Organized by Robert Kjorlein.

1970 *Project South/Southwest*. Fort Worth, TX: Fort Worth Art Center.

PERIODICALS

2007 Bourbon, Matthew. "Vernon Fisher." *Artforum* (September 20), http://artforum.com/archive/id=15835.

2006 Ayers, Robert. "Vernon Fisher." *ARTnews* (April): 144–146.

Ewing, John. "Vernon Fisher: American Tragedy." *Art Lies*, no. 49 (Winter): 121.

Kuspit, Donald. "Vernon Fisher." *Artforum* (February): 211.

Markle, Leslie. "Bird Watching: Vernon Fisher at Mark Moore Gallery." (December 3).

2005 Salcido, Joel. "A Texan in Bern." *Austin Monthly* (December).

2004 Hurt, Cindy. "Vernon Fisher: *Brainiac*." *Art Lies*, no. 41 (Winter): 75.

Tyson, Janet. "Dallas, Texas. Vernon Fisher." *Art Papers* (March–April): 54–55.

2001 Bollen, Christopher. "Vernon Fisher: 'Angel Face'." *Time Out New York* (January 25): 64.

Bourbon, Matthew. "An Artist's Vantage." *NY Arts* (February): 21.

Eagley, Ursula. "Vernon Fisher." *ARTnews* (May): 191.

Korotkin, Joyce. "Short List: Chelsea." *The New York Art World* (February): 12.

Mahoney, Robert. "Vernon Fisher at Charles Cowles." *Art in America* (September): 158.

2000 Bell, J. Bowyer. "Art in a New Century." *Review* (April 1): 91–96.

Berde, Olga. "Ants, Flies & Blondes in the Global Village." *Review* (April 1): 83–86.

Brunetti, John. "Nostalgia as Cultural Discourse: What America's Twentieth-Century Myths Reveal About Ourselves." *New Art Examiner* (January): 18–21.

Colpitt, Frances. "Vernon Fisher at the Glassell School of Art." *Art in America* (June): 130–131.

———. "Report from Houston: Space City Takes Off." Art in America (October): 66–75.

Ennis, Michael. "Northern Exposure." *Texas Monthly* (February): 130–132.

Erikson, Emily. "Preview: U.S. Shorts." *Artforum* (May): 44.

Garcia-Fenech, Giovanni. "Buying the Biennial." *Artnet.com Magazine* (May 30).

———. "Whitney Biennial 2000 Opens." *Artnet.com Magazine* (March 21).

Goodrich, John. "Savvy Industriousness and the Lions of Energy." *Review* (April 1): 79–82.

Gopinath, Gabrielle. "A Patchwork Labyrinth." *Review* (April 1): 56–59.

Silverstein, Joel. "Ten Million Dollars of Fun." *Review* (April 1): 64–67.

1998 Bell, J. Bowyer. "Vernon Fisher." *Review* (May 15): 42–43.

Best, Sherry. "Vernon Fisher." *New Art Examiner* (March).

Muller, Mario M. "Vernon Fisher." *Review* (May 15): 41–42.

Murdock, Robert M. "Vernon Fisher." *Review* (May 15): 40–41.

Yood, James. "Vernon Fisher." *Artforum* (December): 134–135.

1997 Goodman, Alan H. "Bred in the Bone?" *The Sciences* (March/April): 21.

Kutner, Janet. "Vernon Fisher." *ARTnews* (November): 231–232.

1995 Twaddle, Randy. "Vernon Fisher." *Gulf Coast* 8, no. 1 (Winter).

1994 Anderson, Michael. "Vernon Fisher." *Art issues* (September/October): 41.

Bulka, Michael. "Vernon Fisher." *New Art Examiner* (November): 41–42.

Gibson, Eric. "Staking Out Claims." *Art & Antiques* (September 1994): 31–32.

1993 Kelley, Jeff. "Vernon Fisher at Modernism." *Artweek* (August 5): 17.

Ross, Jeanette. "Lone Star Reveries: New Texas Art at the Boise Art Museum." *Artweek* (January 7): 29.

1992 Barden, Lane. "Good Information: Vernon Fisher at the Works Gallery." *Artweek* (October 19): 28.

Lobdel, Diana. "Seeing With All Senses: A Unique View of the Armory Show at the Museum of Contemporary Art." *F Magazine* (December): 6–7.

McConnell, Gordon. "Vernon Fisher: Blank Slate Sky." *Artspace* (January–April): 74–75.

Patner, Andrew. "In Review." *Art and Antiques* (November): 83.

Solomon, Richard. "Occupied Territory." *Inland Architect* (November/December): 4.

1991 Colpitt, Frances. "Vernon Fisher at Barry Whistler." *Art in America* (December): 122–123.

Simpson, Nan Booth. "Art in Focus." *Southern Accents* (June).

Sorensen, Dina. "From Outside the Sphere." *Arts Magazine* (October): 72–85.

1990 Levin, Kim. "Art That Barks, Art That Bites." *Village Voice* (February 20): 103.

McBride, Elizabeth. "Vernon Fisher." *ARTnews* (November): 177–178.

McCombie, Mel. "Vernon Fisher." *Arts Magazine* (February): 82.

Murphy, Jay. "New Orleans." *Contemporânea* (February): 32.

1989 Christensen, Judith. "Vernon Fisher, Images and Text: La Jolla." *Artweek* (March 25).

Davies, Hugh M. "Vernon Fisher: Paintings and Writings." *Artspace* (November/December): 46–53.

Gardner, Colin. "Vernon Fisher: La Jolla Museum of Contemporary Art." *Artforum* (May): 162.

Pagel, David. "Vernon Fisher." *Art issues* (Summer): 24.

———. "Artist's Book Beat." *The Print Collectors Newsletter* 20, no. 2 (May–June).

Porges, Maria. "Navigating By the Stars." *Contemporânea* (September): 101.

———. "Endpapers." *Red Bass*, no. 14.

1988 Finnegan, Patrick. "Washington." *Contemporânea* (September–October): 28–29.

Porges, Maria. "It Was a Dark and Stormy Knight: Jumping the Tracks of Narrative." *SHIFT* (Fall): 50–52.

Risatti, Howard. "Vernon Fisher: Hirshhorn Museum." *Artforum* (November): 150.

1987 Gambrell, Jamey. "Texas: State of the Art." *Art in America* (March): 114–130.

Larson, Kay. "Art." *New York Magazine* (March 9): 112.

1986 Gardner, Colin. "The Unpredictable and the Deconstructive." *Artweek* (June 14): 1.

1985 Cecil, Sara. "New Editions." *ARTnews* (October): 96–97.

Freudenheim, Susan. "Vernon Fisher: At Home on the Ranges." *Artforum* (October): 93–96.

Indiana, Gary. "Vernon Fisher." *ARTnews* (February): 144.

1984 Indiana, Gary. "Vernon Fisher at Barbara Gladstone." *Art in America* (December): 166–167.

Yard, Sally. "The Shadow of the Bomb." *Arts Magazine* (April): 73–82.

1983 Byers, Trudie. "Abilene Homecoming." *Artspace* (Spring): 63.

Evans, Derro. "Profile: A Picture Poet." *Ultra* (November): 58.

Fleming, Lee. "The Corcoran Biennial Second Western States Exhibition." *ARTnews* (May).

Freudenheim, Susan. "Vernon Fisher at Delahunty." *Art in America* (March): 164–165.

Fudge, Jane. "The Second Western States 38th Corcoran Biennial Exhibition." *Artspace* (Fall): 10–13.

Heit, Janet. "The Comic Art Show." *Arts Magazine* (October).

Kutner, Janet. "Portrait of the Artist . . ." *Dallas Life Magazine* (July 24): 8–30.

Lowe, Ron. "Fort Worth Artists." *Artspace* (Spring): 28.

Peterson, William. "Fact & Fiction." *Artspace* (Summer): 66–67.

Princenthal, Nancy. "Vernon Fisher." *ARTnews* (September).

1982 Coppola, John. "Breaking the Code." *SPAN* (March): 40.

Dillon, David. "The Southern Voice." *Artforum* (March).

Freudenheim, Susan. "A Survey of Texas Art: Vernon Fisher." *Arts & Architecture* (Winter): 30.

Reinhart, J. A. "Conversation with Vernon Fisher." *Haute* (September): 24–25.

———. "The Painted Word in the Painter's Words." *Pulse* (November): 27–29.

Silverthorne, Jeanne. "New York: Vernon Fisher at Barbara Gladstone Gallery." *Artforum* (January): 75.

Westfall, Stephen. "Vernon Fisher." *Arts Magazine* (January): 20.

1981 Allen, Jane. "Intellectually Art Dead in New York, Thrives in Regions According to Guggenheim, Whitney, and Hirshhorn." *The New Art Examiner* (April): 1, 9.

Ashberry, John. "An Exhilarating Mess." *Newsweek* (February 23): 82–83.

Burleigh, Robert. "Words as Images." *The New Art Examiner* (April): 14.

Glueck, Grace. "How Emerging Artists Really Emerge: Putting the Biennials Together." *ARTnews* (May): 95–99.

Hughes, Robert. "Quirks, Clamors, and Variety." *Time* (March 2): 84–87.

Kutner, Janet. "You Can Go Home Again." *ARTnews* (December): 113.

Larson, Kay. "The Great American Talent Hunt." *New York Magazine* (February).

———. "Fear of Style." *New York Magazine* (November 9): 64.

Rickey, Carrie. "Curatorial Conceptions." *Artforum* (April): 48–60.

Schwartz, Ellen. "It's the Gospel According to Their Organizers, Not 'The World'." *ARTnews* (April), 122–127.

Thistlewaite, Mark. "Diverse Southern Narratives." *Artweek* 12 (October 17).

Zimmer, William. "Gone Fishering." *SoHo Weekly News* (November 3): 45.

1980 Bee, Maeve. "New Faces/New Images." *Ocular* (Summer): 3–6.

Hoffman, Fred. "Dallas: Vernon Fisher at Delahunty Gallery." *Artforum* (January).

Kalil, Susie. "To See is Not to Understand." *Artweek* (December 20).

Marvel, Bill. "Made in America." *TWA Ambassador* (July): 31–33.

Platt, Susan. "Vernon Fisher." *Arts Magazine* (February): 13.

1979 Dillon, David. "Read Along with Vernon." *D Magazine* (October): 28.

Hoffman, Fred. "New Routes to the Unknown." *Artweek* (October 27).

Kalil, Susie. "Art in Private Places: The Buford Project." *Artweek* (January 27): 19.

1978 Day, Holly. "T for Texas." *Grey City Journal* (May 12).

Katz, Sonia. "Art of Texas." *New Art Examiner* (May 12).

Rifkin, Ned. "The Corsicana Panorama: Ed Blackburn, Vernon Fisher, Jim Malone." *Art Voices/South* (July/August): 61–64.

1977 Kutner, Janet. "Capricious Places." *ARTnews* (December): 102.

1976 Dunham, Judith. "Bay Area/Texas Art Exchange." *Artweek* (February 28).

———. "Vernon Fisher: Painting about Painting." *Artweek* (September 11).

1975 Kutner, Janet. "Dallas: Illusionistic Problems." *ARTnews* (November): 97–100.

Moser, Charlotte. "Termagant Texans." *Currant* (August–September): 6–10.

1973 Hopkins, Henry. "Contemporary Art in Texas: On the Road to Maturity." *ARTnews* (May): 40–45.

ACKNOWLEDGMENTS

I wish to thank:

Julie Bozzi, my wife and best friend.

Anna Allen and the very cool dudes, Jeremy and Moses Fisher.

My first teachers, Claudio Betti and Dick Neidhardt.

And especially Michael Auping, Frances Colpitt, and Ned Rifkin for their thoughtful contributions to this book. Also, Allison Faust, Lindsay Starr, Nancy Bryan, and Victoria Davis at the University of Texas Press.

In addition, Helen Altman, Dotty Attie, Nona and Richard Barrett, Ed Blackburn, Dennis Blagg, Lisa Brown, Devin Borden, Hiram Butler, Laura Carpenter, Dennis Christie, Bonnie Clearwater, Charles Cowles, Hugh Davies, Steve Dennie, Mary Dohne, Talley Dunn, Vernon Faulconer, Richard Flood, Howard Fox, Peter Frank, Susan Freudenheim, Barbara Gladstone, Ron Gleason, Marge Goldwater, Sue Graze, Mr. and Mrs. M. A. Gribin, Madeleine Grynsztejn, Barbara Haskell, Dave Hickey, Fred Hoffman, Henry Hopkins, Jack Lemon, Roberta Lieberman, William Lieberman, Anne Livet, Vicki and Kent Logan, Jim Malone, Hans Mayer, Marty Mayo, Miranda McClintic, Jack Methner, Mark Moore, Christina Patoski, Ted and Mireille Pillsbury, Peter Plagens, Kelli and Allen Questrom, Steve Reichard, Johnny Reno, Alan Schwartzman, Murray Smither, Al Souza, Buzz Spector, Rosalie Taubman, Marcia Tucker, Reagan Upshaw, Barry Whistler, Xiaoze Xie, and the University of Illinois.

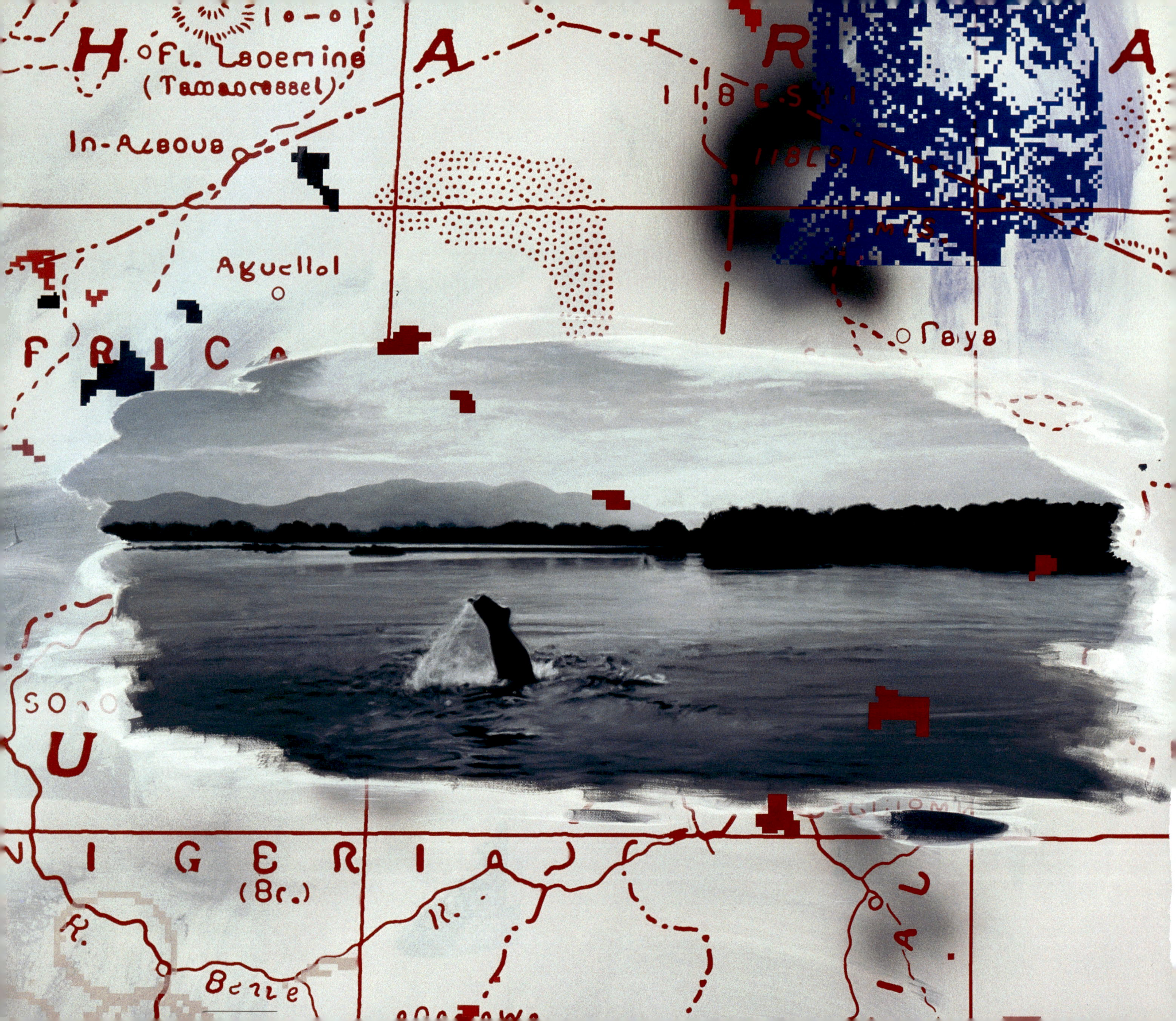

H
A
R
A
In-Azaoua
FRICA
U
NIGERIA
(Br.)

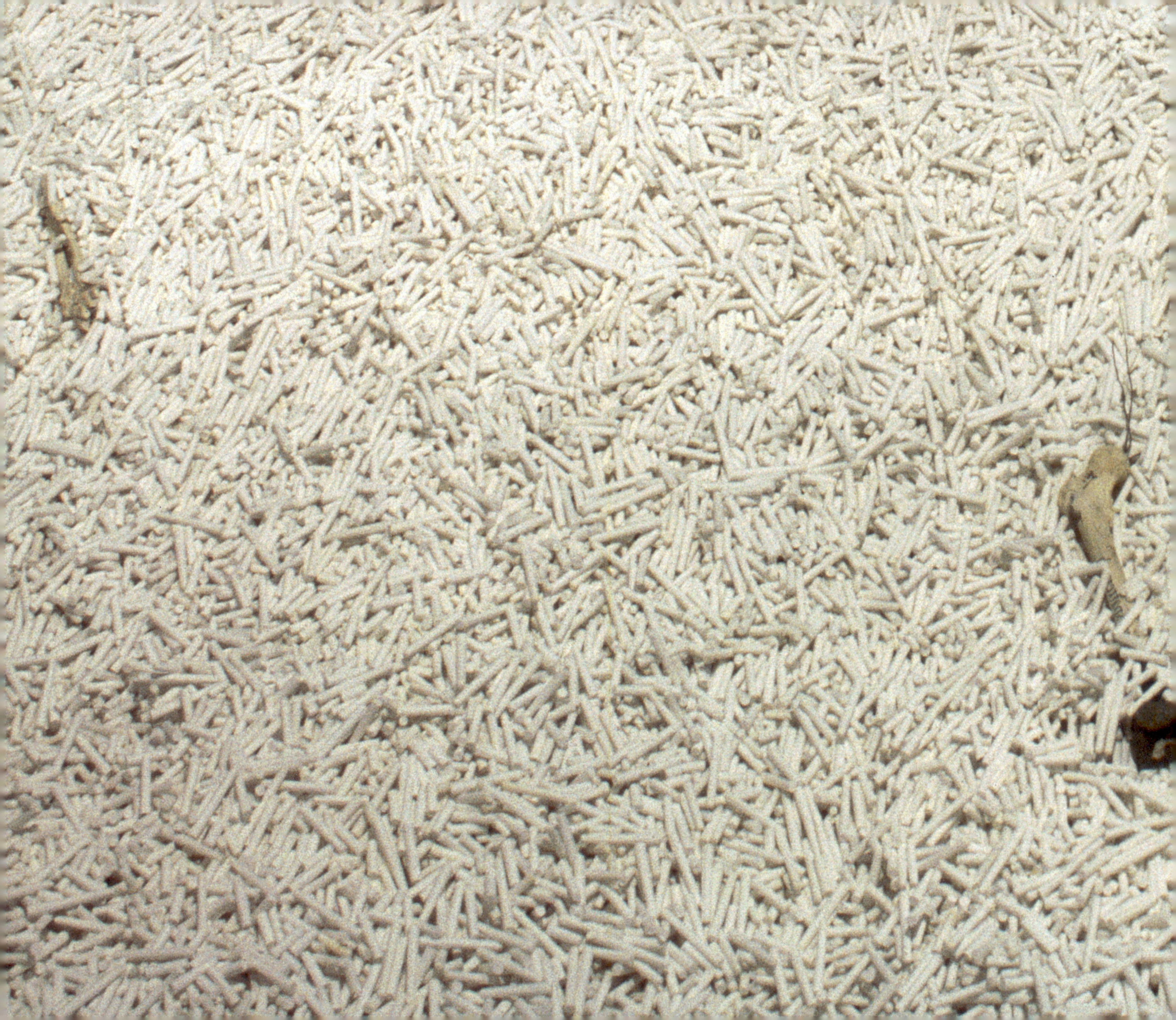